Andean Studies
New Trends and Library Resources

SALALM Secretariat
Benson Latin American Collection
The General Libraries
The University of Texas at Austin

Andean Studies: New Trends and Library Resources

Papers of the Forty-Fifth Annual Meeting of the
SEMINAR ON THE ACQUISITION OF
LATIN AMERICAN LIBRARY MATERIALS

University of California, Los Angeles
UCLA Library
UCLA Latin American Center
May 27–31, 2000

César Rodríguez
Editor

SALALM Secretariat
Benson Latin American Collection
The General Libraries
The University of Texas at Austin

ISBN: 0-917617-69-X

Contents

Andean Resources and Bibliography

Modern Crises Facing Andean Nations

Literary Themes

Cataloging, Bibliographic Control, and Library Services

Accreditation in Latin American Higher Education

Preface

The countries of Latin America's Andean region were very much in the news during SALALM's forty-fifth annual meeting held in Long Beach, California, in May 2000. During the conference, news stories about the decline of democratic rule, the gains of autocratic rulers, and the rise of economic crises appeared almost daily. It could be said that the theme of our conference, "Andean Studies: New Trends and Library Resources," could not have come at a better time. Our theme gave us the opportunity to study and to better understand this troubled region, and it made possible the preparation of many excellent papers by SALALM members and invited guests.

As they face the new millennium, the countries of the Andean region, as well as much of Latin America, have made significant achievements including a partial goal of democracy and economic stability. Even a centuries-old border dispute has been settled between Ecuador and Peru. This border conflict was the last major border dispute in Latin America, and its resolution marks a new era of peace and stability for the area. Nevertheless, there are still many obstacles that face these countries. Democratic ideas are in their infant stage in some countries, and political violence as well as censorship is clearly evident. The social problems caused by poverty, corruption, crime, judicial insecurity, inadequate education and health coverage, and lack of accountability of policy makers are only a few of the issues that Andean nations will have to overcome in the new millennium in order to improve the everyday life of its citizens. The papers presented in this volume examine many of these issues by exploring topics relating to the political, social, economic, literary, and artistic history of the Andean nations.

During the conference, librarians, scholars, book dealers, and publishers from Latin America, the United States, and Europe presented a series of workshops, panels, and roundtables. Many sessions were scholarly in nature covering topics mentioned above, but others dealt with critical issues surrounding bibliographic control, collection development, and the preservation of materials focusing on Andean countries. A number of excellent bibliographies are also included in this volume relating to various Andean themes. In the age of new technologies, some sessions also explored the impact of these advances, and the issues of access to research collections specializing on the Andean region.

To open the conference, we had the great pleasure of welcoming Dr. María Rostworowski as our keynote speaker. For many years now, Dr. Rostworowski has been one of Peru's most brilliant contemporary historians and is undoubtedly one of the great names in Andean ethnohistory. She is a tireless researcher and a prolific author that has published approximately twenty-one books and has contributed some eighty articles published in journals and books on Andean ethnohistory. These works reveal her preoccupation with themes such as the Inca state, the social and economic structure of Peru's coastal region, the ecological wisdom of Andean agricultural practices, the importance of women in pre-Hispanic Peru, the fallacies about the Inca rulers, and the trade routes that linked Peru and Central America. Her book about the true history of Tahuantinsuyu is one of her greatest milestones and reflects her thorough knowledge of the pre-Hispanic Andean world. Dr. Rostworowski set the stage for this conference by providing a general overview of Inca society from its earliest beginnings to the fall of the Inca Empire.

At the end of SALALM XLV, I received many congratulatory remarks about the success of the conference. But it is my sincere belief that the success of any conference is due to the people that participate, not only the organizers and presenters, but also the moderators, rapporteurs, book dealers, and devoted SALALM members. It is also the activities that take place during the annual meeting—the committee meetings, receptions, no-host lunches, library tours, and the friendly exchange of ideas between SALALM members—that enriches the conference, thereby making it a great success.

Nevertheless, there are some individuals that deserve special mention. At this time I would like to extend my heartfelt gratitude to a very hardworking Local Arrangements Committee led by co-chairs Eudora Loh and Barbara Valk. It has been my good fortune to have the opportunity to work with such an exemplary group. The co-chairs deserve a very special thanks because without their leadership and hard work, this conference would not have been possible. I am truly indebted to them for their organizing skills and their patience. My special thanks are also extended to David Block for his good counsel and guidance. I also thank the University of California, Los Angeles; UCLA Libraries; UCLA Department of Spanish and Portuguese; Getty Research Institute; PROMPERU, Comisión para la Promoción del Perú; and the Latin American Center at UCLA for being the gracious hosts of SALALM XLV. This was an auspicious year because the Latin American Center also celebrated its fortieth anniversary, and the SALALM membership was extremely pleased to be part of this celebration.

At this time, I would also like to express my deep appreciation to all presenters for the many fascinating papers and the informative workshops prepared, and to our keynote speaker, Dr. María Rostworowski, who made the long trip from Peru to delight us with her presentation and her presence. Finally, a special thanks to Mark L. Grover and Shannon Thurlow for their invaluable assistance and patience in editing these papers.

César Rodríguez

Andean History Revisited

1. Visión general sobre el Incario

María Rostworowski

Antes de hablar sobre los incas no podemos dejar de lado mencionar el paisaje y el mediocambiante del Perú, por tratarse de un país de difícil y de variada ecología.

El mundo andino no se limita, para nosotros, con la zona de la sierra, sino que comprende también la costa y la selva, con una noción de geografía global. Las tres regiones no se mantuvieron aisladas a través de los siglos y existió un intercambio, una complementariedad, y a la vez un rechazo entre sus habitantes.

La costa, está compuesta por amplios desiertos cortados por ríos que bajan de las serranías. Ellos no tienen un curso regular, y su cauce aumenta durante la temporada de lluvias en las tierras altas. Los valles son fértiles, pero necesitan de sofisticados sistemas hidráulicos para su agricultura. La costa depende del aforo del agua de sus ríos para subsistir y, tiene una subordinación con relación a la sierra. Por ese motivo los serranos pretendían dominar las tierras bajas debido a que el recurso acuífero procedía de las alturas.

En cada valle costeño su historia dependió de esa relación costa-sierra y del lugar adonde se hallaba el centro de poder en una determinada época o momento. Naturalmente a través del tiempo variaron esos centros. Cuando el apogeo de las culturas costeñas, los yungas dominaban sus bocatomas de diversas maneras. A la inversa cuando los serrano dominaban, no existían defensas costeñas.

Ante la torturada naturaleza de desiertos costeños, de quebradas andinas al infinito, de elevadas y heladas punas y de cálidas selvas, el mundo que se ofreció a los primeros habitantes era un mundo duro, difícil, donde el individuo no era nada. Le era imposible luchar solo contra la naturaleza hostil, y para poder vencer tantos tropiezos fue necesario unirse en un esfuerzo para domar el medio ambiente. De ahí surge en los Andes ese espíritu comunitario que caracteriza a sus habitantes y a su cultura, situación que se manifiesta en quechua con la palabra *huaccha*-huérfano, es decir el individuo que está solo en el mundo. Por eso el ideal andino es pertenecer a una familia extendida y numerosa, de la cual se puede obtener ayuda y a la vez ayudar.

A pesar de las dificultades del terreno andino y gracias a la diversidad de sus climas, los Andes fue uno de los centros más importantes del mundo para la domesticación de las plantas útiles al hombre.

El complicado territorio no impidió la existencia del florecimiento de las altas culturas que se distinguen por su desarrollo artístico, y sus diversas tecnologías. Los incas representan la época moderna de las culturas andinas y ocuparon el último siglo antes de la invasión. No es nuestro propósito hablar sobre ese tema; sólo diremos que el historiador inglés Toynbee, en su estudio sobre las civilizaciónes del mundo, señala la andina como una de las originales del universo.

Los Incas deben juzgarse como la etapa moderna del antiguo Perú y los cronistas Cieza de León, Castro Ortega y Morejón (1558) así lo mencionan. El auge cusqueño no duró más de un siglo y fue interrumpido por las huestes de Pizarro.

El conocimiento de las tecnologías andinas conseguidas por las civilizaciones anteriores al Incario, permitieron que los esfuerzos de los incas se centraran en el aprovechamiento de los logros del pasado, para dar a sus conocimientos las dimensiones necesarias para la formación del Estado.

Los soberanos cusqueños no inventaron tecnologías nuevas, sino que se destacan por sus sistemas organizativos y por la planificación exitosa e increíble, obtenida sin poseer escritura y sólo a base del manejo de los quipus. Es lamentable que esta última virtud la hayamos perdido.

Cuando la invasión capitaneada por Pizarro, el país estaba sufriendo de espantosas epidemias de eruptivas y de gripe que se adelataron a la presencia física de los invasores, ellas diezmaron a la población indígena quien carecía de defensas genéticas ante las nuevas enfermedades (Cook 1975).

La baja demográfica fue una verdadera calamidad para el país, y recurrentemente volvían a aparecer a través del tiempo. Las enfermedades en dimensión de pandemias facilitaron la conquista hispana.

Las fuentes para investigar la etnohistoria son naturalmente y en primer lugar las crónicas. Ellas tienen valores distintos según las fuentes usadas por sus autores. Los cronistas, como personajes de los siglos XVI y XVII, tuvieron dificultades para comprender un mundo tan ajeno a ellos y carecían de preparación para el reto. Es frecuente hallar que no comprendían muchas situaciones que se les presentaban.

Aparte de las crónicas, existen una infinidad de documentos en los archivos dejados por la administración española, y son fuentes importantes y menos parcializadas que las crónicas. Representan juicios, testamentos, visitas; o sea, la información local necesaria para elaborar posteriormente la tasa y el tributo que los naturales debían pagar a sus encomenderos.

Sin embargo, toda esta documentación preparada por europeos adolece de defectos de incomprensión de lo andino, de su pensamiento y de su lógica. Además existía la tendencia de los autores hispanos a proyectar su propia cultura judaico-cristiana en sus escritos en lugar de la nativa. Un ejemplo basta para ilustrar nuestro decir. Las crónicas mencionan la herencia del poder de padres a hijos tomando en cuenta la primogenitura. Sin embargo, se percibe que las sucesiones y la herencia en general se otorgaba al "más hábil y suficiente" individuo entre un grupo de candidatos. Podemos afirmar que no existió la primogenitura, ni la bastardía.

En la historia inca no existe el afán europeo por las cronologías. Varios gobernantes fueron excluidos de los relatos por molestar a sus sucesores. Sin embargo, a pesar de que la población era ágrafa, contaban con medios para recordar los eventos, como cantares, que se realizaban durante ciertas fiestas y en las cuales participaban por sus turnos los *ayllus, panacas* o grupos étnicos y que se efectuaban en la plaza principal del Cusco. En ellos narraban las proezas de los jefes de antaño. Además contaban con tablas pintadas que ilustraban los hechos contenidos en los famosos quipus llamados históricos que no se sabe cómo funcionaban.

Habiendo expuesto ciertos conceptos sobre los incas, veremos a grandes líneas su historia. No se puede iniciar el relato con la llegada de Manco Capac y su grupo al Cusco, porque sabemos muy poco de su cronología, faltan trabajos para establecer los movimientos de las etnías, además de arqueología del lugar.

Arrancamos con la llamada historia inca, con el relato de la leyenda de los chancas. Se trataba de un pueblo rudo y aguerrido instalado al norte del Cusco, que había mantenido con los incas repetidos enfrentamientos. El momento les era propicio para atentar contra el poder del viejo inca Viracocha, quien había incorporado a su gobierno a su hijo Urco en calidad de su coregente, para asegurar su sucesión. El Inca y su hijo abandonaron el Cusco a su suerte y se refugiaron en Chita en espera de la rendición de la ciudad. En esas circunstancias surgió la figura del príncipe Cusi Yupanqui, quien decidió defender su ciudad del ataque enemigo.

Con el posterior triunfo de Cusi Yupanqui y su toma del poder con el nombre de Pachacutec Inca Yupanqui se inicia el poderío inca y su increíble expansión. Con la derrota chanca, el círculo de enemigos poderosos que rodeaba al curacazgo Inca quedó desbaratado y nada impedía la expansión cusqueña.

En esos primeros tiempos el inca carecía de poder para ordenar el inicio de las obras necesarias para afianzar su expansión. El cronista Betanzos narra cómo Pachacutec convocó a los señores vecinos, los agasajó con fiestas y numerosos regalos para luego establecer su "ruego" que consistía en mano de obra para emprender los trabajos que consideraba necesarios. Esto indica que el Inca no gozaba de suficiente fuerza de trabajo, ni de poder de convocatoria para ejecutar solo las obras requeridas.

La llamada reciprocidad fue el eje principal del mundo andino y su definición puede ser la siguiente: la reciprocidad fue un sistema organizativo socioeconómico que regulaba las prestaciones de servicios a diversos niveles y servía de engranaje en la producción y distribuciones de bienes. Era un ordenamiento de las relaciones entre los miembros de una sociedad cuya economía desconocía el uso del dinero. Existía en todo el ámbito andino y actuó como un eslabón entre los diversos modelos de organizaciones presentes en el amplio territorio.

El gobierno cusqueño se valió también de la reciprocidad para su expansión territorial. Antes de iniciar el ataque a un señorío, el Inca proponía establecer la reciprocidad, entonces se celebraban fiestas y agasajos, y se solicitaba al curaca su rendición. El señor por conquistar aceptaba la organización socioeconómica inca en lugar de ir a la guerra.

Para un jefe étnico era preferible establecer lazos de parentesco con el Cusco en lugar de luchar, pues tenía todas las probabilidades de ser vencido, despojado de su patrimonio y quizá ser victimado.

La fase de apogeo del Incario se dio con los gobiernos de tres grandes soberanos elegidos por sus cualidades y mérito y no por sucesión de primogenitura, ellos fueron:

Pachacutec Inca Yupanqui	el iniciador
Tupac Yupanqui	el conquistador
Huayna Capac	el estadista

Con ellos se creó el Tahuantinsuyo que significa "Las Cuatro Regiones unidas entre sí", y que comprendía buena parte del Continente sudamericano con cara al Océano Pacífico.

Aspectos organizativos

La sociedad andina era una sociedad fuertemente jerarquizada no solamente entre las culturas serranas, sino también en las de la costa. El territorio estaba dividido en magroetnías, o señoríos, que a su vez se componían de varias pequeñas jefaturas.

Al decir de los cronistas, el Inca Tupac Yupanqui dividió la población en un incipiente sistema decimal. Así en cada macroetnía los habitantes formaban pequeños grupos de diez hombres siendo uno de ellos el jefe. Le seguía una división por *pachaca*, o sea de cien varones con su propio jefe; diez de estas *pachaca* comprendían una *guaranga* de mil hombres.

Sin embargo, existían dos grupos que escapaban al sistema, uno de ellos eran los *mitimaes* enviados lejos de sus lugares de origen para cumplir diversos trabajos para el Estado; podían ser agricultores, guardianes de las fronteras; artesanos especializados, etc., todos marchaban con sus mujeres, hijos y sus propios jefes. En teoría, ellos no rompían sus lazos con sus aldeas de origen, pero en la práctica las distancias eran tan grandes que perdían el contacto con sus pueblos. El segundo grupo estaba formado por los *yana,* o servidores. Algunos autores los han calificado erróneamente de esclavos, en la realidad significaba que se desligaban de sus orígenes y adquirían una cierta movilidad social en las jerarquías establecidas. Podían permanecer como servidores del Inca, de una divinidad o de un señor, pero también convertirse en jefes étnicos a las órdenes directas del soberano sin pasar por la reciprocidad, lo que representó una ventaja para el Inca.

Al no existir el uso del dinero, la riqueza del Estado se apoyaba en la posesión de ciertos recursos que podían ser medidos y contabilizados. Tres eran las fuentes de ingreso del Incario, a saber: la fuerza de trabajo, la posesión de tierras estatales y la ganadería también estatal. El resultado de esas tres tenencias se manifestaba en bienes acumulados en depósitos. Estos bienes permitían al Estado controlar la reciprocidad, clave del sistema organizativo, que facilitó la rápida expansión territorial. Para hacer frente a la demanda de la reciprocidad el Estado debía poseer depósitos colmados, y contar con grandes reservas de subsistencias y de productos manufacturados. Esos bienes eran indispensables para el funcionamiento de la reciprocidad, es decir que con ellos otorgaba el Estado donativos a los señores étnicos para lograr su sumisión. En otras palabras, el capital del gobierno se manifestaba con el acopio de riquezas, ellas sustituían y reemplazaban la existencia del dinero, y eran redistribuídas según las necesidades del Estado.

La fuerza de trabajo

El interés del Incario por disponer y controlar la fuerza de trabajo se debía a la necesidad de ejecutar diversas labores en beneficio del gobierno; esos trabajos eran múltiples, como por ejemplo: la formación de ejércitos para las campañas guerreras; las faenas en los campos estatales; la ejecución de la red de caminos, puentes, etc.

Para conocer los montos poblacionales requeridos, se precisaba de una eficiente planificación y contabilidad de los habitantes del Incario. Es sorprendente cómo los naturales lograron esas metas sin escritura, con sólo la existencia de ábacos, usando un primitivo sistema decimal de casilleros que representaban las decenas, centenas y miles. Sólo los cómputos finales se registraban en los *quipus,* esas cordeletas de distintos largos, colores y nudos.

Existieron los especialistas contadores llamados los *quipucamayoc,* ellos podían informar al Inca, en el momento deseado, las cifras de población que disponía un lugar, las reservas de productos en los depósitos, etc.

La tierra

La posesión de tierras era una de las riquezas más preciadas en el Tahuantinsuyu y su posesión seguía los patrones andinos. Según las crónicas, las tierras se dividían en tierra del Inca, vale decir del Estado; las del Sol y de los hombres del común, o *hatun runa.* Veámos en detalle el reparto.

a) *Las tierras del Inca.* Este tipo de tenencia se hallaba en todo el territorio, y gracias a documentos de archivos sabemos que cada ayllu, o grupo étnico, disponía de ciertos campos para dicho fin, aunque fuesen pequeños. Los campos eran cultivados por la gente local en común y en forma festiva, con música y comida otorgada por el gobierno.

b) La segunda calificación correspondía a *tierras del Sol, o del culto,* también cada *huaca* grande o pequeña gozaba de un campo, cuya dimensión dependía de su categoría, y en él se cultivaba el maíz necesario para la elaboración de las bebidas para sus fiestas.

Por último, el hombre del pueblo poseía sus tierras en común con su ayllu o grupo étnico y el producto le pertenecía sin tener que dar nada como tributo de su parcela de tierra. Un aspecto importante era que el tributo en sí *no existía,* el poblador sólo entregaba su fuerza de trabajo.

Un hecho que hemos hallado en varios manuscritos es la referencia a las propiedades personales o privadas de cada uno de los últimos soberanos. Ellas se extendían en distintos valles y cubrían vastas extensiones. También las *coyas* o reinas poseían bienes personales, pero limitados. A la muerte del Inca sus tierras eran usufructuadas por su *panaca,* o linaje como si el soberano permaneciera en vida.

La ganadería

Los camélidos jugaron un rol muy importante en el desarrollo de las culturas andinas, y se criaron tanto en la sierra como en la costa. Las alpacas y llamas formaban grandes hatos, cuya división siguió la posesión de la tierra. Si no existió en los Andes el delirio sangriento de sacrificios humanos, como en México, fue en parte por la presencia de los camélidos que suplían al hombre.

Depósitos estatales

La fuerza de trabajo que laboraba en las tierras estatales y los numerosos camélidos que pastaban en las punas, permitían llenar los depósitos con bienes acumulados que significaban la riqueza del Estado. Además todo un sistema contable permitía conocer lo conservado en los depósitos, hecho que causó la admiración de los españoles al contemplar el orden y los elevados montos de los bienes acumulados.

Para cubrir las necesidades del Estado, el Incario construyó una red caminera que asombró a los hispanos, pues en aquel entonces no existía nada semejante en Europa. Esta red vial cubría de 30 mil a 50 mil kilómetros, con dos vías principales; una, la troncal de la sierra que iba desde el Cusco a Quito; y el camino a lo largo de la costa con una red de conexiones a lo ancho del territorio. Los ríos se cruzaban con puentes colgantes y también de troncos, según las necesidades. A lo largo de las rutas se levantaban *tambos,* o mesones, que disponían de alimentos y proporcionaban un lugar de descanso.

Los modelos económicos

El modelo económico Inca se ha calificado de redistributivo, debido a las funciones que cumplía el propio gobierno. Esto significa que gran parte de la producción del país era acaparada por el Estado; el cual, a su vez, la distribuía según sus intereses.

a) El modelo económico serrano: sierra sur

La economía sureña del Tahuantinsuyu ha sido estudiada por John Murra (1964, 1967, 1972). Para obtener productos de diversos medio ambientes, los naturales se valían del sistema de enclaves llamados por Murra "Archipiélagos verticals", cuyo núcleo serrano controlaba por medio de colonias multiétnicas, zonas diferentes, situadas en microclimas *distantes.*

Subrayamos la palabra *distante,* para indicar que se hallaban a varios días de camino unos de otros. Estos enclaves son a la fecha clásicos y se situaban en la costa y en la selva, quedando el núcleo en la sierra a varios días de marcha.

Murra en sus trabajos se pregunta cómo se crearon esos enclaves, nosotros a través de varios documentos encontramos que su origen estaba en una conquista.

b) La sierra central

Una situación muy diferente a la del altiplano existía en la Cordillera Marítima Central. Las condiciones geográficas especiales hicieron que los naturales adoptaran un modelo propio. Es importante demostrar cómo una situación diferente se creaba debido a un medio ambiente distinto y hacía variar el modelo. Esta información la obtuvimos en dos documentos para la región de Canta de 1549 y 1553. La zona de Canta, al noreste de Lima, tiene un terreno muy abrupto que a corta distancia goza de climas distintos, lo cual permite producir recursos agrícolas variados.

El Señorío de Canta comprendía ocho *ayllus,* y para atender cultivos situados a diversas alturas y microclimas distantes a un sólo día de camino, idearon un trabajo comunal rotativo y de temporada. Esta trashuancia limitada los llevó a poseer, además de sus pueblos permanentes, unas aldeas comunes habitadas temporalmente, mientras cumplían sus labores en la zona.

Por ejemplo, se dirigían a la puna sobre los cuatro mil metros para sembrar y cosechar una planta llamada *maca* (Lepidium meyenii), o a realizar la esquila de sus camélidos.

En otra época del año bajaban a la región cálida, a las plantaciones de coca (Eritroxylum novogranatense, var. trujillensis) de la variedad de hojas pequeñas que se daba en la costa y era muy estimada. No sólo usaban de sus aldeas trashumantes para la agricultura, sino también para fabricar en común textiles, cerámica, preparar charqui o carne secada al sol, etc. (Rostworowski 1978).

El modelo económico costeño

La especialización laboral

Dado que la economía serrana guardaba relación con el medio ambiente propio a las quebradas andinas y de las punas, es comprensible que la diferente geográfica de la costa propiciase un modelo económico distinto.

Una de las mayores riquezas de los pueblos costeños era el mar, un mar rico en especies ictiológicas. Aquello dio lugar a los grupos de pescadores instalados a lo largo del litoral dedicados sólo a pescar y secar sus productos.

Esa práctica dio lugar a la división de la población costera entre pescadores y agricultores. Un manuscrito sobre el Señorío de Chincha indica, para el valle, una división de sus 30 mil hombres en 10 mil pescadores; 12 mil campesinos y 6 mil "mercaderes", a modo de indios.

Una acuciosa investigación en archivos reveló la situación laboral costeña como altamente especializada. Cada oficio, cada trabajo, era cumplido por determinadas personas, sin que nadie pudiese cambiar su labor por otra; hecho que recibió el apoyo posterior de la administración virreinal.

El intercambio costeño

En las sociedades arcaicas predominaba, según Polanyi (1957), el modelo redistributivo, a pesar de existir en algunos lugares el hábito del intercambio. Este fue el proceso seguido entre los Señoríos costeños y marcó una diferencia con los Señoríos serranos.

La reciprocidad, como una institución, tuvo mayor poder en la costa al emplearse tanto la redistribución como el trueque, que se basaba en equivalencias establecidas y compensaba la falta de algún tipo de producto local. Un estudio empírico de la economía llamada primitiva comprende en sus principales cuadros la reciprocidad, la redistribución y el trueque. Es así que se formó en la costa un trueque local y un intercambio a larga distancia.

El trueque local

La especialización del trabajo obligó en la costa al establecimiento de un trueque local entre sus habitantes para obtener las subsiscencias y los objetos que cada uno *no* producía. En las sociedades arcaicas existía un rechazo a los beneficios en las transacciones que involucraban los alimentos; se limitaban a mantener equivalencias. El trueque a nivel local en un valle costeño no era materia de ganancia, sino a un acomodo necesario al sistema de trabajo especializado imperante en la sociedad.

Intercambio a larga distancia de los "mercaderes" chinchanos

En el Señorío de Chincha mencionamos más arriba, la presencia de seis mil "mercaderes a modo de indios". Naturalmente, la palabra "mercader" no tiene los mismos conceptos que los actuales, ellos trocaban diversos productos por no conocer el uso del dinero.

Según el documento en cuestión, ellos cubrían dos rutas: una terrestre con hatos de camélidos y se dirigían al Altiplano y al Cusco y otra, vía marítima, en balsas hacia el actual Ecuador. Los objetos principales de trueque eran el cobre y el *mullu* (Spondylus sp.) una concha roja de mares cálidos.

Durante el segundo viaje de Pizarro que antecedió al de los acontecimientos de Cajamarca, su piloto mayor Bartolomé Ruiz, apresó una balsa de troncos de gran tamaño que conducía una variadad de mercaderías. Según Anne Chapman (1957) el trueque distante no usó de mercados sino de "puertos", lugares donde se realizaban los intercambios. Ellos desaparecieron inmediatamente después del impacto europeo.

Reflexiones finales

La organización Inca asombró a los europeos y sirvió para crear la utopía de un Estado donde el hambre, la necesidad y la miseria estaban proscritos.

Sin embargo, uno de los motivos del espectacular derrumbe del Incario fue un sordo descontento latente, tanto entre las clases dominates como en el pueblo.

Analicemos los diferentes motivos, ellos se pueden dividir en las *causas visibles* y las *causas profundas*.

Las visibles son bien conocidas, ellas fueron: la guerra fratricida, el factor sorpresa en la embosacada de Cajamarca, la superioridad tecnológica de la armas españolas, es decir los arcabuces, falconetes, las espadas de acero y por último la presencia del caballo.

Sin embargo, existen otros motivos profundos que actuaron en la derrota indígena, a saber: la falta de integración nacional, los naturales no tuvieron la visión del peligro que los amenazaba y sobre todo pesó el descontento de los grandes señores "provincianos" frente a la política Inca, seguidos por el descontento de la gente del común.

Los incas no intentaron anular la existencia de los grandes Señoríos, o macroetnías, porque los cusqueños se apoyaban en las estructuras locales y regionales para gobernar. Al Inca le bastaba recibir el reconocimiento de su poder absoluto que le daba acceso a la fuerza de trabajo que necesitaba, además de la designación, en todo el país, de tierras estatales y del Culto. A partir de estas exigencias, cada macroetnía conservó sus características regionales.

La única medida centralizadora impuesta por el Inca fue la implantación de un mismo idioma para todos los territorios, que los españoles llamaron la "lengua del Inca". El descontento de los señores se basaba en su empobrecimiento, a pesar de los grandes donativos que les otorgaba el estado. En efecto, ellos proporcionaban al gobierno sus mejores hombres para integrar los ejércitos, además de numerosos mitimaes y *yanas* que eran llevados fuera de sus Señoríos. Por su parte, la gente del común estaba igualmente descontenta por tener que participar en las guerras que duraban largo tiempo sobre todo en el Ecuador y en Chile. Otros tenían que partir en calidad de mitimaes y perdían todo contacto con los suyos. Por último, los que quedaban tenían más trabajo para suplir la mano de obra ausente.

El Estado Inca no llegó a plasmarse en una integración nacional y su acción se limitó a su reconocimiento y al aprovechamiento de los recursos humanos y territoriales en poder de los señores étnicos.

Una innegable situación de descontento debió reinar entre los señores y entre las clases populares, insatisfacción que fomentó el deseo de sacudirse de la influencia inca. Estos sentimientos explican la buena acogida otorgada por los naturales a las huestes de Pizarro. Sólo después, con las miserias y los sufrimientos que se abatieron sobre el pueblo durante la Colonia, surgió una añoranza por el pasado inca.

Por esas razones los grandes señores, junto con su pueblo, se plegaron a los españoles y ayudaron con sus ejércitos y con sus bienes a la conquista hispana. Por esos motivos no fue un puñado de españoles quienes doblegaron al Inca, sino los propios indígenas descontentos con la situación imperante, quienes creyeron encontrar una situación favorable para recobrar su pasada libertad. Los indígenas no podían prever los sucesos, ni el arribo masivo de hispanos. Ellos apoyaron a los españoles porque vieron una oportunidad para librarse del yugo inca. La fragilidad de las bases del Estado Inca era excesiva para hacer frente a la rebelión de los grandes señores andinos y a la conquista europea con superior tecnología.

La reacción indígena a los sucesos de Cajamarca y la prisión y muerte de Atahualpa, se produce en 1536 con Manco II, Inca títere nombrado por los españoles para mantener la cohesión del país.

En noviembre de 1535, Hernando Pizarro, hermano del conquistador retornó de España, donde había viajado para entregar el quinto del rey sobre las tasas del "Rescate". El marqués Pizarro ocupado en la recién fundada ciudad de Los Reyes, capital de su gobernación, envió a su hermano al Cusco con el cargo de Teniente Gobernador. Hernando experimentaba una insaciable sed por lograr más riquezas y ejercía constantes presiones sobre Manco II para que le aportara un mayor número de tesoros, por ese motivo permitió al Inca ausentarse del Cusco con el ofrecimiento de traerle más oro.

Manco, con su recuperada libertad, aprovechó de la situación para sublevarse y cercó la ciudad en 1536. Siguieron varios meses de una obstinada lucha de los naturales por apoderarse de su antigua capital, y una porfiada resistencia hispana. La *Relación anónima* sobre aquellos sucesos muestra la división existente entre los naturales. Según la crónica, un ejército atacó también la ciudad de Lima, sede del gobierno español, ellos avanzaron por el llano del río con lucida gente y comenzaron a entrar por las calles de Lima, es entonces que salió la caballería y se entabló la lucha. los caballos no podían avanzar entre los guijarros del río que impedían su defensa. Los españoles principiaron a desmayar por tener pocos efectivos, cuando sorpresivamente los soldados de Manco emprendieron la huida y se replegaron hacia la sierra. La crónica no esclarece el por qué del abandono indígena de la plaza cuando la tenía prácticamente ganada, la situación se explicó cuando a través de un manuscrito de archivo se supo que la jefa étnica de Huaylas llamada Contar Huacho, una de las mujeres segundarias del pasado Inca, envió un ejército de socorro contra Manco II, por ser su hija la concubina de Pizarro.

La falta de sentimiento de nación se manifestó con esta ayuda brindada por la curaca de Huaylas a los invasores. Primó en ella el parentesco y el deseo de la clase dominante indígena de sacudirse y librarse del gobierno inca.

Otro ejemplo de falta de unión y de comprensión de la situación en que se vivía en aquel entonces es la actitud del señor étnico llamado Huacra Paucar, curaca de Anan Jauja quien colaboró con los españoles proporcionándoles todo lo que necesitaban. Les dio víveres y sobre todo gente para transportar las subsistencias y las armas a ambos grupos de los hispanos durante sus guerras civiles.

Su ayuda fue masiva e importante en bien de los europeos y para que los indígenas no trataran de escapar los encadenaban, y si uno caía al abismo, y los hay muchos en la sierra, los demás seguían en su muerte.

El curaca de Jauja apuntaba minuciosamente en sus *quipus* lo que entregaba y años después cuando se estableció la administración española, acudió a la Real Audiencia con sus *quipus,* esas cordeletas con nudos, para pedir una recompensa a la Corona. Quería que se le otorgara por sus servicios una encomienda, naturalmente no recibió nada.

Estos dos ejemplos mencionados muestran la escasa visión de los indígenas de los acontecimientos, ellos no comprendieron los deseos de los españoles de apoderarse de la tierra y de reducir a sus habitantes a una situación de subordinación y de miseria. A Manco II no lo siguieron los grandes señores de la macroetnía, el Inca no contó con el apoyo del país hecho que demuestra que los curacas no se integraron a su rebelión, debido a su descontento.

BIBLIOGRAFÍA

Betanzos, Juan de. 1968. *Suma y narración de los Incas*. Madrid: Biblioteca de Autores Españoles, Ediciones Atlas.

Castro, Fray Cristóbal y Diego Ortega Morejón. 1974. "Relación y declaración del modo que este valle de Chincha y sus comarcanos se gobernaron antes que hobiese ingas y después que los hobo hasta que los cristianos entraron en esta tierra". Edición de Juan Carlos Crespo. *Historia y Cultura* 8:91–104.

Chapman, Anne. 1957. "Port of Trade in Aztec and Maya Civilizations". En Karl Polanyi, *Trade and Market in the Early Empires*. Glencoe, Ill.: The Free Press. Pp. 114–153.

Cook, Noble David. 1975. *Tasa de la Visita General de Francisco de Toledo*. Lima: Dirección Universitaria de Biblioteca y Publicaciones, Universidad Nacional Mayor de San Marcos.

Martín Rubio, María del Carmen. 1987. *Suma y narración de los Incas (segunda parte)*. Madrid: Edición Atlas.

Murra, John V. 1964. "Una apreciación etnológica de la Visita". En Garci Diez de San Miguel, *Visita hecha a la Provincia de Chucuito*. Lima: Casa de la Cultura. Pp. 419–442.

——. 1967. "La Visita de los Chupachos como fuente etnológica". En Iñigo Ortiz de Zùñiga, *Visita de la Provincia de León de Huánuco en 1562, t. 1*. Huánuco, Perú: Universidad Nacional Hermilio Valdizán. Pp. 381–406.

——. 1972. "El 'control vertical' de un máximo de pisos ecológicos en la economía de las sociedades andinas", t. 2. En Iñigo Ortiz de Zúñiga, *Visita de la Provincia de León de Huánuco*. Huánuco, Perú: Universidad Nacional Hermilio Valdizán. Pp. 427–476.

——. 1975. *Formaciones económicas y políticas de mundo andino*. Lima: Instituto de Estudios Peruanos.

Polany, Karl, C. A. Arenberg, y H. Pearson. 1957. *Trade and Market in the Early Empires*. Glencoe, Ill.: The Free Press.

Rostworowski, María. 1970. "Mercaderes del Valle de Chincha en la época prehispánica: un documento y unos comentarios". *Revista Española de Antropología Americana* 5:135–178.

——. 1972. "Las etnías del valle del Chillón". *Revista del Museo Nacional* 38:250–314.

——. 1978. *Señorios indígenas de Lima y Canta*. Lima: Instituto de Estudios Peruanos.

——. 1983. *Estructuras andinas del poder, ideología religiosa y política*. Lima: Instituto de Estudios Peruanos.

——. 1988. *Historia del Tahuantinsuyu*. 5th ed. Lima: Instituto de Estudios Peruanos.

——. 1989. *Costa peruana prehispánica*. 2d ed. Lima: Instituto de Estudios Peruanos.

2. El conocimiento del mundo andino a través de las crónicas

Enrique Marchena Cárdenas

Introducción

El presente trabajo busca presentar un panorama general sobre las crónicas escritas en el Nuevo Mundo, especialmente sobre aquellas gracias a las cuales nos es posible conocer el mundo andino de la época, tema de esta reunión de SALALM.

En vista a la complejidad y amplitud del tema propuesto en esta ponencia, me limitaré a señalar cronológicamente aspectos puntuales de la historia de las crónicas y de los principales cronistas. Sin embargo hay que señalar que, aparte de las crónicas, existían otros documentos como relaciones, cartas y coplas.

La crónica en España

En Europa, y particularmente en España, la crónica había surgido como una rama del árbol épico. La crónica castellana se nutrió de la vieja cepa popular de los cantares de gesta. La crónica medieval tuvo como característica formal, la de ser narración pura, objetividad ajena a toda opinión o juicio reflexivo. Los cronistas repiten invariablemente la misma sucesión de hechos y batallas, con las mismas palabras. No pretenden juzgar ni encontrar una idea general, ni una explicación reflexiva sobre las causas. Las crónicas primitivas son puro relato. Los cronistas viven en el espíritu de los acontecimientos que narran y pertenecen a él. Se jactan de lo que vieron o lo que oyeron decir y de ello deriva su jerarquía en la credibilidad de las fuentes. Pero su cronología y su geografía son deficientes, y tienen toda la vaguedad de las tradiciones populares incluyendo en las gestas los nombres de los soldados que acompañan al jefe de la hueste.

La crónica en América

Se puede decir que la crónica se traslada a indias por encargo real. Las ordenanzas sobre conquistas y descubrimientos, cada vez más humanas y previsoras, prescriben que los aventureros que van a su costa y misión en busca de nuevas tierras, lleven consigo un veedor que haga la descripción de la tierra, de las riquezas de ésta y de los usos y costumbres de sus habitantes.

La crónica soldadesca es parca en la percepción de las costumbres y de las instituciones de los incas. La extrañeza de la vida india se va lentamente desvaneciendo, a medida que se verifica la fusión de los elementos originarios e importados, contrapuestos por la conquista. Durante las guerras civiles la atención de los cronistas está todavía pendiente principalmente de las peripecias de la contienda bélica. La crónica es en nuestra cultura el primer género mestizo. Pasado el estruendo bélico de la conquista o de la guerra civil entre españoles, el cronista castellano se inclina a recoger las tradiciones del pasado indio, a reconstruir la historia de sus príncipes y dinastías de sus jefes e instituciones, y a rastrear, por el interés de la evangelización, sus creencias religiosas, sus ritos, ceremonias y supersticiones gentílicas. La transculturación es palpable sobre todo en el lenguaje castellano que recibe el aporte cotidiano de las lenguas indígenas. Las palabras indígenas, escasas y mal transcritas en las primeras crónicas, van aumentando visiblemente, hasta alcanzar una proporción apreciable en las crónicas de escritores como Cieza, Gutiérrez de Santa Clara, Sarmiento, Murúa y Garcilaso, y ocupar, por último, trozos enteros, oraciones, himnos, haillis o cantos de triunfo, en las crónicas de Cristobal de Molina o de Juan Santa Cruz Pachacutic, indio españolizado y espiritualmente mestizo, hasta llegar a la crónica bilingüe de Guamán Poma de Ayala.

La tradición oral incaica de los cantares y de los quipus se recoge notarialmente en las llamadas informaciones de la Gasca, de Cañete y, posteriormente, de Toledo. Por más que se discuta el mérito y la imparcialidad de estas informaciones, ellas constituyen la única base subsistente de la historia incaica. Cada una de estas informaciones dio origen a crónicas fundamentales sobre el incario: las de Gasca a la crónica de Cieza, las de Cañete a la de Betanzos y las de Toledo a la Historia Indica de Pedro Sarmiento de Gamboa, y a los Ritos y Fábulas de los Incas de Cristobal de Molina.

Una nueva generación de cronistas, en la que aparecen ya algunos criollos y mestizos, reacciona, con natural simpatía y reclamo de la sangre, contra las exageraciones de la tesis toledana. Aunque las informaciones levantadas en 1583 por el virrey Enríquez sostengan todavía las afirmaciones de dureza y crueldad de los incas, contenidas en la encuesta de Toledo, la tendencia de los cronistas post-toledanos, a excepción de Cabello Balboa que copia a Sarmiento y a Molina, es la de poetizar la vida incaica. Los nuevos cronistas inician el ciclo novelesco, que es la decadencia de lo épico, y se hechan a buscar leyendas míticas o "romancescas", como las que llenan las crónicas de Cabello Balboa, Murúa, Montesinos, Anello Oliva (editado recientemente por el Fondo Editorial de la Universidad Católica) y un descendiente de los antiguos collaguas Juan Santa Cruz Pachacutic.

El servicio más trascendente prestado por la crónica castellana a nuestra cultura naciente, es haber salvado nuestra historia incaica de perecer por obra del tiempo y falta de escritura, como pereció la cultura de los pueblos preincaicos que los incas ahogaron y sumergieron en su propia cultura borrando todos los rastros de su contribución y atribuyéndose, por voz de Garcilaso y la tradición imperial cusqueña, todos sus esfuerzos y trofeos culturales, que ahora va restaurando el testimonio mudo de la arqueología. Historia, geografía, ciencia de la naturaleza, lenguaje y alma del primitivo Perú, hay que aprenderlos, pues las obras de los cronistas del siglo XVI son los verdaderos forjadores de la cultura mestiza y original del Perú.

En consecuencia, los cronistas del siglo XVI, desde Cieza a Betanzos hasta Sarmiento de Gamboa, Molina, Cabello Balboa y Murúa, agotaron los testimonios orales de los antiguos quipucamayocs que guardaban la tradición del imperio. Sin embargo, en el siglo XVI aparecen Garcilaso, Santa Cruz Pachacutic y Guamán Poma de Ayala, pero con un afán de ordenación y de síntesis que es el anuncio definitivo de la aparición de la historia.

Es importante señalar que uno de los primeros documentos más relevantes que se publicaron en 1629 es el Epítome de la Biblioteca Oriental i Occidental, Náutica i Geográfica, redactada por Antonio de León Pinelo, siendo publicada su edición facsimilar en Washington con el título de El Epítome de Pinelo, recogiendo entre cartas, relaciones y crónicas un número de 26 obras, siendo las siguientes:

1. Pedro Sancho de la Hoz. *Relación de la conquista del Perú*

2. Miguel de Astete. *Relación del viage de Fernando Pizarro, Desde Caxamalca*

3. Pedro Pizarro. *Relación de la conquista del Perú i su gobierno*

4. Diego de Trujillo. *Relación de la tierra, que descubrio con Pizarro, en el Perú*

5. Diego de Toro. *Comentario del Perú*

6. Francisco de Xerez. *Conquista del Perú.* 1547 (Juan de Sámano)

7. Jodoco Rique (Franciscano). *Relación de sucesos del Perú*

8. Vicente de Valverde. *Relación de las guerras de los pizarros i almagros*

9. Pedro de la Gasca. *Historia del Perú.* 1567

10. Silvio Uvilen. *Historia del Perú.* 1563 (En alemán)

11. Juan Hayo. *Cartas del Japón, India, Perú.* 1605

12. Juan Cristioval Calvete de Estrella. *Comentarios del Perú*

13. Agustín de Zárate. *Historia del descubrimiento i conquista del Perú.* 1555

14. Pedro Cieza de León. *Cronica del Perú.* 1553

15. Diego Fernandez Palentino. *Historia del Perú.* 1571

16. Levinico Apolonio Gandobrugano. *Del descubrimiento de las provincias del Perú, i de sus cosas.* 1567 (En latín)

17. Pedro de Castro. *Relación de la governación de los quixos, en Indias.* 1608

18. Inca Garcilaso de la Vega. *Historia general del Perú.* 1617

19. Vicente Marinero. *Historia del imperio peruano en Latin*

20. Polo de Ondegardo. *De las costumbres, ritos, i ceremonias de los Indios del Perú*

21. Blas Valera. *De los Indios del Perú i sus costumbres i pacificación*

22. Juan de Betanzos. *Historia del origen de los reyes Incas del Perú*

23. Manuel Cabello de Balboa. *Miscelanea antartica, i origen de los Indios i de los Incas del Perú*

24. Inca Garcilaso de la Vega. *Comentarios reales del origen de los Incas.* 1609

25. Josef de Acosta. *Historia natural i moral de las Indias.* 1590

26. Fernando Murillo de la Cerda. *Libro del conocimiento de letras i caracteres del Perú y Mexico.* 1602

Crónicas Perdidas

El Dr. Waldemar Espinoza Soriano, investigador y especialista en la época de la Colonia, sostiene que existen unas mil quinientas crónicas, de las cuales gran número están perdidas, aunque felizmente muchas crónicas y de gran valor han sido rescatadas. Refiere que hay información detallada de más crónicas sobre el Perú que sobre cualquier otro territorio descubierto y conquistado por los españoles. Es por ello que la atención sobre el gran imperio de los Incas es muy basta por los investigadores de todas las latitudes.

Sin embargo, Dr. Raúl Porras Barrenechea hace mención de crónicas que no han sido pubicadas y que están consideradas perdidas sobre la conquista tales como: *La relación del veedor Juan Carvallo,* desde la Isla del Gallo.

- Hay testimonios de la existencia de una Relación y dibujos de la ciudad de Tumbes por el griego Pedro de Candia, uno de los 13 de la Isla del Gallo, pero no ha sido encontrada.
- Fray Jodoco Ricki, autor de una relación que nunca apareció.
- Fray Marcos de Niza es otro cronista dudoso y clandestino cuya crónica sobre la conquista del Perú y particularmente sobre la conquista de Quito tampoco fue hallada.
- Francisco de Chávez escribió una crónica que contendría afirmaciones singulares sobre instituciones incaicas y acaso una versión insólita sobre el proceso de Atahualpa.
- Fray Vicente de Valverde es uno de los 13 de la Isla del Gallo y el más ilustrado acompañante de Pizarro. Fue el primer obispo de Lima y uno de los fundadores de la ciudad del Cusco. No se conserva, sin embargo, carta ni relación alguna sobre los episodios de Cajamarca.
- El fragmento historial del paje de Francisco Pizarro, Fernando de Montesinos, que da cuenta de la personalidad del conquistador, tampoco ha sido encontrado.
- La relación de Fray Luis de Morales sobre los daños y ofensas a los andinos no ha sido publicada todavía a pesar de encontrarse en el archivo de Indias de Sevilla.

Principales Crónicas del Siglo XVI

A continuación comentaré algunas crónicas importantes que dan cuenta del mundo andino y que fueron escritas en los primeros años de la llegada de los españoles a esta parte del continente y que dan fe de los acontecimientos de los últimos años del imperio de los incas, sus costumbres, su organización social, la vida cotidiana, su geografía, etc.

Francisco López de Xerez

Participó como escribano en las dos primeras expediciones dirigidas por Francisco Pizarro, dejando un valiosísimo documento titulado *Relación Samano Xerez*. Esta es una breve relación del primer contacto que hubo entre los peruanos de la costa norte y los futuros conquistadores. Se escribió en 1528, años antes de la toma de Cajamarca, y relata algunas escenas de los dos primeros viajes de Pizarro, realizados entre 1525 y 1527. Francisco de Xerez es el autor, más tarde cronista oficial de Pizarro. Juan de Sámano, secretario de Carlos V, sólo puso su firma en la Relación para darle carácter oficial. Esta Relación es reproducida por Porras en su libro Relaciones Primitivas de la Conquista del Perú en 1967. Luego se publica en el tomo I de la Biblioteca Peruana de los Editores Técnicos Asociados en 1968. Xerez posteriormente, por mandato de Pizarro, escribe la *Verdadera relación de la conquista del Perú*. En este documento incluye las tres expediciones de Pizarro hasta la muerte de Atahualpa. Xerez nos deja muchos y muy valiosos datos etnográficos y geográficos del Perú, la abundancia de oro y plata, el camino real, los edificios de piedra, los puentes colgantes, la alta tecnología textil, la existencia de pastores, la organización política, el uso de la numeración decimal y la autoridad absoluta del señor principal (no utiliza nunca la palabra inca).

Pedro Sancho de la Hoz

Este cronista sucedió a Xerez como escribano de Pizarro y se dirigió con éste al Cusco y redactó un documento referente a las guerras de conquista (julio 1534): *Relación de lo sucedido en la conquista y pacificación de estas provincias de la Nueva Castilla Después que el capitán Hernando Pizarro se partió y llevó a S. M. la relación de Victoria de Caxamalca*. El original se perdió. Sólo existe la edición italiana hecha por Ramusio en 1550. Trata de la actividad militar de los españoles en el período que va desde el enjuiciamiento de Atahualpa (julio 1533) hasta la marcha hacia Jauja, describiendo la ciudad del Cusco y la ceremonia de coronación de Manco Inca. El autor pone más énfasis en la relación de las operaciones militares y considera la guerra de conquista como una empresa para liberar el pueblo de Cusco de la tiranía de los de Quito.

Miguel de Estete

Hay una confusión sobre este cronista, ya que existieron hasta cuatro personajes con el mismo nombre. Este nombre aparece en la relación de españoles que se repartieron el rescate de Atahualpa. Después de la captura de Atahualpa, este cronista acompaña al capitán Hernando Pizarro como veedor hacia Pachacamac, escribiendo *La Relación del viaje que hizo el señor capitán Hernando Pizarro* a manera de diario. Se refiere a los acontecimientos ocurridos en el viaje, señalando el camino real, los puentes, el modo de crianza del ganado; informaciones sobre la sociedad y la religión, el dominio del estado inca; describe la majestad del Inca frente a sus súbditos. En 1535 debió escribir *La noticia del Perú*. El manuscrito se encuentra en el Archivo General de Indias. Luego se editó en 1918 en Quito, en 1938 en París y en 1987 en Buenos Aires.

Agustín de Zárate

Agustín de Zárate no es conquistador y viene al Perú como contador del rey acompañado de su sobrino Polo de Ondegardo, encontrándose ambos en plena guerra civil y obligado por las circunstancias regresa a España escribiendo su crónica titulada *Historia del descubrimiento y conquista del Perú*. Sólo estuvo un año en el Perú (junio 1544–julio 1545). El autor narra con minuciosidad el proceso de las guerras de conquista y las expediciones de aventura, sobre todo las guerras civiles del Perú. También describe las grandes obras atribuídas a Huayna Cápac, como el camino real, el tambo, las ropas y armas, los puentes colgantes, la reedificación del templo del Sol en el Cusco, etc. Esta crónica fue publicada en Amberes 1555, 1563 y 1596; en Venecia 1563; en Sevilla en 1577; Londres 1581, París 1700 y 1740 y en Lima en 1994.

Pedro Cieza de León

Llega al Perú en 1547. El virrey La Gasca lo nombra cronista, teniendo acceso a documentos oficiales. En 1550 acabó de escribir la primera parte de *La crónica del Perú* publicada en Sevilla, luego en Amberes, Venecia, Londres, Buenos Aires, México, Bogotá y Lima en 1973. En el Cusco captó lo más valioso que había de las fuentes orales indígenas. El peruanista Jiménez de la Espada lo llamó *Principe de los cronistas de las Indias*. Es el representante más cabal de la crónica pre-toledana por su figura humana, comprensiva y tolerante. La edición completa fue publicada por la Pontificia Universidad Católica del Perú. La descripción del territorio y de los caminos de la sierra y de los llanos que atravesaban el imperio, y de las ciudades y pueblos que los bordeaban, con los ritos, costumbres, fiestas y vestidos de sus habitantes, sus plantas y alimentos, lo califican como el primer viajero y etnógrafo en tierra peruana. El *Señorío de los Incas* es la primera historia incaica. Su versión del imperio es la más completa y ecuánime. La posición de Cieza es netamente contraria a la de los conquistadores y equilibrada para juzgar a los indios.

Escribe su crónica titulada *La crónica del Perú*. Extenso documento que narra la descripción del imperio, la dinastía de los incas, las operaciones militares, presenta varios mitos en torno a los incas, las guerras civiles. Es el primer cronista que considera este territorio como un "imperio". Su obra describe la geografía de los andes y las costumbres de los indios, la historia de los incas, el descubrimiento y conquista del Perú y las guerras civiles. El libro segundo o *Señorío de los Incas* se publicó en 1873, y luego en 1880 por Jiménez de la Espada. En este libro expone diversos mitos incas, narra la expansión del imperio desde Manco Inca hasta Huáscar y Atahualpa. El tercer libro *Descubrimiento y Conquista del Perú* fue publicado en 1946 en forma incompleta por Jiménez de la Espada. La historiadora Francesca Cantú la publicó en Roma en forma completa gracias a su descubrimiento del manuscrito original en la Biblioteca Apostólica Vaticana. En 1987 fue publicada en Lima (PUC). La cuarta parte trata de las guerras civiles y se compone de cinco libros: *La guerra de las Salinas, La guerra de Chupas, La guerra de Quito, La guerra de Huarina* y la de *Jaquijaguana* publicada en 1877, 1887 y 1984 en Madrid; en 1913 y 1923 en Londres; y en 1991 y 1994 por la PUC en Lima.

Juan Díez de Betanzos

También existían muchos homónimos suyos en los primeros años de vida colonial, sin embargo nuestro cronista llega al Perú en 1535. Casado con Angelina Yupanqui, quien habría sido esposa de Francisco Pizarro. Conocedor del quechua, fue escribano del virrey y tuvo acceso a material oficial que le permitió elaborar su crónica por muchos años olvidada. Aparece con el título de *Suma y narración de los Incas*. En ella describe la genealogía de los incas, las leyendas sobre el orígen de los incas, el gobierno y las obras de cada inca y la infraestructura y organización del estado incaico, el conflicto entre Huáscar y Atahualpa, la conquista española y la rebelión de los incas, desde el levantamiento de Manco Inca hasta su asesinato en Vilcabamba. Colaboró en la composición de la doctrina cristiana para los evangelizadores y de dos vocabularios del quechua que serían la base para la redacción de la obra de Fray Domingo de Santo Tomás: *Gramática de la Lengua General de los Indios de los Reynos del Perú y Lexicon o Vocabulario de la Lengua General del Perú*, publicadas en 1560. Hoy han sido reeditadas por el Centro Bartolomé de las Casas del Cusco. Betanzos colabora con el gobernador Vaca de Castro que pacifica el conflicto entre pizarristas y almagristas. Luego, durante el virreynato de Blasco Núñez de Vela se rebela Gonzalo Pizarro y el cronista simpatiza con el rebelde ocasionándole una serie de sinsabores. Al parecer Betanzos recoge información de la crónica de Cieza por la coincidencia de algunos pasajes de ambos cronistas. La crónica fue publicada en 1987 gracias al descubrimiento del manuscrito en Palma de Mayorca por la historiadora María del Carmen Martín Rubio.

Nota aparte merece la labor del gobernador del Perú don Cristobal Vaca de Castro, quien mandó escribir un documento llamado *Relación de la descendencia y conquista de los Incas,* escrita en la década de los cuarenta. Trata de la historia de la dinastía de los incas y las guerras de los andinos, desde la lucha entre Atahualpa y Huáscar hasta el fin de la rebelión de los incas en 1572. Este documento es conocido como la *Relación de los Quipucamayoc,* ya que fue narrado por los antiguos oficiales cusqueños llamados quipucamayocs y transcrito por Juan Díez de Betanzos y Francisco Villacastín.

Felipe Guamán Poma de Ayala

Cronista andino nacido en San Cristobal de Sondongo en Lucanas, Ayacucho en 1535 o 1536 a muy pocos años de la llegada de los españoles. *Nueva corónica y buen gobierno* es el libro más conmovedor y violento de la historia y de la literatura peruana, terminado de escribir en 1615. Permaneció ignorado durante tres siglos hasta que en 1908 el manuscrito fue descubierto por el bibliotecario alemán Richard A. Pietschman en la Biblioteca Real de Copenhagen. Desde entonces es cada vez mayor el reconocimiento de su extraordinario valor como la fuente más importante para conocer la vida del pueblo andino, desde los albores de sus civilización hasta la primera centuria de la conquista española. En 1936 se publicó en París, posteriormente hubo otras ediciones como las de 1944 en La Paz, en 1956 por Bustíos, 1969 por La Casa de la Cultura, 1990 por el Instituto de Estudios Peruanos y Siglo XXI, en 1993 por Fondo de Cultura Económica en Lima y en 1980 editado por la Biblioteca Ayacucho de Caracas Venezuela. *Nueva corónica y buen gobierno* es una denuncia vigorosa y descarnada contra el régimen colonial, contra el abuso y la dominación impuesta por los conquistadores a la raza vencida y al mismo tiempo una utopía reformista que propone medidas para un buen gobierno y que ponga remedio y fin a la injusticia social. En la crónica, entre otros temas, desfilan leyes incaicas, formas de enterrar a los muertos, vírgenes escogidas, fiestas y ceremonias rituales, comidas, tareas agrícolas de cada mes del año. Da una visión andina de la conquista, quejas por agravios contra los indios, denuncias sobre los abusos de corregidores, encomenderos, sacerdotes, jueces y otros funcionarios españoles. Ofrece también descripciones de ciudades, itinerarios de tambos del camino Cusco-Lima, propuestas al rey de España para un buen gobierno en el Perú. El texto tiene unas 400 ilustraciones que forman parte de las 1,179 páginas de la obra completa.

El Inca Garcilaso de la Vega

Nació el 12 de Abril de 1539 en el Cusco. Hijo del capitán Garcilaso y de Isabel Chimpu Ocllo, sobrina de Huayna Cápac y prima de Huáscar, Atahualpa y Manco Inca. A los 20 años viaja a España y se establece en Montilla durante 30 años. En 1590 traduce del toscano al español los Diálogos de Amor de León el Hebreo. Luego publica La Florida del Inca en 1596, libro de aventuras que trata de la expedición de Hernando de Soto a La Florida y termina con la vuelta de los sobrevivientes a México. Posteriormente escribe *Relación de la descendencia de Garci Pérez de Vargas* en el que expone su estirpe familiar por el lado español y por el lado andino. Su obra más importante es sin duda *Los Comentarios Reales de los Incas* publicada en Lisboa en 1609. Sus principales fuentes son José de Acosta, Pedro Cieza de León, Blas Valera, El Palentino, Gómara, Zárate, entre otros cronistas de la época.

Reales significa verdaderos, porque algunos estudiosos afirman que los cronistas no siempre escribían verdades y era necesario corregirlos. La primera parte de los *Comentarios Reales* corresponde a la descripción de la grandeza del imperio incaico, aunque también hay algo de mestizaje colonial. La segunda parte, más conocida como *Historia General del Perú,* corresponde a la historia de la conquista, de las guerras civiles y del inicio de la colonia. Fue publicada en Córdoba en 1616.

Garcilaso quiso unir ambas historias, la incaica y la conquista española, evitando la escisión (división, rompimiento) que significó la invasión europea.

El prólogo de la primera edición dice así: "A los indios, mestizos, y criollos de los reinos y provincias del grande y riquísimo imperio del Perú, El Inca Garcilaso de la Vega, su hermano, compatriota y paisano, salud y felicidad".

El Perú de hoy, a principios del siglo XXI, sigue oscilando entre la solución social pacífica que sugería Garcilaso y la violenta de Guamán Poma. En cierto modo la utopía mestiza de Garcilaso ha sido guía en el Perú colonial y gran parte de la república. La violencia social que describe Guamán Poma reaparece—o se ve con más claridad—en las últimas décadas del siglo XX. En cuanto al lenguaje, Garcilaso, el revolucionario de bella prosa y Guamán Poma, el revolucionario de híbrido lenguaje, son complementarios. Los dos son el rostro del Perú en formación.

Conclusiones

La crónica es un documento valioso, fuente primera de gran importancia para los estudiosos que siguen tratando de encontrar la verdadera historia del mundo andino. Con la fusión de los aportes culturales entre los españoles y los andinos, se produce la transculturación que da cuenta del proceso de occidentalización y la formación de las sociedades mestizas del presente.

En las crónicas somos testigos del encuentro difícil, doloroso, muchas veces violento; pero que la historia y el tiempo se han encargado de asimilar, debiendo nosotros rescatar aquello que nos sirva de empuje para enfrentar el futuro, reconociéndonos deudores de un pasado sobre el cual debemos reflexionar siempre. Nuestros dos más grandes cronistas: Guamán Poma y Garcilaso son dos claros ejemplos por construir nuestra nacionalidad como peruanos, proceso en contínua transformación.

BIBLIOGRAFÍA

Araníbar, Carlos. *Nueva Crónica y Buen Gobierno*. Lima: I. A. A., 1990.

Carrillo, Francisco. *Enciclopedia Histórica de la Literatura Peruana*. 9 Tomos. Lima: Horizonte, 1999.

Guamán Poma de Ayala, Felipe. *Nueva Córonica y Buen Gobierno. Antología*. Lima: Horizonte, 1998.

Miró Quesada, A. *El Inca Garcilaso*. Lima: Fondo Editorial de la Pontificia Universidad Católica del Perú, 1994.

Pease, Franklin. *Las Crónicas y los Andes*. Lima: Fondo de Cultura Económica, 1995.

Porras, Raúl. *Los Cronistas del Perú*. Lima: Banco de Crédito, 1986.

————. *Fuentes Históricas Peruanas*. Lima: Universidad Nacional Mayor de San Marcos, 1963.

—————. *Las Relaciones Primitivas de la Conquista del Perú*. Lima: Instituto Porras, 1967.

Someda, Hidefuji. *El Imperio de los Incas. Imagen del Tahuantinsuyo creado por los Cronistas*. Fondo Editorial de la Pontificia Universidad Católica del Perú, 1999.

3. Garcilaso de la Vega, nexo de dos mundos

Roberto Vergaray

La ciudad del Cusco fue la Capital de la civilización sudamericana llamada Imperio Incaico o Tawantinsuyo antes de la Conquista española. Quien haya tenido la oportunidad de viajar al Cusco, habrá conocido una de las ciudades más antiguas de América. Un interesante lugar imposible de olvidar.

Los Incas, sus fundadores, la llamaron Qosqo, que en castellano significa ombligo y a semejanza de esta parte central del cuerpo humano, para los incas el Qosqo era el ombligo del mundo, era el centro de su mundo, el Tawantinsuyo.

Hay en ella hermosas muestras de arquitectura en piedra. El contorno de la ciudad primigenia vista desde el aire tiene la forma de un jaguar de colosales dimensiones.

A medida que los conquistadores españoles iban adentrándose de norte a sur en el territorio de los Incas, se repartieron la tierra del espacio conquistado, asentándose y fundando ciudades, utilizando los llanos vacíos y poco poblados de los valles de la costa. Las ciudades eran levantadas con el mismo trazo que estaban acostumbrados a hacer en Europa, partiendo de una plaza central, llamada "Plaza Mayor", alrededor de la cual en cierto orden jerárquico iban asignándose la propiedad de la tierra en la que edificaron sus casonas. Pero al llegar al Cusco se encontraron con una ciudad bastante extensa, ya edificada y con bloques de piedra, algunos tan grandes y pesados que ni los hombres ni aun el tiempo y los terremotos han podido mover.

En el Cusco, los conquistadores se repartieron estas edificaciones incaicas, palacios y templos, utilizándolas como base, sobre las que construyeron sus casas e iglesias al estilo europeo de ese entonces. El resultado de estas construcciones podría sintéticamente ser el ejemplo gráfico del encuentro de los dos mundos, el americano y el europeo, superponiéndose este último sobre el nativo. Es así como vemos esta singular ciudad mitad incaica y mitad española.

Garcilaso de la Vega cuenta que nació en el Cusco el 12 de abril de 1539, primo de Huascar y Atahualpa, los dos Incas que se disputaban el imperio a la llegada de los conquistadores.

Chimpu Ocllo, madre de nuestro personaje, era un familiar más cercano a Huascar el Inca vencido que a Atahualpa, el vencedor, por lo que tuvo que

26

sufrir las vejaciones que sobre la nobleza cusqueña desató el vencedor Atahualpa. La invasión europea acabó por arruinar a la familia imperial quitándoles toda posibilidad de poder, sin embargo, es posible que en lo más íntimo de sus seres sintieran una especie de justicia divina cuando Atahualpa fue ejecutado por las huestes de Pizarro.

Nuestro personaje no fue un hijo reconocido y el nombre que se le impuso, no fue el de su padre Garcilaso de la Vega, sino una mezcla de los de sus antepasados por rama paterna. Así, inicialmente fue conocido como Gómez Suárez de Figueroa.

Aquella nueva era en la que le tocó vivir, de la incorporación de la cultura incaica de sus antepasados maternos, al mundo occidental, mediante la fuerza de las armas, la imposición de la religión católica y de las normas de la España de sus antepasados paternos, fue sin duda una etapa decisiva en su formación espiritual y un sello indeleble de mucho peso en su carácter, siendo la primera lengua que habló, el quechua.

A Gómez Suárez, el mestizo, le tocó entonces, ser espiritualmente la síntesis de aquellos dos mundos completamente diferentes en su cultura. Y su azarosa existencia estuvo cifrada por una larga etapa de búsqueda de identidad, por la lucha interna entre dos herencias, la aborigen y la europea, terminando en ser indio para lo indio y español para lo ibérico o indio para lo español y español para lo indio. Al no encontrar su espacio y sentirse no ser ni una casa ni otra, ni europeo ni aborigen, se manifiesta en él una complejidad espiritual y casi una doble personalidad sin puntos de vista comunes con otros hombres, en la que primaba la melancolía, singular característica del hombre andino.

Aun cuando pasaba mas tiempo con su padre, al parecer su mocedad la transcurrió sin un hogar formal. Situación que empeoró cuando su padre se casó legítimamente con doña Luisa Martel y su madre, simultáneamente, también se casó legítimamente con Juan de Pedroche, soldado o comerciante sin linaje.

A la luz de algunos documentos, el historiador Raúl Porras Barrenechea manifiesta que "probablemente el Capitán Garcilaso casó a la madre del Inka con Juan de Pedroche mientras que él contrae matrimonio con Doña Luisa Martel de los Ríos". Gómez Suárez pierde así su hogar y más adelante perderá también su patria.

Fue testigo de la llegada de los primeros bueyes al Cusco, seres nunca antes vistos en América y admiró por horas y horas la facilidad con que estos animales habrían los surcos en la tierra, en reemplazo de la chaquitaclla o arado de pie de los antiguos peruanos. En su embeleso por observar estos animales trabajando la tierra, se olvidó de asistir a sus clases, con lo que se ganó-doce azotes de parte de su padre y otros doce propinados por su maestro, según las normas pedagógicas de entonces.

Cuenta que disfrutó de las primeras uvas, que en grandes cantidades llegaron por primera vez a su casa y fué encargado de repartirlas entre los amigos de su padre, llevándose a la boca una buena cantidad por el camino. Conoció el trasplante de nuevas especies traídas de España: rosas, olivos, vides, espárragos.

El Capitán Garcilaso, su padre, tomó parte en las guerras civiles al lado de los gonzalistas, aunque, al parecer, obligado a hacerlo. El niño mestizo recorrió un largo camino para espectar la entrada triunfal de los sublevados al mando de Gonzalo Pizarro, vencedores de la batalla de Huajina, grupo en el cual estaba su padre. En el Cusco siguieron largas tertulias y banquetes en casa del gobernador, en las que participó el joven mestizo y conoció, hizo amistad y jugó con los hijos de los conquistadores, muchos de ellos también mestizos, hasta que esta etapa de cierta calma se acabó cuando llegó La Gasca, en nombre del Rey, a sofocar la rebelión con un ejército mejor armado.

Gonzalo Pizarro se entregó y fue decapitado. El Capitán Carvajal, famoso por sus chanzas y agudezas, en la huída cayó del caballo, sus propios soldados lo capturaron y lo entregaron a La Gasca. Fue llevado al suplicio halado por un caballo, a rastras, en un serón o manta. Fiel a su carácter, burlándose de si mismo exclamó "Niño en cuna, viejo en cuna, ¡qué fortuna!"

El niño Garcilaso presenció los castigos físicos, azotes, decapitaciones o descuartizamiento de los vencidos, cuyos restos quedaron expuestos hasta heder en las afueras de la ciudad a modo de advertencia o lección para los que pretendieran alzarse contra la corona. Su padre se libró de todo esto por haber sido el primero en pasarse a las filas de La Gasca antes del encuentro de Xaquijahuana. El triunfador La Gasca participó de las fiestas en su honor y presenció las corridas de toros, desde la casona de los Garcilaso de la Vega.

Sintiéndose Gómez Suárez, íntimamente vinculado a los españoles y por lo tanto al mundo europeo de su padre, sentía también un gran afecto por el desaparecido mundo de su madre, el colosal imperio en que sus directos antepasados gobernaban, aun cuando en los momentos posteriores a la conquista, cuando no acababa de extinguirse el impulso vital de aquella gigantesca civilización conquistada, los incas vencidos gozaban de cierta estima y privilegios. Por ejemplo, en las cercanías del Cusco, en el valle de Vilcabamba, había una pequeña corte formada por los herederos del trono incaico y los aborígenes que compartían la tierra con los españoles, eran reconocidos en su estirpe y eran tratados con consideraciones. Los más distinguidos conquistadores se amancebaron con las princesas incas, al igual que su madre, y los mestizos nacidos de esta unión eran los niños aristocráticos del Cuzco. Todos ellos vivían no sólo del recuerdo de su mundo desaparecido, sino que mantenían muchas de sus costumbres según relataría después Garcilaso "Demás de habérmelo dicho los indios, alcancé y vi por mis ojos parte de aquella idolatría, sus fiestas y supersticiones, que aún en mis tiempos, hasta los doce o trece años de mi edad, no se habían acabado del todo. Yo nací ocho años después que los españoles ganaron mi tierra (Aquí a Garcilaso le brota lo español y es muy gentil cuando dice "ganaron") y, como lo he dicho— continúa—me crié en ella hasta los veinte años, y así vi muchas cosas de las que hacían los indios en aquella gentilidad, las cuales contaré diciendo que las vi", tal como relata en sus *Comentarios Reales,* lib. I, Capítulo XIX, acerca de las postrimerías del Tawantinsuyo.

Gómez Suárez abandona el Perú el 20 de enero de 1560, a la muerte de su padre el Capitán Garcilaso de la Vega, cuando cumple los veinte años de edad y obedeciendo el deseo de éste, quien le dejara en herencia "cuatro mil pesos de oro y de plata ensayada y marcada" para que fuera a estudiar a España, "por que así es mi voluntad por el amor que le tengo, por ser como es mi hijo natural y por tal le nombro y declaro".

Era la etapa en que se consolidaba el Virreinato, rigurosamente estatal y el Virrey Toledo ejecutaba a Tupac Amaru. Entonces viaja a Montilla cerca de Córdoba, donde residía su tío paterno el Capitán Alonso de Vargas, casado con Doña Luisa Ponce de León, hermana del Licenciado Francisco de Argote (quien iba a ser padre del poeta Luis de Góngora y Argote). Sus tíos lo recibieron cordialmente y su estancia en Montilla se prolongó por treinta años.

Gómez Suárez en ese período trató de obtener una renta de la corona buscando el reconocimiento por los servicios prestados por su padre en América y las mercedes que consideraba que le correspondían por la sangre real de su madre, en virtud de la pérdida de todas sus propiedades y beneficios en favor de los conquistadores. Pero no obtuvo sus objetivos, al parecer por que su padre fue contado entre los rebeldes a la corona en las guerras civiles, que podrían calificarse como la lucha política entre el individualismo de los conquistadores contra el poder coherente y centralizador de la Corona.

Su nombre sufre una metamorfosis poco a poco. En una partida de bautismo en la que actúa como padrino, figura y firma como Gómez Suárez de la Vega. Pocos días después, se decide a firmar "Garcilaso de la Vega", como su padre, en momentos que toma la espada para combatir la rebelión de los moriscos en las Alpujarras de Granada, bajo las órdenes del Marqués de Priego, señor de la Villa de Montilla, de marzo a diciembre de 1570 obteniendo cuatro "despachos" o "Condutas" de Capitán, como su padre, dos de Felipe II y dos de Juan de Austria, de las que se sentiría orgulloso.

Pero esta actitud de tomar las armas contra los moriscos levantados ha sido condenada por varios historiadores, dado que los moriscos eran los mestizos españoles, y un mestizo americano como lo era el, en cierto modo eran de la misma causa. Por esto, despectivamente se le denominó Garcilaso de la Vega "matamoros" y a su padre, Garcilaso de la Vega "mataindios".

Luego de este episodio, Garcilaso cuelga la espada y decide tomar la pluma, su verdadera vocación. Sería largo recordar el árbol genealógico europeo de Garcilaso, que entre sus antepasados y parientes, contemporáneos a él, contaba con figuras de las letras españolas, por lo que no sería errado decir que esta vocación por las letras la llevaba en sus genes.

Negados, pues, todos los permisos para retornar al Perú, dedicó sus energías y su tiempo a la lectura y a visitar a los doctos y religiosos.

Emprende la traducción de los *Diálogos de Amor* escritos en italiano por León Hebreo, obra que dedicó al Rey Felipe II, afirmando en el prólogo su personalidad y aparece por primera vez su firma como "Inka Garcilaso de la Vega". Esta obra, fue para él un modelo intelectual por el armonioso despliegue metafísico del autor, así como por la presencia de un afán de integración y un gusto por el equilibrio, de neta raíz renacentista.

Dice José María Arguedas que "Inqa" no significa únicamente emperador. "Inqa" denomina el modelo originante de cada ser, según la mitología quechua. Este concepto se conoce más comúnmente con el término "Inkachu", "Tukuy Kansaq uywakunaq Inqakuna" debe traducirse, pues, por el modo originante de todo ser. De esta manera y para diferenciarse de su padre, nuestro personaje será el "Inka Garcilaso de la Vega", recordando las dos vertientes de su origen, el americano y el europeo.

Se afianza así su labor de escritor, con una modesta pero tranquila situación económica. Se traslada a Córdova donde tuvo un mejor contacto con los doctos amigos y mejor acceso a los libros. Emprende aquí la labor de escribir la historia de la expedición de Hernando de Soto a la Florida, utilizando los relatos que oyó primero, de boca de uno de los actores de aquella frustrada expedición, que había llegado al Perú, el viejo soldado Gonzalo Silvestre a quien importunó con sus preguntas y ansias de escuchar contar sus experiencias, y falleció luego, antes que Gracilazo emprendiera su viaje a España. Esta narración junto con otros documentos que llegaron a sus manos, así como dos relaciones escritas por otros dos testigos de la expedición de De Soto.

La obra apareció luego con el título de *La Florida del Inca* y es sobre todo un tratado de *Historia General del Perú,* pero también tienen un valor literario por que el relato se presenta con adornos novelescos de gran madurez literaria.

Emprende luego la tarea de escribir *Los Comentarios Reales* sin dejar de cotejar sus escritos con los de otros Cronistas como Gómara, Cieza de León o el Padre Acosta. Y, finalmente, la *Historia General del Perú,* hermosa obra que terminó y que fue póstumamente editada, pues falleció el 22 o 23 de abril de 1616, contemporáneamente con Cervantes y Shakespeare.

Es interesante recordar de *Los Comentarios Reales* uno de sus pensamientos "No hay más que un mundo, y aunque llamamos viejo y nuevo mundo por haberse descubierto éste nuevamente para nosotros, y no porque sean dos sino todo uno".

Garcilaso fue el primer latinoamericano que dejó su tierra para nunca más volver y cuya vida, que discurrió entre dos mundo, fue dedicada en síntesis a unir aquellos dos universos.

A Ustd los bibliotecarios latinoamericanistas que también están dedicando sus vidas a tender puentes entre estos dos mundos divididos, puentes que llevan a una mejor comprensión de la cultura latinoamericana, único camino al buen entendimiento y que acortan las diferencias, les tenemos que dar las gracias.

Ojalá no sea lejano el día en que esos puentes nos acerquen más y las diferencias sean menos, que podamos ser todos uno, como lo soñó Garcilaso, un sólo mundo y una sola raza, la raza humana.

4. Hipólito Unanue's Prescription for an Enlightened Philosophy of Diet

Myra L. Appel

During the Enlightenment, Peruvians, especially the residents of Lima, possibly enjoyed a greater diversity of foodstuffs than any other population in Latin America, or for that matter, much of the world. From the many varied ecological niches that created a vast patchwork of environmental life zones throughout the Andes came an incredible bounty of indigenous and introduced foodstuffs. Meat from domesticated European food animals, native birds and Andean vicuñas, rodents and guinea pigs, supplemented by the many species of edible fish, crustaceans, and other fresh and saltwater creatures, supplied *limeños* with such abundance that even the city's poor relied on protein as a dietary staple, according to some scholars.[1] The diversity of fruits and vegetables available for consumption could easily overwhelm any servant or housewife shopping in the bustling *mercados* of the capital. In Peru, the native home of the potato, for example, consumers had access to hundreds of varieties of the tuber that ranged in color from white to yellow or blue to purple, and came in sizes as tiny as a finger to as large as a fist.

To glean the data and insights needed to reconstruct a society's food history, the integrated history of the production, distribution, and consumption of foodstuffs, requires the use of primary source materials beyond cookbooks and compilations of recipes. Furthermore, to examine a society's foodways, the system of beliefs and practices that surround all aspects of food from the point of its origin to the moment it is consumed, demands an even broader survey of documents. A fruitful, untapped source exists in the *Observaciones Sobre el Clima de Lima,* which helps shed light on the history of Peruvian food, dietary practices, and food as medicine during a critical period of political, social, intellectual, and culinary change.

Written by José Hipólito Unanue, one of Peru's most illustrious eighteenth and nineteenth-century intellectuals, essayists, and philosophers, the *Observaciones* publicized his views about the effect of the Peruvian climate on all living organisms. Called the "Father of Peruvian Medicine," Unanue exemplified the Latin American Creole intellectual strongly influenced by Enlightenment ideologies filtering across the Atlantic from Europe. Like many of his contemporaries, he also was receptive to the enlightened thought of North Americans such as Thomas Jefferson and Benjamin Franklin. Among his many careers, Unanue also included those of academician, revolutionary, and, eventually, diplomat. Perhaps Unanue was best known for his participation with several friends and like-minded young limeños in contributing numerous lengthy articles to the *Mercurio Peruano,* the newsprint voice of the Sociedad Académica de Amantes de Lima, published from 1791 to 1794. His essays appeared in many of the paper's 382 issues and included literary and scientific treatises, some of which still remain classics on topics as diverse as the nutritional efficacy of the coca leaf and the data on the ocean tides that lapped the Peruvian coasts. Unanue reached his literary apogee with the publication of his well-known volume *Observaciones Sobre el Clima de Lima.* Written between 1799 and 1805, first published in 1806 and later revised in 1811, the *Observaciones* attempts to refute the fairly prevalent European accusations that New World organisms, both plants and animals (including humans), were inferior to the hardier and more perfect stock of their European counterparts.

Using these sources, along with archival documents, a number of twentieth-century Latin American historians have attempted to assess Unanue's role in the enlightened scientific and medical communities of late-eighteenth- and early-nineteenth-century Peru. More recently, in 1964, John E. Woodham wrote a dissertation examining Unanue's career as a force in shaping and directing Peru's scientific community prior to independence and up to the early years of nation building. Each of these historians focused on the political, medical, and intellectual history that dominated their own specialized academic discipline.[2]

What each researcher overlooked as irrelevant or trivial were Unanue's explicit or implicit commentaries about food and the *mestizaje* process that foodstuffs and their preparation techniques had undergone during the centuries of Spanish influence. Ignored was the role of food in linking the natural world to the social world of early-nineteenth-century Peru and the importance of food as an indicator of ethnic and gender relations, among other things. A man with strong opinions and discerning ethnographic skills, Unanue did not hesitate to set down his views about limeños dietary practices, the medicinal efficacy of certain foodstuffs, and the prescribed dietary regimens that he believed would lead to improved health. These documents are a reservoir of information about who was eating what, when, and sometimes why and how. Unanue's political and literary texts and scientific proofs provide windows into the production, distribution, and consumption of foodstuffs among the Peruvian social and economic strata; various groups of limeños based on age, gender, or ethnicity; and the healthy or the unhealthy people in coastal Lima.

I will focus only on a portion of Unanue's publications. In 1971, the Comisión Nacional del Sesquicentenario de la Independencia del Perú published its monumental eighty-volume set of sources that served as a tribute to

Peru's independence from Spain and an affirmation of its sense of nationalism. Included in this massive set are writings of many of Peru's most famous sons, travel accounts (many in English) of notable North Americans and Europeans, accounts of indigenous rebellions, and political documents. The seventh and eighth volumes contain a large portion of Unanue's voluminous correspondence, an inventory of his estate, including a fairly detailed list of the books in his personal library at the time of his death, and a reprint of the *Observaciones* mined so thoroughly by Woodward and Latin American researchers like Lastres.[3]

Before looking at what Unanue was eating, or recommending that others eat, it is fruitful to look at what he was reading. Although a representative of the Peruvian Creole elite caught up by European Enlightenment ideology, Unanue was perhaps unique in the breadth and depth of his eclectic reading tastes. According to the inventory list compiled at his death, in 1833, his personal library numbered well over one thousand volumes, some bequeathed by Augustín Hipólito Landaburu, a former employer. Unanue added to the solid core of this bequest many other titles published in the nineteenth century during the peak of his literary career, while he was *Protomedicato,* or during his tenure in government service after Peru gained its independence.

Each library reflects its owner's soul, especially in colonial Peru where the exorbitant cost of the printed word prohibited the majority of readers from accumulating a massive collection.[4] Unanue's literary tastes seemingly paralleled many of the other great readers and collectors of his country, but he apparently enjoyed the financial wherewithal, or the contacts, to acquire more titles than many of his fellow bibliophiles. Classic literature and Christian texts appear to have been a favorite of Unanue (or of Hipólito Landaburu). He surely enjoyed history, with books about Spain and volumes written by the most notable Latin American authors dominating the collection. References to dictionaries and grammars of many languages abound on the inventory list, along with numerous other specialized reference works. Books about indigenous peoples, such as the *Arte de la Lengua Maya, Costumbres y Trajes del Perú de Ahora Cuarenta Años,* and the *Arte y Vocabulario de la Lengua Quechua,* attest to Unanue's latent or amateur anthropological interests.

Notable scientific treatises, both for the natural and physical sciences, appear to be his personal acquisitions and, judging by the number appearing in his collection, his favorite reading material. General medical works by Cullen rested alongside Pison's medical text on Brazil and Le Camus's *Medicina del Espíritu.* Not unexpectedly, few significant works written by prominent physicians of the Enlightenment escaped Unanue's collecting reach. Illnesses stressed by the items in the collection included colic, venereal diseases, and problems of the mouth and nasal passages. Humboldt's *Plantas Equinocciales,* Walton's work on the Andean vicuñas, and Candole's volume on plants, along with several pharmacopias, were set beside volumes on geography, chemistry, and astronomy. Of the hundreds of titles, only two, *Tratado Sobre la Caña Dulce* and *Cultivo de las Papas,* specifically addressed food crops. No European cookery guides or cookbooks appeared in the inventory, although these publications were quite prevalent in Europe and available in Peru at this time. Nor was there mention of any Peruvian cookbooks or manuscripts of handwritten compilations of recipes.

To comprehend Unanue's world of food begs for a picture of early-nineteenth-century Lima, Peru's political and culinary center. By 1812, Lima boasted a population of 63,900. Ideological beliefs carried from the Iberian world had merged so successfully with indigenous cultural and religious worldviews that even discerning twentieth-century scholars frequently attributed the Hippocratic humoral classification system of foods to an independent New World origin. From extant original Latin American cookbooks published after 1750, it is obvious that the more economically advantaged limeño enjoyed the traditional Spanish cuisine heavily perfumed and flavored by Arab culinary complexes. Spices such as cinnamon and cloves added heady aromas, while saffron colored the dishes a golden hue. Also obvious is the presence of European foods tempered by the evolution of a French cuisine that eschewed heavy flavors and aromas in favor of more bland, less acidic dishes prepared with copious amounts of fats, especially butter. Here, too, one sees evidence of food mestizaje as indigenous Peruvian ingredients are molded, shaped, and substituted into European recipes, while "traditional" European foodstuffs like chicken, beef, and wheat find new places in variations of indigenous-inspired dishes. Less obvious to a casual reader of these cookbooks is the importance placed by Peruvians on the Hippocratic humors, the proper order for combining dishes to protect the body, and the role of food as medicine.

What can the *Observaciones* tell us? Many things. Unanue's references to the foods and foodways of his time reflect the cultural and social values, implicitly and explicitly. The specific commodities and individual foodstuffs he identifies as salubrious or troublesome for health give an indication of the foods commonly eaten by at least the more privileged colonists in 1806 in Lima. Although actual data are missing, a sense of what economic and political power can afford appears as Unanue describes the gluttony of overeating and specifies certain foodstuffs that are particularly destructive to the human constitution. In looking over the recipes collected in the 1776 publication *Libros de Cocina de Doña Josepha de Eschurrechea,* it is obvious that Unanue had in mind dishes such as the pastel known as *Queque.* With Queque's twenty-five eggs, one pound of flour, one pound of butter, one cup of cognac, and one pound of sugar (flavored only with one spoonful of cinnamon), a steady diet of this high-fat, high-cholesterol, high-sugared food could easily create an imbalance in the body.[5]

Gender relations and elite male attitudes toward at least the more economically advantaged females appear as Unanue stresses appropriate dietary
and exercise behavior and offers advice on the medical concerns common to
the ladies of his economic stratum. Considered by enlightened males, including the growing ranks of professional male physicians, as undisciplined and
self-indulgent, females were often equated with children. There is evidence of
these perceptions as Unanue lays out his preferred soft, bland, pale diet and
inflexible dietary regime for infant and child, wife and mother.

Subtle insights into the systems of production emerge as Unanue makes
reference to the working classes. Implicit are his relatively liberal social views
and a growing concern for public health in Lima as he describes the food practices of the Andean Indians and the black field hands, along with the health
problems they endured. Written partially from Unanue's prejudice and professional campaign toward eliminating the power of Peru's *curanderos,* or native
folk healers, the *Observaciones* emphasizes the tenets of enlightened, ortho-
dox, organized Western medicine and the growing professionalization of
health care, which increasingly censured male and female folk healers.

The *Observaciones* indicates that Unanue himself probably did not enjoy
the extent of the culinary bounty of the dining table savored by many of his
less-disciplined acquaintances and patients. A firm believer in living a moderate life as a means of preventative medicine, Unanue possessed a philosophy
toward diet, alimentation, and foodstuffs that weaves in and out of his
climatic data and expository views about the physical and natural history of
Lima's unique ecological environment. Like twentieth-century historians, he
speaks glowingly of the culinary riches, especially the agricultural bounty of
the countryside, claiming that few cities throughout the world enjoyed a
greater abundance of foodstuffs than did Lima. But he continues by speaking
forcefully against the general attitude toward this largess of produce from the
land and the laxity of certain people in maintaining a dietary program that he
deemed sensible and healthy. He notes, in particular, that women tended to
deviate more frequently from following these principles of good health and
scolds them for indulging immoderately on food that he deemed destructive to
maintaining a sound body and mind. For example, instead of appreciating the
natural bounty of the land, many limeños actually preferred fried pork or other
fatty dishes for breakfast. Other urbanites, particularly the señoras, succumbed
to temptation and could not resist feasting on cheeses, fruits, and floury
sweets.

On the other hand, Unanue does not stint with his praise as he compli-
ments the moderate and disciplined diners in Lima. With pleasure he observes
that the most "orderly" or well-regulated limeños divided their food into three
daily meals. These restrained diners lunched in mid-morning on chocolate
accompanied by pieces of fruit. Unanue, however, could not restrain himself
from adding disapprovingly, yet once again, that some females transgressed by

preferring to feast on cooked pork or other similarly prepared food. Lunch, served in the middle of the day, tended to be more indicative of one's social position as people dined in a style proportionate to their economic wherewithal. For supper, a judicious person always ate his evening meal accompanied by sweet water and the ubiquitous *jicara* of chocolate. Under no circumstances should a person eat during the night, according to Unanue. To violate the night's fast meant risking an upset stomach, acquiring an escalating temperature that would produce night sweats, and, perhaps, even inducing vomiting.

Confident Unanue does not hesitate to share with his readers what he considers the optimal diet tailored to the residents of Lima. Meat, that Peruvian dietary staple seemingly available to all economic classes, receives much attention as a foodstuff and as a therapeutic tool. On a sliding nutritional scale, beef offered more value than did mutton, and the flesh of all sheep offered greater nutritional reward than did meat from birds. In Unanue's schema, pork was the most readily digested meat, but its high-fat content made it undesirable as a daily staple on the dinner table. Meats, deep red in color and from a young animal, provided the most nutrition. Particularly when prepared as a delicious soup, good quality animal protein served as a restorative, or antacid, to people suffering from indigestion. Unanue felt that meats consumed during the middle of the day offered strong positive forces in strengthening the stomach, a view that many who have eaten a steak late at night would probably not refute.

Certainly, Unanue recognized that human beings do not live by meat alone, no matter how highly valued as a marker of social status. A prime directive to his audience and potential patients includes the admonition to dine on what people in the twentieth century label "rounded meals" or a "balanced diet." To complement the hearty flavors and bulk of meat, Unanue felt that people need salads and other vegetable dishes. Another suitable alternative or accompaniment to red or white meats, especially for those unfortunate individuals who were not enjoying good health, was fresh fish from the nearby ocean. Shark and corvina were favored to feed recuperating and weak patients.

Of the fruits of the land, Unanue approved the consumption of both the indigenous and introduced produce. As with all foods, fruits and vegetables should be enjoyed with restraint and moderation. Only a mature harvest, soft, sweet, and replete with sugar, was suitable for the human body. Eating green fruits would cause indigestion, a common observation to us as well as to Unanue. Certain fruits such as melons, watermelons, Guinean bananas, and cucumbers could carry over well into the autumn, especially if sugar was added to the fruit, whether for preservation, taste, or medicinal value he does not say. The tropical *cherimoya,* although tempting and delicious, produced unpleasant side effects for the sick or frail. Peaches, a cultivated crop introduced by Spaniards, also caused undesirable side effects. Unanue continues his catalog of common fruits—the citrus, bananas, and apples—describing in detail the salubrious, as well as the unwholesome, qualities of each.

It is with the pineapple that Unanue finds his perfect fruit and exhibits an almost poetic form in describing the virtues of this succulent plant indigenous to Latin America. He not only comments on its excellent aroma, flavor, and effect upon the stomach, but also adds that it appears in some of the region's most outstanding prepared dishes. Unanue gives us a rare tidbit of a recipe with his instructions to spray strips of meat with wine, dust with cinnamon, and serve with pineapple to create a superb dish. His instructions do not sound out of place in today's *Gourmet* or *Bon Appetit*. Pineapple, a versatile fruit, also contributes a marvelous essence to syrups, fruity tisanes, and other elixirs concocted to improve the humors.

Perhaps Unanue's discussion about the beverages enjoyed by limeños demonstrates most obviously the mestizaje process that had occurred between native foodstuffs and those introduced by the end of this enlightened period. Certainly, chocolate ranks as the prime example of this fusion process. By the end of the eighteenth century, the cacao and water mixture drunk only by the Inca elite in elaborate rituals had evolved into a tasty beverage sweetened with sugar and beaten to a high froth by a wooden chocolate beater, an implement of Spanish design. From the formula, chocolate moved to the free and informal. Citing pure water, a commodity hard to acquire in Peru, as the best of all drinks, Unanue suggests that a glass taken with two or four large bananas, followed by a cup of chocolate, formed the perfect breakfast. He continues his discussions of composed drinks—the *horchatas, guindas,* tisanes—ices, and fruit waters and notes that each had found great popularity in summertime Lima. Certainly, the ices and fruit waters were originally hailed from Europe (with strong influence from Arab gourmets), but in the Americas assumed new flavors with the addition of tasty indigenous fruits.

Fermented beverages found great favor with all of Lima's social strata. Unanue acknowledges the importance of these beverages and divides them into two categories: the *chicha* or native Peruvian beer, and the *guarapo.* Chicha, an indigenous alcoholic beverage based on fermented corn, and guarapo, derived from introduced sugarcane, served as invigorating tonics for Creole, Indian, Negro slave, and mestizo alike in Unanue's mind. Noting that the Europeans and Indians preferred the chicha, Unanue knowingly discusses the efficacy of the two different forms—the sweet and the strong—and recommends the drink for its nutritional value. Among its virtues, he claims that the beverage will facilitate the movement of the soul and the body, and will bring a pleasing contentment. From studying the African field hands, perceptive Unanue notes that they preferred the guarapo. The observant and empathetic physician adds that it was more readily accessible to them and that the powerful raw substance "sustained" the exploited sugarcane workers on the haciendas, because guarapo was one of the few things available to them to make their lives of drudgery more bearable.

But Peruvians also had ample access to other liquors. Unanue points out that the use of these other alcohol-based beverages had "extended greatly in recent years," especially the consumption of *aguardiente*. Unlike chicha and guarapo, warns Unanue, aguardiente caused unpleasant side effects in the body, the mind, and the soul. Reputed to be the catalyst for violence among the Indians, especially the people of the Sierra, aguardiente did not rate a place of favor in Unanue's system.

Numerous indigenous rebellions rocked Peru in the last quarter of the eighteenth century, creating an even greater climate of ethnic and racial fears among the elite limeños. Despite these social upheavals, Unanue maintained his compassion toward the health of Lima's poor and the enslaved and wage laborers on which Peru's agriculture depended. Aware that their consumer choices were more limited to the foodstuffs produced locally, Unanue recommends the foods that their palates and belief systems, as well as their purses, would find more congenial. Presumably, he intended that these instructive dietary notes would be read by persons dedicated to improving the lot of the poor, or by the intellectually curious.

At length he devotes attention to the daily diet of the poor, noting the cultural differences in consumer choice made by the Indians and the Peruvian blacks. The Indians preferred corn and potatoes, their native foods. The field Negroes opted for corn and beans. Unanue lauds the virtues of the potato, claiming the potato as one of the richest gifts given by the Americas to Europe. Maize, too, he notes also changed the culinary world. From corn came a variety of delectable dishes, including *Milanese polenta* and Peruvian *sango*. Beans receive their due and are proclaimed by Unanue to be as delicious as grains. Since the poor of Lima had access to purchasing notable amounts of animal protein, they needed to be on guard against following their propensity in using a spicy seasoning to flavor their meat. To avert potential ill effects, Unanue advises to spice meat only when it is served with vegetables.

The poor, like the affluent urbanites, had the economic means to enjoy chocolate. And once again, Unanue approves of chocolate as a morning beverage when it becomes a "friend of the stomach's." Taken at other times of the day, chocolate could cause dizziness, sadness, or insomnia. His recipe for preparing chocolate includes instructions to make it simple and strong, to use the best Guayaquil cacao, and to prepare it in a horchata until the body becomes accustomed to imbibing the beverage. Unanue labels chocolate as a vegetable, and elevates it to the level of one of the most nutritious of all plants.

This paper presents only a small sampling of the data collected by Unanue. To determine the extent of Enlightenment thought on Peruvian dietary practices requires a comparison with what Europeans were eating at this time and a reading of the texts of noted food authorities like Brillat-Savarin.

At what point did Latin American gourmets look at food in terms of taste and gastronomy rather than in regard for its medicinal or dietetic qualities? A thorough analysis also requires a more extensive examination of when Peruvian food moved to the realm of a cuisine with the growth of a middle class.

NOTES

1. Augusto Ruíz Cevallos, "Dieta Popular y Conflicto en Lima de Principios de Siglo," *Histórica* 16 (1992): 203–220.

2. For a selection of works, see John E. Woodham, "Hipólito Unanue and the Enlightenment in Peru" (Ph.D. diss., Texas Christian University, 1964), and a subsequent article by him entitled "The Influence of Hipólito Unanue on Peruvian Medical Science, 1789–1820: A Reappraisal," *Hispanic American Historical Review* 50 (1970): 696–714. For Latin American publications, see Leoncio I le Mora, *Hipólito Unanue, Padre de la Medicina Americana* (Mexico: Talleres Gráficos de la Nación, 1926); Juan B. Lastres, *Hipólito Unanue* (Lima, 1955); and Marcos Cueto, ed., *Saberes Andinos: Ciencia y Tecnología en Bolivia, Ecuador y Perú* (Lima: Instituto de Estudios Peruanos, 1995).

3. Jorge Arias-Schreiber Pezet, "Hipólito Unanue, investigación, recopilación y prólogo," in *Colección Documental de la Independencia del Peru, Los Ideológos* (Lima: Comisión Nacional del Sesquicentenario de la Independencia del Perú, 1974), vols. 7–8.

4. In his article "The Diffusion of Books and Ideas in Colonial Peru: A Study of Private Libraries in the Sixteenth and Seventeenth Centuries," *Hispanic American Historical Review* 73 (1993): 211–233, Teodoro Hampe-Martínez discusses insights that can be gained from examining the holdings in colonial Latin American book collections.

5. Beatriz Rossells, *La Gastronomía en Potosí y Charcas, Siglos XVIII y XIX, 800 Recetas le la Cocina Criolla* (La Paz: Embajada de España, Fundación "Mario Mercado Vaca Guzmán," Centro de Estudios Sociales, 1995).

5. Sources about the Vaccination Expedition of Charles IV in the Andes

Rafael E. Tarragó

The expedition that King Charles IV (r. 1788–1808) sent in 1803 to his domains in America and Asia with the charge to vaccinate the masses free of charge; to teach how to prepare the smallpox vaccine; and to organize municipal vaccination boards throughout those domains for recording the vaccinations performed and keeping live serum for future vaccinations is one of the least known deeds of the Spanish crown in modern times. In the small corpus of articles and monographs about this expedition, most limit themselves to narrate the expedition's activities in the Spanish domains in the Caribbean, and of those under their director, Dr. Francisco Xavier Balmis (1753–1819), who went to Mexico, Central America, and the Philippines.[1] Relatively few articles include accounts of the activities of those under their subdirector, José Salvany Lleopart (1776–1810), who went to South America.

The purpose of this paper is to review the monographs and articles about the vaccination expedition in general that include accounts of its activities in the Andes, and the specialized works about José Salvany and the activities of the expedition under him in present-day Colombia, Ecuador, Peru, Chile, and Bolivia. I have included in the bibliography references to archives in Spain and South America containing information about the activities of the vaccination expedition under José Salvany in those countries, as well as general histories of the expedition including sizable accounts of the South American section, and specialized monographs and articles dealing with individuals and events related to the section of the expedition under José Salvany in the Andean region.

Motivations for the Vaccination Expedition

The origins of the idea of an expedition that would bring the smallpox vaccine from Europe to Spanish America and the Philippines have been hotly debated. It is a fact that the Council of the Indies in Madrid began discussing the idea of sending a vaccination expedition overseas only after it received several requests for the vaccine from royal officers in the Kingdom of New Granada (present-day Colombia). But it has been argued that King Charles IV was moved to underwrite this expedition after the death of one of his children from smallpox.

Some authors have interpreted the vaccination expedition as an act of enlightened despotism undertaken because King Charles and the Council were influenced by the ideals of the European Enlightenment concerning philanthropy and humanitarianism. This interpretation is argued by R. Ballester in the chapter "Repercuciones y significado de la Real Expedición Filantrópica de la Vacuna," and by Elvira Arquiola in the chapter "La expedición de Balmis y la difusion de la vacuna." Humanitarianism is the motivation attributed to King Charles and the Council in S. F. Cook's "Francisco Xavier Balmis and the Introduction of Vaccination to Latin America." But the losses to the Royal Exchequer due to population decline and labor force disruption caused by smallpox epidemics were also a concern.[2]

On September 1, 1803, King Charles IV sent out a royal order to all royal officers and religious authorities in his American and Asian domains, announcing the arrival of the vaccination expedition and commanding their support to that philanthropic undertaking. The expedition consisted of a director (Dr. Francisco Xavier Balmis), a subdirector (José Salvany Lleopart), and several assistants and paramedics. They carried with them vaccine serum preserved between sealed glass plates, thousands of copies of a treatise on vaccination describing how to vaccinate and preserve the vaccination serum, by Dr. Balmis, and twenty-one children from the orphanage at La Coruña, who carried the vaccine through arm-to-arm vaccinations performed during the journey between Galicia and Puerto Rico. The children in the expedition became crown wards as reward for being live carriers of the vaccine. Therefore inclusion in the expedition must have seemed a godsend to the foundlings.[3]

The vaccination expedition left Spain by the harbor of La Coruña, in Galicia, in the ship *María Pita,* on November 30, 1803, and it reached Puerto Rico in February of 1804. Dr. Balmis was displeased when he learned that the Puerto Rican authorities had gotten the vaccine from the Danish colony of Saint Thomas but, despite his poor relations with the Governor General and his chief doctor, don Francisco Oller, Balmis worked together with them in the organization of a central vaccination board that would record the successful vaccinations performed in Puerto Rico, and would keep live serum for future vaccinations. From Puerto Rico, the expedition went to Venezuela, where, according to R. Archila's *La expedición de Balmis en Venezuela,* the expedition was received with public manifestations of joy by the local authorities, and it was praised in an ode by the Venezuelan poet Andrés Bello.[4] In Venezuela, Balmis decided to divide the expedition into two sections, sending under his subdirector, José Salvany, the assistant don Manuel Grajales, the paramedic don Rafael Lozano Pérez, the nurse don Basilio Bolaños, and four children to Cartagena de Indias, in the Kingdom of New Granada, with the charge to introduce the smallpox vaccination, to teach its application, and to establish vaccination boards throughout Spanish South America.

The Vaccination Expedition in Present-Day Colombia and Panama

The ship *San Luis,* carrying the expedition under Salvany to Cartagena de Indias, wrecked on its way to that port city, and the expeditionaries and their luggage had to be rescued. But they entered within the walls of Cartagena in triumph on May 24, 1804, and began vaccinating at once. From Cartegena, Salvany sent the vaccine to Portobelo and Panama, where thousands were vaccinated. In Cartagena, Salvany established a vaccination board (Junta de la Vacuna) and made the arrangements to take ten children from the city orphanage in order to carry the vaccine through arm-to-arm vaccination to Santafé de Bogotá. The journey in a riverboat up the Magdalena River from the Caribbean coast to Santafé in the highlands was not easy but Salvany would land to vaccinate in every river port where the boat stopped, despite his falling down with an illness that caused him the loss of one eye. It is estimated that in that journey the expedition vaccinated 56,327 people.

On December 18, 1804, the expedition under Salvany arrived in Santafé, where they were welcomed with princely honors by the viceroy of New Granada, don Antonio de Amar y Borbón, and the archbishop of the city. During his stay in Santafé, Salvany met Father José Celestino Mutis, a medical doctor and the head of the botanical expedition in New Granada, who was familiar with the literature about the smallpox vaccination. Popular enthusiasm for the vaccine was immense, an understandable reaction given the fact that two years earlier Santafé had seen a smallpox epidemic, and that the royal authorities in New Granada had been trying ever since to obtain the vaccine.

The expedition left Santafé for Popayán on March 8, 1805, and it stopped in several towns on the way, always vaccinating people. On May 27, they arrived in Popayán where they were received with public manifestations of joy. In Popayán, Salvany formed a vaccination board following the regulations that he had drawn with the cooperation of Viceroy Amar y Borbón in Santafé. Henceforth, he would use this *Reglamento para la conservación de la vacuna* to form vaccination boards. But the expedition did not linger in Popayán because they received word of a smallpox outbreak in Quito. They speeded up their journey to the capital of the Kingdom of Quito (present-day Ecuador), although they stopped to vaccinate and established vaccination boards in the towns that they passed on their way.

Triumphs and Tribulations of the Vaccination Expedition in Present-Day Ecuador and Peru

There is a ten-page account of the activities of the vaccination expedition in present-day Ecuador in the two-volume *Historia de la medicina en el Ecuador,* by Virgilio Paredes Borja.[5] But the account of the Ecuadorian experience of Salvany and his expeditionaries is told in greater detail by Gonzalo Díaz de Yraola in his *La vuelta al mundo de la expedición de la vacuna.* The expedition was received in the outskirts of Quito by the city council and the members of the local Court of Justice *(Real Audiencia)* as well as by the bishop and members of the clergy. The expeditionaries stayed in Quito for two months, because Salvany had fallen ill again, and there they formed a vaccination board following the guidelines drawn at Santafé.

From Quito the expeditionaries went to Cuenca, where they were welcomed with a *Te Deum* in the cathedral, and bullfights, masked balls, and fireworks for three nights in a row. In that city they vaccinated 7,000 people, and Salvany formed a vaccination board. The authorities in Cuenca helped them obtain boys to carry the vaccine to Lima, and the Bethlemite brother Lorenzo Justiniano joined them. The land journey through the Andes from Cuenca down to Piura, in Peru, was as harsh as the rain-soaked river journey up the Magdalena River. They went through villages such as Azogue, Cumbre, Nabón, and Oña where they were welcomed by Native Americans. In the town of Loja, they were welcomed like saviors, and vaccinated 3,500 people.[6]

When the expeditionaries arrived in Piura, they stopped for several days to allow Salvany to recover, but as soon as he felt well, they left for Trujillo. On the way to Trujillo, Salvany fell ill again, and they stopped in a village of Native Americans who asked to be vaccinated. In that village, they were approached by a delegation of Andean gentry from the village of Chocope who wanted to be vaccinated, too. The expeditionaries arrived in Trujillo on January 17, 1806, and there they spent five days and vaccinated 2,761 people. From Trujillo, Salvany sent the paramedic Lozano and Fray Lorenzo Justiniano to vaccinate in the neighboring area, and then he went to the village of Lambayeque, where he was disappointed by the coldness of the welcome that he received from its city council, but he was able to vaccinate 4,000 people. From Lambayeque, Salvany went to Cajamarca, and on the way his beasts of burden were stolen by the hired muleteers, and he lost four days before being rescued by a Native American passing by, who helped him obtain burden animals from a nearby farm. In Cajamarca, he was well received by the city authorities, Native Americans danced in his honor, and a local poetaster read a poem in praise of the vaccine and the philanthropy of King Charles IV. After vaccinating 1,100 people in Cajamarca, Salvany returned to Trujillo, where he reunited with Lozano and Fray Lorenzo, who had gone to vaccinate on their own. Don Manuel Grajales and don Basilio Bolaños, who had separated from Salvany in Popayán in order to vaccinate in the area of Guayaquil, rejoined them before they reached Lima.[7]

On May 23, 1806, the vaccination expedition arrived in Lima. Juan B. Lastres has written about the activities of the expedition in Peru in his monographic work *La salud pública y la prevención de la viruela en el Perú*. In Lima, the expeditionaries did not find the welcome that they had met before, because the vaccine had preceded them there. It had been sent by the viceroy of the River Plata Provinces, at Buenos Aires, the Marquis of Sobremonte.

Indeed, the smallpox vaccine had arrived in the River Plata area from Brazil, in the arms of vaccinated slaves who landed in Montevideo, in the summer of 1805, when Salvany and his expedition were still in present-day Colombia. On August 2, 1805, 22 people were vaccinated in Buenos Aires before the Marquis of Sobremonte, who subsequently sent the serum to northern Argentina, Paraguay, Chile, and Lima.[8] The city council of Lima welcomed the expedition and dined with them, but the council made clear its opinion that their charge was no longer necessary.

Salvany appealed to the viceroy of Peru, don Gabriel Avilés y del Fierro, but his decrees calling for mass vaccinations in Lima were not heeded. The fact is that vaccination was widely spread in that city, although it was not applied free of charge. The serum was sold pressed between two sealed glass plates or dried on pieces of English taffeta, and in the neighboring towns those who vaccinated charged four pesos per person. But Salvany was concerned about the proper administration of the vaccine, and about its institutionalization. Fortunately for the expeditionaries, a new viceroy arrived in Lima on August 20, 1806, don José Fernando Abascal, who supported forcefully their endeavors. Shortly after the arrival of Viceroy Abascal, Salvany had vaccinated 22,726 people in the Kingdom of Peru.

Before Salvany's arrival in Lima, the city council had decided that the serum for the smallpox vaccine should be preserved by Dr. Pedro Belomo, a Lima doctor. Salvany developed a good professional relationship with Dr. Belomo, and through him won the confidence of the scientific community in Lima. Shortly after Salvany's arrival, the University of San Marcos at Lima granted him the doctor degree, and he won public praise from Dr. Hipólito Unanue, one of the most prestigious Peruvian scientists of the time.[9]

The Activities of Grajales in Chile, and Those of Salvany in Present-Day Bolivia

Before leaving Lima in order to continue his mission in Alto Peru (present-day Bolivia), Salvany commissioned Grajales and Bolaños to vaccinate in the areas of Huarochiri, Jauja, Tarma, Huanuco, Pantagua, and Canta in Peru, and to go by sea to the Kingdom of Chile. There is an extensive section about the activities of the vaccination expedition in Chile in Eduardo Salas Olano's *Historia de la medicina en Chile,* but Enrique Laval Manrique's "La viruela en Chile. Desde la Conquista hasta el regreso de Grajales a España en 1825" is a more complete source to what turned out to be the concluding chapter of the saga of the vaccination expedition of Charles IV in South America.

Don Manuel Grajales was the leader of the expedition in Chile. He and Bolaños landed at Valparaiso in November of 1806, and were disappointed by the news that the vaccine had preceded them in Chile. It had arrived from Buenos Aires in September of 1805, and for one year the priest don Pedro

María Chaparro had been carrying out his own vaccination campaign in central Chile. But Grajales, like Salvany, was aware of the importance of institutionalizing vaccination, and proceeded to obtain the assistance of the local authorities in the Kingdom of Chile to establish a vaccination board to keep records of the vaccinations performed and to preserve the serum. Vaccination boards were established by Grajales in Chilean townships.

Salvany sent the assistant Rafael Lozano Pérez to Huancavelica, Huamanga, and Cuzco, before he left for Alto Peru. On his way to La Paz, Salvany stopped in Chincha, Santiago de Almazor, and Ica, where he arrived on April 28, 1809. In Ica, he had to stop for health reasons, but several months later he recovered and continued on his way to La Paz, stopping to vaccinate and establish vaccination boards in Villa Nasca, Acari, Caraeli, Cumaná, Uchumayo, Arequipa, Tiabaya, Sabandía, Puno, Vilqui, Pomata, and Cepita. For a long time it was assumed that he had died at La Paz, from the last mention of his being alive—a record of the city council or Oruro, dated June 7, 1809, thanking him for bringing the vaccine to them.[10] But M. Parrilla Hermida was able to confirm that Salvany died in Cochabamba on July 21, 1810. In his article "Biografía del Doctor José Salvany Lleopart," Parrilla Hermida cites a death certificate issued by the pastor of the church of San Francisco, in Cochabamba, giving an account of the death of Salvany in that city on that date.

The Significance of the Vaccination Expedition in South America

On November 22, 1806, Dr. Edward Jenner, discoverer of the smallpox vaccine, wrote to his friend Rev. Dibbin, in reference to the vaccination expedition of King Charles IV, the following words: "I don't imagine the annals of history furnish an example of philanthropy so noble, so extensive as this."[11] One hundred and sixty years later, William McNeill compared favorably the Spanish behavior in reference to Native Americans and smallpox with that of English crown officers. As an illustrative example of Spanish behavior, McNeill mentioned the vaccination expedition of King Charles IV to Spanish America that instructed local doctors in the new technique to eradicate smallpox, and compared it with the policies of Lord Jeffrey Amherst in Massachusetts, who, in 1763, ordered that blankets infected with smallpox be distributed among enemy Native American tribes.[12] S. F. Cook estimated that, through this one act on the part of the government of Spain, more lives probably were saved than were lost in all the battles of Napoleon, and lamented that it had gone substantially unnoticed and unrecorded by both medical and political historians.[13]

John Z. Bowers included the vaccination expedition of King Charles IV to his American and Asian domains in his article "The Odyssey of Smallpox Vaccination," and several histories of medicine published in Spanish American countries during the 1960s covered that experiment in social welfare. But the number of monographs and articles specifically about the expedition is small.[14] I hope that this paper will foster interest in the activities of the vaccination expedition in the Andean countries.

The Madrid periodical *Semanario de Agricultura y Artes,* published on March 21, 1799, included the Spanish translation of an abridgement of Dr. Edward Jenner's 1798 report on his discovery of the vaccine.[15] That weekly and *La Gaceta de Madrid* were widely read in Spanish America, and the latter published on January 3, 1804, a letter from someone who asserted that the discovery of Jenner had become known in the Kingdoms of the Indies (as Spanish America was then referred to) through the article in the March 21, 1799, *Semanario.*[16] Indeed, King Charles IV sent out the vaccination expedition after receiving repeated pleas for the vaccine from the public authorities in the Kingdom of New Granada. But the most significant charge of the expedition that he sent out was not the vaccine itself, but its institutionalization scheme for teaching the new technology in Spanish America and the Philippines to doctors, barber-surgeons, and *curiosos* willing to participate in vaccination boards that would keep records of the vaccinations performed, and would preserve the serum for future vaccinations—its empowering aim.

Twenty years before the epidemic in New Granada that started the chain of events that led to the outfitting of the philanthropic expedition of Charles IV, the French publicist Nicolas Masson de Morvilliers had asked, "What has Spain done for humankind or the sciences?" in his article "Espagne."[17] It would be interesting to know M. de Morvilliers's reaction to reports of the success of the Spanish vaccination expedition. His article was never corrected, and for one hundred years monumental publication of the French Enlightenment misinformed the educated sectors of the Western world— including Latin America and the United States—by denying this vaccine and other significant scientific achievements of Spain and—by association—of Spanish Americans.

NOTES

1. See José G. Rigau-Pérez, "The Introduction of Smallpox Vaccine in 1803 and the Adoption of Immunization as a Government Function in Puerto Rico," *Hispanic American Historical Review* 69, no. 3 (August 1989): 393–423; J. P. Bantung, "Carlos IV y la introducción de la vacuna en Filipinas," *Anuario de Estudios Americanos* 12 (1955): 75–129; Michael M. Smith, "The 'Real Expedición Marítima de la Vacuna' en New Spain and Guatemala," *Transactions of the American Philosophical Society,* n.s., 64, pt. 1 (1974); and R. Archila, *La expedición de Balmis en Venezuela* (Caracas, 1969).

2. Rafael E. Tarragó, "La financiación de las ciencias y las expediciones científicas en Hispanoamérica bajo los Borbones," in *Technology, the Environment and Social Change,* ed. Patricia Noble, Papers of SALALM XXXVIII, Guadalajara, Mexico, May 15–20, 1993 (Albuquerque, N.Mex.: SALALM, 1995), p. 59.

3. Rigau-Pérez, "Introduction of Smallpox Vaccine," p. 397.

4. Claudio Costa-Casaretto, "Andrés Bello y la Real Expedición Filantrópica de la Vacuna," *Revista médica de Chile* 119, no. 8 (August 1991): 959.

5. Virgilio Paredes Borja, *Historia de la medicina en el Ecuador* (Quito: Editorial Casa de la Cultura Ecuatoriana, 1963), 2:39–49.

6. Gonzalo Díaz de Yraola, *La vuelta al mundo de la expedición de la vacuna* (Seville: Escuela de Estudios Hispanoamericanos de Sevilla, 1948), pp. 74–76.

7. Ibid., pp. 76–79.

8. Ibid., pp. 79–80; Verlarde Pérez Fontana, *Historia de la medicina en el Uruguay* (Montevideo: Rupublica Oriental del Uruguay, Ministerio de Salud Pública, 1967), 3:103–106.

9. See José Hipólito Unanue, *Actuaciones literarias de la vacuna en la Real Universidad de San Marcos* (Lima, 1807).

10. Díaz de Yraola, *La vuelta al mundo,* p. 93.

11. Edward Jenner, "Letter to Rev. Mr. Dibbin of 22 November 1806," in "A Review of the Early Vaccination Controversy with an Original Letter by Jenner Referring to It, and to the Spread of Vaccination to the Spanish Possessions of America, the Philippines and Other European Settlements of the Orient," by Philip King Brown, *California State Journal of Medicine* 12, no. 5 (May 1914): 172.

12. William McNeill, *Plagues and Peoples* (New York: Anchor Press/Doubleday, 1976), pp. 251–252.

13. S. F. Cook, "Francisco Xavier Balmis and the Introduction of Vaccination to Latin America," *Bulletin of the History of Medicine* (Baltimore) 11 (1942): 543.

14. See John Z. Bowers, "The Odyssey of Smallpox Vaccination," *Bulletin of the History of Medicine* (Baltimore) 55, no. 1 (spring 1981): 17–33; R. Archila, *Historia de la medicina en Venezuela* (Merida: Universidad de los Andes, Ediciones del Rectorado, 1966), pp. 155–165; Andrés Soriano Lleras, *La medicina en el Nuevo Reino de Granada durante la Conquista y la Colonia* (Bogotá: Imprenta Nacional, 1966), pp. 166–168; Virgilio Paredes Borja, *Historia de la medicina en el Ecuador,* 2:39–49; Velarde Pérez Fontana, *Historia de la medicina en el Uruguay,* 3:103–106; Ricardo Cruz-Coke Madrid, *Historia de la medicina chilena* (Santiago de Chile: Editorial Andrés Bello, 1995), p. 178.

15. José G. Rigau-Perez, "La difusión en Hispanoamérica de las primeras publicaciones españolas sobre la vacuna, 1799–1804," *Asclepio* (Madrid) 44, no. 1 (1992): 165.

16. Ibid., p. 167.

17. Nicolas Masson de Morvilliers, "Espagne," in *Encyclopedie méthodique: geographie moderne* (Paris: Panckoucke, 1782), 1:565.

BIBLIOGRAPHY

Archival Sources

In this section I include archival sources in Colombia, Peru, and Spain, but I am certain that similar valuable materials could be found in the National Libraries of Quito, La Paz, and Santiago de Chile. Given the involvement of parish priests and municipal officers with the vaccination boards formed by the vaccination expedition, I strongly recommend research in parishes and town hall archives of towns where the expedition is known to have stopped. The actual date of José Salvany's death was discovered through the efforts of the pastor of San Francisco, Cochabamba, who was able to locate the death record for him in the parish archives.

Colombia. Biblioteca Nacional (Santafé de Bogotá) Sección de "Raros y Curiosos":

Manuscritos 169 and 191.

Perú. Biblioteca Nacional (Lima) Oficina de Investigaciones y Fondos Bibliográficos:

Documentos dispersos sobre la vacunación antivariólica y la expedición filantrópica de la vacuna

Anexo I, 1803, Código D13105 Libro de Reales Ordenes y Actas concernientes a la Expedición Filantrópica de la Vacuna. 68ff.

Publicaciones en las colecciones X. Porras y Zegara de la Sala de Investigaciones. Anexo II:

Devoti, Felix, *These medicae de variolis: Pro gradus Bacchalaureatus defendendae, auspice deu preaeside Josepho Hippolyto Unanue.* Lima: Typi Domus Orphaorum, 1803.

Unanue, José Hipólito, *Actuaciones literarias de la vacuna en la Real Universidad de San Marcos.* Lima: Real Casa de Niños Expósitos, 1807.

Spain. Archivo General de Indians (Seville):

Indiferente General, Legajo 1558.

Secondary Sources

Books

Castillo y Domper, J. *Real expedición filantrópica para propagar la vacuna en América y Asia.* Madrid: R. F. de Rojas, 1912.

Días de Yraola, Gonzalo. *La vuelta al mundo de la expedición de la vacuna.* Seville: Escuela de Estudios Hispano-Americanos de Sevilla, 1948.

Frías-Núñez, Marcelo. *Enfermedad y sociedad en la crisis colonial del Antiguo Régimen (Nueva Granada en el Tránsito del siglo XVIII al XIX: las epidemias de viruelas).* Madrid: Consejo Superior de Investigaciones Científicas, 1992.

Lastres, Juan B. *La salud pública y la prevención de la viruela en el Perú.* Lima, 1957.

Ruiz-Moreno, A. *Introducción de la vacuna en América.* Buenos Aires: Universidad de Buenos Aires, Facultad de Ciencias Médicas, 1947.

Salas Olano, Eduardo. *Historia de la medicina en Chile.* Santiago: Imprenta Vicuna McKenna, 1894.

Silva, Renán. *Las epidemias de viruela de 1782 y 1802 en la Nueva Granada. Contribución a un análisis histórico de los precesos de apropiación de mod-elos culturales.* Cali, Colombia: Centro Editorial Universidad del Valle, 1992.

Articles

Arquiola, Elvira. "La expedición de Balmis y la difusión de la vacuna." In *La ciencia española en Ultramar,* edited by A. R. Diez Torre et alii. Madrid: Doce Calles, 1991. Pp. 249–254.

Ballester, R. "Repercuciones y significado de la Real Expedición Filantrópica de la Vacuna." In *La Ilustración Española.* Alicante: Instituto Juan Gil-Albert; Diputación Provincial de Alicante, 1986. Pp. 35–49.

Cook, S. F. "Francisco Xavier Balmis and the Introduction of Vaccination to Latin America." *Bulletin of the History of Medicine* 11 (1942): 543–560.

Costa-Casaretto, Claudio. "Andrés Bello y la Real Expedición Filantrópica de la Vacuna." *Revista médica de Chile* 119, no. 8 (August 1991): 957–962.

Frías-Nuñez, Marcelo. "A propòs de la variole et de la vaccine dans le vice-royaume de la Nouvèlle Espagne." In *Proceedings* of the 32nd International Congress on the History of Medicine. Brussels: Societas Belgica Historiae Medicinae, 1991. Pp. 383–390.

Gicklhorn, R., and H. Schadewaldt. "Sobre la introducción de la vacuna antivariolosa en América." In *Ensayos científicos escritos en homenaje a Tomás Romay,* edited by José López Sánchez. Havana: Academia de Ciencias de Cuba, 1968. Pp. 393–413.

Laval Manrique, Enrique. "La viruela en Chile. Desde la Conquista hasta el regreso de Grajales a España en 1825." *Anales chilenos de historia de la medicina* 9/10 (1967/1968): 203–276.

Lucena Giraldo, Manuel. "Entre el miedo y la piedad: la propuesta de José Ignacio Pombo para traer la vacuna a Nueva Granada." *Asclepio* (Madrid) 41, no. 2 (1989): 127–193.

Parrilla Hermida, M. "Biografía del Doctor José Salvany Lleopart." *Asclepio* (Madrid) 32 (1980): 303–310.

Rumeu de Armas, A. "La inoculación y la vacunación antivariólica en España: V. La Real Expedición para propagar la vacuna en América." *Medicina Española* 4 (1940b): 393–410.

6. African Legacy in Peru

Sara Sánchez

The African slave trade, which lasted nearly four centuries, produced the uprooting and deportation of nearly fifteen million Africans, who by virtue of the trade became mere objects of merchandise. In the Americas, besides providing the labor factor, these enslaved Africans contributed an indelible genetic and cultural imprint that constitutes the so-called third root of most Latin American countries, along with the Spanish heritage and the legacy of their indigenous peoples.

Research geared towards analyzing and disseminating the role of African American peoples in the historical process of the New World has acquired an increasing and deserving significance in the Western Hemisphere in the last four decades. So have ethnic and racial studies to the point that at the Miami Latin American Studies Association (LASA) conference in March 2000, about thirty of the estimated five hundred panels (about 6 percent) dealt entirely with some aspect of race in one or several countries in the Caribbean and Latin America. Other panels like the ones dealing with Latino studies or gender issues partially dealt with racial topics.

The purpose of this paper is to explore and describe the social sciences research conducted on Peru's African heritage, and to discuss and analyze Peru's most significant researchers, thus providing a brief pathfinder of the literature they contributed. This research I hope will offer a starting point for understanding the formative processes of contemporary society in Peru, as well as its social and cultural traits. I also hope that it will serve as an incentive for researchers and other Peruvian specialists to delve deeper and expand the literature and examination of such topics from various perspectives and disciplines.

Both the regular and the contraband African slave trade displaced substantial numbers of Africans to Latin America, the Caribbean, and North America. It is difficult if not impossible to surmise accurately the numbers of enslaved peoples that made it to this continent due to the fact that, since the traders involved illegal practices, many of these figures were not recorded. It is estimated that about 30 percent died in transit. Even with these constraints, conservative estimates have over 10 million people arriving as slaves in the Americas between the sixteenth and the nineteenth centuries. About 1.5 million of those went to Central and South America. The transplantation of so many people transformed the cultures of North and South America and the Caribbean.

Enslaved Africans first reached Peru between 1524 and 1528 in the wake of the first expeditions of the Spanish conquistadores and their armies, and in not insignificant numbers. Slaves accompanied Francisco Pizarro in all his activities and excursions after leaving Panama for the continent.[1]

Black slaves contributed to the campaign to subdue Peru's Inca empire. A Peruvian researcher, José Carlos Luciano Huapaya, has characterized them as *conquistadores a palos* (forced conquistadors),[2] serving as "particularly valuable auxiliaries not only in defeating the native population, but in acculturating the Indians to Spanish ways of living and doing things, not to mention becoming a key ingredient to the supply of labor."[3] Moreover, among the major purveyors of Spanish civilization mainly in urban centers in Peru were the Spanish *encomenderos,* artisans, the Spanish women who came to live in that country, and the ladino African (Latinized blacks brought from Spain, the Caribbean, or other colonies).

Brought up in Spanish culture, residing in Spanish homes, these black ladinos and their descendants served in specialized occupations, acted as intermediaries with the Indians, fought in Spanish armies, and participated in the conquistadores' internal struggles.[4] They also acted as "confidants, accomplices and private messengers,"[5] and they took part in Spanish residential and urban fiestas with their dances and instruments. They therefore earned the mistrust and hatred of the indigenous population by identifying themselves and being identified with the ruling Spanish class, who had conquered and oppressed the natives.

After this initial group, the number of slaves arriving in Peru continued to grow steadily. Indeed by the middle of the eighteenth century, almost half of the population of Lima was of African descent, with Peru being rated as having one of the largest black populations in South America up to the early-nineteenth century. Even though they dwindled in numbers and have been assimilated into the general population, they still have "made a significant cultural contribution in specific areas of Peruvian urban culture."[6] According to the official 1940 census, which was the last to take race into account, 48 percent of the population was black.[7]

The period of political and economic instability from the end of the eighteenth century to mid-nineteenth century saw Lima's slave population diminish considerably, not only as casualties of wars, but through manumissions (self-purchases). Some slaves were able to accomplish this by working extra *(trabajo jornalero),* or by renting themselves out for odd jobs. Other slaves achieved freedom by their owners decreasing their value to facilitate manumission, or granting them emancipation in their wills. Prolonged negotiations between slaves and their masters on the price of freedom were well documented by Christine Hunefeldt, a Peruvian social historian, who in numerous articles and monographs has pursued research on Peruvian slavery, its diminution by degrees, and other colonial social themes. This aspect is also examined extensively in Carlos Aguirre's *Agentes de su propia libertad: los esclavos de Lima y la desintegración de la esclavitud, 1821–1854* (1993).

African presence is most evident in popular urban music and dance, folkloric traditions such as the *danza de los diablitos* de El Carmen and massive religious celebrations in honor of *El Senor de los Milagros.* This last one is an old Peruvian tradition celebrated in Lima in October, which tradition can be traced to the old African *cofradías* (religious brotherhoods) that introduced this cult in the nineteenth century[8] and were described by María Rostworowski in her well-researched 1992 monograph.[9] These cofradías were exported to the Caribbean and to Peru, and were derived from long-standing traditions in Andalucia, which traditions blacks adapted with the blessing of the Church and the Spanish authorities. The real purpose of these Africans was to be able to congregate within this shelter and preserve their own traditions in the guise of Catholic practices, just as they did in Cuba and Brazil. African influences can be perceived even in traditional Peruvian cuisine. Nowadays, African presence is obvious in popular sports such as soccer, where black descendants are prominent, and women Olympic volleyball, both being successful and competitive.

Popular Peruvian language used by Spanish speakers is interspersed with African-derived words. About four hundred of them have been identified by renowned researcher and Afro-Peruvian scholar Fernando Romero in his 1980 book *Quimba, fa, malambo, ñeque,* a painstakingly researched glossary of "afronegrismos."

Until recently it was accepted that Africans had been prominent only in coastal Peru and that black characteristics were not evident in the Andean plateaus. This idea is now regarded as a myth, as African presence was also prevalent in the highland sierras of the interior, since there were slaves working in the mines and in the *obrajes* (textile factories) of the large cities. Black influence was not limited to the narrow coastline of the Pacific but extended to vital urban centers, such as the city of Lima, and covered wide territories. There was a significant African presence in those centers, with the black population and Indian masses both subject to tribute to the Spanish conquistadores.

Now still subject to a subtle kind of discrimination, African heritage Peruvians possess problems that have never been officially recognized, unlike those of the indigenous peoples with the *indigenismo* movement and its aftermath of Indian activism. Not until recently, with several musical and artistic movements, have the blacks been able to rally together as a group for their rights and for intellectual and artistic expression, to the extent that Andre Serbin has posed the question: Why is black power not active in Peru? in one of his essays and analyzed the reason for this lack of racial activism.[10]

In the mid-1950s, the historian José Durand spearheaded a movement along with the brother/sister team of Nicómedes and Victoria Santa Cruz that attempted to revive, collect, and reconstruct the African musical and dance traditions that had disappeared through dissociation and creolization. From the early 1500s to the 1800s, the songs and dances in Peruvian street fiestas were heavily African tinged. According to Fernando Romero, the 1700s marked the beginning of creolization,[11] with marimbas and typical African drums disappearing while Spanish or indigenous instruments took their place. In the nineteenth century, integration progressed rapidly until cultural syncretism in music was achieved. In accordance with these trends at the beginning of the twentieth century, it was difficult to distinguish African characteristics and traits in music. Many song and dance genres disappeared or were syncretized beyond recognition.

The new movement that sprang in the 1950s and peaked in the 1960s, flourishing to the 1980s, tried to isolate African-derived genres that had been diffused while endeavoring to reconstruct many rhythms and choreography using African-based styles. For example, the *marinera,* a typical Afro-Peruvian dance, was isolated and restored as its African predecessor, the *zambacueca*. The origins of these musical and dance genres are still being discussed and analyzed by ethnomusicologists regarding the authenticity of their African provenances.

Research and Publications

There is a wealth of primary sources and historical documentation on Peruvian blacks from the earliest times of the colony in the form of deeds, official correspondence, fiscal records, lawsuits, census data and statistics, marriage licenses, slaves' bills of sale, contracts, bail bonds, wills, and letters of manumission in the Archivo de Indias in Seville and in Peru's archives, such as the Archivo Nacional, the Archivo Arzobispal de Lima, and Archivo de la Cámara de Diputados. In parochial archives in Lima, and especially in Pacific coastal towns devoted to agriculture and largely dependent on African slave labor where it was a more significant fabric of daily life than elsewhere in the Spanish mainland, countless manuscripts and records were generated in daily life and are available to interested scholars. Frederick Bowser, one of the notable historians who has studied this aspect of Peruvian colonial history, wisely cautions scholars that research conducted using these documents needs complementary sources for it can lead to viewing the African, whether slave or free, not as a person but as an object of trade or subject or victim of the law, depicted not as an individual but as something devoid of feeling and with needs unrelated to the body.[12]

The early Indian chroniclers such as Felipe Guamán Poma de Ayala and Inca Garcilaso de la Vega account for the African presence and react to it; but they do not devote a considerable amount of attention to Indian interaction in

Peru's society, except Guamán Poma de Ayala condemns miscegenation while Garcilaso seems to condone *mestizaje,* as discussed by Raquel Chang-Rodríguez.[13]

In other countries, such as Cuba and Brazil, some of the earliest instances of recorded references to African ethnic traditions in print, besides the censuses and the 1681 Leyes de Indias, were narratives and descriptions of travelers and chroniclers who commented on the lascivious dances, the strident music, the loud drums, and the other festive celebrations of the black slaves and their freed brethren. Among others are cited A. F. Frezier's *Lima, 1713,* which describes Lima's population and the more than half Africans or African descendants in a rather contemptuous way commenting on their "evil traits"; Tadeo Hanke's *Lima, 1801,* which also comments on the African population, depicting their customs; and E. de Sartiges's *Lima 1834,* which deplores the situation of African descendants in the early Republic. Finally, Manuel Fuentes in his *Lima: apuntes históricos, descriptivos, estadísticos y de costumbres,* published in Paris in 1867, describes at length African cofradías in Peru and their religious festivities, especially those held for Corpus Christi, in a sarcastic and prejudiced manner.[14]

Among the most noted researchers who have endeavored to explore in-depth the African legacy in this country is Peru's Fernando Romero (born in 1905). A Harvard graduate, Romero became the dean of the National University of San Cristobal de Huamanga, the second oldest academic center in Peru. After retirement, this tireless scholar, diplomat, and traveler became a prolific writer and concentrated his interests in anthropological studies, in which he had become an expert, drawing on his experiences in and out of Peru. From his student days, the African presence in Peru and black culture had captivated his attention. He developed an extensive bibliography that became an important documentation on blacks in Peru, an issue whose analysis is integral to the country's history, national identity, and societal structure. Starting in the late 1930s, Romero wrote numerous articles, such as "Ritmo negro de la Costa Zamba" (1939) in a magazine called *Turismo,* in which he discusses the African influences in Peruvian music, musical instruments, and dance. He followed this with his *Papel de los descendientes de africanos* in 1980, based on a 1974 paper presented at a conference on the role of ethnic minorities in the socioeconomic development of Latin America that took place in Panama. There he provides an overreaching, careful analysis of the role of Afro-Peruvians; their contribution to the social, economic, and cultural evolution of their country; and their adaptation to Peru's society, examining their influence and participation in cofradías, which later evolved into *gremios* (labor unions). Fernando Romero argues that most Africans in Peru did not preserve their religious or magical practices as such, like in Cuba or Brazil; but he underlines the presence of St. Martin de Porras, a mestizo, who became a healer, probably using African skills and healing practices, and who won the love and reverence of Peruvians of all classes, ultimately achieving sainthood. Romero also centers attention on José Manuel Valdes, a mulatto physician, poet, and literary figure, who was exalted even by Spanish literary critic Menendez y Pelayo.[15]

Delving into linguistic studies, Romero wrote *El negro en el Perú y su transculturacion liguistica* (1987) and also *Quimba, fa, malambo, ñeque* (1988). His *Posibles influencias de los lenguajes afronegros en el habla de la costa peruana* (1987) expanded further on this linguistic study. The above-mentioned analysis and glossary of "afronegrismos" or words of African origin used in Peru were edited again in 1990 and republished as a *Diccionario afroperuano*.

This devoted scholar, who is likened to Cuba's Fernando Ortiz or Mexico's Gonzalo Aguirre-Beltrán for his prolific work, versatility, and vast knowledge, dedicated most of his more than ninety years of life to study and understand Peru. Among other topics, Romero examined at length how blacks combined the Spanish and aboriginal languages with their ancient African words to use in their current brand of Africanized-Spanish dialect and influenced even the language of the rest of the population.

In his *Safari africano y compraventa de esclavos para el Perú* (1994), he not only examined slavery and its trade in Peru, but its complete history from its African origins, as well as its repercussions in the Peruvian economy, life, and culture, thereby continuing this line of investigation. In this erudite work, his innovation within Afro-Peruvian studies was that he did not limit himself to the Peruvian experience. With a global outlook, he strove to understand slave traffic in its entirety, going in his research to the ultimate source of the trade, sub-Saharan Africa, where the unfortunate slaves were hunted down to be taken to Peruvian marketplaces. He examined exhaustively the development of the trade, including the international struggles that complicated slave supplies to the viceroyalty of Peru.

Another Peruvian scholar, Emilio Harth-Terré, an architect by profession, due to his interest in the arts and crafts first explored the participation of the colored man in colonial architecture, showcasing the quality of black artistry in carpentry and other skilled arts in his "El artesano negro en la arquitectura virrenial limeña" (1971). His *Negros e Indios; un estamento social ignorado del Perú colonial* (1973) analyzes the relationship between these two ethnic groups as artisans and constructors, and even documents Indian possession and use of black slaves to substitute for them in the *mita* (forced-labor conscription in public works) used as a tribute by their Spanish lords. Harth-Terré discovered that Indians could buy slaves and also participated in the slave trade especially in the early colonial days. Frequently co-authoring with Harth-Terré, Alberto Márquez Abanto also studied skilled Afro-Peruvian and Indian relations in his work.

As far as lengthy, authoritative, mainly historical treatises dealing with Peru's African heritage, the most important volume is James Lockhart's 1968 *Spanish Peru, 1532–1580,* in which he devotes a whole well-researched chapter to Africans in early colonial society. Frederick Bowser, who later followed in his footsteps, focused more closely on African presence, but nevertheless credits Lockhart with magnificently tracing the "complex interaction between Spaniard, African and Indian within the socioeconomic structure of colonial Peru."[16]

Peter Blanchard contributed his *Slavery and Abolition in Early Republican Peru* (1992), which deftly describes the process of abolition, the conditions of the Africans after independence, the complexities and contradictions inherent on their lack of real status, and marginalized assimilation into society after significantly contributing to achieving independence from Spain.

Currently, Peter Klarén's 1999 *Peru: Society and Nationhood in the Andes* updates historical studies on these periods, with the underlying theme of power and inclusion among the Spanish elite, the Indian, the mestizo, and the African descendants in both their ethnic and class dimensions. Drawing on the latest scholarship to date, Klarén effectively analyzes the significant economic, political, and social issues that have shaped Peruvian society throughout its long history.

European researchers were also drawn to Afro-Peruvian studies. In 1975 the French researcher Denys Cuche wrote *Poder blanco y la resistencia negra en el Perú; un estudio de la condicion social del negro en el Perú despues de la abolición de la esclavitud,* wherein he pursues the study of socioeconomic conditions of Peruvians of African descent after their emancipation, though his research is not as rigorously conducted or in-depth as his predecessors'. Jean Pierre Tardieu, another French scholar, has also explored Peru's African dimension in his 1998 *El Negro en el Cuzco: los caminos de la alienación en la segunda mitad del siglo XVII,* where he analyzes blacks' alienation and their lack of identification with other marginalized peoples of the area.

In 1982, a brief but interesting essay by Mirko Lauer, an art historian in Peru, discusses the African influence in plastic arts, highlighting two mulatto painters Francisco (Pancho) Fierro and José Gil de Castro, the latter being the official painter of the independence libertadores from 1810 to 1879. Lauer characterizes Fierro as a true painter of the Peruvian ambiance whose *aquarela* vignettes are reminiscent of Ricardo Palmas's *Tradiciones peruanas* in that they capture a particular moment and characters in Lima, thereby providing a vivid cultural and social testimony of the city in the 1900s as illustrated by his domestic servant scenes and street episodes, with the first realistic images of negritude.[17]

An important development in the study of local minorities and marginalized peoples occurred in 1986 with the Seminario sobre poblaciones inmigrantes, which took place in Lima. As an outcome of this seminar, a two-volume proceedings was published in 1988, which included well-researched and documented essays, such as Lorenzo Huertas's "Esclavitud y economía regional: Huamanga, 1577–1655"; Victoria Espinoza's "Cimarronaje y palenques en la costa central de Perú, 1700–1815"; and Alejandro Reyes Flores's "Esclavitud en Lima, 1800–1840," dealing with the plight of the enslaved African, his descendants, and their internal migrations.

Valuable studies have been forthcoming in recent years, such as *Rebeliones de esclavos en el Peru* (1990) by Wilfredo Kapsoli, *Los mecanismos del comercio negrero* (1980) and *Rutas negreras* (1979) by German Peralta Rivera. Up to the 1990s, Emilio Harth-Terré was still pursuing his studies on colonial blacks.

Peruvian Columbia alumnus and ethnomusicologist Raúl R. Romero, now associate professor at San Marcos University in Lima and head of the Archive of Traditional Andean Music at the Catholic University of Peru, participated in the Conference on Music and Black Ethnicity: The Caribbean and South America, held in Miami in January 1992. Attendance at this event renewed my interest in Afro-Latin American themes, expanding from the base of my own Afro-Cuban bibliographic research.

Besides his very enlightening and well-documented essay published in 1994 as part of the proceedings of this conference, Raúl Romero has authored monographs, articles, and essays in collective works on traditional Andean music, touching on its African influences, including his *La música tradicional y popular* in 1985 and *Música, danzas y mascaras en los Andes* in 1994.

Among other contemporary works worthy of mention are those of Carlos Aguirre's studies on outlaws, maroons, and criminality in Latin America, in which he focuses on Peru, among which is the collective work *Bandoleros, abigeos y montoneros: criminalidad y violencia en el Perú, siglos XVIII–XX* (1990), which he co-edited with Charles Walker and Carmen Vivanco. Also outstanding is his previously mentioned 1993 *Agentes de su propia libertad: los esclavos de Lima,* based on thorough archival research that examines in detail the disintegration of Peruvian slavery. Also to be included are Edgar Montiel's "Negros en Perú: de la conquista a la identidad nacional" (1995); and José Carlos Luciano Huapaya's "African Presence in Peru," published in *African Presence in the Americas* (1995), a thought-provoking essay from an Afro-Peruvian with a typical Indian surname and Spanish forenames—a living example of "syncretism."

Outstanding among the contributions of Peruvian scholars is the very documented and innovative family historical study, Christine Hunefeldt's *Lasmanuelos; la vida cotidiana de una familia negra en la Lima del siglo XIX: una reflexión histórica sobre la esclavitud urbana* (1992). This is an interesting, insightful case study tracing the history of a slave family and their successful efforts at manumission through tireless and prolonged negotiations by the family black matriarch, Manuela. Hunefeldt, a Peruvian historian/sociologist of German extraction, is now associate professor of History at the University of California, San Diego, who has dedicated her endeavors to examine the Afro-Peruvian population, especially on sociohistorical issues about gender and family. Her contributions show "impeccable archival research and theoretical grounding"[18] as rated by Peter Klarén from George Washington University

Current Trends

As previously described, the 1950s featured an African musical and cultural revival centered in Lima, which peaked in the 1960s and flourished into the 1980s. There was "an intense promotion of a black cultural presence at a national level through the mass media (television, radio, videos, recordings and cassettes)."[19]

Despite this movement, Afro-Peruvians do not constitute a distinct ethnic group as defined by the sociologist/anthropologists. They constitute an "undifferentiated mass" as opposed to an ethnic group. Neither do they exhibit clear physical features, characteristics, or distinct traits.[20]

This socioethnic development is due in part to the fact that since intermarriage was a tool for social and economic upward mobility, African ancestry was forgotten and their traditions diffused among the population. Looking for better treatment and future opportunities for their offspring and integration into Peruvian society, African descendants strove for "blanqueamiento" (whitening); so that as early as the seventeenth century, the number of pure Africans decreased to be supplanted by mestizos or *castas* (as persons produced by miscegenation were referred to). Thus according to Lima's official records, 45 percent of the 1820 population was considered to be black; in 1836 it had decreased to 10 percent; and by 1876 it was reported down to only 9 percent.

Even now miscegenation is common with 40 percent of black men and 25 percent of black women marrying whites or mestizos.[21] In colonial times blacks were barred from communicating among themselves freely or interacting freely, as 82.39 percent of them were isolated as servants in Spanish households and did not develop cohesive, shared common values or ethnic identities.[22] To a certain extent this included freed Africans who were hindered from developing cohesiveness by fierce competition and occupational diversity.

As opposed to countries like the United States, Brazil, and Cuba, even in coastal towns where Peruvian slaves were abundant, blacks were isolated in small or middle-sized plantations—a fact that inhibited their interaction and did not bode well for the preservation of social, cultural, ethnic, and musical traditions. Moreover, the diversity of ethnic groups in Africa from which the

Peruvian slave population originated dampened any chances for social interactions based on a common heritage, as happened elsewhere.

After the final abolition of slavery in 1855, the process of emancipation,
which had begun in 1821, was completed. As a result of this, the African
enclaves in Lima were disbanded as the blacks moved away from their distinct
neighborhoods. This scattering of African descendants further diffused, if not
dissolved, them into the general population.

The end result of all this was that Peruvian blacks, young or old, when
interviewed recently did not see themselves as a separate group.[23] Peruvian
blacks still mainly identify themselves with the Creole or Spanish ancestry
groups predominantly composed of Spanish descendants or mestizos, a carry-
over from their tradition from early colonial times of being identified and
identifying themselves with the Spanish conquistadors.[24] This is a result of
their fighting alongside the Spaniards in the conquest of the Incas, in the
Spanish *caudillos'* own civil wars, and even in the independence struggles.
Their plight is that conversely they are not recognized by the Spanish Creoles
as their own, but as a group separate from them by virtue of white racial
discrimination and prejudice. Nor do, in general, African descendants and
mestizos in Peru react as an ethnically and culturally distinct group with an
independent identity and social consciousness. With this attitude, the Peruvian
blacks are rejected both by the majority of the white Creole elites and by the
population of Andean extraction. Recent developments in Peru's socioeconomic and political environment have resulted in heavy indigenous
Andean migrations to the cities, such as Lima and even to coastal towns,
diluting African influence even more.

Conclusion

Historical publications written by Peruvians are scarce, despite a richness
of archival documents about Peruvian blacks and a prominent colonial African
presence reflected in some sixteenth-century manuscripts. Research on
African presence has not been emphasized as much as it should either in
colonial times or in the rest of Peru's history.[25] Most researchers agree there
is still a wealth of analytical research to be undertaken. Even many Peruvian
historians and scholars have neglected Afro-Peruvian studies in favor of
indigenous Andean subjects. There are a few noteworthy exceptions such as
Romero, Harth-Terré, Márquez Abanto, Aguirre, Hunefeldt, and others; but
the potential for more extensive historical research exists in these archives
teeming with documents.

In fact, as late as the 1970s, when a researcher such as the historian
Frederick Bowser was conducting his investigations, he could count mainly on
the first three of the above mentioned authors and on the historian James
Lockhart as the *cimientos* (foundations) for his Afro-Peruvian research.[26] With
Fernando Romero's demise, there seems to be a deferment in Peru as to

conducting and publishing such historical studies on the African heritage per se. On the other hand, there is still a promise of this trend changing; since, as pointed out by a researcher from the Instituto de Estudios Peruanos, the donation of Romero's private library, documents, and manuscripts to this institute has spurred some interest among the younger generations which should bear fruit in the form of substantial contributions to the literature.[27]

As far as other disciplines are concerned, research and publications for a time focused mainly on the colonial period and were largely historical in nature. Very little has been examined or thoroughly analyzed on current times or from an ethnographic point of view. Accomplished and well-researched ethnographic analyses particularly with the current population would be worthwhile developments in Afro-Peruvian studies.

The latest trends in Afro-Peruvian research, in keeping with social and ethnological developments, are heavily weighted towards African influence in music, dance, and folklore as a logical consequence of the integration or diffusion of the African descendants, to the extent that their impact is now most discernible in some centers, features, or folk traditions. Working to expand the scope is an active civil organization created in 1986, focusing on Afro-Peruvian publications and activities, called Movimiento Negro Francisco Congo. Its goals are to promote union among Peruvians of African descent, defend their rights to equality and dignity, and foster the artistic creativity among them. They sponsor festivities and events such as a black Christmas celebration and a black carnival in La Victoria, a traditionally Afro-Peruvian section of Lima. This movement has now been institutionalized into a Centro Francisco Congo and publishes a journal entitled *Bongo,* under the direction of Lilia Mayorga,[28] but, though still carrying out research and publications, receives little or no official support from the government.

After this research on Peruvian publications with an African content, my findings seem to concur with the views and observations expressed by Raúl Romero, the Peruvian musicologist who described the reconstruction and revival of Afro-Peruvian musical traditions at the 1992 Music and Black Ethnicity Conference previously referred to. He deplored that there were severe limitations to the revival and reconstruction of the Santa Cruzes' movement since it did not address the social and political problems of discrimination or the plight of Peruvian blacks as a whole. Up to the 1990s, most of these movements and centers had failed to move the masses and become a lasting foundation for furthering the black cause or the survival of Afro-Peruvian traditions. The problems faced by Afro-Peruvians "went further than these artistic interests." Instead of becoming a clearinghouse for Afro-Peruvian studies or a lasting foundation for furthering the black cause or the survival of their traditions, most of these movements, except for the Centro Francisco Congo, have evolved into commercial ventures without a permanent, deep-rooted impact on the national society and consciousness. In general, they did not succeed in taking root in the African descended communities, but remained an elitist endeavor with musical and choreographic dimensions.[29]

In sum, not discernible in the current literature is a significant revival or trend to study Afro-Peruvian themes in a more interdisciplinary manner, from diverse perspectives and disciplinary points of view, like with the Afro-Cuban or Caribbean literature I have analyzed in prior research. Attempts would be welcomed at comparing the conditions and status of black presence in colonial times and their social and economic conditions now vis-à-vis other Latin American countries with similar characteristics, such as Mexico and Uruguay, in addition to focusing solely on the Peruvian scenario.

Although there is no actual dearth of publications dealing with Afro-Peruvian themes, anthropological, ethnographical publications with a narrower focus, like those of Christine Hunefeldt and Carlos Aguirre, which publications contribute to the elucidation of the characteristics of the actual African population, would be a valuable contribution to Afro-Peruvian research. For example, accounts would be appreciated of the history and current conditions in African descendant enclaves in coastal towns such as Chincha, Cañete, Aucallama, and Zaña, which, to my knowledge, have not been adequately documented and explored. What is lacking is the example of Mexico, where Afro-ethnologists such as those in the Nuestra Tercera Raíz circle headed by Luz María Martínez Montiel have extensively studied the black towns of Veracruz and other coastal regions with local African heritage.

After a careful examination of Peter Klarén's extensive and detailed bibliographic essay at the end of his authoritative book *Peru: Society and Nationhood in the Andes* (1999),[30] the conclusion was reaffirmed that most research on Afro-Peruvians is buried deep within other Andean studies dealing with the following: a particular period in which Africans had some relevance, as in the early colonial times; actions in which they had some intervention, as in Peru's struggles; sectors where they were abundant, as in the sugar plantations or the mines; or socioeconomic studies of the lower classes, as in their criminality and internal migration. Few of these studies deal directly and specifically with the African legacy and their descendants.

Since Peru's black population almost disappeared by integration or assimilation after the abolition of slavery in the mid-nineteenth century, the cultural roots of Peru are more dependent on the contributions of the indigenous peoples than on the few survivals of slave cultures. A final conclusion is that though culturally and demographically, Peru's African legacy is deemed important by many Peruvian investigators and other Latin American researchers, it is not regarded as overwhelmingly significant in the overall picture of Andean studies as it deserves to be considered.

Furthermore, as Edgar Montiel most adequately expresses it: "Nuestra América no ha tomado conciencia de la gravitación del continente africano en la génesis cultural y racial de América Latina. Esta parte de la historia le resulta extraña y casi reniega de ella mentalmente, como latencia de una verguenza étnica originada en la conquista." Montiel goes on to emphasize:

> No hay una mera influencia de Africa en América, sino que constituye un componente relevante de la identidad nacional y americana. La presencia de la raza negra en la composición genética del hombre americano es innegable; otro problema es que no hayamos tomado conciencia de ella, lo que es síntoma de un yo colectivo dominado, avergonzado de sus raíces, por una ilusa "limpieza de sangre."[31]

This resulted from a legacy of the misguided and discriminatory policy of the Spanish colonial mentality that divided and segregated persons into castes and our own unfortunate acceptance, perpetuation, and internalization of this mentality.

SELECTED BIBLIOGRAPHY

Africa en América. México, D.F.: Centro de Estudios Económicos y Sociales del Tercer Mundo, Instituto de Investigaciones Estéticas, UNAM, 1982.

Africa en América Latina, relator Manuel Moreno Fraginals. México, D.F.: Siglo Veintiuno, 1977.

California State University, Los Angeles. Latin American Studies Center. *Black Latin America*. Los Angeles: Latin American Studies Center, California State University Press, 1977.

Coloquio Contribución Africana a la Cultura de las Américas. *Contribución africana a la cultura de las Américas: memorias del Coloquio Contribución Africana a la Cultura de las Americas*. Bogotá: Proyecto Biopacífico-Inderena, Instituto Colombiano de Antropología y Cultura, 1993.

Congreso de Cultura Negra de las Américas. *Primer Congreso de la Cultura Negra de las Américas*. Bogotá: Fundación Colombiana de Investigaciones Folklóricas, 1988.

Conniff, Michael L., and Thomas J. Davis. *Africans in the Americas: A History of the Black Diaspora*. New York: St. Martin's Press, 1994.

Davis, Darien J., ed. *Slavery and Beyond: The African Impact on Latin America and the Caribbean*. Wilmington, Del.: Scholarly Resources, 1995.

Franco, José Luciano. *La presencia negra en el Nuevo Mundo*. La Habana: Casa de las Américas, 1968.

Gray, John. *Ashe: Traditional Religion and Healing in Sub-Saharan Africa and the Diaspora: A Classified International Bibliography*. New York: Greenwood, 1989.

Guillot, Carlos Federico. *Negros rebeldes y negros cimarrones: perfil afroamericano en la historia del Nuevo Mundo durante el siglo XVI*. Buenos Aires: Libreria y Editorial "El Ateneo," 1961.

Knight, Franklin W. *The African Dimension in Latin American Societies*. New York: Macmillan; London: Collier Macmillan, 1974.

Martínez Montiel, Luz Maria. *Negros en América*. Madrid: Editorial MAPFRE, 1992.

Rout, Leslie B. *The African Experience in Spanish America, 1502 to the Present Day*. Cambridge: Cambridge University Press, 1975.

Seminario Internacional sobre la Participación del Negro en la Formación de las Sociedades Latinoamericanas. *La participación del negro en la formación de las sociedades latinoaméricanas*. Bogotá: Instituto Colombiano de Antropología y Cultura, 1987.

Wade, Peter. *Race and Ethnicity in Latin America*. London; Chicago: Pluto, 1997.

Williams, Cortez H. *The Black Experience: An Investigation of the Plight of Blacks in the United States and Latin America from the Fifteenth to the Nineteenth Century*. New Mexico: University of New Mexico Press, 1976.

Research on Peru

Primary Sources

Frezier, A. F. *Lima, 1713*. Reprinted in 1959.

Fuentes, Manuel. *Lima: apuntes históricos, descriptivos, estadísticos, y de costumbres*. Paris: 1867. Reprinted in 1959.

Guamán Poma de Ayala, Felipe. *El primer nueva corónica y buen gobierno; edición critica de John V. Murra y Rolena Adorno: traducciones y analisis textual del quechua por Jorge L. Urioste*.

Hanke, Tadeo. *Lima, 1801*. Reprinted in 1959.

Sartiges, E. de. *Lima 1834*. Reprinted in 1959.

Vega, Garcilaso de la. *Royal Commentaries of the Incas, and General History of Peru*. Translated with an introduction by Harold V. Livermore. Austin: University of Texas Press, 1966.

Secondary Sources

Blanchard, Peter. *Slavery and Abolition in Early Republican Peru*. Wilmington, Del.: SR Books, 1992.

Bowser, Frederick P. *The African Slave in Colonial Peru, 1524–1650*. Stanford: Stanford University Press, 1974.

———. "The Free Persons of Color in Lima and Mexico City: Manumission and Opportunities, 1580–1650." In *Race and Slavery in the Western Hemisphere, Quantitative Studies,* edited by Stanley Engerman and Eugene D. Genovese. Princeton: Princeton University Press, 1975. Pp. 331–368.

Cuche, Denys. *Poder blanco y resistencia negra en el Perú: un estudio de la condición social del negro en el Perú despues de la abolición de la esclavitud*. Lima: Instituto Nacional de Cultura, 1975.

Harth-Terré, Emilio. *Negros e Indios; un estamento social ignorado del Perú colonial*. Lima: Libreria-Editorial Juan Mejia Baca, 1973.

————. *Presencia del negro en el virreinato del Perú*. Lima: Editorial Universitaria, 1971.

Huapaya, José Carlos Luciano. "The African Presence in Peru." In *African Presence in the Americas,* edited by Carlos Moore. Trenton, N.J.: Africa World Press, 1995.

Hunefeldt, Christine. *Lasmanuelos; la vida cotidiana de una familia negra en la Lima del siglo XIX: una reflexión histórica sobre la esclavitud urbana*. Lima: Instituto de Estudios Peruanos, 1992.

Klarén, Peter F. *Peru: Society and Nationhood in the Andes*. New York: Oxford University Press, 1999.

Lauer, Mirko. "Límites de la plástica negra en el Perú." In *Africa en América*. México, D.F.: Centro de Estudios Económicos y Sociales del Tercer Mundo, Instituto de Investigaciones Técnicas, UNAM, 1982. Pp. 108–109.

Lockhart, James Marvin. *Spanish Peru, 1532–1580: A Colonial Society*. Madison: University of Wisconsin Press, 1968.

Millones Santagadea, Luis. "La población negra en el Perú: análisis de la posicion social del negro durante la dominación española." In his *Minorias étnicas en el Perú*. Lima: Pontificia Universidad Católica del Perú, 1973.

Montiel, Edgar. "Negros en Perú: de la conquista a la identidad nacional." In *Presencia africana en Sudamérica,* edited by Luz Maria Martinez Montiel. México, D.F.: Consejo Nacional para la Cultura y las Artes, 1995. Pp. 210–245.

Peralta, German. *Los mecanismos del comercio negrero*. Lima: Kuntur Editores, 1990.

————. *Rutas negreras*. Lima: Universidad Nacional Federico Villarreal, Dirección Universitaria de Investigación, Centro de Investigaciones Históricos Sociales, 1979.

Romero, Fernando. *El negro en el Perú y su transculturación lingüistica*. Editora Milla Bartres, 1987.

————. *El papel de los descendientes de africanos en el desarrollo económico-social del Perú*. La Molina, Perú: Taller de Estudios Andinos, Departamento de Ciencias Sociales, Universidad Nacional Agraria, 1980.

————. *Quimba, fa, malambo, ñeque: afronegrismos en el Perú*. Lima: Instituto de Estudios Peruanos, 1988.

————. *Safari africano y compraventa de esclavos para el Perú, (1412–1818)*. Lima: Instituto de Estudios Peruanos, Universidad Nacional San Cristóbal de Huamanga, 1994.

Romero, Raúl R. "Black Music and Identity in Peru: Reconstruction and Revival of Afro-Peruvian Musical Traditions." In *Music and Black Ethnicity: The Caribbean and South America*. Coral Gables, Fla.: North-South Center, University of Miami; New Brunswick, N.J.: Transaction Publishers, 1994.

Rostworowski de Díez Canseco, María. *Pachacamac y el Señor de los Milagros: una trayectoria milenaria*. Lima: Instituto de Estudios Peruanos, 1992.

Seminario sobre Poblaciones Inmigrantes. Lima: Consejo Nacional de Ciencia y Tecnología, 1987.

Stockes, Susan C. "Etnicidad y clase social: los afroperuanos de Lima, 1900–1930." In *Lima obrera 1900–1930,* edited by Steve Stein. Vol. 2. Lima: Ediciones El Virrey, 1987. Pp. 171–252.

Tardieu, Jean-Pierre. *El negro en el Cuzco: los caminos de la alienación en la segunda mitad del siglo XVII.* Lima: Pontíficia Universidad Católica del Perú, Banco Central de Reserva del Peru, 1988.

Vega, Juan José. "Negros contra Incas." In *Congreso de la Cultura Negra de las Americas.* Bogotá: Fundación Colombiana de Investigaciones Folklóricas, UNESCO, 1988. Pp. 117–119.

Periodical Articles

Bowser, Frederick P. "The African in Colonial Spanish America: Reflections on Research Achievements and Priorities." *Latin American Research Review* 7, no. 1 (1972): 77–94.

Cuche, Denys. "La mort des dieux africains et les religions noires au Perou" (Death of African gods and black religions in Peru). *Archives de Sociologie de Religions* 22, no. 1 (1977): 77–91.

―――. "Le Perou noir entre la tradition et la modernite." *Cahiers des Ameriques Latines* 19 (1979): 249–257.

―――. "Perou negre." *Tiers Monde* 23, no. 91 (July–Sept. 1980): 704–705.

Escobedo Mansilla, Ronald. "El tributo de los zambiagos, negros y mulatos libres en el virreinato peruano." *Revista de Indias* 41, no. 163–164 (Jan.–June 1981): 43–54.

Estenssoro Fuchs, Juan Carlos. "Música y comportamiento festivo de la población negra en Lima colonial." *Cuadernos Hispanoamericanos* 451–452 (Jan.–Feb. 1988): 161–168.

Harth-Terré, Emilio. "El artesano negro en la arquitectura virreinal limeña." *Revista del Archivo Nacional del Perú* 25, no. 1 (1971): 191.

―――. "El esclavo en la sociedad indoperuana." *Journal of Inter-American Studies* 3, no. 3 (July 1961): 297–340.

Hunefeldt, Christine. "Indios y negros en la construcción del nuevo estado republicano: Perú en la primera mitad del siglo XIX." *Cahiers des Ameriques Latines* 10 (1990): 225–235.

MacLean y Estenos, Roberto. "Negros en el Perú." *Letras* 36 (1947): 5–43.

Millones Santagadea, Luis. "Gente negra en el Perú: esclavos y conquistadores." *América Indígena* 31, no. 3 (July–Sept. 1971): 593–624.

Montiel, Edgar. "Los negros en el mundo andino." *Cuadernos Americanos* 36 (Nov.–Dec. 1992): 70–85.

Orellana, Valeriano, D. "La pachahuara de Acolla: una danza de los esclavos negros en el valle de Yanamarca." *Bulletin de l'Institut Francais d'Etudes Andines* 5, no. 1–2 (1976): 149–165.

Romero, Fernando. "Como era la zamacueca zamba." *Turismo* 146 (1939).

―――. "Instrumentos africanos de la Costa Zamba." *Turismo* 137 (1939).

————. "El negro en Tierra Firme durante el siglo XVI." *Actas y Trabajos Científicos del 27 Congreso Internacional de Americanistas* 2 (1942): 441–461.

————. "Ritmo negro de la Costa Zamba." *Turismo* 135 (1939).

————. "La zamba, abuela de la marinera." *Turismo* 141 (1939).

NOTES

1. Frederick P. Bowser, *The African Slave in Colonial Peru, 1524–1650* (Stanford: Stanford University Press, 1974), pp. 21–22.

2. José Carlos Luciano Huapaya, "The African Presence in Peru," in *African Presence in the Americas*, ed. Carlos Moore (Trenton, N.J.: Africa World Press, 1995), pp. 119–130.

3. Peter F. Klarén, *Peru: Society and Nationhood in the Andes* (New York: Oxford University Press, 1999), p. 51.

4. Bowser, *African Slave*, pp. 27–28.

5. Luis Millones Santagadea, "La población negra en el Perú: analisis de la posición social del negro durante la dominacion española," in his *Minorias étnicas en el Perú* (Lima: Pontificia Universidad Católica del Perú, 1973), pp. 17–47.

6. Raúl R. Romero, "Black Music and Identity in Peru: Reconstruction and Revival of Afro-Peruvian Musical Traditions," in *Music and Black Ethnicity: The Caribbean and South America* (Coral Gables, Fla.: North-South Center, University of Miami; New Brunswick, N.J.: Transaction Publishers, 1994), p. 308.

7. Roberto MacLean y Estenos, *Negros en el Nuevo Mundo* (Lima: Imprenta Domingo Miranda, 1948), p. 146.

8. Susan C. Stockes, "Etnicidad y clase social: los afroperuanos de Lima, 1900–1930," in *Lima Obrera 1900–1930*, ed. Steve Stein (Lima: Ediciones El Virrey, 1987), 2:171–252.

9. María Rostworowski de Díez Canseco, *Pachacamac y el Señor de los Milagros: una trayectoria milenaria* (Lima: Instituto de Estudios Peruanos, 1992), devotes a whole chapter besides numerous references to the African legacy.

10. Andre Serbin, "Por que no existe el poder negro en America Latina?" *Nueva Sociedad* 111 (1991): 148–157.

11. Fernando Romero, *Turismo,* 1939.

12. Bowser, *African Slave,* p. xiv.

13. Raquel Chang-Rodríguez, "Coloniaje y conciencia nacional: Garcilaso de la Vega y Felipe Guamán Poma de Ayala," *Caravelle: Cahiers du monde hispanique et luso-bresilien* 38 (1982): 29–43. Chang-Rodríguez interprets chronicler Guamán Poma de Ayala as opposing mestizaje and Inca Garcilaso as recognizing it.

14. Edgar Montiel, "Negros en Perú: de la conquista a la identidad nacional," in *Presencia africana en Sudamerica,* ed. Luz María Martínez Montiel (México: Consejo Nacional para la Cultura y las Artes, 1995), p. 258.

15. Fernando Romero, *El papel de los descendientes de africanos en el desarrollo económico-social del Perú* (La Molina: Taller de Estudios Andinos, Departamento de Ciencias Sociales, Universidad Nacional Agraria, 1980).

16. Bowser, *African Slave,* p. viii.

17. Mirko Lauer, "Limites de la plástica negra en el Perú," in *Africa en América* (México: Centro de Estudios Económicos y Sociales del Tercer Mundo, Instituto de Investigaciones Esteticas, UNAM, 1982), pp. 108–109.

18. Klarén, *Peru,* pp. 152–153.

19. Raúl Romero, "Black Music and Identity," p. 308.

20. Alberto Flores Galindo, *Aristocracia y plebe: Lima 1760–1830* (Lima: Mosca Azul Editores, 1984), pp. 128–137.

21. Stockes, "Ethnicidad y clase social," p. 186.

22. Galindo, *Aristocracia y plebe,* p. 121.

23. Raúl Romero, "Black Music and Identity," p. 311.

24. Luis Millones Santagadea, "Gente negra en el Perú: esclavos y conquistadores," *América Indigena* 31, no. 3 (July/September 1971): 593–624.

25. Juan José Vega, "Negros contra Incas," in *Congreso de la Cultura Negra de las Americas* (1st Cali, Colombia) (Bogotá: Fundación Colombiana de Investigaciones Folklóricas, UNESCO, 1988), p. 118.

26. Bowser, *African Slave,* p. viii.

27. Virginia García, conversation with author, Long Beach, Calif., May 2000.

28. Emma Zevallos, conversation with author, Miami, Fla., March 2000.

29. Raúl Romero, "Black Music and Identity," p. 323.

30. A meticulous examination of Klarén's inclusive bibliographic essay at the end of his *Peru: Society and Nationhood in the Andes* did not produce many instances of books or articles dealing solely with the African presence in Peru.

31. Montiel, "Negros en Perú," p. 214.

Historic Andean Collections

7. Researching "El Virreinato del Perú" in the Northeast

Peter A. Stern

For any historian wishing to undertake research on the viceroyalty of Peru, it is obvious that a visit to a number of archives is in order, beginning with the AGI, the famous *Archivo General de Indias* in Seville. But it is surprising the amount of investigation which the diligent colonial historian can do in the United States, using microfilmed documents from a variety of libraries and university archives. Very often the holdings of institutions reflect the research interests of the professors who have taught there. For example, the core of the Bancroft Library's great Mexican holdings from both the *Archivo General de Indias* and the *Archivo General de la Nación* in Mexico are the direct result of the labors of Herbert Eugene Bolton and his graduate students beginning in the 1930s. My paper will examine the legacy of another professor's tenure at a public institution, that of the eminent Lewis Hanke at the University of Massachusetts, Amherst.

Hanke joined the history department at the University of Massachusetts in 1969, after a distinguished career at the University of Texas at Austin, Columbia University, and the University of California at Irvine. Not quite ready to retire, and forced to do so at age sixty-five by the state of California, Hanke sought an academic refuge and was offered a position at UMass by one of his old students at Harvard, Robert Potash. Hanke taught in Amherst for six years, retiring in 1975. His writings throughout his career reflect his deep interest in many different aspects of Latin American history, particularly the struggle between the exploiters and the defenders of the Native Americans under Spanish rule. This abiding interest resulted in publications such as *All Mankind is One: A Study of the Disputation Between Bartólome de Las Casas and Juan Ginés de Sepúlveda in 1550 on the Intellectual and Religious Capacity of the American Indians,* as well as *The Spanish Struggle for Justice in the Conquest of America.* But Hanke also wrote a number of works specifically on the Andes, including a history of the mining complex at Potosí, *La villa imperial de Potosí: un capítulo inédito en la historia del Nuevo Mundo,* and *Los virreyes españoles en América durante el gobierno de la casa de Austria: Perú.* It was particularly to aid in researching and writing this last work that Professor Hanke created and deposited at the university his collection of microfilm on the viceroyalty of Peru. The seven-volume set on *los virreyes,* part of the *Biblioteca de autores españoles desde la formación del lenguaje hasta nuestros días,* attempts to document the establishment and development of the imperial Spanish government, as represented by the crown's representative in Spanish America, under the Hapsburgs, the House of Austria, between 1535 and 1700. In 1700 the last Hapsburg monarch, the feeble Charles II, died without issue, triggering the War of the Spanish Succession. When the war ended, some fourteen years later, the more potent and vigorous blood of the Bourbons replaced the exhausted Hapsburg *sangre,* and it has occupied the throne ever since.

The enormous Spanish Empire was one held together not by military force, but by laws. Considering Latin America's post-independence propensity for military *coup d'etat* and authoritarian government, it might surprise one to learn that until the Bourbon reforms of the eighteenth century, there were few Spanish military forces stationed in the Americas. Apart from the viceroy's small bodyguard, there was little in the way of a standing army in the Spanish Empire. The Indies, of course, had been conquered for Spain by the conquistadores, who were virtually military and economic entrepreneurs operating under license from the united crowns of Castile and Aragón. The conquest of the Americas could be described as being accomplished by private enterprise, or, perhaps more accurately, by the sort of public-private enterprise partnerships so dear to contemporary politicians. Thereafter, the defense of the realm depended on the "unregulated militia"; that is, every able-bodied man who could bear arms. In particular, the *encomenderos* were obligated to defend the crown when trouble arose; this was one of their obligations under which they received their grants of tributary Indians.

Of course, there were some Spanish military forces in the Indies: the seas were patrolled by the navy, and frontier areas in Chile and northern Mexico were garrisoned by *presidio* troops, almost all raised locally. But by and large, the Spanish held their empire together by custom, bureaucracy, and law, not by arms. This crucial factor often forced the crown, in the person of the crown's representative, the viceroy, to back down in the face of local resistance to some decree or other from Madrid. The most famous example of this was the suspension of the New Laws of 1542. The New Laws regulated the institution of the *encomienda;* and in New Spain, to avoid open revolt (which did occur in Peru), the viceroy was forced to nullify the decrees coming from the Council of the Indies with the now-famous phrase, "*Obedezco pero no cumplo*—I obey but I do not comply." This legalism let the viceroy off the hook—he could report to the king that much as he would like to put into force the crown's law, conditions at the present time prevented him from doing so, and so such decrees that cause unrest were suspended pending clarification from Spain.

The crown also held together its empire with an extensive bureaucracy, and, as Hanke writes, it was a particularly legalistic bureaucracy.[1] Between the king and his representative in America—the viceroy or *virrey,* literally vice-king—were the Council of the Indies and the *Casa de la Contratación.* The latter was both legislature and supreme court for the Indies, and the former the house of trade, regulating not only commercial relations between Spain and its colonies, but also all matters relating to maritime commerce, including emigration from Spain to America. Below the viceroy in America was the *audiencia,* which also combined legislative and judicial functions. The audiencia consisted of a president, usually trained in the law, at least four *oidores* (literally, "those who listen"), who were magistrates, a fiscal or crown attorney, an *alguacil mayor* or chief constable, a chaplain, a solicitor for the poor, assistant attorneys, notaries, and scribes.[2] Below the audiencia were the *cabildos,* town councils. Whereas all viceroys and most oidores were *peninsulares,* the cabildos were the strongholds of the *criollos,* the Spanish born in the Americas.

Attending all officials at all levels were various bureaucrats, in particular the aforementioned notaries and scribes. In an era of limited literacy, the office of the *escribano,* the notary, was particularly important. (The words *notario* and *escribano* were used interchangeably during the colonial period.) The duties of the escribano were spelled out as early as the thirteenth century in the *Siete partidas* of Alfonso X. Clearly delineated in the laws was the difference between an escribano who writes for the king and an *escribano público,* who writes letters of purchase and sale.[3] One historian of the colonial notaries describes *escribanos públicos, escribanos de cabildo, de cámara, ayuntamiento, or consejo, escribanos de naos* (for naval stores and munitions), *escribanos de mayor de armada* (for fleets), *de gobernación, de minas y registros* (for mining records), *de visitas, de la Santa Hermandad,* ecclesiastical notaries, escribanos of the Inquisition, and many others. The ones which concern us for colonial records are the *escribanos de gobernación,* auxiliary functionaries of the governor, viceroy, or captain-general. All such men had to be *de real,* that is, authorized by the crown to be royal notaries. All had to be at least twenty-five years old, Christian, of good birth and character, able to write well, and well versed in *escrivanía*—the scribe's art.[4] Mestizos and mulattos were forbidden the office of notary, although that provision was often ignored, due to severe shortages of trained notaries in the Indies.[5]

All commercial and official transactions had to be done in a legal and prescribed fashion, which meant utilizing the services of the scribes. All contracts and land transfers, for example, had to be written down by notaries. All judicial and administrative proceedings were recorded by these officials. All "public instruments"; that is, legal documents (particularly contracts) had to be on *papel sellado*—official paper, inscribed with the king's seals, which paper was a major source of crown revenue.[6] (The regulations concerning papel sellado are on five pages in the *Recopilación de leyes de los Reynas de las Indias.*) When, in distant outposts of the empire, the authorities might run out of papel sellado, they were forced to write on whatever paper they could obtain. In addition, notaries of the sixteenth to the eighteenth century utilized a type of shorthand in their writing—a system of abbreviations and symbols similar in purpose to modern business shorthand or court stenographers' transcripts— thus forcing colonial historians to learn paleography, the handwriting and codes of colonial-era escrivanía.

It is the work of these escribanos which are read when examining documents from the viceroyalty of Peru. The crown established the viceroyalty as an administrative entity in 1544, following the creation of the first, the viceroyalty of New Spain, in Mexico in 1535. In part, the viceroyalty of Peru was a response to the failure of the Lima audiencia to enforce the New Laws of 1542, but it also reflected a desire of the Spanish monarch (Charles I, Holy Roman Emperor) to assume greater control from Europe of the turbulent American empire. The rough and ready era of the conquistadores was to be replaced by the more dependable rule of the imperial servant. Legally speaking, the immense viceroyalty of Peru consisted of nearly all of Spanish South America, including the Audiencia of Lima, the Captaincies-General of Chile and New Granada, and the Presidencies of Quito, Charcas (Bolivia, Paraguay, and parts of Argentina), and Panama. However, considerable autonomy from Lima proved to be the rule in certain administrative aspects, given the immense distances and difficulty of communication between parts of the Spanish Empire.

The microfilms that Professor Hanke selected in his examination of viceregal administration were for the most part filmed by the Centro Nacional de Microfilm in Madrid. The microfilms were indexed in a three-volume set entitled *Guía de las fuentes en el Archivo General de Indias para el estudio de la administración virreinal española en México y en el Perú: 1535–1700*. This guide to the microfilm briefly describes the contents of each *legajo;* it is in the seven-volume work *Los virreyes españoles en América* that Hanke transcribed in full selected documents which, to his thinking, illuminated important aspects of viceregal government in Peru. Hanke collaborated with Celso Rodríguez on this project, which was published in Cologne and Vienna by the publishing firm Böhlau in 1977. The 335 reels of film which he deposited in the library at the University of Massachusetts were supplemented by another 23 reels of film received later, which were catalogued as *Juicios de residencia, audiencia de Lima, años 1549–1617*. This film was also produced by the Centro Nacional de Microfilm from documents held in the *Sección de Justicia* of the AGI.

Before examining the kind of research that this mass of filmed documents facilitates, it might be well to say a few words about the source of this material, the General Archives of the Indies. Surprisingly, the archive is of relatively late origin; its date of foundation is 1785, when authorities realized that the older *Archivo General de Simancas,* the crown's central archives from the sixteenth century onwards, was inadequate to deal with the flow of paper from the empire. Accordingly, a handsome building, the Commodity Exchange of Seville, built in various phases between 1583 and 1646, was chosen as the site for the new archives, as most of the trade in commodities had moved from Seville to Cádiz, and the building had fallen into disuse. From October 1646, all documents generated from state agencies such as the Council of the Indies, the House of the Indies (or *Casa de la Contratación*), the trading *consulados,* and the Secretariats of State and the Indies were deposited there. All documents dated from before 1760 were sent to the new archives; documents from after that date remained the property of the bodies which had issued them.[7] The millions of documents housed in the archives are organized according to the "principle of provenance"; that is, by the bodies which issued them. The archives are divided into fifteen sections, eleven of them by provenance, and the remainder by historical criteria. The administration of justice, governance, and economics of the empire are the subjects of the divisions into which the sections are divided.

The purpose of Hanke's project, as he relates at the beginning of his *Guía,* is to discover whether or not the Spanish government was beneficial or prejudicial to the inhabitants of the Americas. Was Spanish rule "better" or worse than that of the English, French, and Portuguese empires? (Hanke seems to have left out the Dutch in his question.) The only way to even try and answer this question, wrote Hanke in the introduction to his catalogue, was to examine how imperial government worked. Through viceregal correspondence, one can examine every aspect of political, social, and economic interaction of Spaniards with Spaniards, other Europeans, Native Americans, and the other diverse castes of the empire—mestizos and mulattos of every variation: the tribute gathered from the encomienda Indians, the silver production from the mines at Potosí, the risings of black slaves, the encounters with foreign corsairs off the Pacific coast, the friction with ecclesiastical authorities over power and money, the actions of the Inquisition, the interaction with members of the audiencia and the cabildos, the population of cities, towns, and Indian villages, and a thousand other topics.

The material is organized by class, first in *registros,* which contain instructions from the viceroy as well as decrees issued in response to petitions from individuals wanting to recover property or change their status. A large number of viceregal documents, which were particularly illustrative of the social order and interaction of the colonies, were reprinted in a superb five-volume collection by Richard Konetzke entitled *Colección de documentos para la historia de la formación social de Hispanoamérica, 1493–1810.*[8]

Another type of colonial document is the *residencia,* a type of investigation which was ordered by either the crown or the Council of the Indies. Residencias were usually carried out at the end of a colonial official's tenure of office to see whether malfeasance or other misconduct had taken place. It was a period when people could also lodge complaints against the departing official. Residencias could also be conducted at any time that circumstances warranted it; thus the Spanish crown had a permanent "special counsel" at its disposal. Besides residencias, there were *visitas,* literally visits from high officials down to the provincial level. Visitas could be civil, ecclesiastical, or even military in nature. Hanke introduces his section on imperial residencias by commenting that so many complaints were lodged against royal officials that if one were to believe them all, one would assume that every crime known to man was being committed in the Indies, and that thousands of letters were being sent back to Spain to inform the king and royal officials of the horrors which were being perpetrated in the empire.[9] Hanke characterizes the crown's attitude as almost sadistic in its insistence on believing the worst of its own American officials, and the Council of the Indies had little faith in the honesty of any imperial official. One viceroy commented acidly that in America one was received with bows and shown the way out with arrows.[10] But a fiscal, Francisco López de Caravantes, one of the most honest and efficient financial officials Peru ever saw, swore that the Spanish crown lost more riches "as a consequence of dishonest and inefficient administration than any other cause."[11] Residencias could drag on for years, and ruined many a man, leaving some officials disgraced and penniless. One *proceso* against the Conde de Castellar in the seventeenth century left 37,000 folios of documents in its wake.[12]

The Peruvian documents are also invaluable in gaining a sharper picture of the economic development of the Indies. Financial accounts run from the establishment of the viceroyalties of Mexico and Peru until the end of the colonial era. They delineate the sources of royal revenue and the purposes to which it was put. Each viceroyalty had a central treasury, with a network of subtreasuries; in Peru there were fourteen *cajas,* including ones in Arequipa, Cuzco, Potosí, Huancavelica, and La Paz. Until 1700, cajas in Buenos Aires, Paraguay, and Chile were subordinate to Lima as well.

What kind of data do the documents reveal? The sources of imperial wealth were numerous: *quintos y diezmos,* the famous king's "fifth" paid on silver and gold (traditionally, usually only a tenth); the *media anata,* a fee consisting of half a year's salary paid by prospective officials to secure official positions; the *avería,* taxes levied on all imports and exports at Seville in order to support the *flotas* or fleets; the *almorifazgo,* another customs duty levied both in Spain and in the Americas; *alcabalas,* sales taxes; and special taxes levied on salt, papel sellado, playing cards, aguardiente and *pulque,* tobacco, and many other items. The revenue was spent on salaries of royal officials and bureaucrats; the costs of war; *situados,* or special subsidies paid to support presidios in Chile guarding against the Araucanian Indians, and forts and naval ships in the Caribbean guarding the empire against English, Dutch, and French incursions and pirates; loans; and alms and charities supported by the viceroy.

Records of the regional treasuries show the monies remitted to Mexico City and Lima; the imperial treasury accounts show the revenues sent back to the metropolis.[13]

Hanke also includes biographies and bibliographies of each of the twenty-four men who served as viceroy in Peru, including the date he took office in Lima and the date he died, a brief description of the highlights of his term of office, and the results of his residencia. It was in particular the instructions that one viceroy would pass to his successor and the residencies that interested Hanke,[14] almost as if the complaints registered against the king's representatives in America and the advice that a weary leave-taker would impart to his successor might reveal more than voluminous dry and routine correspondence.

Leafing through the thousands of entries contained in the three-volume *Guía,* one is awed by the vast scope of matters—political, judicial, economic, and administrative—with which the viceroys had to deal. Just one section, Folio 178, of the correspondence of Francisco de Toledo (1569–1581) with King Philip II refers to letters dealing with the punishment of *caciques* (native chieftains), the province of Chile, *corregimientos* (economic and administrative Indian districts), gold and silver, the *Casa de Moneda,* encomiendas, the criminal courts, complaints and succession of encomenderos, the Holy Office (Inquisition), *malas costumbres,* residencias of justices and other officials, jails, the baptism of slaves, *yanaconas* (Indian workers living outside tribes or communities), and the division of lands.[15] Other entries in the *Guía* refer to "Indians of war who are on the frontier of Christians in Peru," excesses of the monastaries, the supply of mercury to the mines at Potosí, the university in Lima, the sale of offices, the salaries of oidores, the construction of churches, the raids of English corsairs, the discovery of new islands, a rebellion in Santa Cruz, the stocking of royal granaries for the Indians' benefit, the supplying of enough natives to work the silver and mercury mines, *negros cimarrones* (escaped black slaves), arguments among bishops, the position and influence of the Jesuits in the viceroyalty, charity for the poor and the establishment of hospitals, the dispatch of fleets back to Panama, the declarations of English sailors captured in Chile, artillery destined to defend Callao and Lima, the building of ships in Guayaquil, a journey overland to Brazil from Tucumán to trace silver smuggling out of Spanish territory into that of the Portuguese, excommunications, prohibitions against trespassing in Indian towns—and thousands upon thousands of petitions from people desiring, requesting, begging for, renouncing, and requesting offices and positions.

The cumulative effect of such a vast catalog of the minutiae of colonial life can be numbing, but there is no doubt that the enormous mass of documents record the very essence of life during the nearly three hundred years of the colony. Hanke's project was, not surprisingly, not the first to transcribe the papers of various viceroys of Peru. Only a few examples are *Memorias de los vireyes que han gobernado el Perú durante el tiempo del coloniaje español,* published in Lima in 1859; another scholar assembled *Relaciones de los vireyes y audiencias que han gobernado el Perú* (Lima, 1867); and a third is *Papeles de los gobernantes del Perú* (Madrid, 1921). But the Hanke project is an exceptional example of the meticulous assembling and cataloguing of Latin American documents which give us rich research sources. The universities in which the great postwar generation of historians taught are lucky to have benefited from the kind of labors no longer performed today. But a new generation will, one hopes, turn its attention to these collections and bring new technologies to bear which will make their availability and dissemination more widespread than their authors could ever have imagined. The technology already exists to put enormous quantities of historical data online in digital form; what is lacking is the money to do so in any sustained fashion. That collections like those assembled by scholars like Lewis Hanke and Herbert Eugene Bolton will someday be available through the Internet is a distant dream, but one well worth working towards.

NOTES

1. Lewis Hanke, *Guía de las fuentes en el Archivo General de Indias para el estudio de la administración virreinal española en México y en el Perú, 1535–1700,* 3 vols. (Köln, Wien: Böhlau, 1977).

2. Lyle N. McAlister, *Spain and Portugal in the New World, 1492–1700* (Minneapolis: University of Minnesota, 1984), p. 190.

3. Jorge Luján Muñoz, *Los escribanos en las Indias Ocidentales: En particular en el reino de Guatemala* (Guatemala: Instituto Guatemalteco de derecho Notarial, 1977), p. 3.

4. Ibid., p. 20.

5. Ibid., p. 26.

6. See Ley xviii, título xxiii, Libro VIII, *Recopilación de leyes de los eynos de las Indias,* 3 vols. (Madrid: Ediciones Cultura Hispánica, 1973), 3:107–109.

7. Pedro González García, introduction to *Discovering the Americas: The Archive of the Indies,* ed. Pedro González García (New York: Vendome, 1997), p. 19.

8. Richard Konetzke, *Colección de documentos para la historia de la formación social de Hispanoamérica, 1493–1810,* 5 vols. (Madrid: Consejo Superior de Investigaciones Cientificas, 1953–).

9. Hanke, *Guía de las fuentes,* 1:39.

10. Ibid., 1:40.

11. Quoted in Engel Sluiter, "Francisco López de Caravantes' Historical Sketch of Fiscal Administration in Colonial Peru, 1533–1618," *Hispanic American Historical Review* (1945), 25:225–226; cited in ibid.

12. Hanke, *Guía de las Fuentes,* 1:40.

13. John Te Paske, "Las cartas cuentas como fuente para la historia de los virreinantos del Perú y Nueva España, 1521–1700," in Hanke, *Guía de las fuentes,* pp. 45–46.

14. Robert Potash, conversation with author, University of Massachusetts, Amherst, May 22, 2000.

15. Hanke, *Guia de las fuentes,* 3:16.

8. Press Coverage of "Campesinado Boliviano" in the Late 19th Century

Darlene Waller

It was my intent in proposing this paper and is my intent in presenting to continue to inform my colleagues and scholars about the research possibilities using the Latin American newspapers collection at Archives and Special Collections in the University of Connecticut's Thomas J. Dodd Research Center. I will not describe the entire newspaper holdings in detail. A description of major holdings in Special Collections for the study of Hispanic history and culture can be found in the collection's searchable web database at http://norman.lib.uconn.edu/LatinPapers. The database can be searched using a single element or a combination of elements including paper title, city or country of publication, and publication date or date span. I will point out, however, that the strength of the collection is represented by Bolivian papers—most dating from the late-nineteenth century. With this in mind, I have focused my research on but a few years in this period of Bolivian history in which a variety of land tenure and agrarian reform issues were considered and implemented. Campesino uprisings and subsequent brutal government responses followed these reforms typically resulting in blood baths wiping out thousands of rural citizens.

In the first years of the Bolivian republic, there was no policy to create and/or increase feudal latifundios in the rural communities, but this practice changed drastically in the later years of the developing nation. Successive leaders starting with the Dictator Melgarejo in 1864 and extending through the 1950s implemented a variety of agrarian reforms. Not until the 1950s did Bolivia finally end its policy of agrarian feudalism. As the rights of freedom and landownership were threatened, the revolutionary democratic campesino movement advanced against the new tendency toward feudalistic policies.

In fact, the entire second half of the nineteenth century was a period of great political turmoil in Bolivia. During this time, often referred to as the "caudillo" period, a variety of Bolivian military officers and generals vied with one another for control of the state. In a twenty-nine-year period between 1850 and 1879, Bolivia had nine presidents, all of which were overthrown and replaced with equally tyrannical fellows.

The period started with Colonel Manuel Belzú from 1848 to 1855 who was considered Bolivia's first populist caudillo, because his policies favored Indians and the oppressed classes. Belzú instituted a nationalistic mining code and protectionist economic legislation, the new 1851 Constitution, and the 1854 national census. In 1855, Belzú passed power to his son-in-law, Jorge Cordova, who remained in office for only two years at which time he was overthrown by General Agustín Morales and José María Linares. At this point Linares became Bolivia's first civilian president. Linares stayed in office from 1857 to 1861 and brought sweeping fiscal, administrative, and judicial reforms. These reforms, of course, aggravated the power elites causing chronic unrest. In order to thwart continual coup plotting, Linares turned to harsh dictatorship, but he was eventually overthrown by members of his own cabinet in 1861 and replaced by the minister of war, General José María de Achá. Achá's government differed little from that of his predecessor's and has, perhaps, come to be known as the most violent caudillo due to the "Massacre of Loreto" in which seventy opposition politicians were executed. In December 1864, Achá was deposed by Mariano Melgarejo, the most infamous of Bolivia's tyrants.

Melgarejo is remembered as squandering large amounts of state funds and other resources such as the sale of 40,000 square miles of Bolivia's rich Matto Grosso lands to Brazil and the loss of Bolivia's rights to valuable nitrate deposits in Atacama province. His social and economic policies supported free-trade capitalism and the new mining oligarchy. The extremely unpopular land decree of 1866, which seized and sold communal Indian lands, provoked bloody peasant uprisings and subsequent merciless government repression and massacres.

Melgarejo was overthrown in 1870 by General Agustín Morales, president from 1870 to 1872, who later annulled the agrarian reform, temporarily restoring lands to the indigenous population, and renegotiated unequal foreign agreements made by Melgarejo. Morales, however, became as authoritarian as his predecessors furthering the general policies of Melgarejo and was subsequently killed and replaced by Tomás Frías, a lawyer from Sucre, prior to the election of Adolfo Ballivián in May 1873. After the sudden death of Ballivián in 1874, Frías was then brought back to the presidency. Frías stayed in power until overthrown by Hilarión Daza in 1878. Daza would be the last of Bolivia's military caudillos before the outbreak of the War of the Pacific in 1879.

During the second half of the nineteenth century, the ruling party press predominated in many countries of Latin America. Serving the oligarchy, the primary objective of these newspapers, which served as the official voice of the regime, was to form public opinion, seeking support to further specific social and economic policies and political interests. The cultural and scientific press, where and when they were published, remained outside the struggles for political power, and offered different reflections of the complex, changing societies of nineteenth-century Latin America. Many of these non-political papers started as business enterprises initially connected with a small society or a family. In general, papers were written in a fashion that did not make them accessible to the masses. They were directed and written by and for the Creoles who had studied in schools and universities of England and Europe. In Bolivia, due to constant political turmoil of the time, as well as to the scarcity of publishing resources, both financial and material, not as many newspapers were published as in other parts of Latin America. Yet, despite these obstacles, a large number of papers were established, even though many did not survive the first year.

The newspaper collection at UConn was acquired as a gift from the American Antiquarian Society in 1993 and represents extensive collecting on their behalf during the early decades of the twentieth century. The bulk of the collection was obtained from the Lichtenstein expedition to South America in 1914. It was there that Lichtenstein learned of a library owned by Donato Lanza y Lanza. In his report entitled "A Trip to South America," in which he describes his work to gather South American materials, Lichenstein offers the following details about Lanza y Lanza and the collection acquisition:

> This gentleman had at one time been the leader of the Conservative Party in Bolivia, but on account of financial reverses had lost this position and finally offered his large collection which he had inherited from his uncle, Nicolas Acosta, to the Bolivian Government. Congress had actually voted an appropriation of twenty thousand bolivianos for the purchase of this material, and the collection at the time of my arrival in Bolivia had been housed for some time in the Library of the Bolivian Senate. The Government, however, found itself unable to pay Lanza, with the result that he finally sold the collection to me for 9,550 bolivianos ($3724.00).[1]

Subsequent additions to the newspaper collection were made in 1916 with a transfer of eighty-three volumes (or several thousand issues) of Latin American newspapers from the Harvard College Library. In 1926, newspapers from the islands of the West Indies became part of the collection after an extensive research and acquisition trip by the then president of the American Antiquarian Society, Waldo Lincoln. Most of the newspapers date from the nineteenth century and are listed in detail in Steven Charno's *Latin American Newspapers in United States Libraries, A Union List* and Waldo Lincoln's *List of Newspapers of the West Indies and Bermuda*. However, the most efficient and accurate way to determine holdings at UConn, since it seems that several papers found their way out of the AAS before the collection was gifted to UConn, is via the web-searchable database that I mentioned earlier.

Given the vast number of titles and issues of Bolivian newspapers in the collection for the late-nineteenth century, I have concentrated my survey on only a small number of years for this presentation. This review focuses on the last few years of the Melgarejo *sexenio* and the beginning of Morales's success to gain support for his fight to revindicate lands to the indigenous population. Hence, I am considering from about 1868 to 1872. I focused my review on reports and commentaries addressing issues of agrarian reform, and social and political responses to these policies during this five-year period, including seizure of peasant lands, subsequent uprisings and massacres, change of governments, and restoration of lands to the campesinos. This was also a period in which a variety of papers appeared to channel the divergent political messages and opinions of the various factions vying for power.

Thus far, I have reviewed ten newspapers from La Paz, Sucre, Potosí, and Cochabamba. Most papers in the collection for this period were published in La Paz. I have found a number of references to *campesinado boliviano* in articles, official documents, reports, letters, and editorials printed in the pages of these newspapers. I would like to offer just a sampling of the journalistic references uncovered during my survey.

Throughout 1869, *La Situación,* published in La Paz from 1869 to 1870 and is one of the official papers serving the Melgarejo administration, provided continual coverage of events concerning issues of land seizure and sales offering official opinion to support the disentailment policies of the regime.

In the issue for February 26 in a section entitled "Crónica de la Ciudad," a letter to the editors from a citizen in Cochabamba supports the government repression of uprisings in Cochabamba and Sucre indicating that just a small number of malcontents had risen up in protest. The letter offers reasons as to why these malcontents joined the revolt: "unos por su tenacidad en las banderas de lo oposición, a otros por la mediocridad de su importancia personal, y a otros por su nulidad absoluta."[2]

On May 29 of the same year, an article on "La Venta de Tierras de Comunidad" defends the practice of disentailment and selling community lands to white folk so they can better the land and advance agricultural production! And I quote: "Dividir claramente la propriedad y entregarla a la raza blanca para que la adelante y mejore."[3]

On September 9, 1869, *La Situación* contained another piece that questions the sanity of these rebellious enemies of the state:

> A los enemigos del actual orden de cosas ni les falta el deseo de los trastornos y del cambio, tampoco las falta buen juicio para comprender la locura a que se lanzarián intentando una rebelion. ¿Para que levantar las masas si en pocas horas el bravo y leal Batallon 4 vendria a hacerlas entrar en su beber . . . ?[4]

An article in the October 9 issue of *La Situación* emphasizes the need for peace, or the need to avoid protest against government policy, to solve all of society's problems.

La paz—he ahí la sola aspiración, la única esperanza de rejeneración para esta patria gastada por las rebeliones y las luchas. Las revueltas esterilizan el trabajo, secan la industria, degradan el corazon, enjendran el odio y la venganza. La paz garantiza el trabajo, es fuente que da vida a la industria, mata el rencor y enjendra la fraternidad.[5]

A lengthy piece in the November 15 issue of the same year details unrest in *el campo* and refers to the *farsa revolucionaria* and the subsequent military repression. This same article goes on to discuss Agustín Morales's instrumental role in the most recent uprisings, which article is not a very favorable description from the current regime's perspective:

La insidiosa conducta de Morales en armonía con sus bastardas miras se ha dirijido a remover los elementos mas torpes para apoyar en ellos su poder y su ambición.

La indiada y las masas han sido llamadas por el, antes que el pueblo sensato (wise) e ilustrado, para secundar sus planes.

Ha inficionado esa clase ignorante, la ha engañado para esplotar su furor y lanzarla contra los propietarios territoriales, so pretesto de contribuciones sobre el capital y desapropio de terrenos privilejiados.

Hé aqui la guerra mas sangrienta de una casta a otra, de una clase de la sociedad contra la otra.—La guerra social no la guerra política—La guerra contra las propiedades adquiridas, no contra el Gobierno solo.

¿Puede envilecerse mas la politica, puede desmoralizarse mas la clase ignorante que proclamándola de este modo?

Millares de bolivianos de todos colores políticos han adquirido lejitimamente los terrenos del Estado en virtud de una lei nacional, y un caudillo menguado [coward] viene a arrebatar esas propiedades alhagando con el ofrecimiento de ellas a la clase mas ciega.

Apenas se ha realizado la venta de esos terrenos, la industria agricola ha aumentado, los capitales han crecido, y la producción es tan exuberante que es incomparablemente superior a la de años anteriores.

Uno de los timbres de gloría de la administración actual es la realización de la venta de tierras del Estado, pensamiento que ningun Gobierno pudo realizar a pesar de sus ventajas, por la debilidad de sus esfuerzas.[6]

The battle of January 15, 1871, marks the victory of Morales ending the Melgarejo tyranny. A survey of the daily publication *El Noticioso,* published in La Paz, 1870–1871, and subtitled "Organo de los intereses nacionales," reveals a shift in support from Melgarejo to Morales. A January 18 report highlights Indian involvement in the capture of Melgarejo and assurance that Megarejo minister, Muñoz, will soon be captured due to the dedicated vigilance of the Indian population in Achocalla: "Muñoz no ha ganado aun el estranjero, y pronto caerá tambien prisonero, porque la vigilancia de los indios y del pueblo, es mayor que la de Argos."[7]

Also printed in this issue is a proclamation from Morales, "el jefe supremo de la Revolución" to the people dated January 16, thanking them for their participation in the rebellion and for their heroic deeds in the battles.

Several issues of *El Noticioso* published later that week report personal narratives of episodes of the January 15 battle and record—in some detail— the flight of Melgarejo including many references to Indian involvement in tracking him through Laja, Tiaguanaco, and Guaquifué before losing the pursuit as Melgarejo escaped across the Peruvian border.

La Libertad, published from 1871 to 1872 in La Paz, printed articles both criticizing and supporting the sale of communal peasant lands. The March 25, 1871, issue carried an article signed only by *unos bolivianos* in Sucre entitled "Necesidad Urjente de Revisitas en las Provincias," which refers to the land decree of 1866 as one of the most arbitrary and unjust acts that the ill-fated government of Melgarejo could have executed. These "bolivianos" emphasize the importance of the *contribución indijenal* to the nation's economy and demand immediate return of lands to the peasantry: "que los indígenas comunarios entren inmediatamente en posesión de los terrenos de que fueron despojados por la avidez (greed) de la administración pasada."[8]

On May 27 of the same year, *La Libertad* printed another article defending the sale of communal lands. The author, a Favian Trujillo, cites a variety of publications he has read and concludes that the sale of these lands is better for the country and its economy, and, in fact, beneficial to the indigenous population.

> He ahi nuestra opinión inspirada tan solo por el amor al órden y á la prosperidad pública, y hemos quedado mas persuadidos en nuestras convicciones al leer los distintos folletos que han sido escritos en las demas ciudades de la República. Al ver que será una medida salvadora de la casta indijenal y de los pobres. Está visto, la venta de comunidades, conviene a los indígenas, al Estado, á los pobres, á la agricultura, á la finanza, á la tranquilidad del país y á la civilización y la voluntad de todos los Bolivianos.[9]

Some of the richest material I found appeared in *El Republicano* (La Paz, 1870–1871). In thirteen successive issues from June 13, 1871 to July 11, 1871, there appeared two lengthy ongoing series dedicated to commentary on restoring lands to the campesinos. The first was "Venta de las Tierras de Comunidad," by Bernardino Sanjines, and the other by José María Santiváñez was entitled "Revindicación de los Terrenos de Comunidad." The latter article starts as a letter from Santiváñez to his brother. In the letter Santiváñez says:

> Querido hermano:
>   Dedicado desde tu juventud a los trabajos agrícolas, has vivido al lado del indio y podido observar de cerca los infinitos males que agovian a esta clase desvalida. Hate inspirado su suerte el mas tierno interés, y le has protejido contra las injusticias, abusos y vejámenes de todo linaje de que es

víctima, prodigándole al propio tiempo en su lecho de dolor los cuidados mas solícitos. A tí, pues, debo consagrar el presente trabajo, destinado a defender los derechos de esta desventurada raza, peor tratado por el gobierno de la república de 1868, que lo fué por la monarquía absoluta del siglo XVI.

Acéptalo como una prenda de mi cariño.

Tu hermano—

José María Santiváñez

Cochabamba, Mayo de 1871[10]

Santiváñez then goes on to present an extensive historic review of agrarian policy in Bolivia. The series of articles includes the following section titles: I. Constitución de la propiedad territorial bajo el imperio de los Incas; II. La Conquista.—Encomiendas y repartimientos.—Concesión de tierras a los pobladores y a los indios.—Leyes protectoras de las tierras de los indios y de las Comunidades; III. Derecho de realengo; IV. Terreno de comunidad.—Su importancia social y economica, etc.; V. Medios propuestas para resolver la cuestion; VI. Despojos de los terrenos de comunidad—Levantamiento de los indios—Atrocidades cometidos en la repression—Trastorno social; VII. Fáz económica de la cuestion; VIII. Consideraciones de justicia y equidad en favor de los comunarios; IX. Vicios insanables de que adolecen las ventas de terranos de comunidad; X. Legalidad emanada de la sanción de los congresos; and XI. El Indio.

In his conclusion Santiváñez provides an epilogue in which he cites and systematically refutes information from a variety of publications that appeared during the course of his writings in *El Republicano*. He also reviews several land-reform decrees declared by the Constitutional Assemblies between 1826 and 1871.

While I have not specifically identified José María Santiváñez, in an article entitled "La Circular de 1er de Setiembre. Terrenos de Comunidad," published later that same year, on October 14 in *El Illimani* (another paper published in La Paz in 1871), Santiváñez is referred to in the following manner: "Plumas concienzudas, ilustradas y de esperiencia como la del Dr. José María Santiváñez, han demostrado hasta la evidencia, la justicia en que descansa la ley de que nos ocupamos."[11]

To conclude, despite my brief review of only ten newspapers thus far, I was pleased with the journalistic accounts I was able to uncover that provide useful information for research on agrarian reform issues and specific events such as peasant lands seizures, subsequent uprisings and massacres, changes of government, and temporary restoration of lands to the *Indígenas* in Bolivia between 1868 and 1872. The next step in this research will be to complete a review of all relevant papers I have identified from the collection for this four year period. Additionally, a more significant contribution to the discourse on late-nineteenth-century Bolivian social and political history will be to expand this study to cover the entire caudillo period, starting in 1848 with Belzú, known for his policies favoring Indians and the oppressed classes, right up through the presidency of Hilarión Daza and the outbreak of the War of the Pacific.

NOTES

1. Waldo Lincoln, "Report of the Librarian," *Proceedings of the American Antiquarian Society* 25 (October 1915): 322.

2. "Cronica de la Ciudad," *La Situación* (La Paz) 1, no. 17 (febrero 26 de 1869): 4.

3. "La Venta de Tierras de Comunidad," *La Situación* 1, no. 26 (mayo 29 de 1869): 1.

4. "La Paz," *La Situación* 1, no. 44 (setiembre 9 de 1869): 1.

5. "Revista para el Interior," *La Situación* 1, no. 48 (octubre 9 de 1869): 1.

6. "La Situación," *La Situación* 1, no. 54 (noviembre 15 de 1869): 1.

7. "Crónica de la Capital," *El Noticioso* (La Paz) 1, no. 26 (enero 18 de 1871): 1.

8. Unos Bolivianos, "Necesidad Urjente de Revisitas en las Provincias," *La Libertad* (La Paz) 1, no. 1 (marzo 25 de 1871): 1.

9. Fabian Trujillo, "Venta de Comunidades," *La Libertad* 1, no. 11 (mayo 27 de 1871): 4.

10. José María Santiváñez, "Revindicación de los Terrenos de Comunidad," *El Republicano* (La Paz) 1, no. 41 (junio 22 de 1871): 3.

11. "La Circular de 1er de Setiembre. Terrenos de Comunidad," *El Illimani* (La Paz), no. 5 (octubre 14 de 1871): 1.

BIBLIOGRAPHY

Alvarez, Jesús Timoteo, and Ascención Martínez Riaza. *Historia de la Prensa Hispanoamericana*. Madrid: Editorial MAPFRE, 1992.

Antezana Ergueta, Luis. *Las Grandes Masacres y Levantamientos Indígenas en la Historia de Bolivia (1850–1975)*. La Paz: Libreria Editorial "Juventud," 1994.

Contribución a la Historia del Periodismo en Bolivia. Sucre: Universidad de San Francisco Xavier, 1962.

Irusta Medrano, Gerardo. *Periodismo y Revolución Nacional*. La Paz: Imprenta Papiro, 1983.

Klien, Herbert S. *Bolivia: The Evolution of a Multi-Ethnic Society*. 2d ed. New York: Oxford University Press, 1992.

Lincoln, Waldo. "Report of the Librarian." *Proceedings of the American Antiquarian Society* 25 (October 1915): 320–329.

Urquidi Morales, Arturo. *Las Comunidades Indígenas en Bolivia*. Cochabamba: Editorial "Los Amigos del Libro," 1970.

9. Our Man in Peru: The Hiram Bingham Papers at Yale University

David Block

The Hiram Bingham papers at Yale consist of two large record groups in the Sterling Memorial Library: the Bingham Family Papers, group #81 comprising 51 feet and 8 inches, with a guide by Randall C. Jimerson and Rena R. Weiss; and the Yale Peruvian Expedition papers, group #664, with a guide by Jimerson and an extent of 16 feet.

Bingham was born in 1875 in Hawaii, and was the son and grandson of pioneering Protestant missionaries to the islands. In 1900, he married Alfreda Mitchell, a granddaughter of Charles Comfort Tiffany. Together they had seven sons. Bingham was a graduate of Andover, Yale, Berkeley, and Harvard. He was an early advocate of Latin America as a legitimate area of academic study, and between 1905 and 1924, he held positions at Princeton and Yale, including curator of Yale's collections on South American history.

World War I effectively ended Bingham's academic career. With the U.S. entry into the conflict, he joined the Air Service and served in France. On returning to civilian life, Bingham entered politics, was elected lieutenant governor of Connecticut in 1922 (while still on the faculty at Yale), and then governor of the state in 1924. But a month after his election, Bingham offered himself as a candidate in a special election and was elected a U.S. senator. January 1925 was a busy month. In Jimerson's words, "On January 7, 1925, Bingham took the oath of office as Governor of Connecticut, gave the longest inaugural address on record and resigned."[1] This precipitous political ascent was matched by an equally steep decline. Bingham was defeated in a bid for reelection in 1932 and never stood for public office again. He stayed in Washington as a businessman and insider, and occasionally served in bureaucratic capacities. Bingham died in the District of Colombia in 1956.

Hiram Bingham III was a family man, never at home; a rugged individualist, who lived on his wife's inheritance; and a senator who thought it was proper to invite a Connecticut manufacturer's lobbyist into executive session of the Finance Committee (his colleagues disagreed, by the way, and censured him, which was the last time this would happen before Joe McCarthy). Hiram Bingham had his foibles, but he also had his moments.

On July 24, 1911, while leading the Yale Peruvian Expedition, Bingham reached the magnificent structures, now called Machu Picchu, and that story, illustrated by photographs taken from that time, is the jumping-off point for my presentation. It is a well-known story told by the "discoverer" himself in several works, including *Lost City of the Incas* (1948)[2] and, more recently, in biographical accounts by two of his sons.[3] But it is worth the retelling for several reasons. It is a good story, and a very picturesque one, even ninety years after its first rendition. It also offers an example of a period of great transition in the Andes and a transition from a Victorian, imperialistic domination of politics and scholarship to one where nationalism asserted itself in government and research.

Although it is not immediately apparent from reading Bingham's accounts—he does not offer a comprehensive treatment until a decade has passed—there were actually three Yale Peruvian expeditions, all in a relatively narrow range of the Peruvian Andes along the 73rd meridian between 13° and 16° south latitude.

1. The Yale Peruvian Expedition (1911)—consisting of Bingham and six other North Americans, including the to-be-eminent geologist Isaiah Bowman.

2. The Peruvian Expedition of 1912, under the auspices of Yale University and the National Geographic Society—a better-financed trip with ten members, underwritten by a $10,000 grant from the National Geographic Society.

3. The Peruvian Expedition of 1914–1915, under the auspices of Yale University and the National Geographic Society, again underwritten by the society, which expedition was the largest and least successful.

Why Bingham should have chosen Peru at all is something of a mystery. His historical research to the time of the first expedition treated the ill-starred Scottish colonization of Darien[4] and Bolivar's campaigns in northern South America, which research is well documented in the manuscript "Journal of an Expedition across Venezuela and Colombia," in the Bingham Family Papers.[5] Bingham offers a quixotic explanation for his choice in the first pages of his *Inca Land*. He describes a fascination with Andean civilization, first stirred by a "marvelous picture" of a suspension bridge across the Apurimac River in one of Ephrim Squire's travel accounts. Then, once at the Apurimac, on a round-about trip to the Second Panamerican Scientific Conference in Santiago, he was tantalized by the idea of discovering the rebel Inca Manco's last capital, Vilcabamba.[6]

In the documents that propose the 1911 expedition, Bingham lays out three objectives: to discover Manco's capital, to reconnoiter the uncharted region along the 73rd meridian, and to climb Mount Coropuna to determine if it was the highest peak in the Andes. Bingham sailed for Peru early in 1911 and reached Cuzco in June. Then, after contracting mules and provisions from a local merchant, Cesare Lomellini, Bingham led his team, now joined by a Peruvian gendarme identified only as Sergeant Carrasco, into the Urubamba Valley.

The region downriver from the famous Inca redoubt of Ollantaytambo had been opened to pack traffic ten years before by Peruvian engineers who incised a roadbed along the same route that carries today's tourist trains.

On July 23, most of the team was camping on a piece of level ground called Mandor Pampa. While in Cuzco, Bingham had learned of this location and that its "owner," Melchor Arteaga, claimed that substantial ruins occupied the heights above his lands. Arteaga appeared in the camp that day and offered to lead Bingham up the steep cliffs the next morning. July 24, 1911, dawned overcast, and Bingham wrote in his diary that Arteaga had to be coaxed into the climb by the offer of a Sol piece, the equivalent of a week's wages, for his trouble. At 10 A.M., Arteaga, Bingham, and Sergeant Carrasco set out from Mandor Pampa.

The first impediment was the Urubamba River. The explorers' camp was on the east side and the cliffs were on the west. Arteaga knew of a bridge that spanned the waters, at least in the dry season, and demonstrated how to cross it. Bingham attributed the mestizo's technique to "prehensile toes." (Unfortunately, no photos of Bingham's traverse—he refused to remove his shoes and crossed the bridge on his hands and knees—have survived.) Now across the river, the trio spent the rest of the morning scaling the cliffs, following paths cut through the undergrowth by the people they would soon meet.

Around noon, Arteaga, Carrasco, and Bingham finished their climb and came upon two men, know to posterity as Richarte and Alvarez, who cultivated lands on the cliff tops and provided Arteaga with a part of their harvest in exchange for their use of the property. According to his remembrances, Bingham was most interested in the cool water and comfortable seating offered by his hosts, but was persuaded to climb just a bit farther under the guide of a child, now know only as "the boy."

The discovery of Machu Picchu would mark the height of Bingham's career in Peru, but at the ripe old age of thirty-six, he apparently had no idea of its significance. He descended the cliffs on the afternoon of the twenty-fourth and said nothing about what he saw to the rest of his party. In a letter written to his wife the next day, Bingham seems more absorbed in the logistics of his expedition than in his discovery: "I climbed a couple of thousand feet to a wonderful old Inca city called Machu Picchu. The man who owns this land (or rents it) told me about it and offered to act as our guide." Clearly, Bingham's thoughts are elsewhere as he breaks off this description to relate: "the mules are found, we are off."

Just what Bingham thought of what has come to be called Machu Picchu on July 24, 1911, cannot be reconstructed unequivocally. His journal entry "Fine Ruins" is cryptic but the extra pressure with which the words were penciled into the notebook makes them stand out on the page.[7] The journal also holds a rough sketch of the ruins with outlines and dimensions of the major buildings. So while Bingham left Machu Picchu after only a few hours of reconnoiter, he did not leave unimpressed.

Bingham saw enough on July 24 to know that Machu Picchu was not the lost Inca capital he was looking for. His principal documentary research for the expedition had been to read a translated version of the seventeenth-century history of Peru, given to him by Carlos A. Romero. Antonio de la Calancha's account, *Crónica moralizada del Orden de San Agustín en el Perú,* describes the visit of two Augustinian priests to Manco, Inca's headquarters, "where a spring flowed from beneath a great, white rock." There was no white rock or Inca capital, so Bingham and his team left Mandor Pampa the next day and trekked farther down the Urubamba. A month later, they returned to Cuzco and traveled south for their climb of Mount Coropuna. Bingham would not return to the site for more than a year.

In hindsight, the 1911 expedition was something of a folly. Coropuna proved not to be the tallest mountain in the Andes, and Bingham's brave men were beaten to the top by a sixty-two-year-old suffragette, Annie S. Peck, who is reported to have celebrated her conquest of the mountain by unfurling a yellow banner inscribed "VOTES FOR WOMEN." Adding insult to injury, a much ballyhooed cache of prehistoric animal bones turned out to be the remains of cattle slaughtered to serve the Cuzco meat market. Ironically, the 1911 expedition *did* reach the last Inca capital, but Bingham proved unwilling to label it as such.

In 1912, Bingham recruited a new team and returned to Cuzco. With Coropuna scaled, the second expedition centered its efforts on clearing and charting Machu Picchu and with mapping the high passes of the region. The 1912 expedition also began excavations in Peru, exploring a series of burial caves at Machu Picchu and turning up artifacts in the Cuzco region. Though this activity went unnoticed at the time, it would set off a chain of events that were to bring Bingham to grief.

The Peruvian Expedition of 1914–1915 was intended to build on the other two expeditions, to definitively map Machu Picchu, and to carry out extensive excavations in the Urubamba Valley. An advanced party preceded Bingham to Cuzco and established a base camp at Ollantaytambo, which locals derisively called "Yanquihuasi." Bingham joined his vanguard in 1915 and ran headlong into Peruvian opposition to his activities.

In the spring of 1915, the Cuzco and Lima presses became spaces contested between those who accused the Yale Peruvian Expedition of pillaging national treasure and those who denied it, who supported Bingham. In June, a

delegation of Peruvians, led by the young Luís Valcárcel, paid a visit to
Ollantaytambo and asked to see the expedition's archaeological permit. The
evidence of excavation was plain to see in a series of cases that lined the walls
of Yanquihuasi, but the third expedition, like its predecessors, had no permit.
Peruvian law was of long duration and explicit. As early as 1822, a
provisional government published laws that regulated excavations in national
territory and the exportation of artifacts.[8] By 1915 Peru had a statue of
cultural patrimony, requiring written permission and presentation of duplicate
pieces of artifacts to the National Museum, and a presidential decree stating
that *only* duplicates could be taken out of the country. Public accusations that
the expedition was violating Peruvian law and, worse, secretly shipping
treasure out of the country, coupled with the temporary departure of
Bingham's most powerful advocate, Augusto B. Leguía, from the Peruvian
presidency, effectively ended the third expedition. Bingham spent the rest of
1915 defending himself in the press, lobbying government officials, and
gaining permission to take the expedition's artifacts back to New Haven.

     Bingham and his biographers have attributed Peruvians' opposition to the
expedition to petty jealousy on Valcárcel's part and to the refusal of the Wilson
administration to take a firm stance against Germany after the sinking of the
Lusitania.[9] Neither dispute the essential facts of the case—for example, the
expedition had no permit to excavate when one was required—and both
discount the importance of Peruvian events. Valcárcel offers a different
interpretation. His *Memorias,* published in 1961, defends Bingham as the true
discoverer of Machu Picchu, against the subsequent claims of Peruvians, and
debunks the charges of archaeological pillage.[10] Documents from the time of
the events record Valcárcel's testimony that he and his associates from the
Comisión Histórica had never actually made accusations themselves, rather
they investigated those of others. He goes on to explain that none of the
charges against the expedition and Bingham—the export of treasure, the
endangering of monuments, and the abuse of Indian labor—could be
substantiated.[11]

     What Bingham failed to recognize was the strength of nationalist senti-
ment in Peru. The first decades of the twentieth century mark the assertion by
Peruvians of their political and cultural rights in the international community.
The Guillermo Billinghurst regime, which succeeded Leguía's, was very
unsympathetic to foreign economic interests and insisted that foreigners
observe Peruvian law. This period also marks a changing of the guard in cultural affairs from a European directorate, personified by Max Uhle, to
Peruvians, Julio Tello and José Sabogal. Perhaps the best visual images that I
can offer to illustrate this change are the paintings of Sabogal and Jorge
Vinatea Reinosa who visited the highlands and painted sympathetic images of
the native people. Artistic nationalism peaked in the centennial celebrations of
Peruvian independence in 1925 produced several architectural monuments

such as the Museo de la Cultura Peruana, but it was very much in earlier decades, even though it took a while for foreigners to understand it.

Hiram Bingham III returned once more to Peru. In 1948 he was invited to Machu Picchu for the opening of the road that carries tourists from a railway station on the Urubamba to the ruins. I do not know what he said at the dedication; his speech is not a part of Record Group #61. But I carried away a number of insights in Peru from my two days at Yale.

A New Critic would have a field day with Bingham's writings. Peru was usually portrayed in them as dirty and corrupt, and references to Peruvians' drunkenness abound. Bingham's lack of concern for native people as anything but subjects is palpable. While the North American participants of all three expeditions and the members of the Peruvian elite are fully named and often biographied, Sergeant Carrasco, Richarte, and "the boy" are all that Bingham's accounts hold of these rather pivotal participants in the "discovery." And with the exception of the archaeological labor force active at Machu Picchu, Bingham seems to have limited his Peruvian employees to one, the Spanish and Quechua speaking "assistant to the director," Ricardo Charaja, from the third expedition. As far as I know, Bingham's texts have not been examined as cultural markers, but there has been a small movement to recast Bingham in the mold of Indiana Jones. "Raiders of the Lost City" and *Hiram Bingham and the Dream of Gold,* a couple of works from the 1980s, should give readers an idea of this line of interpretation.[12]

Bingham never became an expert on Peru. Despite his pioneering interest in Latin America, he never seemed to have learned the region's languages. His bibliographies, compiled at Yale, show German and French citations, but no Spanish ones outside of translated works.[13] Thus, Bingham was severely constrained in his vision of Peruvian history, despite working at a time when scholars such as Raúl Porras and Horacio Urteaga were editing many of the classic accounts of the early colony. He never included a trained archeologist on the expeditions, although excavation was among their principal enterprises. As a result, the lasting scholarly impact of Bingham's research was minimal. His claims for Machu Picchu, which over time became in his mind both Manco's capital and Tampu-toco, the first capital of the Incas, were as preposterous as his identification of prehistoric bones had been.

In Peru, Bingham's reputation has never fully escaped the charges that he stole a part of the national patrimony. Pillage is now part of the standard tourist guide's description of the North American expeditions, but serious Peruvian scholars have begun to investigate the old rumors again. I have nothing to add to the debate; I found neither gold nor silver at Sterling Library. But I think that it is important to cite Valcárcel's testimony on these matters. Valcárcel was one of the three men appointed by Cuzco's prefect to investigate accusations that Bingham had discovered treasure at Machu Picchu and spirited it out of the country. In his memoirs, Valcárcel relates that he personally examined the expedition's artifacts, interrogated Peruvian citizens in the Cuzco region, and traveled to Puno and La Paz in search of evidence of clandestine shipments through Bolivia. He concludes: "los únicos restos o materiales trasladados fuera de Machu Picchu habían sido los que permitieron las autoridades nacionales pertinentes. Era evidente, pues, que no se extrajeron objetos de oro, plata o cobre . . . lo demás no fueron sino simples rumores."[14]

Exoneration of the Yale Peruvian Expedition begs the question of what Bingham may have done on his own account. In fact, Valcárcel seems to have had second thoughts on this issue when in an interview to El Sol given in August 1916, he suggests that while Bingham's excavations had uncovered nothing more than bones, ceramics, and stones, he believed that Bingham purchased artifacts of gold and silver while in Peru and somehow exported them through Peruvian ports.[15] The expedition archives in New Haven hold numerous examples of Peruvians offering their collections to the visiting North Americans. One note offers to divulge the location of Manco Capac's legendary golden chain, with the secretive aside, "which is not in Lake Titicaca but in a ravine near Ayacucho." But others are less fantastic, and it seems that Bingham may have yielded to their blandishments, for in 1916, Yale's treasurer offered to try to find a donor to purchase Bingham's "very valuable collection of antiquities, including some very beautiful textiles representing the civilization of the Southern Peruvian Coast."[16]

I read Bingham not so much as a scoundrel but an anachronism: a scholar who favored exploration to research, a Latin Americanist who never learned Spanish, a North American out of touch with the nationalism of twentieth-century Latin America. But he certainly had his one, shining moment.

NOTES

1. Randall C. Jimerson and Rena R. Weiss, *Bingham Family Papers* [typescript guide to Manuscript Group 81] (New Haven, Conn., 1979), p. 5.

2. Bingham's other book-length accounts are *Inca Land* (Boston and New York: Houghton Mifflin, 1922) and *Machu Picchu, a Citadel of the Incas* (New Haven and London: Yale University Press, 1930).

3. Woodbridge Bingham, *Hiram Bingham, a Personal Memoir* (Boulder, Colo.: Bin Lan Zhen Publishers, 1989); Alfred Bingham, *Portrait of an Explorer* (Ames: Iowa State University Press, 1989).

4. Hiram Bingham, "Virginia Letters on the Scots Darien Company, 1699," *American Historical Review* 10, no. 4 (July 1905): 812–815. Hiram Bingham, "The Early History of the Scots Darien Company," *Scottish Historical Review* (January 1906): 110–127.

5. Bingham Family Papers, Series V, box 36, folder 4.

6. Hiram Bingham, *Inca Land,* pp. 1–2.

7. The journal is the entire contents of Yale Peru Expedition, III, 18, 1.

8. Ramiro Matos, "Punto de vista de la arqueología," in *Patrimonio cultural del Perú* (Lima: Fomciencias, 1986), p. 68.

9. Alfred Bingham, *Portrait of an Explorer,* pp. 305–306.

10. Luis Valcárcel, *Memorias* (Lima: Universidad Catolica, 1961), pp. 152–153, 185–186.

11. "Preguntas a que contesto el Dr. Valcarcel, Presidente del Instituto Historico," Yale Peruvian Expedition, Group 664, I, 2–25.

12. Alfred H. Bingham, "Raiders of the Lost City," *American Heritage* 38, no. 5 (1987). Daniel Cohen, *Hiram Bingham and the Dream of Gold* (New York: M. Evans, 1984).

13. Hiram Bingham, "The Possibilities of South American History and Politics as a Field For Research," *Monthly Bulletin* (International Bureau of the American Republics, Feb. 1908). "Books Carried to Peru," Yale Peruvian Expedition, I, 2, 1.

14. Valcárcel, *Memorias,* pp. 185–187.

15. "Por la Historia Nacional," *El Sol* [Cuzco], August 14, 1916, p. 1.

16. George Parmly Day to Hiram Bingham, January 31, 1916, Yale Peruvian Expedition, Group 664, II, 16–286.

10. Preserving Andean Collections: Progress and Challenges of Microfilm Preservation

Fernando Acosta-Rodríguez

Introduction

While libraries in the United States have for decades been microfilming Latin Americanist bibliographic resources, little is known about what has been preserved and what remains to be done. Previous studies by Harvard University's Dan Hazen have provided an initial assessment of what has been so far accomplished and have laid the groundwork for further analysis. More than anything, these studies demonstrate the need to continue documenting progress and identifying neglected areas. They also suggest the need for increased levels of institutional coordination.[1]

With those principles in mind, this report provides an initial assessment of the current state of preservation microfilming of Andean history collections held collectively by libraries in the United States. The findings are based on the data gathered during an ongoing two-year preservation project funded by the National Endowment for the Humanities (NEH) to microfilm materials from the New York Public Library's Latin American history collections. Hopefully, the presented data will shed some light on how much has already been preserved, and may suggest areas to be targeted by future efforts. After a description of the project and the presentation of its findings, a conclusion and some recommendations will be offered.

Project Description

The New York Public Library's NEH-funded preservation project, June 1999–May 2001, is microfilming materials published between 1800 and 1950. The scope includes monographs, periodicals, and pamphlets on (1) the overall history of Latin America, (2) the history of individual South American nations, and (3) material documenting the African Diaspora in Latin America. It is anticipated that the project will preserve 11,754 volumes.

Materials to be microfilmed are selected by means of a title-by-title inspection where items on brittle, highly acidic paper stock are identified.

Titles are not reformatted if an existing archival master negative film is located in RLIN, OCLC, and occasionally other appropriate sources.

This report deals only with the preservation work that has already been completed for materials on the history of the Andean nations.[2] Covered collections are those dealing with the history of Chile, Colombia, Ecuador, and Peru. All of them include North American, Latin American, and European imprints. The Bolivian and Venezuelan history collections were not included because their selection has not yet been completed. In the spirit of institutional coordination advocated by this report, the microfilming of the Bolivian collection has been postponed until another NEH-funded project for the preservation of Bolivian collections is completed by the University of Pittsburgh Library System.[3]

Findings

This section reports on three aspects of the project's findings: (1) How much has been microfilmed by country and type of material; (2) how much has been filmed by year of publication, type of material, and country; and (3) what institutions have done most of the previous preservation microfilming.

From the outset, it is recognized that one of the report's deficiencies is the nature of the sample. Though NYPL's collections are among the most extensive, they do not represent a definitive bibliography on Andean history. In fact, previous studies have established that no library collection can make such a claim.[4] Nevertheless, NYPL holds a large proportion of mainstream and secondary sources, as well as a very large amount of marginal materials such as regional publications and ephemera that have been collected by only a few if any other libraries in the United States. In other words, though the sample is admittedly biased, it is large enough to make it worth looking at. At least, this is the case with the monograph samples analyzed in the report. Serial and pamphlet samples are much smaller, thus more problematic.[5]

Data by Country and Format

The compiled data reveals that among the four South American countries covered in this report, Colombia is the country with the highest proportion of titles for which preservation microfilming has been completed. Of the 351 monographs identified as potential candidates for microfilming, 200 (57 percent) of the total had already been microfilmed. Of the 21 serial titles selected, 8 (38 percent) were already available on microfilm. None of the 18 pamphlets selected in this area had been reformatted, or at least this was not indicated by the major bibliographic utilities.

Table 1: Colombia. Titles Selected for Microfilming by Format

	Monographs	Serials	Pamphlets	Total
Selected titles[a]	351	21	18	390
Previously filmed[b]	200	8	0	208
% Previously filmed	57%	38%	0%	53%
To be filmed by NYPL[c]	151	13	18	182

a. Selected titles refer to the total number of titles identified as potential candidates for microfilming.
b. Previously filmed refers to the number of titles already available on microfilm among those identified as potential candidates for microfilming.
c. To be filmed by NYPL are those titles that had not been previously filmed by any library.

Statistics for materials on Chilean history show that, in comparison to Colombia, a somewhat smaller percentage of monographs had already been microfilmed: 51 percent or 250 out of 488. However, the percentage of Chilean serials previously microfilmed is higher (47 percent) than that of Colombian serials. No pamphlets were selected in this area.

Table 2: Chile. Titles Selected for Microfilming by Format

	Monographs	Serials	Pamphlets	Total
Selected titles	488	15	0	503
Previously filmed	250	7	0	257
% Previously filmed	51%	47%	—	51%
To be filmed by NYPL	238	8	0	246

In the case of Peru, it was found that almost half (49 percent) of the 385 monographs selected had already been microfilmed. But it is the low percentage of previously microfilmed serials and pamphlets that is surprising. Only 2 out of 11 serial titles or 18 percent were found to be available on film already. None of the 8 selected pamphlets had been filmed.

Table 3: Peru. Titles Selected for Microfilming by Format

	Monographs	Serials	Pamphlets	Total
Selected titles	385	11	8	404
Previously filmed	187	2	0	189
% Previously filmed	49%	18%	0%	47%
To be filmed by NYPL	198	9	8	215

The history of Ecuador was by far the most neglected in terms of the preservation microfilming previously done by U.S. libraries. In contrast with the other Andean nations covered in this report, only 14 percent or 19 out of 137 monographs had been microfilmed before this project. The proportion of microfilmed serials and pamphlets is once again very low. Only 1 out of 10 serial titles and none of the 19 pamphlets had been previously reformatted.

Table 4: Ecuador. Titles Selected for Microfilming by Format

	Monographs	Serials	Pamphlets	Total
Selected titles	137	10	19	166
Previously filmed	19	1	0	20
% Previously filmed	14%	10%	0%	12%
To be filmed by NYPL	118	9	19	146

Data by Country, Year of Publication, and Format

In order to determine whether microfilming institutions have emphasized or neglected the preservation of publications produced during particular periods in the history of these four countries, the compiled data was broken down into six consecutive twenty-five-year periods. All of the materials selected for preservation microfilming were assigned to one of the six periods according to the year of publication. Serial titles that overlapped among two or more of the twenty-five-year periods were accommodated in the one where most available issues had been published.

The percentage of Colombian history monographs already preserved on microfilm is consistently high throughout all time periods with rates fluctuating between 54 and 61 percent. The percentage of serial titles on film is consistently low. Three of the 9 (33 percent) serial titles published between 1876 and 1925 had been filmed. There is a slight improvement among titles published between 1926 and 1950 with 5 out of the 12 (42 percent) titles having been filmed. With pamphlets, the findings are more dramatic. None of the 18 titles selected, all published between 1876 and 1950, had been previously filmed by any institution.

Table 5: Colombia. Titles Selected for Microfilming by Publication Year and Format

Publication Year		Monographs	Serials	Pamphlets	Total
1800	Selected titles	12	0	0	12
to	Previously filmed	7	0	0	7
1825	% Previously filmed	58%	_	_	58%
	To be filmed by NYPL	5	0	0	5
1826	Selected titles	17	0	0	17
to	Previously filmed	10	0	0	10
1850	% Previously filmed	59%	_	_	59%
	To be filmed by NYPL	7	0	0	7
1851	Selected titles	18	0	0	18
to	Previously filmed	11	0	0	11
1875	% Previously filmed	61%	_	_	61%
	To be filmed by NYPL	7	0	0	7
1876	Selected titles	35	1	1	37
to	Previously filmed	19	0	0	19
1900	% Previously filmed	54%	0%	0%	51%
	To be filmed by NYPL	16	1	1	18
1901	Selected titles	77	8	6	91
to	Previously filmed	42	3	0	45
1925	% Previously filmed	55%	38%	0%	49%
	To be filmed by NYPL	35	5	6	46
1926	Selected titles	192	12	11	215
to	Previously filmed	111	5	0	116
1950	% Previously filmed	58%	42%	0%	54%
	To be filmed by NYPL	81	7	11	99

In the case of Chilean history, all of the 4 monographs published between 1800 and 1825 that had been identified as potential candidates for microfilming were already available on microfilm. The lowest proportion of microfilmed material was found among monographs published between 1826 and 1875. Only 33 percent of the monographs published between 1826 and 1850, and 42 percent of those published between 1851 and 1875 were already available on film. For works published between 1876 and 1950, the rate consistently stays slightly above 50 percent.

The contrast is more striking among serial publications. Of the 3 pre-1901 serial titles identified, none of them were available on microfilm. For twentieth-century serial publications, only 2 out of 5 (40 percent) titles published between 1901 and 1925 have been microfilmed. The rate goes considerably higher for the 1926–1950 period with 5 out of 7 or 71 percent filmed.

Table 6: Chile. Titles Selected for Microfilming by Publication Year and Format

Publication Year		Monographs	Serials	Pamphlets	Total
1800	Selected titles	4	0	0	4
to	Previously filmed	4	0	0	4
1825	% Previously filmed	100%	_	_	100%
	To be filmed by NYPL	0	0	0	0
1826	Selected titles	6	1	0	7
to	Previously filmed	2	0	0	2
1850	% Previously filmed	33%	0%	_	29%
	To be filmed by NYPL	4	1	0	5
1851	Selected titles	36	1	0	37
to	Previously filmed	15	0	0	15
1875	% Previously filmed	42%	0%	_	41%
	To be filmed by NYPL	21	1	0	22
1876	Selected titles	90	1	0	91
to	Previously filmed	48	0	0	48
1900	% Previously filmed	53%	0%	_	53%
	To be filmed by NYPL	42	1	0	43
1901	Selected titles	187	5	0	192
to	Previously filmed	96	2	0	98
1925	% Previously filmed	51%	40%	_	51%
	To be filmed by NYPL	91	3	0	94
1926	Selected titles	165	7	0	172
to	Previously filmed	85	5	0	90
1950	% Previously filmed	52%	71%	_	52%
	To be filmed by NYPL	80	2	0	82

In the case of Peruvian history, it is interesting that only 7 out of the 18 (39 percent) pre-1851 monographs selected for preservation microfilming were already available on film. The only period with a noticeably high proportion of microfilmed monograph titles (58 percent) is from 1876 to 1900. Other time periods fluctuate between 42 and 50 percent. Because the sample is so small, little can be discerned of serial publications and pamphlets when analyzed by the year of publication.

Table 7: Peru. Titles Selected for Microfilming by Publication Year and Format

Publication Year		Monographs	Serials	Pamphlets	Total
1800	Selected titles	6	0	0	6
to	Previously filmed	3	0	0	3
1825	% Previously filmed	50%		_	50%
	To be filmed by NYPL	3	0	0	3
1826	Selected titles	12	0	3	15
to	Previously filmed	4	0	0	4
1850	% Previously filmed	33%	_	0%	27%
	To be filmed by NYPL	8	0	3	11
1851	Selected titles	38	1	3	42
to	Previously filmed	16	1	0	17
1875	% Previously filmed	42%	100%	0%	40%
	To be filmed by NYPL	22	0	3	25
1876	Selected titles	40	1	2	43
to	Previously filmed	23	0	0	23
1900	% Previously filmed	58%	0%	0%	53%
	To be filmed by NYP	17	1	2	20
1901	Selected titles	112	3	0	115
to	Previously filmed	56	1	0	57
1925	% Previously filmed	50%	33%	_	50%
	To be filmed by NYPL	56	2	0	58
1926	Selected titles	177	6	0	183
to	Previously filmed	85	0	0	85
1950	% Previously filmed	48%	0%	_	46%
	To be filmed by NYPL	92	6	0	98

As the previously shown data previewed, a very low proportion of Ecuadorian history materials on all formats and from all time periods have been microfilmed.

Table 8: Ecuador. Titles Selected for Microfilming by Publication Year and Format

Publication Year		Monographs	Serials	Pamphlets	Total
1800	Selected titles	0	0	0	0
to	Previously filmed	0	0	0	0
1825	% Previously filmed	_	_	_	_
	To be filmed by NYPL	0	0	0	0
1826	Selected titles	1	0	3	4
to	Previously filmed	0	0	0	0
1850	% Previously filmed	0%	_	0%	0%
	To be filmed by NYPL	1	0	3	4
1851	Selected titles	2	0	3	5
to	Previously filmed	0	0	0	0
1875	% Previously filmed	0%	_	0%	0%
	To be filmed by NYPL	2	0	3	5
1876	Selected titles	15	0	2	17
to	Previously filmed	3	0	0	3
1900	% Previously filmed	20%	_	0%	18%
	To be filmed by NYPL	12	0	2	14
1901	Selected titles	31	6	0	37
to	Previously filmed	5	1	0	6
1925	% Previously filmed	16%	17%	_	16%
	To be filmed by NYPL	26	5	0	31
1926	Selected titles	81	4	11	96
to	Previously filmed	11	0	0	11
1950	% Previously filmed	14%	0%	0%	11%
	To be filmed by NYPL	70	4	11	85

Before closing this section, some comments should be made about the challenge that emerged early in the project regarding the handling of early-nineteenth-century materials. It was quickly realized that the widely held assumptions about the good paper quality of imprints from that time period are misleading. Though many of the reviewed titles were published on high quality paper and did not require reformatting, a considerable amount of them were in poor condition and did demand preservation attention. This was particularly true of Latin American and U.S. imprints, in contrast to European ones. These observations suggest that this period cannot go unexamined by future preservation projects.

A related issue was assessing the artifactual value of those items before making reformatting decisions. Guidelines used for European and U.S. imprints seemed inadequate because of the distinctiveness of Latin American history. Since no standard guidelines exist for evaluating these collections, special attention was given to every item published before 1850 and to items published during prominent periods in the history of specific nations.[6] Factors such as the presence of fine illustrations were taken into consideration, but the determining criteria was paper condition. Perhaps imprints from these time periods represent a fertile ground for the selection of titles for digitization.

Main Microfilming Institutions

This section briefly indicates which U.S. libraries have been the main producers of preservation microfilm for materials on the history of the four Andean nations evaluated. It should be noted that the preservation work produced by the New York Public Library before the implementation of the current project is not reflected in this section even though NYPL has been identified among the "first tier" of library-based filmers of Latin American materials.[7] The data was not gathered because of the nature of the selection procedure.

For titles on Colombian history, the University of Florida Libraries came out as the most prominent producer of preservation microfilm. Other prominent contributors were the University of California at Berkeley, the Library of Congress, and the University of Texas at Austin.

With Chilean history collections, four institutions stood out. These were the University of Texas at Austin, the Library of Congress, the University of California at Berkeley, and the University of North Carolina. UT-Austin was the main contributor.

Cornell University was by far the most significant contributor of preservation microfilming for materials on Peruvian history. Harvard University, the University of California at Berkeley, the Library of Congress, and the University of Texas at Austin were prominent in this case too.

In the case of Ecuador, only the University of California at Berkeley and the University of Texas at Austin stood out.

Even though only the major preservation-microfilm producers are mentioned here, it should be pointed out that smaller contributors have made a great difference. Even though their individual contributions may not stand out, in combination they have filmed a large segment of all the work so far completed.

Conclusions and Recommendations

As a whole, the data presented shows that a significant proportion of monographs has already been microfilmed by U.S. institutions in the area of Andean history. This proportion will be considerably higher after the completion of NYPL's preservation project. The challenge for future projects will be to identify what remains to be done in the area of Andean history as well as in other areas. Accomplishing this task will not be easy because, as has been previously demonstrated, monographs are widely scattered among U.S. libraries (not to mention institutions in Latin America and Europe) and no core collection or combination of core collections holds every title of importance to Latin American research.[8] The question then is how are the librarians going to effectively complete the preservation of these collections without losing a valuable portion of their cultural and intellectual heritage. It seems like the answer lies in institutional cooperation and coordination. This will be particularly crucial in saving materials held by libraries that have no preservation mandate or the adequate capacity to individually handle this challenge.

Another important conclusion derived from the gathered data is that substantial preservation work remains to be done in the preservation of serial publications. Even though the serial samples previously presented in this report are very small and consequently problematic, additional data so far gathered for serials published in Latin America as a whole suggest that larger samples would not reveal much higher percentages of serials already being microfilmed. So far only 17 out of 126 titles (13 percent) selected as candidates for preservation microfilming had been already reformatted. The picture becomes worse when considering that many of the selected serial runs are incomplete and that it often is very difficult to locate other institutions that hold the missing volumes.

A similar situation is true of pamphlet collections. Though the previously presented sample is minuscule, a much larger sample of pamphlets that was not classified by country reveals that a great deal remains to be done. Only 275 out of the 1884 pamphlets so far selected (15 percent) have been filmed. Such a low rate may be misleading because other libraries such as Princeton and Yale filmed large pamphlet collections. But it is not know if the reason for the low rate is because there is little overlapping among the collections, or because records for individual titles have not been loaded on the major online bibliographic utilities.

A final conclusion derived from the data is that previous preservation-microfilming efforts have neglected certain subject areas. The case of Ecuador clearly illustrates this. Such neglect may be the result of a lack of academic or research interest among Latin Americanists including librarians. It is not unreasonable to assume that other countries, regions, or subject areas have also been neglected. Additional analysis is required to identify and target those areas.

It may be that librarians are reaching a point in which a collective preservation strategy that involves coordination and planning among U.S. libraries has become necessary to secure the preservation of their combined Latin American collections. With few exceptions such as the Latin American

Microform Project (LAMP) and the Intensive Cuban Collecting Group (ICCG), most preservation efforts have followed a model of individual institutional efforts that focus on preserving the holdings of specific library collections.[9] While this may continue to be the most viable alternative for some time, it may not be long before a collective approach becomes imperative.

NOTES

1. Dan C. Hazen, *The Production and Bibliographic Control of Latin American Preservation Microforms in the United States* (Washington, D.C.: Commission on Preservation and Access, 1991), pp. 16–17.

2. For the purposes of this report, the Andean region is understood in broad geographic terms and not as a region with particular sociocultural characteristics. Included are all the countries where the Andes form part of the national territory.

3. A brief project description is available at http://www.nypl.org/research/LANE/preservation.htm.

4. Dan C. Hazen, *The Bibliographic Control and Preservation of Latin Americanist Library Resources: A Status Report with Suggestions* (Washington, D.C.: Association of Research Libraries, 1994), p. 15.

5. The smallness of the serial sample derives from the fact that under the Billing's classification system used by NYPL, most serials and pamphlets have not been classified by country. All the Latin Americanist titles have been lumped together. Figures shown by the work already completed show that the findings wouldn't be meaningfully different.

6. Informal conversations with colleagues in other libraries indicate that different dates (for example, 1830 and 1850) are used as guidelines.

7. Hazen, *Production and Bibliographic Control,* p. 11.

8. Hazen, *Bibliographic Control and Preservation,* p. 17.

9. Peter T. Johnson and Francisco J. Fonseca, "Cuban Serials and Primary Source Collections: A Bibliography of Microfilm Negatives," *Cuban Studies* 22 (1992): 231–247.

Andean Resources and Bibliography

11. Early Printed Books Containing Andean Languages in the British Library

Geoff West

What follows forms part of a much larger and more ambitious project to record the provenance of the British Library's collection of pre-1801 Hispanic books. The work has been tackled piecemeal: by author, by subject, by auction sale or donation, or simply by a result of an inquiry. At present the information is not held on a database, but it has recently been proposed that one be created. The aim is not simply to amass data for its own sake, but to enable research into fashions of collecting, the contents of libraries, and the methods of the book trade. Hopefully, some evidence of this scholarly inquiry will emerge from this paper.

Various sources exist within the British Library to establish provenance. First, there is the accession data within the book itself: an ownership stamp and, since 1850, a date stamp. The color of the ownership stamp indicates the mode of acquisition (purchase, donation, or legal deposit), and because different designs of stamp were used at different periods, the ownership stamp will also indicate an approximate date of accession. An actual date stamp is invaluable, because the purchase invoice will bear the same date and the majority of invoices have survived. An invoice will reveal the bookseller and possibly more information besides. From 1837 to 1850, each item acquired was annotated with the date of accession and with a running number of items accessioned on that day. This information enables consultation of the accessions register, which will disclose the bookseller, or donor, and occasionally additional facts. For this period the collection of invoices is not complete, and for the period before 1837, only a very few have survived. For donated books, records stretch back to 1756, three years after the foundation of the British Museum by an act of Parliament.[1] Finally, there are the minutes and reports of the various Keepers of Printed Books to the British Museum Trustees, which minutes and reports ask for special funds for notable purchases and then record success or failure. Besides these documentary sources, the usual evidence of ownership—bookplates, armorials, and manuscript annotations—may of course be present.

In this paper, I have looked at the library's holdings of printed books from the colonial period containing Andean languages. These are listed in the

appendix in order of accession.[2] There may be omissions (the pre-1975 catalogue cannot be searched by language), but I have checked my list against
Norman A. McQuown's *Catalogue of American Indian Language Printed
Books in the British (Museum) Library in London*.[3] McQuown's list is not
itself complete, but it does at least provide a cross-check. His information on
provenance is minimal.

Knowledge of the provenance of the earliest books to have entered the
museum's collections is obviously the least complete unless the earliest books
form part of a named collection. The earliest book containing Andean languages (no. 1) was one of the books of Sir Hans Sloane, the museum's
founder. The type of ownership stamp, the presence of two early shelfmarks,
and, in particular, the signature of William Godolphin on the title page are
proof of this fact.[4] The next item (no. 2) to have entered the museum could
have done so at any time before 1834, when the type of ownership stamp it
bears ceased to be used. The next title on the list, Valdivia's *Arte y gramática
general* was most probably acquired between 1834 and 1837. It might be
cheating from a linguistic point of view to have included this item, as the language described is Araucanian, and thus not Andean, according to many clas-
sifications with the exception of that of Joseph H. Greenberg.[5] The book was
purchased at the sale of Richard Heber's library (150,000 volumes), which
took place over those three years, 1834–1837.[6] According to his own note in
the book, Heber had purchased it in 1824 at the sale of the library of the
Spanish Arabist, José Antonio Conde. The date of accession of Febrés's *Arte
de la lengua general del reyno de Chile* (no. 4) can be estimated by the
absence of an ownership stamp. It probably entered the museum between late
1835 and the end of 1836 when no books were stamped.

Further imprints from colonial Lima entered the library of the British
Museum surprisingly early in its history, that is, before the "boom" in the
acquisition of foreign material in the second half of the nineteenth century. In
January 1843, 8 works in 6 books were purchased from the London bookseller
Thomas Rodd the Younger. The books were part of a sizeable consignment of
some 350 titles of which approximately 185 titles were printed in Peru
between 1585 and 1839. The museum's accessions register states that a book
or books were "purchased at Sampayo's sale."[7] This refers to the sale that took
place in Paris in November 1842 of books belonging to a late M. de Sampayo.
His collection comprised "livres en différentes langues sur l'histoire et la littérature de l'Espagne, du Portugal et de leurs colonies."[8] So far, unfortunately,
I have failed to identify this man. In no library catalogue that I have seen does
he have a given name, nor is he identified in the introduction to the catalogue.
However, there is a greater problem as far as the library's books are concerned:
only a few of the titles listed in the museum's register appear in the sale catalogue. In fact, none of the books that I have listed in the appendix as having

been acquired on January 11, 1843, figures in it. Two conclusions are possible. First, M. de Sampayo's library was much larger than it appears from the catalogue and Rodd purchased some books in advance of the sale. Alternatively, the books purchased by the museum consisted of a small number of Sampayo's books, plus many others from Rodd's stock, that is, from another sale, or sales.

With one exception (nos. 6 and 6b), all the books described in the appendix as acquired on January 11, 1843, were offered in Rodd's printed catalogue of 1843, and it can be assumed that the museum bought them some time between the bookseller's sending the catalogue to the printer and the catalogue's appearance.[9] Other items from the catalogue were accessioned on the same date.

The Rodd family had had many dealings over the years with Spanish material. Rodd the Younger had, for example, acquired 117 books from the Iriarte Library from Thomas Thorpe in 1826; the books were acquired by Richard Heber and subsequently by the Bodleian.[10] Rodd was also responsible for the sale of some of Juan de Iriarte's († 1771) manuscripts to the museum in March 1843.[11] Clearly he had ample access to books from Spanish libraries. However, there is one possible specific source for the Peruvian material, which is not a Spanish library. In 1842 the books of the late Amédée Chaumette des Fossés (1782–1841) were auctioned in Paris.[12] A notable polyglot, he was a member of several learned societies in France. He also served as a diplomat overseas, most significantly in Peru (first as "inspecteur du commerce," then as consul general). During fifteen years there, he added considerably to his library, collecting both manuscripts and printed books. He died of fever before being able to return to France. Rodd most certainly acquired a quantity of the Peruvian material that was purchased by the museum at the Chaumette des Fossés sale, as the coincidence of date and titles, particularly of early-nineteenth-century works, is overwhelming. All of the early Peruvian imprints in Rodd's catalogue were also in that of Chaumette des Fossés, so it is probable, but not conclusive, that they were his books that the museum purchased from Rodd.

The next significant acquisition of books containing indigenous American languages came in December 1846. Fortunately, there is reliable information concerning their provenance. The museum purchased 22 titles from the Berlin bookseller Adolphus Asher for £91 14s.[13] Asher was probably the most important supplier of foreign books to the museum in the nineteenth century and worked with Antonio Panizzi, Keeper of Printed Books (1837–1856) and Principal Librarian of the British Museum (1856–1866) to create a world-class research library.[14] All of the books purchased from Asher in December 1846 came from the collection of Henri Ternaux-Compans (1807–1864), the majority bearing the distinctive ram's head device and the initials "H. T." tooled on the covers. Ternaux, nephew of the man who made a fortune introducing cashmere to France, was a diplomat, traveller in South America, and from 1844 to 1848, député for Loire-Inférieure. He was also a great bibliophile and has been described as the first collector of Hispanic Americana.[15] He appears to have bought and sold books constantly throughout his collecting career. However, in 1844, according to Wagner, he sold much of his library to Obadiah Rich, a London-based American bookseller. Many of these books are now in the John Carter Brown Library, Providence, Rhode Island; his manuscripts are in the New York Public Library.[16] Ternaux must have retained some books, as Asher was selling them to the museum in late 1846, or Rich sold some to Asher. This is not impossible because Brown bought the Ternaux-Compans books, not from Rich, but from another prominent American bookseller Henry Stevens. With one exception all the titles on Asher's invoice relate to indigenous Latin America and 17 of the works were written in or concern native languages. Besides Quechua and Aymara, the languages are Cumana, Guarani, Nahuatl, Huastec (Mayan), and Otomi. Their dates of publication range from 1595 (Rincón, *Arte mexicana*) to 1810 (Sandoval, *Arte de la lengua mexicana*).

The museum's interest in acquiring books in exotic languages is evident also in the acquisitions made in December 1863. The two editions of Torres Rubio's *Arte de la lengua quichua* (nos. 23 and 24) and Estevan Sancho de Melgar's *Arte de la lengua . . . quechua* (no. 25) were bought from the booksellers T. & W. Boone. Their invoice indicates that these came from a massive sale in Ghent in May–June that year. The languages of the approximately 150 items acquired range from Basque to Yoruba via Malabar, Mordvin, Otomi, and Tamil. The books belonged to Pierre Léopold van Alstein (1792–1862), an avid collector of linguistic books, particularly of Oriental languages, and associate professor *(agrégé)* at the University of Ghent.[17] The sale catalogue notes that 2 out of the 3 books (nos. 5161 and 5162) purchased by the museum had belonged to Amédée Chaumette des Fossés.

Before passing to arguably the most notable purchase of the museum in the nineteenth century, it should be noted that just one item (no. 29) containing Andean languages was acquired at the second (1892) Heredia sale, and accessioned on July 14, 1892 *(Vocabulario en la lengua . . . quechua).*[18] One book (no. 30) was then purchased from Maisonneuve in 1893. After that nearly a century elapsed before Avendaño's *Sermones* (no. 31), in Spanish and Quechua, was purchased for the British Library by Quaritch at the sale of the collection of the bookseller Lionel Robinson at Sotheby's (June 26–27, 1986). The book had belonged to Sir Thomas Phillipps and was part of the residue of the Phillipps collection acquired by Robinson and his brother, William H. Robinson.[19]

The most notable, and intriguing, purchase was the book accessioned on October 13, 1891. This consisted of copies of 3 out of the first 4 books printed in Lima: a catechism in Spanish, Quechua, and Aymara; a confessor's manual, similarly trilingual; as is the third item, another catechism. The other, *Pragmática sobre los diez dias del año* (Ciudad de los Reyes [that is, Lima]: Antonio Ricardo, 1584), the statute authorizing the corrections to the calendar following the Gregorian reforms, was the first to be published.[20] The report to the Trustees (September 23, 1891) by the Keeper of Printed Books, Richard Garnett, records how the museum's purchase was secured:

> The extraordinary good fortune which has permitted such an acquisition to be made at such a price [£30] is due before all things to the courtesy of Señor J.T. Medina, the eminent Chilian [*sic*] bibliographer, who in March this year presented the Museum with his privately printed catalogue of books printed in Lima up to 1810. Mr Garnett thought it right that Señor Medina's kindness should be acknowledged by a special letter of thanks from himself. . . . He took occasion to enquire whether Señor Medina knew of a copy of the first South American book existing in Europe and was informed that one was in the possession of M. Maisonneuve, a bookseller in Paris. This volume was procured . . . and upon its arrival was discovered to contain not merely the first South American book, but the second and third also.[21]

The price, at £30 including commission, inevitably struck Garnett as a bargain, although the museum already possessed copies of 2 out of the 3 works contained in the volume. The museum had paid £120 at the Andrade sale in 1869 for a copy of the first surviving book printed in Mexico, Juan de Zumárraga's *Doctrina breve* of 1543 or 1544. The Lima volume had belonged to Chaumette des Fossés (1843), subsequently to Alstein, being auctioned at Ghent in the sale of his books in 1863.[22] Where it was between then and 1891 and why it was offered for just £30 to the museum remain a mystery.

So far, I have dealt with the "when" and "from whom" of my title, but there remains the "why." The museum's acquisitions policy from the time of Panizzi onwards is best described as omnivorous. The Keepers of Printed Books and of Manuscripts bought to the limits of their annual budgets and beyond through special bids. They sought copies of every major work of scholarship or imagination from every country of what they considered the civilized world and in as many editions as possible. The most famous expression of the museum's acquisitions policy is that of Thomas Watts, Keeper of Printed Books (1866–1869), to the effect that the museum desired to acquire the best collection of books in every European language outside their country of origin.[23] It also desired examples of the output of every printing press in the history of the book, and examples of printing in every language, however minor or exotic. This policy can be likened to that of contemporary collectors of natural history specimens, fossils, or rocks. The books considered were important on at least three counts: they were major works of scholarship or of historical significance, they were printed on presses important for the history of the book in South America, and they recorded exotic languages.[24]

APPENDIX

Early Printed Books Containing Andean Languages in the British Library, London
Arranged in order of accession

1753
1 ORE, Luis Gerónimo de
Symbolo Catholico Indiano, en el qual se declaran los mysterios
dela Fè contenidos en los tres Symbolos Catholicos, Apostolico,
Niceno, y de S. Athanasio. Contiene assi mesmo una descripcion del
nuevo orbe, y de los naturales del. Y un orden de enseñarles la doctrina Christiana en
las dos lenguas Generales, Quichua y Aymara, con un Confessionario breve y
Catechismo de la communion.
Lima: Antonio Ricardo, 1598.
C.58.e.9
Godolphin—Sloane

Before 1834
2 QUICHUA
Arte, y Vocabulario en la lengua General del Perú llamada Quichua,
y en la lengua Española.
2 pt. En los Reyes [i.e. Lima]: Francisco del Canto, 1614.
C.58.b.3.(1.)
not known

1834–1836
3 VALDIVIA, Luis de
Arte y Gramática general de la lengua que corre en todo el Reyno
de Chile, con un Vocabulario, y Confessonario . . . Juntamente con
la Doctrina Christiana y Cathecismo del Concilio de Lima en español,
y dos traduciones del en la lengua de Chile, etc.
3 pt. Lima: Francisco del Canto, 1606.
C.63.e.3
Conde—[Evans]—Heber

[ca. 1835–1837]
4 FEBRÉS, Andrés
Arte de la Lengua General del Reyno de Chile, con un dialogo
Chileno-Hispano muy curioso: a que se añade la Doctrina Christiana, esto es,
Rezo, Catecismo . . . lo más en Lengua Chilena y Castellana: y
por fin un vocabulario Hispano-Chileno, y un Calepino
Chileno-Hispano mas copioso.
Lima: En la calle de la Encarnación, 1765.
621.a.29
not known

June 29, 1842
5 PRADO, Pablo de
Directorio espiritual en la lengua Española, y Quichua general
del Inga.
Lima: Jorge López de Herrera, 1641.
C.58.a.13
[Smith]

January 11, 1843
6 BERTONIO, Ludovico
Arte breue de la lengua Aymara, para introducción del arte grande
de la misma lengua.
pp. 30. Roma: Luis Zannetti, 1603.
C.33.d.19.(1)
+
6b BERTONIO, Ludovico
Arte y Grammatica muy copiosa de la lengua Aymara. Con muchos,
y varios modos de hablar para su mayor declaración, etc.
pp. 348. Roma: Luis Zannetti, 1603.
C.33.d.19.(2)
[*Rodd*]

7 DOMINGO, *de Santo Tomas*
Grammatica, o Arte de la lengua general de los Indios de los
Reynos del Perú.
Valladolid: Francisco Fernández de Córdoba, 1560.
C.33.c.35.(1)
+
7b DOMINGO, *de Santo Tomas*
Lexicón, o Vocabulario de la lengua general del Perú.
Valladolid: Francisco Fernández de Córdoba, 1560.
C.33.c.35.(2)
[*Rodd*]

8 LIMA, Concilio Provincial
Tercero Cathecismo y Exposición de la Doctrina Christiana, por
Sermones. Para que los Curas y otros ministros prediquen y
enseñen a los Yndios y a las demas personas. Conforme a lo que
en el sancto Concilio Provincial de Lima se proveyo. [Span.,
Quichua, Aymara.]
Ciudad de los Reyes: Antonio Ricardo, 1585.
C.53.d.8
[*Rodd*]

9 LITURGIES
Latin Rite. Rituals. II, Local, Perú

Rituale, seu Manuale Peruanum; et Forma brevis administrandi apud
Indos sacrosancta Baptismi, Poenitentiæ, Eucharistiæ, Matrimonij,
& Extremæ Unctionis Sacramenta. Iuxta ordinem Sanctæ Romanæ
Ecclesiæ. Per R. P. F. Ludovicum Hieronymum Orerium . . .
[Span., Lat., Quichua, Aymara, etc.]
pp. 418. Neapoli: Giovanni Jacobo Carlino, 1607.
C.52.c.13
[*Rodd*]

10 MARBAN, Pedro
Arte de la Lengua Moxa, con su Vocabulario y Cathecismo.
2 pt. [Lima]: Imprenta Real de Joseph de Contreras, [1702].
621.a.34
[*Rodd*]

11 PEREZ BOCANEGRA, Juan
Ritual formulario, e Institución de Curas, para administrar a los
naturales de este Reyno, los santos Sacramentos del Baptismo,
Confirmación, Eucaristia, y Viatico, Penitencia, Extremaunción y
Matrimonio. Con advertencias muy necessarias. [Span. and Aymara.]
Lima: Gerónimo de Contreras, 1631.
1219.i.5
[*Rodd*]

December 12, 1846
12 BERTONIO, Ludovico
Arte de la lengua Aymara, con una silua de phrases de la misma lengua,
y su declaración en Romance.
pp. 241. Iuli: Francisco del Canto, 1612.
C.38.c.53
Parish—Ternaux-Compans—[Asher]

13 BERTONIO, Ludovico
Confessionario muy copioso en dos lenguas, Aymara, y Española, con una
instrucción a cerca de los siete Sacramentos de la Sancta Yglesia, etc.
pp. 350. Iuli: Francisco del Canto, 1612.
C.58.a.15
Ternaux-Compans—[Asher]

14 BERTONIO, Ludovico
Vocabulario de la lengua Aymara, etc.
2 pt. Iuli: Francisco del Canto, 1612.
C.58.e.6
Ternaux-Compans—[Asher]

15 GONZALEZ HOLGUIN, Diego
Vocabulario de la lengua general de todo el Perú llamada lengua
quichua, o del Inca. Corregido y renovado conforme a la
propriedad cortesana del Cuzco. Dividido en dos libros, etc.
2 pt. Ciudad de los Reyes: Francisco del Canto, 1608.
C.58.e.5
Ternaux-Compans—[Asher]

16 HUERTA, Alonso de
Arte de la lengua Quechua general de los Yndios de este Reyno
del Pirú, etc.
En los Reyes [i.e. Lima]: Francisco del Canto, 1616.
C.58.e.4
Ternaux-Compans—[Asher]

17 LIMA, Concilio Provincial
Confessionario para los Curas de Indios. Con la instrucción contra
sus Ritos: y Exhortación para ayudar a bien morir: y summa de sus
Privilegios; y forma de impedimentos del Matrimonio. Compuesto y
traduzido en las Lenguas Quichua, y Aymara. Por autoridad del
Concilio Provincial de Lima, del año de 1583.
3 pt. Ciudad de los Reyes: Antonio Ricardo, 1585.
C.53.c.59
Ternaux-Compans—[Asher]

18 ROBERT [Bellarmino], Saint, Cardinal, Archbishop of Capua
[Dichiarazione più copiosa della dottrina cristiana; Polyglot]
Declaración copiosa de las quatro partes mas essenciales, y
necessarias de la doctrina christiana . . . con las adiciones del
Maestro Sebastian de Lirio . . . Traducida de lengua Castellana en
la general del Inga por . . . Bartolome Iurado Palomino, etc. [Span.
and Quechua.]
ff. 136. Lima: Jorge López de Herrera, 1649.
3504.ee.29
Ternaux-Compans—[Asher]

19 TORRES RUBIO, Diego de
Arte de la lengua Aymara.
Lima: Francisco del Canto, 1616.
C.58.a.14.(1)
+
19b LIMA, Concilio Provincial
Catecismo en la lengua Española y Amara del Pirú. Ordenado por
autoridad del Concilio Provincial de Lima, y impreso en la dicha
ciudad el año de 1583.
Sevilla: Bartolomé Gómez, 1604.

C.58.a.14.(2)
Ternaux-Compans—[Asher]

20 TORRES RUBIO, Diego de
Arte, y Vocabulario de la Lengua Quichua general de los Indios de
el Perú. Que Compuso el Padre Diego de Torres Rubio de la Compañia
de Jesus. Y añadió el P. Juan de Figueredo de la misma Compañia.
Ahora nuevamente Corregido, y Aumentado en machos [*sic*] vocablos . . . Por
un Religioso de la misma Compañia.
Reimpresso en Lima: Imprenta de la Plazuela de San Christoval, 1754.
826.a.13
Ternaux-Compans—[Asher]

21 VALDIVIA, Luis de
Arte, y Gramática general de la lengua que corre en todo el Reyno
de Chile, con un Vocabulario, y Confessionario.
Sevilla: Tomás López de Haro, 1684.
C.58.a.11
Ternaux-Compans—[Asher]

December 1846/January 1847
22 TORRES RUBIO, Diego de
Arte, y Vocabulario de la Lengua Quichua general de los Indios de
el Perú. Que Compuso el Padre Diego de Torres Rubio de la Compañia
de Jesus. Y añadió el P. Juan de Figueredo de la misma Compañia.
Ahora nuevamente Corregido, y Aumentado en machos [*sic*] vocablos . . . Por
un Religioso de la misma Compañia.
Reimpresso en Lima: Imprenta de la Plazuela de San Christoval, 1754.
G.7452
Grenville (don.)

December 29, 1863
23 TORRES RUBIO, Diego de
Arte de la lengua Quichua.
Lima: Francisco Lasso, 1619.
C.33.a.50
Chaumette—Alstein—[Boone]

24 TORRES RUBIO, Diego de
Arte de la lengua Quichua . . . Nuevamente van añadidos los Romances,
Cathecismo pequeño, todas las Oraciones, los dias de fiesta
ayunos de los Indios, el Vocabulario añadido, y otro Vocabulario
de la lengua Chinchaisuyo. Por . . . Iuan de Figueredo, etc.
ff. 114. Lima: Joseph de Contreras y Alvarado, [1700].
C.33.a.49
Alstein—[Boone]

25 MELGAR, Estevan Sancho de
Arte de la lengua general del Ynga llamada Qquechhua.
Lima: Diego de Lyra, 1691.
1568/3528
Chaumette—Alstein—[Boone]

April 9, 1864
26 SANCHO DE MELGAR, Estevan
Arte de la Lengua general del Ynga llamada Qquechhua.
Lima: Diego de Lyra, 1691.
Imperfect; wanting first two leaves of dedication; t.p. mutilated.
1568/3092
A.T. Barnard (don.)

March 25, 1874
27 GONZALEZ HOLGUIN, Diego
Gramática y Arte nueva de la lengua general de todo el Perú,
llamada lengua Qquichua, o lengua del Inca, etc.
Ciudad de los Reyes: Francisco del Canto, 1607.
C.58.e.14
[Tross]

October 13, 1891
28 LIMA, Concilio Provincial
[Doctrina Christiana, y Catecismo para instrucción de los Indios
y de las demas personas, que han de ser enseñadas en nuestra
santa Fe. Con un confessionario, y otras cosas necessarias para
los que doctrinan . . . Compuesto por auctoridad del Concilio
Prouincial, que se celebro en la Ciudad de los Reyes, el año de
1583. Y por la misma traduzido en las dos lenguas generales, de
este Reyno, Quichua, y Aymara.] [By Joseph de Acosta.]
ff. 84. Ciudad de los Reyes: Antonio Ricardo, 1584.
Imperfect; wanting the title page and parts of the first two
preliminary leaves.
C.53.c.26.(1)
+

28b LIMA, Concilio Provincial
Confessionario para los Curas de Indios. Con la instrucción contra
sus Ritos: y Exhortación para ayudar a bien morir: y summa de sus
Privilegios; y forma de impedimentos del Matrimonio. Compuesto y
traduzido en las lenguas Quichua, y Aymara. Por autoridad del
Concilio Provincial de Lima, del año de 1583.
3 pt. Ciudad de los Reyes: Antonio Ricardo, 1585.
C.53.c.26.(2)
+

28c LIMA, Concilio Provincial
Tercero Cathecismo y Exposición de la Doctrina Christiana, por
Sermones. Para que los Curas y otros ministros prediquen y
enseñen a los Yndios y a las demas personas. Conforme a lo que
en el sancto Concilio Provincial de Lima se proveyo. [Span.,
Quichua, Aymara.]
Ciudad de los Reyes: Antonio Ricardo, 1585.
C.53.c.26.(3)
Chaumette—Alstein—[Maisonneuve—Dulau]

July 14, 1892
29 MARTINEZ, Juan
Vocabulario en la lengua general del Perú llamada Quichua, y en
la lengua Española. Nueuamente emendado y añadido de algunas
cosas que faltauan por el Padre Maestro Fray Juan Martinez, etc.
2 pt. En Los Reyes [Lima]: Antonio Ricardo, 1604.
Includes: Arte de la lengua general del Perú, llamada Quichua.
C.63.a.13
Heredia—[Cohn]

August 3, 1893
30 VILLEGAS, Alfonso de
Libro de la Vida y milagros de Nuestro Señor Iesu Christo en dos
Lenguas, Aymara y Romance, traducido de el que recopilo el
Licenciado Alonso de Villegas, quitadas, y añadidas algunas
Cosas, y acomodado a la capacidad de los Indios. Por el padre
Ludovico Bertonio, etc.
pp. 660. Iuli: Francisco del Canto, 1612.
C.58.d.23
[Maisonneuve—Dulau]

August 30, 1986
31 AVENDAÑO, Fernando de
Sermones de los misterios de nuestra santa Fe Católica, en
lengua castellana, y la general del Inca. Impugnanse los errores
particulares que los indios han tenido . . . Por el Doctor Don Fernando
de Avendaño, etc.
2 pt. Lima: Jorge López de Herrera, [1648?].
Lacks leaves 35–42.
C.189.bb.9
Phillipps—Robinson—[Sotheby—Quaritch]

Missing or Destroyed Books
1* LIMA, Concilio Provincial
Tercero Catecismo, y exposición de la doctrina Christiana por
sermones, paraque los curos . . . enseñen a los Indios . . .
conforme a lo que se proveyó en el Santo Concilio Provincial de
Lima el año pasado de 1583. Mandado reimprimir por el concilio
Provincial del año de 1773. [Span. and Quichua.]
[Lima, 1774?].
4425.aa.14

2* LITURGIES
Latin Rite. Rituals. II, Local, Perú
Rituale, seu Manuale Peruanum; et Forma brevis administrandi apud
Indos sacrosancta Baptismi, Poenitentiæ, Eucharistiæ Matrimonii
& Extremæ Unctionis Sacramenta, Juxta ordinem Sanctæ Romanae
Ecclesiae. Per R. P. F. Ludovicum Hieronymum Orerium . . .
Accuratum: et quae indigent versione vulgaribus Idiomatibus
Indicis . . . aut per ipsum translata, aut ejus industria
elaborata. [Span., Lat., Quichua, Aymara, etc.]
pp. 418. Neapoli: Giovanni Jacobo Carlino, 1607.
D-3365.g.3

3* VILLAGOMEZ, Pedro de, Archbishop of Lima
Carta pastoral de exortación e instrucción contra las idolatrias
de los Indios del Arçobispado de Lima por . . . Don P. de
Villagomez. A sus visitadores de las idolatrias, y a sus
vicarios, y curas de las doctrinas de Indios. [*With sermons in Spanish and Quechua.*]
Lima, 1649.
D-4425.g.15

NOTES

1. The donation records are held by the Central Archives of the British Museum, although the British Library Archives have the departmental copies of reports of donations from about 1836 onwards.

2. The individual records are largely as they appear in the British Library's pre-1975 catalogue (commonly known as the General Catalogue) with necessary alterations in order to haronize entries created at different periods. The provenance information is of course additional. Previous owners are printed in italic, and booksellers and auction houses are in italic within square brackets.

3. Norman A. McQuown, *Catalogue of American Indian Language Printed Books in the British (Museum) Library in London,* Microfilm Collection of Manuscripts on Cultural Anthropology, Ser. XXVIII, no. 152 (Chicago: University of Chicago Library, 1975).

4. Many of Sloane's Hispanic books belonged previously to William Godolphin, British Ambassador in Madrid from 1671 until 1678 when he was removed from office for his pro-Catholic tendencies. I am grateful to my colleague Alison Walker for this information. The two early shelfmarks are those used in Montagu House, home of the British Museum from its

foundation until 1845 when it was finally demolished. On Sloane's library in general, see M. A. E. Nickson, "Books and Manuscripts," in *Sir Hans Sloane. Collector, Scientist, Antiquary, Founding Father of the British Museum,* ed. Arthur MacGregor (London: British Museum Press, 1994), pp. 263–273.

5. "The General Classification of Central and South American Languages," in *Men and Cultures. Selected Papers of the Fifth International Congress of Anthropological and Ethnological Sciences. Philadelphia . . . 1956,* ed. Anthony F. C. Wallace (Philadelphia: University of Pennsylvania, 1960), pp. 791–794.

6. Richard Heber's library was sold largely by Sotheby's. See *Bibliotheca Heberiana. Catalogue of the Library of the late Richard Heber,* 13 parts (London, 1834–1837).

7. British Library Archives, DH 52/11, Department of Printed Books Accessions Register, Jan. 11, 1843.

8. *Catalogue d'une belle collection de livres en différentes langues sur l'histoire de la littérature de l'Espagne, du Portugal et de leurs colonies, provenant de la Bibliothèque de feu M. de Sampayo* (Paris: Colomb de Batines, Libraire, 1842).

9. *Catalogue of Books and Manuscripts, recently added to, or selected from the stock of Thomas Rodd* . . . (London, 1843).

10. See the important article of Nigel Glendinning, "Spanish Books in England: 1800–1850," *Transactions of the Cambridge Bibliographical Society* 3 (1959–1963): 86.

11. See Barry Taylor, "An Old Spanish Tale from Add. MS. 14040, ff. 113r–114v . . . ," *British Library Journal* 22 (1996): 172.

12. *Catalogue des livres imprimés et manuscrits composant la bibliothèque de feu M. Amédée Chaumette des Fossés* (Paris: H. Labitte, 1842). The biographical information that follows is derived from the useful "Notice sur M. Chaumette des Fossés," *Catalogue,* pp. v–viii.

13. British Library Archives, Department of Printed Books Accessions Register, Dec. 12, 1846.

14. On Asher, Panizzi, and the British Museum, see David Paisey, "Adolphus Asher (1800–1853): Berlin Bookseller, Anglophile, and Friend to Panizzi," *British Library Journal* 23 (1997): 131–153.

15. Henry R. Wagner, "Henri Ternaux-Compans: The First Collector of Hispanic-Americana," *Inter-American Review of Bibliography* 4 (1954): 283–298; also Henry R. Wagner, "Henri Ternaux-Compans: A Bibliography," *Inter-American Review of Bibliography* 7 (1957): 239–254.

16. See Wagner, "First Collector," pp. 294–297; and Henry R. Wagner, "Hispanic Americana in the John Carter Brown Library," in *Essays Honoring Lawrence C. Wroth* (Portland, Maine: Anthoensen Press, 1951), pp. 423–455.

17. See the introduction (pp. ix–xii) to the sale catalogue, *Catalogue des livres et manuscrits formant la bibliothèque de feu M. P. Léopold van Alstein* (Gand: Imprimerie et Lithographie de C. Annoot-Braeckman, 1863).

18. *Catalogue de la Bibliothèque de M. Ricardo Heredia, Comte de Benahavis, Deuxième Partie: Belles-Lettres* (Paris: Ém. Paul, L. Huard et Guillemin, 1892), lot 1508.

19. *The Collection of the Late Lionel Robinson, Esq.* . . . . (London: Sotheby's, 1986), lot 257.

20. Just two copies survive: one in the John Carter Brown Library, the other at Harvard University Library.

21. British Library Archives, DH 2/46, 50, Correspondence, Trustees' Minutes and Reports of the Keepers of Printed Books, Sept. 23, 1891.

22. *Catalogue . . . Chaumette des Fossés,* lot 72; *Catalogue . . . van Alstein,* lot 742. The latter indicates that this is the Chaumette copy. The descriptions fit the British Library copy.

23. "The object . . . has been to bring together . . . the best Russian library out of Russia, the best German out of Germany, the best Spanish out of Spain, and so for every language, from Italian to Icelandic, from Polish to Portuguese." These famous words are in fact contained in a letter from Watts to Antonio Panizzi, Principal Librarian, in which he sought (unsuccessfully) for promotion (British Museum Central Archives, CE 4/69, 176. Original Papers, Feb. 20 1861. A microfilm copy is held in the British Library Archives).

24. I should like to thank my colleagues John Hopson (British Library Archivist) and Barry Taylor (Early Printed Collections) for their valuable comments on the printed version of this paper; and Michael T. Hamerly for generously allowing me to read the printed text of his paper, "Catalog of Peruvian Imprints of the Colonial and Independence Periods Held by the John Carter Brown Library," summarized at SALALM XLV.

12. La Biblioteca del Instituto de Estudios Peruanos

Virginia García

La Biblioteca y el devenir institucional

El Instituto de Estudios Peruanos, IEP fue fundado en 1964 en Huampaní, localidad ubicada en las afueras de Lima, por un grupo de connotados intelectuales peruanos, como Francisco Miro Quesada, Luis E. Valcárcel, José María Arguedas, María Rostworowski, José Matos Mar, Augusto Salazar Bondy, Sebastián Salazar Bondy, Jorge Bravo Bresani y John Murra. Reunía así a un conjunto de destacados historiadores, etnohistoriadores, filósofos, economistas y antropólogos, quienes motivados por un diálogo interdisciplinario intentaban comprender y explicar las diferentes perspectivas del desarrollo en el Perú y América Latina. Poco tiempo después se incorporan los sociólogos Julio Cotler y Giorgio Alberti y el lingüista y crítico literario Alberto Escobar.

Definida jurídicamente como una organización no gubernamental de desarrollo, el IEP siguió y en buena medida orientó las principales discusiones de las ciencias sociales peruanas, principalmente el conocimiento de la realidad andina, gran parte de nuestra historia prehispánica, colonial y republicana, las identidades culturales, los mecanismos de dominación interna y las alternativas de transformación. Buscando atender los requerimientos de la información y el debate sobre estos temas la Biblioteca del IEP se iría formando como un área de vital importancia para la institución.

La Biblioteca comenzó originalmente a organizarse a partir de textos cedidos por los fundadores de la institución, así como de donaciones recibidas de algunas instituciones. En sus momentos iniciales la Biblioteca tuvo un carácter más bien informal e incluía apenas unos 500 títulos constituidos principalmente por publicaciones nacionales sobre economía y estadística; publicaciones francesas sobre economía, planificación y desarrollo y publicaciones de ciencias sociales norteamericanas.

El desarrollo de los proyectos de investigación llevados a cabo en el IEP propició el incremento continuo de los materiales bibliográficos; de tal suerte que, a fines de la década de los setenta, la Biblioteca contaba ya con materiales bastante significativos sobre la problemática rural, economía nacional, migraciones e historia. Las primeras publicaciones que el IEP empezara a producir contribuyeron a organizar una política sostenida de canje institucional que desde la década de los noventa se constituiría en su principal fuente de enriquecimiento de la colección bibliográfica.

El apoyo financiero de diversas instituciones, principalmente norteamericanas, implicaría la adquisición de material de apoyo para los proyectos de investigación. Asimismo, el creciente desarrollo editorial potenciaría la política de canjes.

La realidad peruana de los años ochenta y parte de los noventa obliga a redefinir las líneas de investigación del IEP tomando como eje tres temas: el desarrollo económico con equidad, el fortalecimiento de las instituciones democráticas y el respeto por la diversidad cultural del país. Asimismo, la crisis económica y la violencia política fueron problemas centrales examinados con rigor y precisión científica.

En este marco, cobran auge las áreas de economía, ciencia política, antropología, historia y sociología, produciéndose importantes publicaciones que trataban de descifrar los álgidos problemas de la sociedad nacional de entonces. Como en lustros anteriores, libros del Instituto se convertirán en verdaderos "clásicos" sobre la problemática nacional. Años más tarde, el desarrollo de la dimensión de género significará la apertura de una nueva línea de investigación institucional, reflejada en un rubro bibliográfico cada vez más creciente. Acompañando este proceso de reflexión académica renovada para estos años la Biblioteca ha aumentado enormemente su fondo bibliográfico, debido a que publicaciones sobre ciencias sociales más importantes de América Latina, Europa y los Estados Unidos enriquecen constantemente sus colecciones, llegando a desbordar la capacidad física de sus instalaciones. En efecto, la Biblioteca del IEP, a comienzos de los años noventa empezará a perfilarse como uno de los acervos bibliográficos más importantes de las ciencias sociales en nuestro país.

Las nuevas condiciones del financiamiento hacen además que el IEP participe en redes de investigación, incursione en programas cortos de capacitación y atienda el estudio de realidades específicas para la implementación de políticas gubernativas, beneficiándose nuevamente su acervo bibliográfico.

Paralelo a estos procesos, en las últimas dos décadas el prestigio de nuestro sello editorial ha estimulado a muchos investigadores que no pertenecen a la institución, a publicar sus trabajos bajo el auspicio de nuestro centro académico. Esta corriente, sumada a la permanente producción de títulos prestigiados y de gran receptividad, como los de la serie *Historia Andina,* han hecho posible una política editorial relativamente fértil, haciendo que hoy el IEP tenga más de 259 títulos de libros y 110 títulos de documentos de trabajo publicados lo cual redunda en una política más amplia aún del canje de publicaciones.

Organización y servicios

La Biblioteca del Instituto de Estudios Peruanos es actualmente un centro de información especializado en bibliografía destinada a la investigación de problemas sociales del Perú y América Latina. Está dirigido especialmente a atender los requerimientos de nuestros investigadores, afiliados extranjeros, profesores universitarios, y estudiantes de últimos años de universidades nacionales y del exterior.

Una parte importante de nuestros usuarios son investigadores y estudiantes de universidades foráneas que elaboran trabajos sobre el Perú. En muchas ocasiones, la Biblioteca les proporciona materiales únicos, no existentes en otras bibliotecas del país. Igualmente existe una creciente demanda de parte de investigadores y estudiantes nacionales, debido a problemas de acceso a fuentes bibliográficas y severas insuficiencias en sus bibliotecas. De esta manera, la Biblioteca del IEP va prestando un servicio cada vez más reconocido en el área de las ciencias sociales.

En la actualidad la Biblioteca cuenta con más de catorce mil publicaciones principalmente de las áreas de ciencias sociales y economía. Se cuenta además con 400 títulos de publicaciones periódicas, de los cuales 250 son colecciones completas. Es una biblioteca especializada en ciencias sociales, considerada como la segunda en importancia en el país después de la Pontificia Universidad Católica del Perú. La principal fuente de ingresos bibliográficos corresponde al canje, el cual se efectúa con más de 100 instituciones peruanas y del exterior. Las donaciones significan también una preocupación constante de nuestra gestión, sobre todo de bibliotecas o colecciones importantes de personalidades e intelectuales amigos del IEP. El depositario se beneficia con el cuidado y seguridad de sus obras y nosotros nos beneficiamos, sin desembolso adicional, con recursos importantes y muchas veces únicos, como es el caso de la colección sobre el Alianza Popular Revolucionaria Americana, APRA, (partido político peruano), afronegrismo donada por el Dr. Fernando Romero y la colección de la Dra. María Rostworowski, sobre etnohistoria actualmente en proceso de automatización. De igual manera durante el presente año, de acuerdo a un convenio con el BID, nuestra colección se ha visto incrementada con sus publicaciones. En cuanto a la adquisición de títulos, tomamos en cuenta no solamente la producción capitalina y extranjera, sino también la del interior del país. El acopio de la producción internacional en ciencias sociales y otras disciplinas afines, considera igualmente las tesis universitarias que se producen sobre nuestro país en los centros académicos del exterior. Un porcentaje menor proviene de las adquisiciones por compra. De los 400 títulos de publicaciones periódicas sólo el 3% se adquiere por suscripción, correspondiendo el 60% al canje y el 37% restante a donaciones.

Estadistica de adquisiciones

Libros	1997	1998	1999
Canje	378	510	764
Donación	142	221	213
Compra	56	42	103

Pub. Periódicas			
Canje	84	127	182
Donación	68	60	86
Suscripción	8	7	5

La colección se encuentra totalmente automatizada utilizando el software CD /ISIS y el Macrothesaurus de la OCDE especializado en ciencias sociales. En el área de historia se ha incorporado términos específicos en historia del Perú. Contamos con cinco bases de datos, lo que en conjunto hacen algo más de 17,000 registros bibliográficos: IEPBIB, monografías, separatas y artículos de revistas, COPUSE, títulos de revistas; ESTADI, estadísticas y censos; ROMERO, colección especializada en afronegrismos y USUAR, base de uso interno.

En 1999 las consultas ascendieron a 3, 902 entre personas e instituciones que asisten a la Biblioteca a través de consultas telefónicas, referencia, préstamos interbibliotecarios, DSI (Diseminación selectiva de la información) y correo electrónico, lo que para una biblioteca especializada es un volumen bastante exigente. La Biblioteca cuenta con convenios para préstamos con centros de información en temas afines a los nuestros, con quienes comparte una red virtual de diferentes servicios, lo que amplía nuestra disponibilidad de servicio.

Los usuarios pueden consultar la Biblioteca directamente o hacer un contacto inicial con nuestra colección a través de nuestra base de datos que se encuentra disponible en la página Web del Instituto (http://iep.perucultural.org.pe) Asimismo, tenemos acuerdos suscritos con universidades que carecen de material bibliográfico en ciencias sociales. Es mediante estos canales que un número significativo de estudiantes universitarios, docentes e investigadores accede a nuestra colección.

Según nuestras estadísticas de servicio, el promedio de consultas al año en la Biblioteca ha sido:

Años	1997	1998	1999
Consultas	2577	3444	3902

Aparte de los servicios ya existentes, se pueden ofrecer adicionalmente la elaboración de catálogos especializados, así como la edición de bibliografías comentadas por nuestros especialistas en áreas de demanda. Dentro de nuestros servicios ofrecemos también nuestra Alerta bibliográfica mensual, la cual se distribuye electrónicamente a todos nuestros usuarios internos y externos y de forma impresa a las instituciones con las que mantenemos canje de publicaciones.

En términos del personal, se ha dado un proceso de profesionalización creciente. A mediados de los ochenta sólo se contaba con un investigador a tiempo parcial bajo cuya responsabilidad se encontraba la Biblioteca. A principios de los años noventa la Biblioteca comienza a organizarse de modo más sistemático debido a la presencia de un profesional en bibliotecología. Este proceso se ha consolidado finalmente y en la actualidad esta labor es realizada por una Lic. en Bibliotecología y una asistente de la misma especialidad aceptando también en ocasiones pasantías de estudiantes nacionales y extranjeros en el área.

En suma, desde su modesto inicio como un pequeño fondo bibliográfico, la Biblioteca del Instituto de Estudios Peruanos ha recorrido un largo camino para transformarse en lo que actualmente es: una de las bibliotecas especializadas en las ciencias sociales más importantes del país. Y si bien está claro que, para incrementar sus fondos, la biblioteca se ha beneficiado por partida doble de la orientación principal que tiene el IEP, tanto por el lado de la investigación cuanto por el de la actividad editorial; también es cierto que con el tiempo y esfuerzo profesional ha logrado constituirse en una las piezas claves del quehacer del IEP, pero hemos llegado al punto en el cual debemos dar un salto cualitativo y cuantitativo, para lo cual estamos empeñados en buscar un financiamiento permanente.

BIBLIOGRAFÍA

Instituto de Estudios Peruanos. *Memorias 1985–1996.*

Rodríguez Pastor, Humberto. *La antropología del Perú.* Lima: Concytec, 1995.

13. "Nothing in Peru is Permanent": Iturriaga Cia. and the Peruvian Book

Mark Grover

Introduction

A few years ago when Roberto Vergaray from Iturriaga Cia. came to visit the Harold B. Lee Library at Brigham Young University, I took him to see the Peruvian history book section. It was a pleasure to watch his joyful reaction as he examined the collection and recounted events related to his experiences obtaining the books we were finding on the shelves. When we moved to the literature section his reaction turned to tears as he watched a student use the collection and was able to see firsthand the role these important Peruvian books had in the library's collection. The books he supplied are an important element in the process of expanding knowledge and appreciation of Peru worldwide.

I watched these emotions with absolute understanding and appreciation, for I also go into the collection and am moved as I handle books with which I have a personal attachment and history. I have vivid memories of events associated with the acquisition of the collection. I remember with fondness students and faculty who used the books we had acquired. My experience watching Roberto's obvious affection for the books of Peru made me appreciate the fact that for the most part Latin American librarians and bibliographers are privileged to work with dealers and booksellers who have similar concerns and appreciation for the Latin American book. We do not work with large computerized book companies with impersonal workers and bottom-line management concerned more with the profit than with the book. We are fortunate to associate with small companies in which the owners are personally involved in all aspects of the business. Most of all, they are close friends who love the books and culture of Latin America.

One of the most successful of these small companies is that of Iturriaga Cia. from Lima, Peru. It is a small operation that has weathered a variety of political and economic challenges and as a result has provided Peruvian books, both rare and new, to libraries worldwide for more than fifty years. Theirs is a history that deserves recognition.[1]

129

Schwab

The story began with a student who was not sure what he wanted to do for a profession and his concerned parents who hoped that getting him out of Germany might help him decide. Federico Schwab was born in the city of Amberg, Bavaria, in 1902. He joined the German army as a teenager and fought in the First World War. Sent to Northern Africa, he became fascinated with different cultures and gained an appreciation for travel. Unfortunately, however, he lost his sight in one eye during one of the battles of the war. After leaving the military, he attended universities in Munich and Berlin between 1919 and 1925, but his studies failed to take a significant direction. He took classes in library science, archival science, and the cultures of the Americas, but failed to get a degree. His parents suggested a period of travel in hopes that he would find direction in his life. After time in southern Europe, he decided to go to South America to see for himself the native peoples that had so interested him in school. His first stop in 1926 was Montevideo, Uruguay.

Without monetary assistance from home, he was soon in financial straits and had to find work. Jobs took him to Buenos Aires, Argentina, and La Paz, Bolivia, where he experienced firsthand both Indian culture and the difficult manual work of the Standard Oil fields in Charcas. While in Bolivia he became acquainted with two Peruvian musicians, Carlos Sánchez Málaga and Roberto Carpio. Because of their influence and persuasion he made one final stop in Lima, Peru, before finding a home. Here he hoped to spend time learning about Inca culture. He arrived in Peru near the end of 1930.[2]

He became involved in a variety of activities related to culture, education, and libraries. While waiting for a position to open at the Universidad Nacional, he went to the Peruvian Amazon close to the River Perené, where he studied indigenous language and culture and made money in a variety of ways, including catching butterflies to sell to collectors. When he returned to Lima his hoped-for job at the Universidad Nacional had not materialized, so a modest position was found in the library at the Universidad de San Marcos. There he became a colleague and friend of the great Peruvian historian Dr. Jorge Basadre, who was director of the library.[3]

The two became close friends and confidants. Both had a great love for books and libraries as did most of the Peruvian intellectuals of the time. They influenced each other in their work both as librarians and historians. Schwab went to work editing the *Boletín de la Biblioteca Universitaria* where he published numerous bibliographies. He maintained the position of director of the library from 1940 to 1960. Basadre also had Schwab translate into Spanish important German publications on Peruvian archaeology and ethnology.[4] Schwab also taught German at the Facultad de Filologia y Lenguas. As a result of his activities, Schwab became acquainted with many of the influential Peruvian academics of his time. It was with great satisfaction that in 1941 he

was nationalized a citizen of Peru. His visits to Germany were always followed with appreciation when he returned to where he considered to be his
real home, Peru.

One other activity of Schwab was important in the intellectual history of
Peru. One day the geographer, politician, and diplomat Emilio Romero saw
that the workers were cleaning out the basement of the Palacio del Gobierno
and that a large collection of books and documents of the old Tribunal del
Consulado de la Real Hacienda was to be destroyed. Reacting quickly he was
able to save all the records and find a place for their protection. With this collection Romero founded the "Archivo Histórico del Ministerio de Hacienda,"
which eventually became the "Archivo General de la Nacional." Schwab was
hired to organize and catalog the collection of more than 500,000 documents,
which task he was able to accomplish in just over four years. He was the director of the archive from 1942 to 1959. The quality of his work and pattern of
organization became the standard for Peruvian archival methodology.[5]

While teaching German at the Universidad de San Marcos and working
for the Archivo Nacional, he also occasionally worked with the largest academic bookstore in Lima called Libreria Internacional doing catalogs of rare
books. It was in this position that he realized the market that existed for
Peruvian books throughout the world. His relationship with the owner was not
particularly positive, so he began looking for an alternative way to earn extra
money. That opportunity came in a surprising way. A musician friend Enrique
Iturriaga won the 1947 Premio Nación de Música, which prize was 5,000
soles. The day he won the prize he had tea at the Donofrio restaurant and met
Schwab. Iturriaga showed him the check and indicated he did not know what
to do with the prize money. Schwab suggested they use it to open a rare book
business and sell Peruvian books to the exterior. Enrique Iturriaga liked the
idea so much that he endorsed the check and gave it to Schwab on the spot.
Thus in 1948 Iturriaga Cia. began operation in a small converted home on
Carabaya 973, of. 9, close to the Plaza San Martin.

Since Schwab continued to work at the Archivo Nacional and the
Universidad de San Marcos, he wanted to avoid the issue of conflict of interest as much as possible. He felt it best that his name not be used in conjunc-
tion with the company. That concern was legitimate since at one time, in fact,
he was falsely accused of selling documents that were owned by the Archivo
Nacional. Enrique was well known in Peru for his music and was willing to
have his name used for the company. Enrique Iturriaga only worked for two
years with the company and after 1950 had a limited involvement in the business, eventually selling his part (30 percent) to Schwab.[6]

It was a small operation run almost exclusively by Schwab. In a small
office space they had two bookshelves, a desk, a couple of chairs, and a type-
writer. Along with Iturriaga, one assistant worked with him, Geraldo

Escarsena, who worked with Schwab at the bookstore. His expertise was in secretarial work.

One of Schwab's assistants at the Archivo was Luiz Muro Arias, a young historian and paleographer who eventually went to Mexico and worked with Silvio Arturo Zavala at El Colegio de México. Luiz's younger brother Roberto Vergaray Arias had begun studying medicine at the Universidad de San Marcos, but due to financial difficulties left school to work as a bank teller. Roberto had been greatly influenced by his brother since childhood as they talked about books and history. Luiz would occasionally allow Roberto to examine the documents on which he was working at the archive. The family also had a large book collection of more than one thousand volumes in their home. In 1957 Luiz persuaded Roberto to leave the bank and begin working with Schwab.

In the beginning they only worked two hours a day at the office and all three continued to work at other jobs. The three worked well together because of different but complementary abilities. Schwab was the academician who had contacts with scholars and writers throughout the country. Through these contacts he became aware of books and collections in Peru that were available for purchase. He would negotiate for the collection and then do the descriptive annotation for the books that would be offered for sale. Geraldo was a detailed person who had little interest in the business, but was willing to spend the hours necessary on descriptive and clerical tasks. Roberto enjoyed the commercial and personal aspects of the business. He enjoyed interaction with people and appreciated the entire process of obtaining books and collections and getting them sold.

Schwab started the business as a rare books' dealer and had little interest in anything other than antiquarian books. That was the business he knew and felt comfortable doing. When he put together a list of books for sale, however, he would occasionally include a small section (3–4 books) of recent publications that interested him. Recognizing how many orders they began receiving for the new books, Roberto, who did not have the same intense interest in rare books, realized there was an international market for newly published books from Peru. Schwab was not interested, but gave permission to Roberto to expand into this part of the book trade as much as he wanted. So in 1960 the first separate list of recently published books was mailed. The response to the catalog was much greater than expected, far-out distancing the normal response to the rare books catalog. One obvious financial advantage was that they could fill orders for several copies of the same new book whereas there was generally only one copy of each of the rare items available.

It did not take long for the recent book business to become the main source of income for the company. Orders for books continued to increase as more and more libraries became interested in buying Peruvian books. The Seminar on the Acquisition of Latin American Library Materials (SALALM) had just met for their first annual meeting in 1956 and interest in building Latin American library collections in the United States grew with each annual meeting. More importantly, the rise to power of Fidel Castro ninety miles from the United States border awoke interest and concern in U.S. universities for the neglected countries to the south. Latin American centers were organized, students trained, and faculty hired, which improvements greatly increased the presence of Latin America on U.S. campuses. Libraries were given larger budgets to be used for the purchase of Latin American materials to supports these new programs. Iturriaga was ready and willing to provide the desired materials.[7]

The Peruvian Book

The methods and ways of selling books from Peru have varied. The firm order from lists sent out by the company has always been the most important method of acquisition used by most libraries. The important program of cooperative acquisition, LACAP, established by Stechert-Hafner with the help of SALALM worked closely with Iturriaga. Probably the most important, financially successful method was that of the approval program in which the company sent to libraries books that fit a specific subject profile without having to be ordered, but with the opportunity of returning the item for a full refund. The first such arrangement for Iturriaga was with Emma Simonsen from Indiana University. She visited Lima and explained in detail the way it should function and wrote up the contract, since it was a new idea to Roberto and Schwab. That was followed shortly by agreements with the University of Wisconsin and Cornell University. Approval programs have increased to the point that in the year 2000 the company had agreements with twenty-five libraries, the largest contract valued at more than $15,000 a year.

Methods of obtaining the books have also evolved and changed. At first Roberto and Schwab found out about new books primarily by going to the large bookstores. They would purchase one copy of each volume, bring it back to the offices, and make the catalogs. When the orders arrived they would return to the bookstores and purchase the numbers needed. With time they were able to determine how many books would probably sell and started purchasing the determined number ahead of time. They then started going directly to the publishers who would generally sell books in bulk at a lower price. They also maintained contact with authors who would call them as new books were published. The company's reputation as the largest exporter of books to the exterior was well known and has helped ensure good coverage of imprint books. Trips were also taken to regional publishing centers of Cuzco, Trujillo, and Arequipa to find books that did not make it to Lima.

Roberto was made manager of the company in the mid-1960s. As the company expanded so did their need for space. Soon the small office on Carabaya was too small and they moved to the second floor of a building on

Jiron Ica 441, of. 109. With time they continued to expand until they bought the entire first floor of the building which had ample space for the business. They expanded from three to nine full-time employees at one time.

Challenges

Schwab only worked with the international market because he believed financial dealings were more secure with libraries in the United States and Europe. However, working with exports, the company has occasionally been confronted with complications caused by political problems in Peru. Three such events provide examples of the challenges that exist in exporting books out of Peru.

In 1968 the military took over the Peruvian government under the direction of General Juan Velasco Alvarado. During this socialist movement with strong nationalist tendencies, the government attempted to distance the country as much as possible from the United States and dollars. A set of stringent and elaborated regulations was instituted that seriously hampered, complicated, and frustrated all export businesses in the country. Exportation of anything anywhere in the world except to the communist block countries was affected. The government prohibited bank accounts in the exterior as well as accounts in dollars. The export of books was put into the same category as coffee or sugar, requiring the filling out of special declaration forms for each package. Special permits had to be purchased for each shipment and taken to the bank in order to deposit money. Dollars had to be exchanged within a few days of receipt. Each step required an unusual amount of paperwork that significantly increased the amount of work required. A further complication was that the government declared that any book older than twenty years was part of the national patrimony and could not be exported. The company had to rely on just the sale of new books for a while.

Iturriaga's business was seriously hampered. Schwab became so demoralized that he offered to sell the company for the small price of two thousand dollars. Roberto suggested patience and began to determine exactly how to work within the new regulations and system. His comment to Schwab was "Nothing in Peru is permanent." Within about four months a new method of operation was established and the company was able to successfully conduct business within the new governmental regulations. Those regulations lasted for just over two years when the process of the exportation of books was eased considerably.

A second crisis occurred as the result of the growth of terrorism and violence due to the activities of the Sendero Luminoso, the guerilla movement that gained control of some of the country beginning in the mid-seventies. The appearance of this movement actually highlighted one of the difficulties working with books in a country like Peru. Often the most important research materials for scholars are the less substantial ephemeral materials that are not part

of the normal book industry. Getting those materials requires extra work and
creativity. Spending time on the street collecting was often the only way those
materials were obtained. Often Roberto had to establish contacts with participants in the movement who would then supply the desired materials. Members
of the movement were generally happy to supply materials to Iturriaga once
they realized those materials were going to international collections to be used
by researchers. The political result of those contacts, however, particularly
with leftist groups, could be damaging to the company if the government
became aware of the materials being collected. As suppliers of revolutionary
materials, the company was considered to be part of the political process.
When those materials were received in the office, they were immediately
sent out.

Schwab had a friend in the Sendero Luminoso movement, Silvia
Arredondo, widow of José María Arguedas, who supplied him with materials
until her arrest. Afterward it was much more difficult to get the ephemeral
writings of the movement. They also maintained contact with other important
groups or parties such as the Apristas.

The primary effect of Sendero Luminoso on Iturriaga was to decrease the
number of books being published and to restrict movement of company representatives into regional centers to purchase books. The urban violence became
personal when Roberto was close enough to a bomb blast at the post office,
near the Palacio de Gobierno, that the force of the explosion knocked him to
the ground. He learned to avoid getting too close to public buildings. Schwab
again became concerned that the movement would become so strong that it
would gain political control of the country and effectively impede the international book trade. Again Roberto's sage advice was given, "Nothing in Peru is
permanent."

A third major problem occurred within the first year of Alberto
Fujimore's presidency in 1991. Shortly after he took over the presidency, the
government instituted an economic program meant to move the country onto
a stronger international economic footing. Part of this program was a loosen-
ing of economic controls and a privatization of the economy, which caused an
immediate increase in the price of all consumer goods especially books. The
initial program to connect the sol to the dollar resulted in a serious shock to
the economy. Books that cost ten dollars were all of a sudden valued at one
hundred dollars. Roberto refused to purchase any books for about four months,
recognizing his inability to sell any of the overpriced books to his customers.
He had to sell some property just to keep from going under. He did not sell a
single book for four months. The price eventually came down to a reasonable
level and the company again began to sell books.

A more recent crisis caused by the privatization of the post office
resulted in a significant increase in shipping costs making the sending of
books by mail prohibitive. Roberto found it cheaper to airship the books to

Miami and then mail them from the United States. These types of political and social problems definitely made the business of exporting books interesting.

Recent Events

Schwab remained significantly involved in the company, in particular the rare books component, until 1976 when illness caused by prostate cancer began to seriously limit his activities. He also struggled with cataracts and glaucoma in his right eye, which made it difficult for him to see. Roberto continued to bring him to the office or take work to him at his home until his death on December 24, 1986. Thus ended the life of a great Peruvian patriot whose work has spread information and goodwill about Peru throughout the world. His widow, Delfina Valencia, an internationally known doll maker, remained in Peru for four years until poor health persuaded her to return to her home country of Chile where she eventually passed away in 1994. Before leaving Peru she sold her share of the company to Roberto.

Though Iturriaga worked primarily with libraries affiliated with SALALM, Federico Schwab never once attended any of our meetings, even though he was often invited. He did not enjoy travel nor did he see the need for personal contact, feeling all could be done through the mail. Roberto disagreed and began attending SALALM with the 1988 meeting in Berkeley and has been a regular attendee ever since.

Conclusion

Ours is an interesting profession. We work with objects that have great emotional value. As Federico Schwab believed, every book with which he worked with was almost sacred. We build libraries so that students and faculty will have access to information that they need. By collecting books we ensure that ideas thought up and written in places and cultures far removed from our own will reach the students and faculty of our universities. The attainment of our goals is made possible by our friends and colleagues in Latin America who sell us books. Combined we are able to change the lives of our patrons.

To illustrate this sacred trust that both librarian and bookseller have, allow me to end with a statement of Roberto Vergaray.

> It is a personal great satisfaction to know that our company has been part of the development of important libraries. It is very fulfilling to realize that the product of our work is found in all parts of the world. Knowing that a Peruvian book is being used and well conserved in important libraries is what is important to me. I am very pleased our company has helped this happen for more than fifty years.

NOTES

1. Most of the information for this paper came from Roberto Vergaray, "Oral History," interview by author, Miami, Florida, March 3, 2000, copy in possession of the author.

2. Estuardo Núñez, "Federico Schwab (1902–1986)," *Alma Mater* 15 (May 1998): 75–79.

3. Jorge Basadre, *Recuerdos de un bibliotecario peruano* (Lima: Editorial Historia, 1975), p. 22.

4. Examples of translations by Schwab are Hermann Trimborn, "Las clases sociales en el Imperio Incaico," *Revista de la Universidad Católica* 14–18 (1936–1937); Richard Pichard Pietschmann, *La "Historia índica" de Pedro Sarmiento de Gamboa* (Lima: Universidad Nacional Mayor de San Marcos, 1964); Ernst W. Middendorf, *Las lenguas aborígenes del Perú. Proemios e introducciones al quechua, al aimará y al mochica* (Lima: Facultad de Letras, Universidad Nacional Mayor de San Marcos, 1959); and Ernst W. Middendorf, *Perú: observaciones y estudios del país y sus habitantes durante una permanencia de 25 años* (Lima: Dirección Universitaria de Biblioteca, Universidad Nacional Mayor de San Marcos, 1973).

5. Emilio Romero, "El Archivo Histórico de Hacienda," *Revista del Archivo General de la Nación* 6 (1982): 51–52. See the catalogs he produced: *Catálogo de la sección colonial del Archivo histórico* (Lima: Imprenta Torres Aguirre, 1944) and *Catálogo de la sección republicana* (Lima: Imprenta Torres Aguirre, 1945, 1946).

6. Interestingly, Iturriaga has become more well known internationally in the book trade than for his music. Enrique Iturriaga is eighty-three years old, continues to be the Director del Conservatorio Nacional de Música del Perú, and lives in the Miraflores section of Lima.

7. See Mark L. Grover, "Latin American History: Concerns and Conflicts," *The History Teacher* 21 (May 1988): 349–365.

14. Andean Countries on Video: Bolivia, Ecuador, and Peru

Nelly S. González

Introduction

During the last fifteen years, the study of Latin America through visual media in academic institutions has increased immensely. Academic libraries have long been developing quality collections of Latin American videos in social sciences and humanities to support the general undergraduate curriculum and to respond to specific research needs in disciplines dealing with Latin American subject matter. The development of Latin American video collections stems from the unprecedented growth in the 1960s of Latin American studies and academic interest in all aspects of Latin American life. The Latin American "continent-and-a-half" came under increasing scrutiny from diplomats and intelligence operatives, and it also aroused the intellectual curiosity of a growing number of scholars. This coincided with the consolidation of Castro's socialist revolution in Cuba and the possibility of Goulart's in Brazil, along with an increasing number of upheavals and changes. Cinema prospered in Latin America as a component of social transformation as militant clandestine documentary groups recorded in video their struggle for political orientation and freedom of expression. Ana María López states:

> In all Latin American nations, the 1960's were years of cultural and political effervescence, and the cinema—conceived of as an aesthetic, cultural, and political/ideological phenomenon—was self-consciously immersed in the maelstrom of popular and intellectual debates. In Brazil, Argentina, Chile, Cuba and Bolivia cine clubs, film societies, film magazines, and museum exhibitions mobilized an active interest in national film culture and amateur filmmaking as committed activities.[1]

The Andean countries, which constitute the cradle of Inca civilization, contain large groups of indigenous people who are descendants of the Aymara and Inca etnias.[2] These groups, not yet integrated into the national life of each country, were at the peak of their struggle for recognition. Thus, in Bolivia, the "Revolución Nacional" (1952) marked a complete change in the economic and social conditions of the country. The Revolución Nacional was "undoubtedly the most significant event in Bolivian history during this century."[3] It meant a change in the structure of its society and the struggles for cultural, political, and economic improvement. All of these changes were recorded through documentaries. The creation of the "New Latin American Cinema" became the vehicle for the advancement of the cinematic movement. This was the period of emerging news documentaries by PBS and the BBC as well as the U.S. commercial television networks NBC, CBS, and ABC. Because of its inexpensive cost, mobility, and accessibility, cinema provided an enormous opportunity for development.

The purpose of my paper is to present the state of the video industry in the Andean countries of Bolivia, Ecuador, and Peru. I will highlight the unique historical contexts that affected the development of the video industry in these countries, and I will list some of the major publications that have documented the evolution of Andean cinema. Next I will briefly touch on some of the challenges that academic libraries have faced in building video collections and the steps that have been taken to address these challenges. Lastly, I will provide a select bibliography of Andean videos, some of which are included in the University of Illinois's collection.

Bolivia

Historians and filmmakers conclude that the Revolución Nacional of 1952 was a watershed in Bolivian history. It marked the beginning of a complete change in the status quo of the nation, resulting in the start of a Bolivian social revolution that continues to evolve today. Lawrence Whitehead states that 1952 was a profound upheaval in which a wide struggle for mass participation in politics and socioeconomic modernization took place.[4] Bolivia and other Latin American governments "supported cinema as a tool of cultural self-discovery."[5] With this support, revolutionary cinema was born in Bolivia.

Alfonso Gumucio Dagrón, in his *Historia del Cine Boliviano,* states that his book is a "history of a cinema without history,"[6] and explains that this medium of communication began with a series of experiences that culminated with very few films and a number of frustrated and disenchanted producers. Part of this frustration is attributable to much of the pioneering work not being documented and to the lack of bibliographic control of Bolivian films produced during this era. According to Dagrón, there are two periods in the development of this industry: 1904–1938 (first period), and 1938–1982 (second period). I imagine that if he were to write an update to his work, the third period would be 1982 to date, which is undoubtedly the most prolific. Carlos D. Mesa Gisbert, in his *Intento de aproximación al cine boliviano,*[7] opens with an essay on the history of the Bolivian cinema that complements the work done by Dagrón. The book also includes a debate in which he mediated among scholars, filmmakers, amateurs, and aficionados of cinema. In it the participants discussed all the problems and frustrations related to this cinematic art, as well as film genres, directors, ideological frontiers, film boundaries, and the complexities involved with appreciating and understanding film.

Jorge Ruíz also has a place among the pioneers of Bolivian cinema. He produced several documentaries, and his ethnological film *Vuelve Sebastiana* (1953) centers on the "Chipaya" community and its social context.[8] This film has been considered to be the best of its genre. Jorge Sanjinés was another person who ventured into the business side of the film industry, creating his company Ukamau Limitada, which was successful in the production of the films *Ukamau* and *Yawar Mallku*. Ruíz and Sanjinés were joined by Antonio Eguino, and they became influential in the development of Bolivian cinema. Raúl Rivadeneira Prada refers to this media as "alternative cinema"[9] and recognizes the development of alternative film into alternative video, claiming that the creation of the "Movimiento del Nuevo Cine y Video Boliviano" is recognition of this evolution. Carlos D. Mesa Gisbert credits Jorge Ruíz, Oscar Soria, Jorge Sanjinés, and Hugo Roncal as the forerunners of the new Bolivian cinema and refers to Antonio Eguino as the best producer in the last twenty years.[10]

Ecuador

The cinema in Ecuador did not flourish as it did in other Latin American countries, nor was it considered as part of the cultural expression of the country. The cinema was not contemplated in the *Ley de Patrimonio Nacional,* nor was it included in art books and other means of communication. However, Ecuador did institute a "Cinemateca Nacional." Thus, cinema was an activity done by amateurs. In June 1979, the *Primer Encuentro Nacional de Cineastas* took place (organized by the Departamento de Cine de la Universidad Central, Quito, Ecuador). The participants' task was to collect cinematic works and video productions of the last five years and to work for legislation supporting this emerging industry. They also pledged to support the Asociación de Autores Cinematográficos.

Ecuador's cinema "aficionados" had an awakening after the *Conferencia General de la Organización de las Naciones Unidas para la Educación, la Ciencia y la Cultura,* held in Belgrade from September 23 to October 28, 1980. One of the resolutions of the conference stated that "la necesidad de salvaguardar las imágenes en movimiento que son una expresión de la personalidad cultural de los pueblos y que, debido a su valor educativo, cultural, artístico, científico, e histórico, forman parte integrante del patrimonio cultural de una nación."[11] Ecuador, as a member state of UNESCO, accepted the challenge and Benjamín Carrión of the Casa de la Cultura Ecuatoriana compiled a chronology of cinema in Ecuador from 1849 to 1986.[12]

The year 1981 proved to be important in the development of Andean cinema. The Casa de la Cultura Ecuatoriana and the Cine Club Ciudad de Quito organized the *Primer Encuentro de Cineastas Andinos.* Delegates from Venezuela, Colombia, Peru, and Bolivia attended this conference, as well as more than one hundred delegates from Ecuador. This meeting was important because of the collaboration that took place with institutions such as the Acuerdo de Cartagena, Convenio Andrés Bello, and the Andean Pact. These institutions were created for the advancement of the economical, educational, and social conditions of the region. During the conference some Andean cinema productions were shown, and representatives from the different cine clubs of the region met to exchange ideas.[13]

More than twenty films were presented at another conference, the *Ciclo de Cine Ecuatoriano,* organized by the Municipio de Quito. Ecuador was also present at the *II Festival Internacional del Nuevo Cine Latinoamericano,* and presented the documentary *Los hieleros del Chimborazo,* which won "mención especial" in La Habana, in 1980.[14]

There is a great deal of enthusiasm that remains for this art form, and hundreds of films have been produced in the form of documentaries, literary adaptations, musicals, etc. Unfortunately, the great majority of them have yet to be transferred to video. A list of films produced in Ecuador from 1949 to 1986, containing about 398 productions, which consist of documentaries, informational, educational, children's, and various other themes, is included in *Cronología de la cultura cinematográfica.*[15]

Peru

Peru had the first taste of cinema as early as 1897 with the presence of the President of the Republic Nicolás de Piérola at a cinema show at the Jardín Estrasburgo de la Plaza de Armas, Lima.[16] After this presentation, however, cinema in Peru remained largely ignored. In their analysis of the development of independent video in Latin America, Karen Ranucci and Julianne Burton see a future for this important instrument of communication in Peru. They state that "video in Peru is still in its infancy, but two recent organizations testify to an impressive degree of interest and potential."[17] Peru did indeed have a late start in legislating the cinema industry. In *Ley 19327 de fomento a la industria cinematográfica (marzo 28, 1972),* authorities provided some direction on the activities that would help develop the country's cinema industry.[18] In 1986 the Center for the Study of Transnational Culture-IPAL was formed. Its purpose was to research media and new technologies and to organize a video network. The idea was to promote research on the cinema of all Latin American countries. This endeavor had the support of UNESCO, which that same year helped them to start publication of the bilingual (Spanish/English) NTC/NCT Newsletter (New Communication Technologies). This publication addressed such topics as computer use and cable television. The Videoteca Alternativa was formed in 1986, and through collaboration and joint efforts with IPAL, they organized Peru's first video festival. Another achievement since the seventies is the organization of associations of independent filmmakers. According to Ranucci and Burton, the Grupo Chaski is composed of around thirty independent filmmakers and during the 1990s was the largest production collective in Latin America.[19] In Peru, the independent and national film and video makers created innovative and authentic works portraying their own realities. Thus, themes of urban cinema depicting the realities of city life were dramatically different from themes in rural cinema depicting peasant life in the rural communities.

Beginning in June 1980 and continuing throughout the year, the forerunners of the cinema industry met to discuss the state of this media in Peru. Among them were Isaac León Federico de Cárdenas, Juan M. Bullita, Nelson García, Ricardo Bedoya, José C. Huayhuaca, Reynaldo Ledgard, and Carlos Rodríguez. They concluded their "mesa redonda" in a positive manner, looking forward to better times and the development of a national cinema. Other important contributions such as Ricardo Bedoya's *100 años de cine en el Peru: Una historia crítica*[20] and *Un cine reencontrado: Diccionario ilustrado de las películas peruanas*[21] are serious works providing very good sources for research into Peruvian cinema.

Challenges in Building Video Collections

The Latin American video industry has expanded enormously in the last few decades and the university community has been struggling to keep up with the large number of videos that are produced each year. According to the Association of Research Libraries (ARL), although it has been more than twenty years since the introduction of this new media, video collections and services in research libraries still remain uneven in size and quality.[22] Librarians believe that one of the reasons for this slow start in developing media collections was the lack of bibliographic information tools on media materials, making it very difficult to acquire them. This lack of bibliographic information was even more pronounced with regards to Latin American video materials. Dolores Moyano Martin, editor of the *Handbook of Latin American Studies,* accepted the responsibility of providing information about Latin American media and began including a film section in the *Handbook* in the mid-1970s. Professor E. Bradford Burns from UCLA was given the task to write the film section, which appeared in volume 38 (1976).[23] When volume 42 (1980) of the *Handbook* was published the editors decided to alternatively include Folklore and Film in the volume designated for the humanities.[24] Thus, Humanities volume 48 (1986) contains an excellent film section written by Randal Johnson.[25] This was a testimonial to the immense popularity of Latin American films. However, with volume 52 (1990) the editorial board decided to stop including this section because they felt there were enough dedicated publications for the bibliographic control of this medium "due to the metamorphosis from an 'emerging area of study' to a field that has come into its own."[26]

Since then the ARL has taken the initiative to address the problems related to collecting video materials in academic libraries. In 1990 and 1995, the ARL conducted surveys inquiring about universities' video collections policies as well as the video services that they provided. The survey results indicated that the main obstacles of developing video collections included budgeting, cataloguing, space, and video personnel staffing. Librarians were afraid to extend their budget to acquire videos, which were sometimes very expensive. Cataloguing was also a problem, since the cataloguing of videos had to comply with the standards for cataloguing nonprint materials, thus requiring technical expertise in this area. Most university libraries also had space problems due to the special considerations needed for the shelving of videos. Finally, media collections needed to have a media specialist librarian, and university libraries could not allocate the funds to staff this new position.

Although there are still many challenges involved in the development of Latin American video collections in academic institutions, librarians have come a long way in the last few decades to improve both the size and quality of their collections. Modern bibliographic information tools have facilitated their awareness of the wealth of Latin American videos available, and thus their "wish lists" have grown by leaps and bounds. Now it is just a matter of addressing the budgetary and other problems in order to make those wish lists a reality.

Conclusion

As the information revolution evolves, libraries have to be the avant-garde in the collection of video materials. In particular, libraries with strong Latin American collections need to make as much of an effort in building their video collections as they do in building their collections of Latin American books and serials. Jerry W. Carlson states:

> The most distinguished Latin American films are often just as hard to find in Latin America as in North America. In Latin America, as in most of the rest of the world, the products of the Hollywood studios dominate the screens. Even so, the videocassette revolution has given many films a second life and the possibility of circulating among interested filmgoers who cannot take a week away from work to attend the Cartagena Film Festival or a retrospective at New York's Museum of Modern Art.[27]

Often the only access to these hard-to-find videos is via an academic library, so it is important that Latin American librarians realize the importance of building their video collections in order to capture these indelible images of Latin America unavailable in mainstream video outlets. No one can question that videos provide a vivid experience and a lasting impression on viewers. By building strong video collections, libraries can ensure that these experiences and impressions will be available to the many generations to come.

NOTES

1. Ana Maria López, "An 'Other' History," in *New Latin American Cinema*, ed. Michael T. Martin (Detroit, Mich.: Wayne State University Press, 1997), p. 135.

2. Raúl Rivadeneira Prada, *El cine alternativo en Bolivia* (La Paz: Signo, 1994), p. 9.

3. Riordan Roett, "Bolivia," in *Latin America and Caribbean Contemporary Record, v. 1, 1981–1982*, ed. Jack W. Hopkings (New York: Holmes & Meier, 1983).

4. Lawrence Whitehead, *The Cambridge History of Latin America*, ed. Leslie Bethell (New York: Cambridge University Press, 1991), 8:542.

5. Patricia Aufderheide, *Encyclopedia of Latin American History and Culture*, ed. Barbara A. Tenenbaum (New York: Charles Scribner's Sons, 1996), 2:161.

6. Alfonso Gumucio Dagrón, *Historia del cine boliviano* (México: Filmoteca de la UNAM, 1983), p. 11. This work was also published by Editorial Amigos del Libro (Cochabamba, Bolivia) in 1982 as part of the series of *Enciclopedia Boliviana*.

7. Carlos D. Mesa Gisbert, coord., *Cine boliviano, del realizador al crítico* (La Paz: Editorial Gisbert, 1979), p. 13.

8. Carlos D. Mesa Gisbert, "Cine boliviano 1953–1983: Aproximación a una experiencia," in *Tendencias actuales en la literatura boliviana*, ed. Javier Sanjinés C. (Minneapolis, Minn.: Institute for the Study of Ideologies & Literature, 1985), p. 203.

9. Rivadeneira Prada, *El cine alternativo en Bolivia*, pp. 37–43.

10. Mesa Gisbert, *Cine boliviano*, p. 185.

11. *Cronología de la cultura cinematográfica* (1849–1986) (Quito, Ecuador: Casa de la Cultura Ecuatoriana "Benjamín Carrión"), p. 69.

12. Ibid., p. 7.

13. Ibid., p. 55.

14. *Los hieleros del Chimborazo*, dir. Gustavo and Igor Guayasamin, 16 mm, color (Quito, Ecuador: Banco Central del Ecuador).

15. *Cronología de la cultura cinematográfica* (1849–1986), pp. 93–101.

16. Enrique Pinilla, "Panorama del cine peruano," in *El cine peruano visto por críticos y realizadores*, ed. Balmes Lozano M. (Lima: Cinemateca de Lima, CONCYTEC, 1989), p. 9.

17. Karen Ranucci and Julianne Burton, *The Social Documentary in Latin America*, ed. Julianne Burton (Pittsburgh, Pa.: University of Pittsburgh Press, 1990), p. 206.

18. José Perla-Velaochaga, *Notas sobre el régimen de fomento cinematográfico, la publicidad en el Perú* (Lima: Centro de Teleducación, Universidad Católica del Perú, 1975).

19. Karen Ranucci and Julianne Burton, "On the Trail of Independent Video," in *The Social Documentary in Latin America*, p. 205.

20. Ricardo Bedoya, *100 años de cine en el Peru: una historia crítica* (Lima: Universidad de Lima, 1994).

21. Ricardo Bedoya, *Un cine reencontrado: Diccionario ilustrado de las películas peruanas* (Lima: Fondo de Desarrollo Editorial, Universidad de Lima, 1997).

22. Kristine R. Brancolini and Rick E. Provine, *Video Collections and Multimedia in ARL Libraries: Changing Technologies* (Washington, D.C.: Association of Research Libraries, Office of Management Services, 1997), p. 5.

23. Dolores Moyano Martin, ed., *Handbook of Latin American Studies* (Austin: University of Texas Press, 1976), 38:59.

24. Ibid., 42:xvii.

25. Ibid., 48:59–77.

26. Ibid., 52:xxii.

27. Jerry W. Carlson, "Twenty-Five English Language Books That Discuss Latin American Film and Video," in *Review: Latin American Literature and Arts* 46 (fall 1992): 60.

APPENDIX

Andean Countries on Video: Bolivia, Ecuador, and Peru: A Bibliography

Bolivia

The Aymara: A Case Study in Social Stratification (1983)
Director: Ira R. Abrams
29 minutes; color; VHS
Coast Telecourses
Looks at the division that is caused by economic and social issues in northern Bolivia. Relationships between the Spanish-speaking mestizos and the indigenous Aymara Indians are examined.

The Aymaras of Bolivia (1989)
Director: Mike Lavery
28 minutes; color; VHS
Maryknoll World Video Library
At an ancient Aymara ceremony, two missionaries working with Aymara Indians share their views about the culture, land, and life.

Las banderas del amanecer (1983)
Directors: Jorge Sanjinés and Beatriz Palacios
100 minutes; VHS
Latin American Video Archives
Includes testimonies from workers and peasants who struggled against the Bolivian dictatorship from 1979 to 1982.

Blood of the Condor (1972)
Director: Jorge Sanjinés
72 minutes; VHS
Latin American Video Archives
This is one of the most controversial films ever produced in Latin America, which film documents a control program that sterilized Quechuan women without their knowledge or consent. The film was not shown in Bolivia until violent protest forced its release.

Bolivia (1989)
Director: Stan Walsh
color; VHS
Teacher's Discovery
This video allows its viewers to visit and discover Bolivia's unique culture through description and travel.

Bolivia (1993)
Producer: Shelburne Films
20 minutes; color; VHS
Altschul Group
Bolivians believe that their location on earth was chosen by Mother Earth and Father
Sun, and claim that the ancient city of Tiahuanaco credence its advanced culture. This
film also examines the aura surrounding this pre-Incan city. Furthermore, it describes
how Bolivia is dealing with the transformations that modernization brings.

Camino de las almas (1989)
Director: Eduardo Lopez Zavala
32 minutes; color; VHS
(Bibliographic information available from Coroma Hisbol)

The Courage of the People (1990)
Director: Jorge Sanjinés
90 minutes; VHS
Latin American Video Archives
This documentary film reenacts the 1967 miners' strike in the town of Siglo XX when
the Bolivian army launched a surprise attack upon the miners and their families. Many
of the original strikers and their families have roles in the story. The film is unambigu-
ous about its leftist politics and is critical of U.S. imperialism. It was originally released
in 1971 as a 16 mm motion picture.

Cuestion de fe (1995)
Director: Marcos Loayza
88 minutes; color; VHS

Ernesto "Che" Guevara: The Bolivian Diary (1998)
Director: Richard Dindo
94 minutes; color; VHS
Fox Lorber Home Video
A documentary based on Guevara's diary of his futile eleven-month attempt to incite a
Bolivian revolution in 1967.

How We See It
Producer: World Gospel Mission
28 minutes; color; VHS
World Gospel Mission
A video synopsis of the World Gospel Mission ministries in Bolivia.

I Have Spent My Life in the Mines: An Autobiography of a Bolivian Miner (1980)
Directors: Roy Loe and June Nash
40 minutes; color; VHS
Cinema Guild
Juan Rojas, a second-generation miner, and his wife provide a personal description of

their way of life in the Bolivian mines. A few scenes are dramatized, and show working conditions in the mines and the Indians' way of life. Rojas was a miner from 1934 to 1971. The video was originally produced as a 16 mm film in the 1970s.

Jonás y la ballena rosada (1994)
Director: Juan Carlos Valdivia
92 minutes; color; VHS
(Bibliographic information available from Instituto Cervantes)

Mama Coca: The Other Face of the Leaf (1994)
Director: Gabriela Martínez Escobar
26 minutes; color with b&w; VHS
East Bay Media Center
The Aymara Indians of Bolivia discuss their daily and sacred uses of the coca leaf. The video explains the Agro-Yungas project launched by the U.S. government, which replaces the coca crops with coffee. It also examines why the farmers do not want to participate.

Mirrors of the Heart (1993)
Director: Raul Julia
60 minutes; color; VHS
Annenberg/CPB Project
One in a series of programs looking at contemporary Latin America. This program focuses on identity, race, and ethnicity in Bolivia, the Dominican Republic, and Haiti.

La muerte del Che Guevara (1986)
Director: Lewis E. Ciannelli
92 minutes; color; VHS
Condor Video
An investigation into the capture and execution of the *guerrillero* who shook the world with his revolutionary ideas and actions. Che's diary is the background for scenes of guerilla life. Che and nine of his men are eventually all that remain. Hunted by a group of specially trained rangers, they cannot hope to escape.

The Music of the Devil, the Bear, and the Condor (1989)
Director: Mike Akester
52 minutes; color; VHS
Cinema Guild
Takes us to the heart of the Andes to observe the mood of the annual music festivals, showing ceremonies of the Aymara Indians who dress as devils, bears, and sacred spirits that come to life at carnival time. Inca mythology is described, as well as its presence in the lives of the Aymara.

Orphans of the Sun: Magic Healing, Magic Death (1986)
Director: Douchan Gersi
46 minutes; color; VHS

Gaylord Production Company
Explorers are on a quest to find the last of the Incas. In part two, the explorers discover healers capable of curing tuberculosis.

Para recibir el canto de los pájaros (1995)
Director: Jorge Sanjinés
90 minutes; VHS
Latin American Video Archives
A group of young filmmakers visit an Indian community to shoot a film about the conquistadors of the sixteenth century. As a result of their prejudices and ways of dealing with the native inhabitants, they end up repeating the same attitudes and biases they intended to condemn in their film.

The Principal Enemy (1974)
Director: Jorge Sanjinés
100 minutes; VHS
Latin American Video Archives
An examination of the life of the Quechua and Aymara Indian nations located in the Andean mountain ranges of Bolivia, Peru, and Ecuador. A leader recounts the centuries-long struggle his people have endured against the Spanish invaders and later the North Americans.

Ritual Encounter (1998)
Director: Ana Uriarte
40 minutes; color; VHS
TV Cultura
This ethnographic documentary shows the "dansaq," or dancers, impersonating the "Alacrán," the "Halcón," and the "Paqary" who dance during the Quechua Water Festival that coincides with the Catholic Festival for Saint Isidore, the Farmer.

The Secret Nation (1989)
Director: Jorge Sanjinés
120 minutes; VHS
Latin American Video Archives
Set in the mountains of Bolivia, this film chronicles a complex story of politics, morality, loyalty, and betrayal concerning the effort of the Quechua people for national identity and survival in contemporary Bolivia.

The Spirit Possession of Alejandro Mamani (1995)
Director: Hubert Smith
27 minutes; color; VHS
Filmmakers Library
In a Bolivian village, a village elder discusses his belief that he is haunted by evil spirits that are driving him to his death.

Taypi Kala: Six Visions (1994)
Director: Jeffrey D. Himpele
14 minutes; color; VHS
University of California Extension Center for Media and Independent Learning
This video follows several cultural groups who have gathered at Tiwanaku, located on the high plateau of present-day Bolivia. The film is made up of five parts showing different cultural accounts that define this mythical place.

Ukamau (1966)
Director: Jorge Sanjinés
70 minutes; VHS
Latin American Video Archives
A beautiful Aymara peasant woman is raped and killed while her husband is gone. Just before dying she names her killer. A year will have to pass before her husband can exact revenge somewhere in the beauty of the Andes. This, Sanjines's first feature film, earned him the Great Young Directors award at Cannes in 1966.

Wanted, Butch and Sundance (1993)
Director: David Dugan
57 minutes; color; VHS
WGBH Video
Documents the adventurous hunt for the physical remains and graves of Butch Cassidy and the Sundance Kid. The film attempts to answer the question of how they died and where they were buried.

Women of Latin America Series—Bolivia: Coca, Food for the Poor (1997)
Director: Carmen Sarmiento
13 videocassettes, 60 minutes each; color; VHS
Films for the Humanities
Bolivia: Coca, Food for the Poor is an installment in a series that examines Latin America through its women. Some of them run drugs across borders, fight in guerilla armies, give birth to children in poverty, search for sons and daughters who have disappeared during political oppression, and generally bear the burden of a third-world existence.

Ecuador

Columbus Didn't Discover Us (1992)
Director: Robbie Leppzer
24 minutes; color; VHS
Turning Tide Productions
Filmed at the First Continental Conference of Indigenous Peoples held in Ecuador in July 1990, Native Americans from North, Central, and South America hold a discussion on the impact the Columbus legacy has had on the lives of indigenous peoples.

A Continent Crucified: Ecuador (1985)
Director: Jack Pizzey

30 minutes; color; VHS
Landmark Films
Pizzey examines the dilemma of the division within the Catholic Church in Ecuador through its annual explosion of guilt during the Holy Week. But in the Andes, Pizzey sees in the missionaries a new threat to the church that may eclipse its entire future.

Ecuador (1982)
12 minutes; color; VHS
Lucerne Media
Looks at the hot Ecuadorian climate where an array of cultures thrives in the diverse terrain.

Ecuador (1991)
20 minutes; color; VHS
Journal Films, distributed by Altschul Group
Examines the social life and customs of Ecuador, as well as descriptions, travel, and the geography of the country.

Ecuador (1996)
Director: Francoise Gall
77 minutes; color; VHS
National Syndications, Inc.
Filled with authentic train travel, this exciting trek through Ecuador takes the viewer on a complete rail tour of the country.

The Ecuador and the Galapagos Islands Experience (1995)
Director: Peter Boyd MacLean
47 minutes; color; VHS
International Video Network
View the Amazon from above on an old army plane, watch the land slide by from the roof of a train, and bathe in hot water from a volcano, as traveler Justine Shapiro shares her experiences in Ecuador and the Galapagos Islands.

Fuera de aquí (1977)
Director: Jorge Sanjinés
110 minutes; VHS
Latin American Video Archives
A Christian group comes to dwell in the lands of an Ecuadorian peasant community. They preach that the end of the world is near and material possessions are useless. They convince some peasants to believe and to give their land to them. Soon after the Christians leave, the owners of a transnational company who claim that the land belongs to them visit the community. A struggle follows to get the peasants' land back.

Heaven, Hell, and El Dorado (1985)
Director: Jack Pizzey
30 minutes; color; VHS

Landmark Films
With a trader's truck Jack Pizzey plunges down the Andes into the Amazon basin, then by dugout canoe, steamer, and light plane he slides downriver among fortune hunters and people who may be their victims.

Minga: We Work Together (1981)
Director: Don Whyte
13 minutes; color; VHS
World Visual Educational Resources
A documentary on the customs and daily life of an Indian tribe in the Andes of Ecuador.

Nomads of the Rainforest (1984)
Director: Adrian Warren
60 minutes; color; VHS
WGBH Educational Foundation
Details an anthropological study of the Waorani Indians of the Amazon River in Ecuador.

South America: Volume 1, Ecuador (1993)
Director: Patti Ernst
23 minutes; color; VHS
Ernst Interactive Media Publications
An interdisciplinary study of Ecuadorian culture as seen through children's eyes.

The Tigress (1990)
Director: Camilo Luzuriaga
80 minutes; color; VHS
International Film y Circuit Inc.
This film, adapted from a story by José de la Cuadra, shows three sisters who are the proprietors of a cafe in an isolated area of Ecuador.

Time of Women (1985)
Director: Monica Vasquez
20 minutes; color; VHS
Women Make Movies Inc.
A detailed look at the impact of national economic policies on rural women. The film examines an Ecuadorian village populated almost totally by women because their husbands have been forced by economic necessity to look elsewhere for work.

Valdivia: America's Oldest Civilization (1990)
Director: Peter Baumann
43 minutes; color; VHS
Films for the Humanities
Investigation of the culture, arts, and lifestyle of the five-thousand-year-old city of Valdivia in ancient Ecuador, the oldest civilization in the Americas.

Weaving the Future (1997)
Director: Mark Freeman
24 minutes; color and b&w; VHS
Documentary Educational Resources
A contemporary study of the Otavalo Indians, an indigenous community living in the Andean highlands of northern Ecuador. Focuses on their fiscal success selling their weavings and crafts internationally.

Peru

Abisa a los compañeros (1980)
Director: Felipe Degregori
90 minutes; color; VHS
(Bibliographic information available from Instituto Cervantes)

Alias, La Gringa (1992)
Director: Alberto Durant
100 minutes; color; VHS
Facets Video
Feature film about life on a high-security prison island in Peru. Chronicles the adventures of la gringa, an affable criminal capable of escaping from any jail.

The Ancient Peruvian (1990)
Director: James Sage
29 minutes; color; VHS
International Film Foundation
Explores the Chavin, Paracas, Nasca, Mochica, Tiahuanaco, and Inca cultures of Peru, all pre-Colombian civilizations. Provides analysis from present-day archaeology and in-depth studies of ancient textiles, pottery, and gold.

Anda, corre, vuela (1995)
Director: Augusto Tamayo
95 minutes; color; VHS
(Bibliographic information available from Instituto Cervantes)

The Best of Peru (1987)
Director: F. David Clarke
30 minutes; color; VHS
International Video Projects
This program focuses a light on the people, major cities, history, and culture of Peru.

Blood and Treasure in Peru (1996)
Director: Bram Roos
50 minutes; color; VHS
A&E Home Video
The rich burial site of the Mochica Indians at Sipán in Peru came to the attention of

archaeologists when a grave robber revealed its location. Tells the story of this pre-Incan civilization as it is revealed in its graves and artifacts.

La boca del lobo (1990)
Director: Francisco J. Lombardi
111 minutes; color; VHS
Cinevista Video
A study of a violent encounter between the Peruvian Army and the Maoist Shining Path movement that occurred in Chuspi, a small, isolated village in the Andes.

The Bridge of San Luis Rey (1986)
Director: Rowland V. Lee
89 minutes; color; VHS
New World Video
An unusual story, set in eighteenth-century Lima, Peru, about a rickety bridge spanning a deep gorge for years, which suddenly breaks and sends five people plummeting to their deaths.

Caidos del cielo (1989)
Director: Francisco J. Lombardi
125 minutes; color; VHS
K-Films Video
Based on the novel *Los Gallinazos sin Pluma* by Julio Ramon Ribeyro.

Central and South America: Mexico, Nicaragua, Peru, Venezuela (1995)
Director: Horoaki Ohta
55 minutes; color; VHS
Multicultural Media
A video collection of folk music and dances from Central and South America.

Children of the Earth Series: South America Close-up, Peru Brazil (1997)
28 minutes; color; VHS
MaryKnoll World Productions
The segment included on Peru shows the village and school life of a thirteen-year-old Aymara Indian girl.

La ciudad y los perros (1987)
Director: Francisco J. Lombardi
135 minutes; color; VHS
Condor Video
Four angry cadets in a Peruvian military academy set off a chain of events that starts with a theft and ends with murder and suicide.

Cuentos inmorales (1978)
Director: Francisco J. Lombardi

90 minutes; color; VHS
(Bibliographic information available from Instituto Cervantes)

Dancing With the Incas: Huayno Music of Peru (1991)
Director: John Cohen
58 minutes; color; VHS
University of California Extension Center for Media and Independent Learning
Explores the lives of three Huayno musicians in contemporary Peru torn between the
national military and the Shining Path guerilla movement. The film also traces the roots
of Huayno music as well as its contemporary forms.

Discovering the Moche (1976)
Directors: Christopher Donnan, Richard Cowan, and William Lee
25 minutes; color; VHS
University of California Extension Center for Media and Independent Learning
Explores the art and iconography of the Moche people, an ancient Indian group of Peru.

Fernando de Szyszlo de Perú pinta un cuadro (1980)
Director: José Gómez-Sicre
21 minutes; color; U-matic
Museum of Modern Art of Latin America
After presenting some of the artifacts and masks of the artist Szyszlo, the film shows
him preparing and painting a picture.

Fire in the Andes (1985)
Director: Ilan Ziv
35 minutes; color; VHS
First Run/Icarus Films
In 1983, eight Peruvian journalists were murdered in the Andes. Marxist revolutionaries (the Shining Path), the government military, and local peasants were all blamed in
one form or another. This video investigates what took place, as well as examines the
thousands of disappearances and political murders that have happened in Peru.

La fuga del chacal (1992)
Director: Augusto Tamayo
90 minutes; color; VHS
(Bibliographic information available from Instituto Cervantes)

The Golden Coach (1993)
Director: Jean Renoir
103 minutes; color; VHS
Interama Video Classics
A video release of the 1952 English original version of the motion picture. Camilla is
the star of a commedia dell'arte troupe touring and performing in colonial Peru in the
early-eighteenth century.

Gregorio (1986)
Directors: Fernando Espinoza, Stefan Kaspar, and Alejandro Legaspi
60 minutes; color; VHS
The University of Iowa
Grupo Chaski's story of an Andean boy and his family who leave their mountain village in search of a better life in Lima.

El grito (Ojos de Perro) (1982)
Director: Alberto Durant
90 minutes; color; VHS
Condor Video
Compelled into rebellion against the tyrannical regime of a ruthless landowner, sugar plantation laborers form the first union in the country.

Inca Cola: Lima Peru Today (1985)
Director: Jack Pizzey
30 minutes; color; VHS
Landmark Films
Describes life in Lima and how Lima is perceived as the center for a modern Inca revival. Explains the difficulties faced by the people of Peru, and illustrates chances for the future.

The Incas (1988)
Director: Tony Kahn
58 minutes; color; VHS
PBS Video
Examines the work of three archaeologists currently excavating in Peru for clues to how the Incas lived. Describes the history, culture, and technological achievements of the Incan Empire.

The Incas Remembered (1986)
Director: Peter Jarvis
60 minutes; color; VHS
Monterey Home Video
Traces the history of the ancient Incan civilization from its beginnings to its demise at the hands of the invading Spanish conquistadors. Respectfully examines its scientific and architectural achievements.

In the Footsteps of Taytacha (1985)
Directors: Peter Getzels and Harriet Gordon
30 minutes; color; VHS
Documentary Educational Resources
Follows a group of Quechua musicians and dancers as they leave their secluded villages high in the Peruvian Andes and join throngs of other highlanders on the annual religious pilgrimage to the sacred peaks of Qoyllur Rit'i.

In the Shadow of the Incas (1990)
Director: Gottfried Kirchner
43 minutes; color; VHS
Films for the Humanities
The history of ancient Andean Indian civilizations in Peru and northern Bolivia is dis-
covered by examining the archaeological evidence that remains at various sites.

Juliana (1989)
Directors: Fernando Espinoza and Alejandro Legaspi
90 minutes; color; VHS
Grupo Chaski ZDF
A Peruvian feature film in Spanish.

Malabrigo (1986)
Director: Alberto Durant
90 minutes; color; VHS
Cinema Guild
Dramatization of social and economic changes in a coastal Peruvian village.

Manu: Peru's Hidden Rain Forest (1997)
Director: Alex Gregory
60 minutes; color; VHS
PBS Home Video
Following the eastern edge of the Peruvian Andes is the great river Manu at the heart
of one of the world's greatest natural secrets—the Manu Biosphere Reserve.

Mario Vargas Llosa: The Story of the Novelist who would be President (1990)
Director: Nicholas Shakespeare
60 minutes; color; VHS
Cinema Guild
Profiles the life and work of Mario Vargas Llosa, one of the world's greatest contem-
porary novelists, who made an unsuccessful bid in 1990 for the presidency of Peru.

Martin Chambi and the Heirs of the Incas (1986)
Directors: Paul Yule and Andy Harries
50 minutes; color; VHS
Cinema Guild
A full-blooded Indian, Martin Chambi made numerous trips into the countryside to
photograph Indian culture. Today, his work constitutes a moving record of an ancient
civilization under the influence of European colonization.

Maruja en el infierno (1983)
Director: Francisco J. Lombardi
90 minutes; color; VHS
(Bibliographic information available from Instituto Cervantes)

Miss Universe in Peru (1988)
90 minutes; color; VHS
Democracy in Communication
This film documents the contest and its effects on real life for women in Peru.

Mountain Music of Peru (1984)
Director: John Cohen
41 minutes; color; VHS
Cinema Guild
Shows the folk music, culture, and lifestyle of the people of Qeros, high in the Peruvian Andes.

Muerte al amanecer (1977)
Director: Francisco J. Lombardi
90 minutes; color; VHS
(Bibliographic information available from Instituto Cervantes)

Muerte de un magnate (1980)
Director: Francisco J. Lombardi
90 minutes; color; VHS
(Bibliographic information available from Instituto Cervantes)

Mujeres del planeta (1982)
Director: Maria Barea
30 minutes; color; VHS
Women Make Movies Inc.
Women of the squatter settlements of El Planeta in Lima, Peru, discuss their lives and challenges. This film shows their efforts to make better lives for themselves and their families in the face of hostility and indifference from the government and the upper class.

La muralla verde (1990)
Director: Armando Robles Godoy
110 minutes; color; VHS
Facets Video
The story of a young settler and his wife and son who try to escape the bureaucracy of their life in Lima by starting a farm in the Peruvian jungle, only to experience more difficulties.

Mysteries of Peru: Enigma of the Ruins (1993)
Director: Peter Spry-Leverton
50 minutes; color; VHS
Atlas Video
Part of a documentary series honoring the achievements of pre-Inca civilizations, this film inspects the ruins of ancient civilizations that thrived along Peru's coastal deserts.

NELLY S. GONZÁLEZ

Mysteries of Peru: The Lines (1993)
Director: Peter Spry-Leverton
50 minutes; color; VHS
Atlas Video
Part of a documentary series honoring the achievements of pre-Inca civilizations, this
film looks at the Nazca lines and vast animal figures drawn by ancient Peruvians in the
flat desert floor.

The Mystery of Machu Picchu (1996)
Director: Bill Kurtis
58 minutes; color; VHS
Films Inc.
Documents a Peruvian expedition that offers new findings about the mystery of Machu
Picchu, the famous lost city of the Incas.

The Mystery of the Lines (1994)
Director: Bill Kurtis
30 minutes; color; VHS
Films Inc.
Chicago-based astronomer Phyllis Pitluge and German scientist Maria Reiche discuss
their theories that the Nazca lines of Peru were actually part of a prehistoric agricultural
calendar.

Ni con Dios ni con el diablo (1989)
Director: Nilo Pereyra
90 minutes; color; VHS
(Bibliographic information available from Instituto Cervantes)

Not the Numbers Game (1996)
Director: Nupur Basu
43 minutes; color; VHS
Bullfrog Films
Shows how several developing countries have progressed in holding up their end of the
agreements signed at the Cairo Conference on Population and Development.

Paucartambo: The Rest of the River (1989)
Director: John Armstrong
60 minutes; color; VHS
Wombat Film and Video
The story of a group of kayakers who return to Peru to finish running the river that
defeated them two years prior because of extremely high water.

Peru: Between the Hammer and the Anvil (1997)
Directors: Audrey Brohy and Gerard Ungerman
51 minutes; color; VHS
Films for the Humanities and Sciences

Recounts the history of the Peruvian guerrilla group Sendero Luminoso, the Peruvian government's struggle against it, and the government's own brutality against the population. Also examines this conflict's effects on the economic and social conditions of Peru today.

Peru: A Golden Treasure (1992)
Director: Gordon J. Hempel
53 minutes; color; VHS
International Video Network
Travels to archaeological sites in Cuzco, Chan Chan, Lima, Machu Picchu, and other areas of Peru.

Peru of the Conquest: Where the Clock Stopped (1990)
Director: Gottfried Kirchner
43 minutes; color; VHS
Films for the Humanities
An exploration of the Colca valley—from the churches in Arequipa to the ruins, terraces, irrigation canals, and countless other fascinating structures built by the ancient Indians of Peru.

Peruvian Weaving: A Continuous Warp for 5000 Years (1980)
Director: John Cohen
25 minutes; color; VHS
University of California Extension Center for Media and Independent Learning
In this film the late Dr. Junius Bird of the American Museum of Natural History follows the beginnings of the Peruvian weaving tradition back to a pre-ceramic period.

Qeros: The Shape of Survival (1979)
Director: John Cohen
50 minutes; color; VHS
Cinema Guild
Looks at the life and hardships of the Andean nomads called the Qeros. This film outlines their methods of subsistence, their rituals and beliefs, and the discrimination and prejudices they have undergone.

Reportaje a la muerte (1993)
Director: Dany Gavidia
90 minutes; color; VHS
(Bibliographic information available from Instituto Cervantes)

El rey (1987)
Director: Juan Carlos Torrico
90 minutes; color; VHS
Madera Cinevideo
The story of a hero who unselfishly aids the people during the Mexican Revolution.

Secrets of Lost Empires: Inca (1997)
Director: Michael Barnes
60 minutes; color; VHS
WGBH Video
Explores what methods the Incas used to construct their citadels in the Andes, and how they built their suspension bridges out of only grass.

Seeds of Tomorrow (1985)
Director: Graham Chedd
58 minutes; color; VHS
Coronet Film and Video
Visits Ethiopia, Greece, and Peru to examine the genetic heritage of our foods and the current lengths taken to save the seeds that plant-breeders use to engineer new and better crops.

La selva (1993)
28 minutes; color; VHS
PICS/University of Iowa
Focuses on the peoples and industries of the rain forests of Peru.

Sin compasión (1994)
Director: Francisco J. Lombardi
90 minutes; color; VHS
(Bibliographic information available from Instituto Cervantes)

Todos somos estrellas (1993)
Director: Felipe Degregori
80 minutes; color; VHS
Facets Video
Todos Somos Estrellas is a fictional television game show in Lima, Peru. This film is an account of the Huambachano family, faithful watchers of the show who dream of the day their application will be accepted and they'll be presented with the chance to earn millions.

La vida es una sola (1992)
Director: Marianne Eyde
85 minutes; color; VHS
Films Transit
Depicts the brutality and violence perpetrated by both sides in the struggle between the Peruvian military and the Shining Path guerillas, and how this struggle affects a mountain village.

Villa El Salvador: A Desert Dream (1989)
Directors: Luc Cote and Robbie Hart
50 minutes; color; VHS
Cinema Guild

Gives an in-depth examination of Peru's Villa El Salvador, one of Latin America's best-organized squatter settlements.

Voices of Latin America (1991)
Director: David McCullough
59 minutes; color; VHS
PBS Video
Introduces the viewer to Latin American writers including Garcilaso de la Vega, Sor Juana de la Cruz, José Marti, Jorge Luis Borges, and Elena Poniatowska. Filmed on location in Mexico and Peru. Hosted by David McCullough.

Washington—Peru: We Ain't Winning (1992)
Director: Shari Robertson
58 minutes; color; VHS
Ophidian Films
Examining the experiences of a disintegrating society made worse by the abstract exercise of power from Washington, this documentary explains the growing crisis and its implications for all involved.

Where Land is Life (1990)
Director: Mark Saucier
28 minutes; color; VHS
Maryknoll Productions
Documents the struggle of the indigenous people of the Lake Titicaca region of Peru in reclaiming the land of the area as their own.

The World Through Kids' Eyes (1997)
67 minutes; color; VHS
Maryknoll Productions
An intimate and thoughtful look into the hopes and realities of children from all over the world. In Peru, the focus is on child workers.

Yaro Civilization (1990)
Director: Gottfried Kirchner
43 minutes; color; VHS
Films for the Humanities
Older than the Incas, but eventually dominated and assimilated by them, the empire of the Yaros is astounding. This program familiarizes the viewer with this largely unknown civilization and its artifacts.

Other Sources

It should be noted that there are no comprehensive bibliographies of Latin American video titles that are current. However, *The New Latin American Cinema: An Annotated Bibliography, 1960–1980,* compiled by Julianne Burton, can be of some use for older titles. Also, the most recent 23d edition of *The Video Source Book* contains descriptions and reviews of many Latin American titles.

BIBLIOGRAPHY

ABC-CLIO. *Video Rating Guide for Libraries*. Santa Barbara, Calif.: ABC-CLIO, 1990.

The Cinema Guild. *Latin American Studies Videos: New Offerings and Current Best-sellers from the Cinema Guild*. New York: The Cinema Guild, 1997.

Illinet Online. University of Illinois Online Library Catalog. Urbana, Ill. (March 22–April 13, 1999).

Instituto Cervantes. *Video Library Catalogue*. New York: Pine Graphics, 1997. Also at http://www.cervantes.org.

Latin American Video Archives. *LAVA Catalog*. New York: International Media Resource Exchange, 1999. http://www.lavavideo.org/lava/Welcome. cfm.

Maryknoll World Productions. http://www.maryknoll.org/MALL/VIDEO/video.htm. Accessed March 29, 1999.

Sennyey, Pongrácz. *Bibliography of Latin American and Caribbean Videos*. Urbana: University of Illinois Illipaths Series, 1996.

WorldCat. OCLC. http://www.ref.oclc.org/FSIP. Accessed March 22–April 13, 1999.

Modern Crises Facing
Andean Nations

15. ¿Continuará el Sendero?: The Shining Path after Guzmán

Peter A. Stern

September 12, 1992, was day 4,498 of People's War in Peru. Since achieving "strategic equilibrium" with the government in July of the previous year, the "Communist Party of Peru by the Shining Path of the Thought of José Carlos Mariátegui," known simply as *Sendero Luminoso,* had forged ahead on relentlessly in its drive to topple the government of Alberto Fujimori. A thoughtful observer might have noticed that Sendero Luminoso had largely abandoned its efforts at encircling cities from the countryside in the classical Maoist style and was instead concentrating, with its customary ruthless efficiency, on expanding its efforts in Lima's urban slums, known colloquially as *pueblos jóvenes.* But *limeños* simply knew that the fear and violence, which had long plagued distant provinces like Ayacucho and Puno, had come to the capital. Less than two months earlier a car bomb containing 600 kilos of dynamite had exploded in the upper-class suburb of Miraflores, killing twenty-two people in their houses, injuring more than two hundred, and flattening part of the district. More bombs followed, one of them destroying Channel Two's television station. Lima waited in dread for more strikes by the seemingly unstoppable Shining Path, led by its enigmatic philosopher king, Abimael Guzmán Reynoso.

But on this day fortune was to favor Alberto Fujimori, *el chinito,* the Japanese-Peruvian president who had five months earlier suspended parliament and enacted his own *autogolpe.* Alberto Fujimori was about to be the beneficiary of an enormous stroke of luck, although he had done nothing to merit it or to create the conditions that brought it about.

Even before unconstitutionally assuming supreme power, Fujimori had given free reign to the Peruvian military and, in particular, military intelligence or SIN *(Servicio de Inteligencia Nacional)* to conduct the antiguerrilla war without regard to human rights or international opinion. The army and SIN received the president's support, the SIN particularly under the influence of the Fujimori's *eminence grise,* Vladimiro Montesinos, a shadowy and unsavory character, once cashiered from the Peruvian army, and accused of being both a *narcotraficante* and a CIA informant. Meanwhile, the DINCOTE, or *Dirección Nacional Contra el Terrorismo,* part of the Peruvian national police, struggled using old-fashioned methods to try to track down the elusive *Presidente* Gonzalo. Within the national police, the *Grupo Especial de Inteligencia* (GEIN) was formed as a counterinsurgency intelligence elite. Eschewing the military's practice of torture, and the police's practice of rounding up suspects at random and then shaking them down for money, the GEIN represented a significant advance in a crucial element of the counterinsurgency effort, namely, intelligence. Detection of Sendero cadres went up in Lima after GEIN was formed. This group scored a real coup in June 1990, when a raid turned up portions of the Central Committee archives and the famous "Zorba the Greek" videotape, in which a tipsy Guzmán was caught dancing at a party—the first evidence that Presidente Gonzalo was even alive (Guzmán had not been seen in public since going underground in the early 1970s).[1]

Guzmán was known to be living somewhere in the Lima metropolitan area, as his psoriasis did not permit him to stand the conditions of the high Andes. DINCOTE had received information from an informer that Guzmán was hiding in a house in Surco. They tapped phones and searched garbage, normal police procedures, to try to locate the house where he was staying. One such tap indicated that the Central Committee of Sendero was about to meet, and watchers concentrated their efforts on the house at Calle Uno 459, Surquillo. It was rented in the name of a dancer, Maritza Garrido Lecca. Thirty officers, under the command of police General Antonio Ketín Vidal, raided the house. As the DINCOTE agents rushed into the room where Guzmán was sitting down watching television, "Comrade Miriam," Elena Iparraguierre, Sendero's number two, fought with the police.

"Enough with violence," shouted Presidente Gonzalo, "Calm!"

"Who are you?" Iparraguierre asked the agents.

"We are DINCOTE," they replied.

"You are the ones who killed my three sons," he said, referring to three *senderistas* killed in Canto Grande prison, an action in which the police had played little or no part. "Be considerate of President Gonzalo," shouted the highly strung Iparraguierre.

It was a highly dramatic moment for the police, overjoyed that *El Cachetón*, "Big Cheeks," had been taken. "Big Cheeks has fallen; ¡viva el PIP!" shouted an officer into his radio. Some of the cops cried with emotion.

When General Vidal entered the house, he politely exchanged pleasantries with Guzmán. "Doctor Guzmán, you believe in the dialectic. There are times when you win, and times when you lose. This time it's your turn to lose."

"I have only lost a battle," Guzmán is supposed to have replied. "You, General, know that the Party is everywhere in Peru. We've advanced sufficiently that we can't lose now."[2]

But Guzmán, the master strategist, was wrong. His arrest began the downfall of the Shining Path, a movement which had placed a great deal of faith in the myth of Presidente Gonzalo. The cult of personality which Guzmán had allowed to develop around himself was now to prove one of his party's greatest weaknesses. For the moment the tactical advantage lay with the government, no thanks to President Fujimori and his military. Standing orders to the police were that Guzmán was to be immediately turned over upon capture to the SIN. But Vidal disobeyed the orders and saved Guzmán's life. He called a press conference to announce the capture of Sendero's leader; by the time military intelligence officers arrived, several hours later, to take possession of Guzmán, it was too late to dispose of him in secret, as they would have preferred to do. Fujimori was out of the capital on a fishing trip when Guzmán was arrested, and he was furious at Vidal for not notifying him first. General Vidal was to pay for his audacity; when decorations were handed out for Guzmán's capture, Vidal was conspicuously passed over, and he retired shortly after the raid. Peru was stunned; in affluent Miraflores, limeños honked their car horns and hung out Peruvian flags.

Seized in the raid, it was rumored, were computer disks with more than six thousand names of party members and sympathizers. Hundreds of people were arrested within days of Guzmán's capture. President Gonzalo himself was displayed before the press in a specially built cage, dressed in a ludicrous black-and-white striped prison uniform that resembled something out of a Hollywood movie of the 1930s. (It was not customary Peruvian prison garb.) By this time he had recovered his customary poise and yelled at the reporters, urging his followers to continue the struggle. Contrary to what one might expect from a Latin American military, Guzmán was treated courteously after his arrest, and was not tortured. Used to being treated as royalty, he retained a bourgeois liking for wine and classical music. His interrogation revealed some interesting facts, such as that his mother had wished to have an abortion, as he was illegitimate *(un hijo natural)*. He still resented her for this. He admitted to being Presidente Gonzalo, and justified his crimes against Peruvian society by saying, "I am an atom of the universe. I have lit a bonfire; if I don't finish it, someone else will."[3]

What to do with Abimael Guzmán posed a challenge. Since the Peruvian constitution only allows the death penalty to be imposed for treason in time of war, he could not be executed, as many would have preferred. He was tried before a military court, and the sentence was a foregone conclusion: life in prison. But the Peruvian press openly discussed the dangers of holding Guzmán, and the absolute need to isolate the senderista leaders. Peru even thought it might need to copy the West Germans by building a special prison to hold Guzmán and his court, as the Germans had built a special facility for the Baader-Meinhof gang.

Only eleven days after Guzmán was captured, in the United States the Subcommittee on Western Hemisphere Affairs of the Congressional Committee on Foreign Affairs held hearings on "the Shining Path after

Guzmán." Gustavo Gorriti, a journalist who had covered Sendero for Caretas since the very first months of the war in 1980 (and who wrote the first full-length history of the group), gave a striking and prescient testimony. Gorriti noted that unlike other revolutions, which developed cults of personality around their leader after victory, Sendero developed a species of hero worship before the struggle even began. Gorriti also remarked that other fundamentalist groups, like the Hezbollah in Lebanon, survived the loss of their spiritual leader. He predicted that saving the life of Abimael Guzmán would now become the party's first priority, taking precedence over continuing the insurgency.[4]

Gorriti's prediction was soon a reality; no sooner was Guzmán sentenced to life imprisonment than "International Committee(s) to Defend the Life of Dr. Abimael Guzmán" sprang into existence in Europe and America. So did *A World To Win,* the glossy magazine of the Maoist Revolutionary Internationalist Movement (RIM), published in Belgium, turn its attention from People's War to defending the life of Doctor Guzmán. (After "the fall," senderista supporters stressed Guzmán's academic title.) "Move Heaven and Earth to Defend the Life of Chairman Gonzalo," declared an article in the first issue to appear since the capture. The RIM called upon people all over the world to defend Gonzalo's life.

> Millions of people worldwide who despised imperialism were looking to Chairman Gonzalo and the people's war he is leading to batter down the old social order and bring fresh revolutionary winds of liberation that know no bounds among the oppressed. The capture of the Chairman was a bitter blow to revolutionary people the world over, and the danger to the comrade's life is extreme. Defending the life of Chairman Gonzalo means defending the right of the slave to rebel.

The creed concluded by exhorting once again all revolutionaries to "move heaven and earth to defend the life of Chairman Gonzalo! We need Comrade Gonzalo at his post, in the forefront of the Revolution in Peru and the International Communist Movement! Fight for his Liberation!"[5]

Nevertheless, the RIM was not entirely distracted from its goal. A few days after Guzmán's capture, it faxed a document entitled *Construir la conquista del poder en el medio de la guerra popular.* In it, the party acknowledges that the process of constructing revolution may bring disequilibrium, and they must plan for such a situation. As Chairman Mao taught, "We pick up our dead, treat our wounded, and continue fighting." "The party can never be paralyzed because it is clear on the course to follow, and it is united."[6]

But the unity of Sendero Luminoso was shortly to be fatally fractured. Sendero's number three, Oscar Ramírez Durand, Comrade Feliciano, took control of what was left of the Lima metropolitan committee. Attacks by the Shining Path, which dropped drastically in the wake of the September arrest, began to increase again. A new offensive began in November, and armed strikes *(paros armados)* showed that Sendero still could make its presence felt in the slums around Lima, even if defections and surrenders were up in some areas of the country.[7]

It was the second thunderbolt of the war that shook the party to its very foundations. One year after his capture, Abimael Guzmán appeared in a video on Peruvian television (courtesy, of course, of the Fujimori government), beardless, thinner, and fitter-looking than at the time of his capture, and called for peace talks with the government! In two letters subsequently released to the press, Guzmán addressed Fujimori as the Peruvian Head of State (a gesture Sendero had never made before), and acknowledged that Fujimori had succeeded in "recomposing" the Peruvian state. Four other senderista leaders in jail subsequently wrote letters supporting their leader's call for the party's cadres to avoid engaging in "adventurist" actions, which would impede the implementation of a peace accord. While Guzmán did not speak of a cease-fire, the call to his cadres to avoid violence effectively signaled a totally new path for the *Pardio Comunista del Peru* (PCP). The fact that Fujimori released these letters days before a referendum on a new constitution (which would grant him wider powers) looked to many like political manipulation. But virtually all political analysts in Peru agreed that Guzmán's letters looked like political capitulation, and that the war was over.[8]

But the pundits had reckoned without taking into account either the determination of Sendero's new number one, Comrade Feliciano, or the resiliency and flexibility of party ideology. The new Central Committee denounced Guzmán's letters as a sinister farce mounted by the SIN. Who knew what pressures President Gonzalo had been subjected to in prison? Sendero mounted a series of attacks around Lima in the days after the publication of the letters, as if to drive home the point that Guzmán may not in fact have the capacity to effectively control the party from behind bars.[9]

Any pronouncement of victory seemed to be premature. Occasions such as the centennial of Mao's birth in December 1992, and municipal elections in January 1993 provided Sendero with the opportunity to mount renewed offensives; indeed, assassinations and car bombs continued, showing that the war was far from won. After all, the conditions out of which Sendero had emerged were at best, only slightly alleviated in the Peruvian cities and countryside. Indeed, a retired general and former military commander in Ayacucho pointed out that as long as levels of poverty, unemployment, infant mortality, and frustration and impotence among the young remained high, it would require only a leader, an ideology, and a party to fan the flames of revolution once again.[10]

In fact, after a long period in which the situation remained cloudy even to longtime Sendero observers, it became clear that Guzmán's call for a suspension of People's War had caused a split in the ranks of the party. Many senderistas, particularly those imprisoned in Canto Grande and other Peruvian jails, remained faithful to President Gonzalo. Others rejected his orders, and were determined to continue waging war to bring down the Peruvian state. The *gonzalistas* were renamed *Sendero Blanco;* the rejectionists *Sendero Rojo.*

The split between Red and White Shining Paths represented more than just disagreements on tactics. It illuminated a division over strategy, which went back years before Guzmán was captured. Astute Senderologists had noted a shift in tactics in the early 1990s, from a strict adherence to classical Maoist doctrine, which emphasized slow and steady advancement in the countryside, and an encirclement of cities from rural areas completely under insurgent control, to an overwhelmingly urban strategy. This abandonment of the Maoist blueprint may have reflected overconfidence on the part of Sendero's leadership. Their communiques reflected a belief that the collapse of the Peruvian state was imminent. Doubtless, they felt that the government's ineptitude at counterinsurgency would continue. The protracted People's War, which was supposed to last decades, would clearly be over in two to three years—a tremendous acceleration of the party's timetable.[11] There were those who differed from Guzmán in this regard, but they were effectively silenced by the party's dialectical process.

In January 1993, the government leaked a handwritten manuscript of Guzmán to the press, which manuscript illuminated his decision to alter course. Far from abandoning his faith in the ultimate victory of the party, Guzmán simply was changing tactics in light of altered circumstances, that is, his imprisonment. He did not denounce armed struggle, since, quoting Chairman Mao, "war is the highest form of class struggle." Communism, he believed, is the ultimate destiny of mankind, but now he predicted that the victory would take decades, instead of years (quite a reversal from his confidence *antes de la caída!*). He acknowledged the temporary ideological and political victory of imperialism (capitalist restructuring and worldwide neoliberalist policies), but believed that it was only temporary, and by the turn of the century would slow down. He predicted a return to great revolutionary struggles several decades hence, by the middle of the twenty-first century.[12]

In regard to his own situation, Guzmán justified his strategy change in strictly Leninist terms, in which the centrality of the party's leadership is unquestionable. "We believe," he wrote,

> that new, complex and very serious problems have arisen recently, present-
> ing the Communist Party of Peru with fundamental questions of leadership,
> and this is precisely where our party has received the harshest blow. . . .
> Thus, in these circumstances, the party and principally its leadership, is pre-
> sented with the need to take today a new and great decision, and, just as yes-
> terday we struggled to initiate the popular war, today with equal firmness
> and resolution we should struggle for a peace agreement.[13]

With the leader behind bars, out of touch with the cadres and thus unable to direct the party according to the correct political line, there was no possibility of developing People's War, only maintaining it. Guzmán went further, criticizing Comrade Feliciano's leadership and analysis of objective conditions. The Fujimori government selectively released these new "Gonzalo thoughts" and went so far as to fly Sendero's top leaders from prison to prison to meet and discuss the changed party strategy; Fujimori even made the gesture of presenting Elena Iparraguierre with a surprise birthday cake. The government's strategy was simple: Guzmán's seeming surrender would generate division and strife within the party and weaken the Shining Path.[14] In this strategy, Fujimori's government was correct, but the divisions were not enough to fatally wound the PCP. Reconstituted, the Red Path continued to prosecute the war. Since Guzmán could only control the White Path, and do nothing to influence the *felicianistas,* he had nothing with which to bargain, a weakness which ended the possibility of any peace negotiations with the Fujimori administration.

Another significant element in the prosecution of the war by the PCP was financial. With Sendero still very active in the coca-producing Huallaga Valley, the party would continue to have access to virtually unlimited amounts of cash, both from its "taxes" and "protection" of departing drug flights and from its direct involvement in the coca trade. One journalist reported that police believed that Sendero had a "war chest" of forty million dollars from taxes on the coca trade.[15] A former Drug Enforcement Agency (DEA) agent in Peru who had personally raided the Shining Path's jungle drug labs put Sendero's annual revenue at anywhere from fifteen to thirty-five million dollars.[16] A financial base of that scale has given Sendero, as it has Burmese, Afghan, and Colombian rebels, considerable independence. Exactly where the money has gone is a mystery, which has never been solved. It is highly possible that the production of *A World to Win,* which surely cannot finance itself through sales, is subsidized by the revolution's coca money, and other moneys may flow to support the Maoist International worldwide.

The key point is that as long as Sendero holds part of the Huallaga Valley and has access to the coca trade, it can remain a viable force, although eventually it may be so corrupted by drug money as to cease operating as a revolutionary force and become a purely mercenary gangster operation. Although a great deal of low-level fighting has taken place in the jungles of the Huallaga, the government has never been successful in rooting out either Sendero or MRTA, the Túpac Amaru Revolutionary Movement.

As the split between White and Red Senderos widened, the party fractured both inside the Peruvian prison system and throughout the countryside and shantytowns. "Down with the false peace" *(abajo la falsa paz)* is a slogan painted on many a wall; in *la lucha de las murallas,* the reply is "Repudiate the campaign against the peace accord" *(Repudiar la campaña contra el acuerdo de paz)*. Both Blanco and Rojo Senderos have resorted to dialectical arguments to support their positions. Guzmán and his supporters inside the prisons condemned attacks and other actions taken by the Rojos as "adventurism," "desperate acts," and "provocations" by deviationists. They were condemned as "ultraleftists following the false banner of maintaining a fight to the death," and "revisionist opportunists" whose actions actually helped the government.[17] Such an "alliance," they declared, threatened the life of the party itself, promoting its destruction. The Rojos struck back, characterizing the Blancos' support of a peace accord with the government as "a rightist opportunistic line." Some even advocated a *gonzalismo sin Gonzalo;* that is, continuing to follow *pensamiento* Gonzalo, but with the realization that Presidente Gonzalo has become Doctor Guzmán—almost as if the party's deity had been reduced to a mere mortal once again.[18] To political observers, the two opposing "lines" signaled the existence of two Senderos.

The war, of course, continued in both city and countryside. Attacks on police posts and patrols, particularly in the Huallaga, have continued, as have bombings in and around the Lima metropolitan area. But although the level of violence has decreased markedly from its high in the early 1990s, the Shining Path has shown a surprising resiliency in the face of an increasingly successful counterinsurgency mounted by the government's security forces. Several factors that have helped Sendero have been the autocratic Fujimori's increasing unpopularity, and the growing deterioration in the economic situation as the neoliberal policies of the government hurt the average citizen. One journalist noted that while Sendero may be in retreat militarily, it has launched an underground political comeback, attempting to gain footholds in the unions and neighborhood community organizations, which it had both formerly scorned and savagely attacked in the early 1990s.[19] "Sendero has ceased to be a destabilising factor," said José Arieta.

> They are no longer a threat to national security, as they were before 1992. But they are now involved in a camouflage campaign, building a political base in universities, unions, and neighborhoods. They have learned the lessons of the past. Militarily, they are in strategic retreat. But as prices go up, and wages don't, and more and more Peruvians go hungry, Sendero is cashing in on people's frustrations. Whenever there's a rally or a march, there are six or seven Sendero radicals to stir people up.[20]

Carmen Rosa Balbi, author of an essay on urban poverty and political violence in Peru,[21] seconds Arieta's view of Sendero. In an effort to reconstruct Sendero's legitimacy with the masses, the PCP is making an effort to reintroduce itself into neighborhood organizations and make its presence in the *barrios* more widespread and open. This is also a response to the government's complete inaction in the *barrios populares* and pueblos jóvenes in regard to providing any level of social services.[22]

These, of course, are classic guerrilla tactics, to which Sendero reverted once "strategic equilibrium" was lost. "Work with the masses," urged a captured party document. Whatever is left of the PCP is steadfastly convinced that what it terms "Yankee free markets"—the edifice of neoliberal globalization, which includes the IMF and World Bank—will create conditions under which the Peruvian people will turn once again to the party as their savior.[23] But sociologist Enrique Obando denigrates this forecast; Sendero has reckoned without the people, who he says have rejected the Shining Path's extreme methods. Sendero, he believes, will remain a terrorist movement without the support of the masses.[24] Few will forget or forgive Sendero's callous and horrifying murder of community activist María Elena Moyano in February 1992.[25]

And one by one, members of the party's Central Committee have been picked off, captured by the army and the security forces, tried before closed military courts, and sent to join Abimael Guzmán in the prison of the naval base off Callao. In December 1996, Elizabeth Cárdenas Huayta, allegedly "Number Two" in Sendero after Comrade Feliciano, was arrested.[26] The supposedly crowning blow came on July 14, 1999, when Comrade Feliciano himself was captured by security forces in the department of Junín, along with three women identified as Comrades Olga, Rita, and Raquel.[27] Four days later he was shown to the press in Lima, where he raised his fist in a socialist salute, but refused to talk to journalists. He was sentenced by the Consejo Supremo de Justicia Militar to life imprisonment for treason to the *patria*. But just two days after Feliciano's capture, according to a news report, Filomeno Cerrón Cardoso, a shadowy figure known as Comrade Artemio, was reported to be next in line and ready to replace Feliciano.[28]

In fact, according to senderologist Carlos Tapia, Ramírez Durand's capture will have far less impact than the government might have hoped. "Feliciano," he said, "may have been the symbolic head of Sendero Luminoso, but Artemio was the real power in the guerrilla movement. He will be able to replace Feliciano easily."[29] Little is known about the Shining Path's new leader; newspapers in Peru cited intelligence reports that said he is tall, in his late thirties, and is known for his ambition and aggressive personality. He was a mid-level commander in 1992, and escaped capture by hiding in the Peruvian Amazon. He rose quickly through the thinning ranks of Sendero's leadership, gaining power as a collector of "war taxes" from coca traffickers. It is money from drug traffickers that keeps Sendero going, said Tapia. Retired police general Hector J. Caro (a former DINCOTE director) explained that after Guzmán's capture, the guerrillas had only two areas of strength: one in Ayacucho's highlands, and the other in the Alta Huallaga. With Feliciano's capture, the Ayacucho area has been largely pacified, leaving only the Huallaga as a senderista stronghold. He characterized Cerrón Cardoso as a military hard-liner who cut his teeth exhorting money from coca traffickers and lumbering firms, and who lacks a grasp of Marxism and ideology that his predecessors had.[30]

So is the Shining Path a Hydra, growing a new head each time another is lopped off? Is the party a self-regenerating organism, which will never die as long as there are believers in *pensamiento Gonzalo?* The answer is not a simple one. All observers declared Sendero gravely wounded after Gonzalo's capture in 1992, and virtually all have declared it effectively neutralized after Feliciano's in 1999. But for a movement which has been declared dead and buried, the Shining Path marches on.

A Lexis-Nexis search shows a good deal of activity since the beginning of the year 2000 on the part of the *Partido Comunista del Perú* as well as by the security forces. On February 24, 2000, Sendero blacked out the whole of metropolitan Lima by dynamiting a power line.[31] Also in February, a riot by jailed senderistas in Yanamayo prison in Puno ended with one prisoner dead and a dozen policemen injured.[32] The inmates were demanding that they be treated as prisoners of war rather than as criminals.

On March 13, four senderistas were captured in the department of Pucallpa by marines.[33] Three more guerrillas were detained by antiterrorist police in the department of Piura on March 17.[34] On March 20 a band of senderistas murdered an evangelical pastor of the Pentecostal Assembly of God in the jungle department of San Martín, some 650 kilometers northeast of Lima.[35] On March 23 a clash between a patrol and guerrillas in the Ayacuchan jungle left one soldier dead.[36] On March 25, police captured four supposed guerrillas in the department of Lambayeque.[37] On March 30, two columns of guerrillas occupied villages in the San Miguel district of Ayacucho, in the Apurímac valley, calling upon the people not to vote in the elections of April 9.[38]

On April 6, one policeman was killed and two wounded in a firefight with senderistas in Tutumbaru, 100 kilometers northeast of Ayacucho. The police were on an antidrug patrol at the time of the ambush.[39] On April 9 a band of senderistas burned election documents in Uchiza and Tocache in San Martín in order to block people from voting in that day's presidential and municipal elections.[40]

But Sendero's activities in the countryside have been severely curtailed by the activities of the peasant self-defense patrols, the *rondas campesinas,* more formally known as the *Comités de Autodefensa Civil,* or CAD's. Carlos Iván Degregori and Orin Starn, among others, believe that the crucial role of the rondas has never been properly acknowledged. It was the "massification" of the patrols from Ayacucho to Junín, they argue, which ultimately forced Sendero to revert to a primarily urban strategy, to its eventual cost.[41] The rondas have not been disarmed, let alone disbanded, and in both rural and urban areas, they act as a deterrence less to terrorism and subversion, than to petty crime and juvenile delinquency. The Fujimori government passed legislation which placed the CAD's under the direct control of the armed forces, and charged them with not only combating subversion and drug trafficking, but also with supporting the military, security forces, and national police in the tasks of pacification and economic development.[42] The state has retained control of the lethality of the rondas by limiting their access to arms. Shotguns, issued in limited numbers first by the García and later by the Fujimori administrations, gave way to antiquated Mauser rifles, which were not given, but sold to peasant communities. The military also limited their dispensation of ammunition to the rondas to keep them dependent. Thus the patrols are at a disadvantage vis-à-vis the guerrillas, who have automatic weapons captured from the military and bought with drug money.[43]

In this way the government has done its best to ensure that there can never be a peasant uprising, which was initially a fear when the option of arming the peasants was first raised in the early 1980s. But some rondas have bypassed the limitations that the authorities have tried to place upon them; communities not in the sierra, but in the jungle areas of Apurímac have used money earned from coca sales to buy modern arms on the black market. Also, patrols that operate jointly with the military against the guerillas are given assault rifles, hand grenades, and even land mines—weapons which the majority of the highland rondas would never be permitted to possess.[44]

An article in *Caretas* in 1999 profiles a typical ronda in Ayacucho, where sixty adults and younger men patrol by night, mostly armed with wooden staffs. Their primary concerns are no longer armed terrorists, but gang members who dare to trespass on their territory, whom they catch when they can and turn over to the police. Their role can also be that of a neighborhood watch: a boy comes crying to the patrol, asking them to come to his house and stop the beating his father is giving his mother; a woman asks them to catch the delinquent who has stolen a chicken; a drunk disrupts a soccer match on a nearby field. These malefactors are conducted to the local jail where they spend twenty-four hours cooling their heels. Product of a terrible violence, the patrols now exist as a vital part of their rural communities, and despite what the government wishes, they are likely to continue to function if only by popular demand.[45]

Nevertheless, Sendero continues to advance on whatever front it can. Of late, much like the Zapatistas, it has taken to the Internet to wage People's War by proxy. "Committees to Support the Revolution in Peru" with a Berkeley, California, P.O. Box number, "The People's War in Peru—Information about the Communist Party of Peru," and "Sol Perú" are web pages extolling Abimael Guzmán, the party, and its struggle against imperialist capitalism, complete with portraits of the leader, and information on where to buy CDs and cassettes of music sung by party fighters.[46] As one writer commented sarcastically, even as Sendero continues to lose on the ground, it celebrates its imagined "virtual" triumphs in cyberspace.[47]

A World to Win continues to try to pump up enthusiasm, exhorting readers to "Perservere Through the Swirling Currents of the Two-Line Struggle," and "Unite the People Against the Fascist, Genocidal, and Country-Selling Dictatorship by Further Developing People's War." The latest issue of *AWTW* has a statement, dated July 1999, on the capture of Comrade Feliciano. The capture is painful, it declares, for the Revolutionary Internationalist Movement, and for all the world's Maoists, revolutionaries, and progressive people. After the arrest of Chairman Gonzalo in 1992, Comrade Feliciano assumed the responsibility of leading the Central Committee through this "bend in the road." Since then the PCP has never faltered in continuing People's War. The party has persevered despite the Right Opportunist Line, which has emerged from the party's ranks, and has insisted that the war should be abandoned in the face of hard blows. But this plan would mean abandoning the masses of Peruvians, from which the party has always drawn its strength. It has been the Central Committee's steadfastness and grasp of Marxism-Leninism-Maoism that has enabled it to find ways to continue the revolution. The statement calls for people everywhere to support the People's War in Peru, oppose the criminal Fujimori regime, and support the resistance of those heroic prisoners of war who are holding out against torture, abuse, horrendous conditions, and other forms of pressure to force them to make peace with the U.S.-backed regime.[48]

What follows are my own conclusions about the Shining Path and its future, formed by almost a decade of reading about the movement. It is clear that Sendero no longer presents a "clear and present danger" to Peruvian society. It is also evident that the party can and probably will fight on indefinitely, sustained by the drug money of the coca trade. Peru faces a low-level war stretching indefinitely into the future, in what might have been termed "Colombianization" before the recent escalation of that struggle began to threaten the very foundations of Colombia.

It seems inconceivable that Abimael Guzmán, Oscar Ramírez Durand, or any other members of Sendero's top leadership will ever be amnestied or released from prison, certainly not while Alberto Fujimori is in power. The men and women responsible for more than 35,000 killed in the war will not be easily forgiven. While more than 5,000 Peruvians sought amnesty under a government initiative and are at liberty today, none of the thousands of senderistas, blancos and rojos, in Canto Grande and other jails have been released. Do they have enough faith in their leader and their cause to sustain a lifetime behind prison walls? *Posiblemente, pero nadie sabe.* The pictures and recordings made inside the senderista wings of Peruvian jails showed men and women who were like acolytes of a new religious order. With their prison walls adorned with political slogans and hagiographic portraits of their leader, they marched and sang with a zealous sense of purpose:

Presidente Gonzalo es el guía
Con el pueblo del mundo triumfarán
Luminoso sendero transitamos
Lucharemos sin tregua al final

For many in the movement, the tenants of what the party calls *Marxismo-Leninismo-Maoismo-Pensamiento Gonzalo* is more than a political ideology; it is a faith with all the tenants of a religion, with both a godhead and a fanatical army of true believers. And for those who have been immersed in the dialectic, baptized with new names and reborn in the party, there is a terrible certainty: as long as there is one true believer, be he or she only a single individual buried deep in the cells of a Peruvian jail, the capitalists and imperialists of this world should tremble in fear.

NOTES

1. Lewis Taylor, "Counter-Insurgency Strategy, the PCP-Sendero Luminoso and the Civil War in Peru, 1980–1996," *Bulletin of Latin American Research* 17, no. 1 (January 1998): 51.

2. For an extensive account of the raid which arrested Guzmán, see "Fundamentalismo de la sangre," *Caretas,* no. 1228 (September 17, 1992): 10–24, 75.

3. "Criterio rayado," *Caretas,* no. 1229 (September 24, 1992): 10–15, 32.

4. U.S. Congress Committee on Foreign Affairs, Subcommittee on Western Hemisphere Affairs, *The Shining Path After Guzmán; The Threat and the International Response. Hearing, 102nd Congress, 2nd Session, September 23, 1992* (Washington, D.C.: GPO, 1992).

5. Committee of the Revolutionary Internationalist Movement, "Move Heaven and Earth to Defend the Life of Chairman Gonzalo," *A World to Win,* no. 18 (November 1992): 8–9.

6. Communist Party of Peru, Central Committee, "The Revolution Continues to Advance," *A World to Win,* no. 18 (November 1992): 34–36.

7. David Montoya, "Sendero Luminoso: la guerra no ha terminado," *Quehacer,* no. 80 (November–December 1992): 60–64.

8. Jo-Marie Bury and José López Ricci, "Shining Path After Guzmán," *NACLA Report on the Americas* 28, no. 3 (November–December 1994): 6–7.

9. Ibid., p. 7.

10. Sinesio Jarama, "Perú: un país subversive," in *Juicio a Abimael: Sendero, ideología y realidad,* ed. Raúl Vento García (Puebo Libre, Peru: Agenda 2000 Editores, [1993]), pp. 13–23.

11. Taylor, "Counter-Insurgency Strategy," p. 51.

12. Bury and López Ricci, "Shining Path After Guzmán," p. 7.

13. Quoted in ibid., pp. 7–8.

14. Ibid., p. 8.

15. Linda S. Robinson, "No Holds Barred," *U.S. News & World Report* 113, no. 12 (September 28, 1992): 49–50.

16. Steven G. Trujillo, "Peru's Maoist Drug Dealers," *The New York Times,* April 17, 1992, p. A27.

17. Hernando Burgos, "Un nuevo camino, dos senderos," *Quehacer,* no. 87 (January–February 1994): 31.

18. Ibid., p. 32.

19. See "Sendero Luminoso contra los ONG's," *Ideéle,* no. 35 (March 1992): 19–22.

20. Phil Davison, "Shining Path Emerges to Take Peru by Stealth," *The Independent* (London), July 27, 1996, p. 9.

21. Carmen Rosa Balbi, "Pobreza urbana y violencia política en el Perú: Sendero Luminoso," in *América Latina: violencia y miseria en el crepúsculo del siglo,* comp. Carlos Figueroa Ibarra (Puebla: Instituto de Ciencias Sociales y Humanidades, Benemérita Universidad Autónoma de Puebla and the Asociación Latinoamericana de Sociología, 1996), pp. 65–88.

22. Ibid., pp. 86–87.

23. Inika O'Hara, "Yankee Free Market Means More Misery for Peru's People," *A World to Win,* no. 20 (1995): 18–21, 87–88.

24. Enrique Obando, "Al final de Sendero," *Debate* 16, no. 79 (September–October 1994): 16.

25. See Robin Kirk, "Murder in a Shantytown: Shining Path's War on Hope," *The Nation* 254, no. 12 (March 30, 1992): 412–414; also "In Memoriam: María Elena Moyano," *Connexions,* no. 39 (1992): 18–19, among others. The Revolutionary Communist Party launched a scurrilous attack on María Elena Moyano's life and work with a pamphlet entitled *The Myth of Saint Moyano: Exposure of the Role of a Counter-Revolutionary "Martyr"* [Cambridge: Revolution Books, n.d.].

26. "Report: Police Capture Top Peru Rebel," United Press International, December 7, 1996.

27. "Fujimori anuncia la captura del líder terrorista 'Feliciano,'" Efe News Services (U.S.), July 14, 1999.

28. "Peru Rebels to Get New Leader," Associated Press, July 16, 1999. In an ironic twist of fate, Ramírez Durand's wife, Ernestina Hinostraza, alias *Camarada Marcia* or *Camarada Diana,* a member of the *Comité Principal* of Ayacucho-Huancavelíca-Apurímac, was captured at the end of the year, in a dawn raid by police and the SIN on December 25. "Capturada esposa de 'Feliciano,' mando político de Sendero," Efe News Services, December 26, 1999.

29. David Koop, "'Money Man' for Peru Rebels to Take Over after Leader's Capture," Associated Press, July 16, 1999.

30. Ibid.

31. "Apagón en Lima fue causado por voladura de torre eléctrica," Efe News Services, February 24, 2000.

32. "Motín dejó un muerto y 44 heridos, según el gobierno," Efe News Services, February 29, 2000.

33. "Capturados cuatro terroristas de Sendero Rojo," Efe News Services, March 14, 2000.

34. "Detienen a tres presuntos senderistas en operación antiterrorista," Efe News Services, March 17, 2000.

35. "Senderistas asesinan a un pastor evangelico en zona selvática," Efe News Services, March 20, 2000.

36. "Muere un soldado en enfrentamiento con 'senderistas' en la selva," Efe News Services, March 23, 2000.

37. "Capturan a cuatro senderistas en el norte peruano," Efe News Services, March 25, 2000.

38. *Latin American Andean Group Report,* April 4, 2000, p. 6.

39. "Un policía muerto y dos heridos en ataque senderistas en Ayacucho," Efe News Services, April 6, 2000.

40. "Sendero Luminoso quema documentos de electores en la selva," Efe News Services, April 9, 2000. Recall that *inicio de lucha armada* began on May 17, 1980, with the destruction of ballots in Chuschi.

41. See Carlos Iván Degregori, José Coronel, Ponciano del Pino, and Orin Starn, *Las ron das campesinas y la derrota de Sendero Luminoso* (Lima: IEP, 1996).

42. Decreto Legislativo 741 *(Ley de Reconocimiento de los Cómites de Autodefensa),* chapter 1, articles 1–3, and Decreto Supremo 077 *(Reglamento de Organización y Funciones de los Cómites de Autodefensa),* chapter 1, articles 3–16; cited in Mario A. Fumerton, "Rondas Campesinas in the Peruvian Civil War: Peasant Self-Defense Organizations in Ayacucho," LASA 2000 presentation, p. 17.

43. Fumerton, "Rondas Campesinas in the Peruvian Civil War," pp. 17–18.

44. Ibid., p. 18.

45. Fernando Vivas, "Ayacucho 99: Las rondas," *Caretas,* no. 1568 (May 20, 1999): 48–52, 86.

46. See http://www.csrp.org/index.html and http://www.blythe.org/peru-pcp/.

47. Eduardo Toche, *Quehacer,* no. 120 (September–October 1999): 82–84, at http://www.sendero.org.

48. "Statement on the Capture of Comrade Feliciano," *A World to Win,* no. 25 (1999), frontispiece.

16. A Still Unreconciled Chile Faces the Millennium: The Pinochet Crisis

Anne C. Barnhart-Park

In 1998, Spain asked Scotland Yard to detain General Augusto Pinochet Ugarte, who was staying at a London hospital; Spanish Judge Baltasar Garzón wished to extradite Pinochet and have him face charges for genocide and crimes against humanity for actions that occurred while he was president of Chile. Three months later, Jack Straw, British Home Secretary, agreed to allow Pinochet to be extradited to Spain; the ruling was challenged and in March of 2000, the former president of Chile was allowed to return home.

During the sixteen months Pinochet was under house arrest in London, arguments were made for and against his extradition. During the hearings challenging Straw's December 1998 ruling, evidence of Pinochet's alleged involvement with human rights violations was entered into the public record. Spanish officials charged him with thirty-five counts of torture and conspiracy to torture.[1]

Other countries (Belgium, France, and Switzerland) also filed petitions to extradite the retired Chilean commander-in-chief of the armed forces. Argentinean officials have reopened the 1974 assassination case of General Carlos and Sofía Prats. A fear, perhaps valid, raised by both sides is that some military leaders are capitalizing on the anti-Pinochet sentiment and using him as a scapegoat. Some former military allies of Pinochet have begun speaking against him. Those involved in the Letelier car bomb (1976, Washington, D.C.) and the Caravan of Death (in 1973 when at least seventy political prisoners were tortured, then executed by a roving hit squad) have implicated Pinochet, giving the United States the information it needs to prosecute the former president if it so chooses.

Pinochet is even being persecuted at home. A panel of twenty-two judges has decided (13-9) that the Senator-for-life[2] can be stripped of his immunity and put on trial for abuses committed under his government. There are 110 lawsuits currently lodged against the eighty-four-year-old general. Pinochet's lawyers have promised to file an appeal. Because of his failing health, it is likely that Pinochet will die before any of the suits actually goes to trial.

Regardless of the outcome, it cannot be ignored that this man has created a national and international crisis. On the national level, Chileans have divided loyalties—a condition vividly demonstrated in the 1999/2000 presidential election.[3] The global community is also trying to decide what to do with him: should gross human rights violations be prosecuted? Was Chile in a "state of war" for the seventeen years of Pinochet's rule? If he should be tried, should it be at a national or international level? Does the 1978 Amnesty Law of Chile stand? If his own people have granted him immunity, do other countries have to respect that? Can Chile revoke his immunity? Can the world trust that Chile will be able to bring him to justice?

While the newspaper articles give some background information about why Pinochet was arrested, they fail to provide a deep analysis of the horrors of the Pinochet dictatorship, the realities of the Chilean transition to democracy, and the frustration of those who are still seeking justice for the victims of human rights violations. This bibliography presents the reader with a means of accessing the above information and offers tools for taking it to a more profound level.[4]

There is a great deal of Chilean narrative and drama (some more fictionalized than others) that depicts the society under the dictatorship as well as the struggle for self-definition during the transition. This bibliographic guide aims to provide a social and historical context for today's current events and this generation of literature.

Because of the specificity of the topic, there are no traditional "reference" works that fit neatly into this bibliography since the bibliographies of Chilean history that exist are all too old to encompass these recent events. Therefore, texts were targeted that were determined to be key texts in the disciplines of economics, sociology, anthropology, political science, peace studies, and history that represent different ways of approaching today's Chile.

This bibliography guide includes monographs in English and Spanish covering a wide range of social science disciplines. While compiling the guide, I found that arranging the works by academic discipline seemed too contrived and limiting. Instead, I have attempted to group the items together by topics that relate to investigating the current human rights issues of Chile. The ten topics I have identified are the following:

  I. Chilean History (pre–September 11, 1973)

  II. Chilean History (September 11, 1973–1988)

  III. General Augusto Pinochet Ugarte

  IV. Military Regimes

  V. Human Rights Bibliographies

  VI. Human Rights—Chile

  VII. Specific Cases of Human Rights Violations in Chile

  VIII. Latin America—The Transition to Democracy

IX. Chile's Transition to Democracy
X. Justice and Reconciliation
While I attempted to create logical groupings, these, too, are sometimes a little arbitrary—the borders are often blurry and some titles could be in more than one category.

I limited my scope to monographs, even though I realize that articles would add insight especially since new developments are added every day. I would like to see this project continued to include a thorough search through the journal literature. I realize, however, that bibliographies are incomplete by nature, especially when addressing such a timely and dynamic topic as this one.

The Texts[5]

I. Chilean History (pre–September 11, 1973)

In order to understand what is happening today in Chile, London, and Spain, it is necessary to look at Chile's history. Brian Loveman's *Chile: The Legacy of Hispanic Capitalism* remains the primary text for Chilean history. The book was first published in 1979, and the second edition was released in 1988. This book offers solid background to Chile's history, a user-friendly index, and an introductory bibliographic essay. It should be considered a standard text in the discipline. A new edition will probably be published in 2001.[6]

In 1986, Clodomiro Almeyda published *Chile: más allá de la memoria,* the proceedings of a September 1985 Universidad Nacional Autónoma de México conference of the same name. By starting with quotes by Salvador Allende and Pablo Neruda, Almeyda indicates to us that he is not a Pinochetista. The contributors (Almeyda, Anselmo Sule, Jorge Carpizo, Volodia Teitelboim, Pablo González Casanova, Pedro Vuskovic, Hugo Mivanda, Alejandro Witker, Jaime Suárez, and Hugo Zemelman) have all written essays about Chile in which a main theme is a great deal of nostalgia about Allende and his government.

II. Chilean History (September 11, 1973–1988)

Lois Hecht Oppenheim's *Politics in Chile: Democracy, Authoritarianism, and the Search for Development* (1993) attempts to be the first text of its kind to address the socioeconomic and political history of Chile under both Allende and the dictatorship. The author (at the time of publication: professor and chair of the Department of Political Science, Lee College, University of Judaism, Los Angeles) includes a hefty bibliography divided into subcategories such as "General books about Chilean politics" and "Books focusing on Chile under the military and the transition to democracy." Her bibliography alone is a valuable starting place for researchers. Her text includes some firsthand experiences (the author lived in Chile during the coup) that are unfortunately often buried in her notes. While the book does work, as the author states it, in "broad strokes," it offers a good basic sociopolitical spectrum for the twenty-year period she covers.

During the Pinochet regime, Chile's economy was a laboratory for the University of Chicago's School of Economics. Many works about the dictatorship focus on the economic policies of that time. Phil O'Brien and Jackie Roddick published *Chile: The Pinochet Decade: The Rise and Fall of the Chicago Boys* with the London Latin American Bureau in 1983. The text focuses on the economic experiments of the Chicago Boys in the context of their efforts to correct the economic crisis begun under Allende. The book presents basic statistical information for easy reference as well as a chronology and list of political parties and trade unions. The text also contains many political cartoons. Unfortunately, the book does not specify the origin of the cartoons, so it is impossible to fully appreciate them without knowing their original context.

Juan Gabriel Valdés published his Princeton dissertation as *Pinochet's Economists: The Chicago School in Chile* (1995). He explores the background of the Chicago Boys, their influence in Chile's economy, and their impact through the transition. Using the economic crisis of 1982 as a dividing point, the author discusses the two phases of "neo-liberal revolution." In the first phase, the reforms were imposed repressively as ideology was transferred from the United States to Chile. The second phase is described as "progress towards a stable economy, and the return to democracy" (15). Valdés also covers, in broad strokes, the roles of the Chicago Boys during the transition. He identifies where they still hold influence, "be it through rightwing parties, consultancy firms or think-tanks" (254) or be it through the nomination in 1989 of former Treasury Minister Hernán Büchi as the Pinochetista candidate as "the last political expression of the technocrats' endeavor to govern Chile purely from an economic perspective" (262).

The Brookings Institution and the United Nations Research Institute for Social Development co-sponsored Javier Martínez and Alvaro Díaz's publication, *Chile: The Great Transformation* (1996). While this text is not as groundbreaking as Valdés', it is interesting to note the authors' bias. The authors of this work endeavor to show how Chile's economic transformation was an isolated case because the authors fear that the same repressive methods will be used in different countries hoping to pull themselves out of an economic crisis.

Much of the literature about life under the dictatorship has been written by journalists. Perhaps, because of their training, journalists are able to get closer to people and expose a more human side of this time. A Chilean journalist and literary critic who was also a Communist Party senator, Volodia V. Teitelboim, secretly returned to Chile during the dictatorship after having been exiled. His book *En el país prohibido* (1988) describes his clandestine return home. Teitelboim's book is playful as he starts with a quote by Pinochet about how dangerous Teitelboim is:

> [Teitelboim] fue quien escribió las más fantásticas patrañas sobre el lugar de los relegados. Era un experto en lavar cerebros a los chilenos ingenuos, exponiendo su ideología demagógica con apariencia de hombre bonachón y afable, que más parecía cura de pueblo que comunista. Este agente soviético disfrazaba con una facilidad impresionante su traición a Chile, y en cada oportunidad en que encontraba circunstancias propicias hacía creer a los chilenos las dulzuras del comunismo, al que ensalzaba con su adormecedor "canto de sirena."
>
> El hipócrata y extraño personaje, ese tartufo, verdadero artífice del embuste y la calumnia, que escribía las más fantásticas patrañas, experto en lavar cerebros a los chilenos ingenuos, demagogo con apariencia de hombre bonachón y afable que más parecía cura de pueblo que comunista, ese agente soviético, que entonaba un adormecedor "canto de sirena," se proponía entrar a Chile (7).[7]

The text itself presents vignettes of Teitelboim's travels through his country and his impressions of life under the dictatorship. While the topic is serious, the author's writing is enjoyable as he draws on his literary background generating witty chapter titles such as "El Coronel tiene quien le telefonée."[8]

Another journalist was part of the interesting pair that teamed up to create *A Nation of Enemies: Chile under Pinochet* (1993). Pamela Constable was a reporter for the *Boston Globe* and her co-author, Arturo Valenzuela, was the director of Latin American Studies at Georgetown University. The text is complemented by detailed notes and a useful index. While their viewpoint has an anti-Pinochet bias, the text tries to address the different groups of people affected by and participating in the dictatorship. Each chapter covers a different group: the soldiers (background of the structure of the armed forces), the dictator, the law, the technocrats, the rich, and the poor. While the book includes interesting candid interviews with members of each group, the authors speak in such generalizations as to force the reader to question their conclusions. The greatest flaw of this work is that one can read the entire book from cover-to-cover and never know that Chile has an indigenous population (and a sizeable one at that!).

Like Constable, Mary Helen Spooner is a journalist who lived in Chile for nine years. There she worked as a freelance correspondent and was able to interview citizens, politicians, Pinochetistas, and supporters of the opposition. In *Soldiers in a Narrow Land: The Pinochet Regime in Chile* (1994), her primary focus is on the military as she draws on Pinochet's words, newspaper accounts, and personal interviews with those involved. As a result of her years of experience living in Chile, during which she gathered materials, this work wonderfully and tragically bears witness to the culture of dictatorship in Chile.

In his annotation in the *Handbook of Latin American Studies,* Michael Fleet notes that Ascanio Cavallo, Manuel Salazar Salvo, and Oscar Sepúlveda Pacheco's important publication, *Chile, 1973–1988: la historia oculta del régimen militar* (1989), "offered Chileans their first real look at the regime's inner workings. It took the country by storm, selling out its first (1988) edition of more than 10,000 copies in a matter of weeks, and winning that year's Interamerican Press Society's Human Rights prize" (HLAS volume 55, item# bi92011812). The authors, all journalists, display years of research in this 600-page volume, written in the style of their profession with short easy-to-skim paragraphs. While there is a fairly detailed table of contents (listing fifty-three titled chapters), an index would have been of great help to the readers. Hidden in the text are useful informational charts with titles such as "Jefes de zonas en Estado de Emergencia" and "Primer Gabinete," but because of the lack of an index, this information gets lost. The book ends with a dramatic chapter about the victory of the No on October 5, 1988.

Around the same time as Cavallo, et al., Grinor Rojo and John J. Hassett published another anthology entitled *Chile: Dictatorship and the Struggle for Democracy* (1988). The introduction's tone alerts the reader that the authors all share an anti-Pinochet perspective. This work was written in anticipation of the 1988 plebiscite (which the authors imply might not happen).

In 1998 Patricia Verdugo published *Interferencia secreta,* a book with an accompanying compact disc. The premise of this publication is that someone secretly intercepted and recorded communications between the heads of the armed forces on September 11, 1973. The compact disc contains the recordings of these communications, and the book has transcriptions to compensate for the poor sound quality, though I cannot verify the authenticity of the recordings. The book also contains chapters on the golpe and on Allende. Verdugo uses the recordings to paint a portrait of a troubled Pinochet, one who was uncertain about the golpe and whom the other golpistas did not trust since he was so high ranking under Allende. She also shows the others as cowardly traitors.

III. General Augusto Pinochet Ugarte

While Pinochet is the main figure in most of the books about Chile from 1973 to the present, there are also several books dedicated to him. Raquel Correa and Elizabeth Subercaseaux are two journalists who conducted five three-hour interviews with General Pinochet. In *Ego sum Pinochet,* the writers present a Pinochet who is both loved and hated in this text of interview transcripts interspersed with biographical information. From the text it is obvious that Pinochet was controlling the interviews and carefully selecting what he said. When they pressed him about human rights, however, more revealing comments were made by the controversial leader, such as his defensive cry: "¡Yo no soy un dictador y mi gobierno no ha atropellado los Derechos

Humanos! ¡Todo lo contrario!" (13).[9] Perhaps some of the more chilling comments that help shed light on some of the frustration felt today by the Chileans were Pinochet's thoughts about how Hitler was not 100 percent responsible for the actions of the SS since they were not the army and Hitler might not have known what the SS was doing (41). This eerily mirrors Pinochet's relationship with the DINA (the Chilean secret police).

Another series of interviews with the general was published in 1999 by María Eugenia Oyarzún, *Augusto Pinochet: diálogos con su historia: conversaciones inéditas*. Oyarzún is a journalist, and in her questions to Pinochet she refers to previous interviews they conducted in the 1970s. She obviously has a history working with Pinochet, and that coupled with the fact that the conversations that make up this text occurred over the course of three years (from July 1995 to March 1998) creates a familiar tone between the participants. In Correa and Subercaseaux's book, Pinochet seems more defensive. Several years later, when Oyarzún begins interviewing the ex-president of the "gobierno de las Fuerzas Armadas y de Orden" (11), one hears the voice of a more relaxed Pinochet. This text provides an interesting opportunity to hear Pinochet speak about his life. There are examples of his arrogance: "Si Cristo perdonó a sus verdugos, ¿cómo no voy a poder perdonar yo, que soy un pobre hombre, a los que son más pobres de espíritu que yo . . . ?" (12). And, he uses the book as an opportunity to promote his political agenda and his role in Chile's economic success. He also briefly reflects on Chile's history of amnesty laws as well as his assessment of the transition governments. At the end of the book, Oyarzún asks him about the noise being made by Baltasar Garzón (Pinochet had not yet made his fateful trip to London). Pinochet is confident as he states that he was not responsible for any human rights violations and that such charges cannot be substantiated.

General Pinochet has also contributed to his biographical literature with his multivolume series *Camino recorrido: memorias de un soldado* (volume 1, 1990; volume 2, 1991; volume 3, part 1, 1993; volume 3, part 2, 1994). These are not brief memoirs; each monograph is 300–400 pages. Volume 1 starts with his childhood and continues through the coup. Subsequent volumes have a chapter dedicated to each year of his rule with subdivisions for special events such as "First press conference" and "First anniversary of September 11": more than 1200 pages of soundbites with no apologies and no regrets. When writing about controversial topics, such as the Letelier case, the author simply assumes the reader is familiar with the case and merely summarizes Chile's policies and actions regarding the situation. While he includes a lot of statistics—especially about alleged arms holdings of "terrorists"—he offers no citations or bibliographic references.

From the reading of bits and pieces of this text, it is very understandable why many people want Pinochet to be tried for his actions. He does not seem to understand that he did anything wrong. In his contributions to HLAS, Michael Fleet shares that he, too, became tired of the egomania:

> Another volume in Pinochet's seemingly endless reconstruction of his years in power, this time covering the period 1981–1986 . . . In this final(?) install-ment of his memoirs, Pinochet. . . . (HLAS volume 55, item# bi94012424; HLAS volume 57, item# bi96002832)

Pinochet's monographic series irritated many people. A year after the final(?) part was issued, Jaime Castillo Velasco published a response, *¿Hubo en Chile violaciones a los derechos humanos? Comentario a las memorias del General Pinochet.* The author presents himself as a moderate—he opposed Allende but did not whole-heartedly support the coup. The author is disgusted that Pinochet refused to own up to his deeds and that people claim that Chile "está reconciliado" (is reconciled). Castillo Velasco refuses to accept that human rights violations were part of "war" and he pulls quotes from Pinochet's memoirs to show double-talk and contradictions. While this text has an angry tone, it represents well the astonishment with which many Chileans received Pinochet's version of events.

The above cited HLAS annotation for Mary Helen Spooner's book men-tioned another text about the general himself: José Antonio Gurriarán, *Chile: el ocaso del general* (1989). Gurriarán is a Spanish journalist who wrote *¿Caerá Allende?* in 1972. Part of the press pool in Santiago at the time, the author starts his text with the "golpe blando"—"soft coup," the plan to nullify the referendum by inciting riots between the No and the Sí in 1988 to justify military action. The journalist presents material in the form of various inter-views. While not directly related to the fall of Pinochet, the excerpts from his 1972 interviews with Allende (previously unpublished, per Allende's request) about the then-president's perceptions of the military were fascinating as seen through the lenses of hindsight. Gurriarán also interviews General Leigh, head of the air force under Pinochet and supporter of the No. Relevant to today's controversy is an interview with Adolfo Suárez, the first democratically elected president of post-Franco Spain. Suárez compares the transitions to democracy in both countries, but never mentions human rights issues.

IV. Military Regimes

While Pinochet is still the main character in these books, some authors focus more on the military in Chile. Pablo Corlazzoli wrote a cross-cultural study, *Los régimenes militares en América Latina: estructuración e ideología: los casos de Brasil, Chile y Uruguay* (1987). In his introduction, the author promises to look at how three entities (United States, Latin American nations, and multinational corporations) interact during military rule. His primary focus is on national security doctrines. Because of the lack of an index or detailed table of contents, it is difficult to make use (or sense) of this text.

In *Los militares en el poder: régimen y gobierno militar en Chile 1973–1986* (1987), Augusto Varas analyzes the military government by considering the history of civil-military relations in Chile. He also looks at Chile's armed forces as a means of national defense under the dictatorship.

While the two previous texts do provide useful information, they pale when compared to Karen L. Remmer's *Military Rule in Latin America*. This oft-cited work, published in 1989, has two parts: part 1 contains comparative perspectives on military rule in Latin America; part 2 covers military rule in Chile. The author does not address human rights violations. Instead, she begins by focusing on the nature of authoritarianism in general and then moves to use Chile as a case study. Her solid text is supported by numerous figures and tables and more-than-ample notes at the end of each chapter.

Pamela Lowden focuses on the role of the Roman Catholic Church in Chile under the dictatorship in her book *Moral Opposition to Authoritarian Rule in Chile, 1973–90* (1996). Focusing on the activities of the Vicaría de la Solidaridad, Lowden looks at the role of the Roman Catholic Church in Chilean politics in the face of human rights violations and how this organization helped bring about the return to democracy in 1990. She starts with the Roman Catholic Church and human rights in general, then brings her discussion to Chile looking at the Committee of Cooperation for Peace, and then into the Vicaría. Although Cardinal Raúl Silva was still alive at the time of this publication, much of the book reads as a eulogy to him.[10]

V. Human Rights Bibliographies

I discovered that there are numerous published human rights bibliographies. Here I will list the ones I reviewed in chronological order.

In 1976, the Public Administration Students Association of the University of Arizona published *Human Rights, Bureaucracy and Public Policy: A Selected Bibliography—1976*. This is a topical bibliography aimed at students, researchers, instructors, administrators, and policy analysts in public organizations. The scope was determined by student interest and covers the United States, 1965–1976. No government documents, newspapers, or nonprint materials are included. It is indexed by author but is not annotated.

The Vicaría de la Solidaridad, a human rights group affiliated with the Catholic Church in Chile, published *Estudio bibliográfico sobre derechos humanos* (1978). With no limits on publication language, this bibliography is based on works found in Chilean libraries with each specific library indicated by the entry. The 399 references to books, journal articles, and chapters from monographs are also topically arranged and include a section called "Chile and human rights." A small percentage of the entries is annotated. Since the authors were publishing this in Chile under the dictatorship, they could not openly challenge the government. They do indicate subversively that there is a problem with human rights in Chile through annotating a much higher percentage of the materials specifically about human rights in Chile. This book does not have an index.

International Human Rights: A Bibliography 1970–1975 (revised edition) was published in 1980 by the Center for Civil and Human Rights, University of Notre Dame Law School. It is a revision of *1970–1975 International Human Rights Bibliography*. The audience is "legal scholars, political scientists, [and] moral philosophers" (iii). The unannotated entries are arranged by articles with an author, articles with no author, monographs with an author, and monographs with no author. There are no articles from newspapers or popular magazines. This collection does not duplicate United Nations documents and it avoids U.S.-specific material even though it does include U.S. foreign policy as it relates to human rights. It is indexed by subject, country/area, and collection. There are ten entries for Chile.

In 1983, the Center for the Study of Human Rights at Columbia University released *Human Rights: A Topical Bibliography*. Its scope is "scholarly books and articles on human rights drawn primarily from the disciplines of law, the social sciences, and philosophy" (xi). The works included are all published in English through 1981 (with a few added from 1982) and are "likely to be found in most university and large public libraries" (xi). The works are arranged by topic and subcategories and listed in unannotated entries. There is an author and subject index, but it was hard to pinpoint Chile-specific titles. I was able to identify five. Because of its arrangement, this bibliography is not designed for area-specific research but for topical explorations and cross-cultural analyses. The concluding chapter conveniently includes the addresses for organizations one could contact for further information.

Fact-finding missions can be found in Berth Verstappen's *Human Rights Reports: An Annotated Bibliography of Fact Finding Missions* (1987). This guide is divided by geographic region with indices for country, publisher, and keyword. IGO and NGO fact-finding mission reports from 1970 to September 1986 are included, but government delegations and investigative journalism are not. There are twenty-eight well-annotated entries for Chile.

Gregory J. Walters has written a well-annotated bibliography, *Human Rights in Theory and Practice: A Selected and Annotated Bibliography* (1995). The audience is primarily students doing research and the entries are divided first by type, then by topic. There are indices for author, subject, and geographic location. The only entry for Chile is *Report of Chilean National Commission on Truth and Reconciliation*, which I will refer to later in this bibliography.

VI. Human Rights—Chile

In 1974, journalist Sergio Villegas published *El estadio: once de septiembre en el país del Edén*. This edition, which claims to be the first book published after the coup, was published in Buenos Aires and later parts of it (especially the gripping chapter about Neruda's death) have been reproduced in journals of other countries. The entire book is about the first month after the bloody coup that left Pinochet in power.

The author starts with a quote from a Víctor Jara song, so immediately the reader knows that he is not a Pinochetista.[11] This testimonial literature is mostly a series of interviews—clandestinely held in friendly homes, on airplanes while the interviewee was travelling to a new home in exile, and in an embassy behind closed doors. A large percentage of the testimony is about the horrors that occurred inside the Estadio Nacional, which was used as a detention and torture center by the secret police. In 1990 the first Chilean edition of this book was published and Chileans were officially allowed to read what other countries had learned years earlier about the repression.

Jacobo Timerman is a name well known to scholars of Latin America. In 1981 he wrote *Preso sin nombre, celda sin número (Prisoner without a Name, Cell without a Number)* documenting his experiences as a prisoner of the ruthless Argentinian secret police during the "Dirty War." In the late 1980s Timerman travelled to Chile and wrote *Chile: el galope muerto,* based on his experiences and conversations. In this book he paints a grim, terrorized nation through strong emotional descriptions. Most chapters end with a testimony presented by a Chilean to the America's Watch Committee or Amnesty International.

U.S. journalist Tina Rosenberg has travelled through and lived in many parts of Latin America. Her 1991 book, *Children of Cain: Violence and the Violent in Latin America,* was published by Penguin Books as sensationalist literature with a back cover that reads, "Talking to hit men, guerillas and torturers—an award-winning journalist goes behind the scenes to present 6 vivid haunting portraits in Latin America." Once the reader moves beyond the marketing on the book jacket, the reader can find a well-written, chilling narrative. The last chapter is about Chile, "The Pig's Tail" (333–387). It describes in frighteningly honest detail how easy it became for citizens of Chile to ignore the crisis during the dictatorship. The economic boom successfully kept the middle class anesthetized. This chapter is largely a confessional from a middle-class man who had supported Allende but who relished the "good life" under Pinochet (color televisions, new cars) too much to let himself think about what was really happening. Rosenberg includes a bibliography with both general and country-specific sources.

Immediately before the plebiscite of 1988, the Centro de Información y orientación of the Comisión chilena de derechos humanos published *Derechos humanos y plebiscito.* The audience is vaguely defined as social and political groups in Chile and the rest of the world. It discusses in general terms human rights violations in Chile, but the text is not very accessible.

Another pre-plebiscite publication is María Eugenia Rojas's *La represión política en Chile: los hechos.* Covering from 1973 to 1983, the author depends heavily on the Vicaría de la Solidaridad for her information. As the title suggests, she presents all the material as "fact," using no hesitant or emotional language. She describes the creation and desolation of the DINA and the CNI and includes lists of types of torture as well as the names and dates of many of the detained-disappeared. Since it was published in Madrid, it appears that the purpose of Rojas's book is to promote the Vicaría material to a wider audience.

Physicians for Human Rights also published an account of human rights violations in Chile on the eve of the plebiscite (in which the authors have little faith). Written in the wake of the 1985 fact-finding mission by the American Committee for Human Rights (ACHR), *Sowing Fear: The Uses of Torture and Psychological Abuse in Chile: A Report by Physicians for Human Rights* is based on interviews with human rights workers, victims, and medical professionals in Chile. Unlike Rojas's contribution, this publication does not offer lists of cases (except of physicians who were tortured or abused for treating victims of torture), but draws on a few cases to support its statements as it explains how the Constitution of 1980 provided a cover for abuse. Where this report is groundbreaking is in its coverage of psychological terror and its aftermath on victims as well as their families, exploring treatment and therapy options for these survivors. Also included is a listing of organizations that are involved in victims' rights.

Marjorie Agosín edited *Surviving Beyond Fear: Women, Children, and Human Rights in Latin America,* which she divided into: "Women's Political Mobilization Around Human Rights" and "Children and Human Rights." Both sections include chapters on Latin America as a whole and specific chapters about Chile, Argentina, and El Salvador. Agosín's goal was to document gender-specific torture because, as she notes in the introduction, many human rights organizations do not tally gender differences in their statistics. She claims that the psychology of torture is different based on gender and age.

In the chapter "Subversive Mothers: The Women's Opposition to the Military Regime in Chile," Patricia M. Chuchryk traces the history of two women's groups in Chile that responded to the repression: Mujeres democráticas and the Agrupación de los Familiares de Detenidos-Desaparecidos. The former of these was started in October of 1973 in meetings disguised as tea parties and knitting sessions. Since the military tended to ignore women in general, these meetings were not suspected. The latter group formed in 1974 and later worked with the Vicaría de la Solidaridad.

Jennifer G. Schirmer's contribution to Agosín's work is "Chile: The Loss of Childhood." Similar to the work of Physicians for Human Rights, Schirmer explores the psychological effects of repression. She focuses on the residents/patients of a rehabilitation home for children showing symptoms of psychological stress due to repression. Some of the children were themselves physically tortured, while others were psychologically tortured as they were forced to watch their parents' suffering. Still others were children of the detained-disappeared and developed psychological problems due to the disappearance of a parent.

Once Pinochet was no longer president, many reports on human rights violations were published in Chile. Judge René García Villegas shares his personal narrative in *Soy testigo: dictadura, tortura, injusticia* (1990). García Villegas tells of his personal knowledge of those tortured without presenting any real new information and with no noticeable organization. While difficult to navigate, this book is interesting because it is written by someone who tried to change the judicial system from within. While on the bench, Judge García Villegas questioned the complicit role of the judicial system during the dictatorship. This book reprints letters written by the judge denouncing the *Corte Suprema* for failing to act; he was reprimanded for his actions and forcibly removed from the bench in 1990, on the eve of the transition. Also included are letters written on his behalf by the International Commission of Jurists, U.S. Senator Tom Harkin, the American Bar Association, the Asociación Americana de Juristas (Canadian Section), and the International Human Rights Law Group. Mark Ensalaco (whose work is covered later in this essay) values García's text because it "provides a glimpse of how, even in the second decade of the regime, the courts could not intervene to save those the secret police had arrested from torture" (220). Ensalaco also refers to another book that is entitled *Memorias de un magistrado*, by José Cánovas (Santiago: Emisión, 1989).

Patricio Cueto Román wrote *Atrapado en su red* (1992) in which this exiled Chilean law student charts the actions of the Comisión fiscalizadora de la Democracia Cristiana and their actions (mostly verbal) regarding human rights abuses. There is no bibliography and no citations, so the reader has no way of knowing on what the author bases his text since he was living in Germany when all these actions allegedly took place.

Some of these reports named individuals who were victims of such abuses under the dictatorship. Eugenio Ahumada, Javier Luis Egaña, Augusto Góngora, Carmen Quesney, Gustavo Saball, Gustavo Villalobos, and Rodrigo Atria seriously investigated these abuses and published the three-volume work *Chile: la memoria prohibida: las violaciones a los derechos humanos 1973–1983* (1989). The authors attempt to present the "most significant cases" of human rights violations in Chile. They utilize interviews and statistical data to document the abuses. While no bibliography is included, each of the forty-nine chapters of this work has detailed notes at the end. This is a key source because of its extensive details. Unfortunately, there is no index.

While Aylwin's commission was at work officially making its report, León Gómez Araneda published *Tras la huella de los desaparecidos* (1990). Unfortunately, the edition I was able to review was so poorly bound that sometimes the binding actually covers the words or the words go off the edge of the page. This gives the reader a possibly ironic feeling that this text has somehow been censored. Gómez Araneda denounces human rights violations in Chile as he interviews survivors, identifies major detention and torture locations, and lists names of those who were known to have been at these locations before disappearing. He concludes with a sobering list of 682 disappeared Chileans, along with the date and place (if known) they were last seen. Since he offers no citations for his assertions, the reader is to deduce that the information was gathered from the interviews and Vicaría de la Solidaridad documents. There is also an interesting list of banned books.

After nine months of investigating, the Commission on Truth and Reconciliation released its official report. The three-volume result, *Informe de la Comisión Nacional de Verdad y Reconciliación,* was published in 1991. The two-volume English translation (by Phillip E. Berryman), *Report of the Chilean National Commission on Truth and Reconciliation,* was released in 1993. It identifies its mission: "The Commission's task was to draw up as complete a picture as possible of the most serious human rights violations that resulted in death and disappearances which were committed by government agents or by private citizens for political purposes . . ." and, when possible, to determine the fate of the disappeared (2). Information was gathered by investigators travelling extensively around the country, interviewing those who wanted to be heard. The Commission's methods are clearly spelled out.

The *Report* offers a list of forms of human rights violations, then detailed accounts of such violations by the government, region-by-region, victim-by-victim. Clearly stating the victims' names, the *Report* maintains this format divided by periods (1973, 1974–1977, 1978–1983, 1984–1990), and it includes the reactions of Chileans, the Catholic Church, the media, and international observers. There is some quoted testimony from families and friends of victims as well as proposals for reparation. Unresolved cases are also identified.

Unfortunately, this monumental work has no name index, so the reader has to know the time period and region when looking up a name. It is impressive that the Commission could generate such documentation in a short period of time. Gregory J. Walters expresses similar sentiments in his bibliography: "The achievement of the Commission is remarkable. . . . The report is offered as a model of response to the political and ethical dilemmas that must be faced as a country moves from dictatorship to democracy" (104–105).

Asserting that there is no consistency in the numbers of detained-disappeared provided by the Commission on Truth and Reconciliation, the Agrupación de familiares de detenidos-desaparecidos, and the Vicaría de la Solidaridad, Elías Padilla Ballesteros attempts to provide more concrete statistics in *La memoria y el olvido: detenidos desaparecidos en Chile* (1995). The author presents a lot of statistics in different formats (tables and graphs). He maps data about the victims (gender, marital status, age, occupation, region, date, and political affiliation) as well as where they were detained and by whom (the army or the DINA). He also maps where victims were arrested (at home, family's home, friend's home, on the street, or at work). He denounces precincts where the detained-disappeared were held. Then he lists the victims, more than 1200, by name. The author hopes that this type of information can generate a public cry for accountability and ensure proper burials for the dead and punishment for the guilty.

One of the most organized works on human rights violations in Chile is *Determinants of Gross Human Rights Violations by State and State-Sponsored Actors in Brazil, Uruguay, Chile, and Argentina 1960–1990* by Wolfgang S. Heinz and Hugo Frühling (1999). As human rights specialists, Heinz and Frühling include in their book interviews with generals and officers as well as the text of "secret" documents. Each country is given 150–200 pages plus a bibliography of 10–20 pages. The very detailed table of contents and the thorough index make this text one of the easiest to use for the topic. The section on Chile includes pre-1973 political violence (and human rights abuse) which is important historical information usually left out of books that try to make it look as if human rights violations only occurred under Pinochet. In order to truly begin to comprehend why there was a military coup in Chile, it is crucial to know about the abuses during the Allende years. Like *Nation of Enemies,* Heinz and Frühling's book includes a discussion (brief) of the civil-military tensions brewing in the 1960s. Human rights violations are presented in tables as well as in the text facilitating research. One can also find useful administrative charts for the DINA. The problems in Chile concerning bringing those involved to justice due to the Amnesty Decree of 1978 and other Pinochet-sponsored laws that protect the guilty are briefly addressed.

Mark Ensalaco's *Chile under Pinochet: Recovering the Truth* also contains valuable new insight. In his introduction he states that he set out to write "a political history of the repression and the official efforts to recover the truth about it" (x). A law professor, Ensalaco is a little hard to follow because the events he describes are not in a consistently chronological order. When a new topic is introduced, the author jumps around in time to place that topic in its context. His information about the repression does not present the reader with anything groundbreaking. His book excels in its discussion of the investigations and efforts to expose the truth. He includes brief reports of the United Nations' work on human rights in Chile, and notes that UN Special Rapporteur for Chile, Costa Rican jurist Fernando Volio Jiménez, was politically very anticommunist and that this might have affected his objectivity. Ensalaco states that Americas Watch openly criticized his report of the Chilean situation, accusing him of sins of omission (171–174). Ensalaco also gives detailed accounts of the plebiscite of 1988. He includes sensitive interviews with Laura Novoa, Raúl Rettig, José Zalaquett, and Jaime Castillo about their work on the

Commission on Truth and Reconciliation. These interviews about their work, the participants' analyses of its successes and failures, and their reactions to the governments of Aylwin and Frei are what make this work unique. While it was published in 2000, it contains no mention of Pinochet's arrest. Unfortunately, one will never get to hear all of their reactions to his arrest since Raúl Rettig died of a heart attack on April 30, 2000.

VII. Specific Cases of Human Rights Violations in Chile

While many of the above listed sources do include lists of names of victims, some books focus solely on one or a few individuals who were tortured or murdered by government agents. A case that caused an international incident was the detention and torture of British physician Sheila Cassidy. She was arrested in 1975 for giving medical attention to a wounded leftist. Her detention caused an international uproar that led the United Kingdom to remove its ambassador from Chile. Cassidy was eventually released, and she has published an account of her experiences, *Audacity to Believe* (1977). She narrates the story of her activities in Chile, her faith, her arrest, her torture, and her release. This is a strong, first-person narrative.

In 1992, after the dictatorship was over, a doctor who worked with Cassidy, Mario Terrazas Guzmán, wrote *¿Quién se acuerda de Sheila Cassidy? (Crónica de un conflicto religioso-político-diplomático)*. He relies a great deal on translated quotes from Cassidy's own testimony (including translations of twelve entire chapters). His goal seems to be to remind Chileans that the situation has not been "reconciled" and that they should not so quickly forget their recent horrific past. This work appears to be the first publication in Chile of Cassidy's account.

Since the Orlando Letelier case was the first incident of international terrorism in the United States, it has received a lot of attention. Edmundo del Solar published *Orlando Letelier: Biographical Notes and Comments* (1978) in which he presents a biography of Letelier's political life and describes what led up to the September 21, 1976, assassination. This book, written by Letelier's uncle, also includes information about the U.S. investigation of the DINA's involvement in the crime.

Rafael Rodríguez Castañeda, a journalist who teaches at the Universidad Nacional Autónoma de México, wrote *El asasinato de Orlando Letelier* in 1979. This Spanish text covers the history of Letelier, the planning and execution of his murder, and the subsequent investigation. It does not contain any new information, but it is important because the story is told in Spanish.

Riding in the car with Orlando Letelier were Ronnie and Michael Moffit. Michael escaped unharmed, but Ronnie was killed. Michael and Letelier worked together for the Institute for Policy Studies, which later published a report of the Letelier investigation, *Assassination on Embassy Row* (1980).

In 1986 María Olivia Monckeberg, María Eugenia Camus, and Pamela Jiles (journalists) wrote *Crimen bajo estado de sitio*. This work chronicles the detention and murder of José Manuel Parada, Manuel Guerrero, and Santiago Nattino. The text contains information about the three victims, and the authors rely on interviews with family members and colleagues to paint portraits of the individuals.

Another amazingly brutal human rights violation is documented in Patricia A. Verdugo's *Rodrigo y Carmen Gloria, quemados vivos* (1986). This is an emotional account of Rodrigo Rojas Denegri and Carmen Gloria Quintana, who were doused with kerosine and burned alive in the street by government agents in Chile. The narrative is terrifyingly gripping as it describes how Rodrigo later died, but Carmen Gloria survived with burns on over 60 percent of her body. Verónica Denegri (Rodrigo's mother) has been exiled since 1977 and is currently with Amnesty International telling this story.

VIII. Latin America—The Transition to Democracy

There are few texts that study post-dictatorship Latin America in general. Ronaldo Munck's *Latin America: The Transition to Democracy* (1989) focuses on the Southern Cone with chapters on Argentina, Brazil, and Uruguay. There is no chapter devoted to Chile because the topic, when this book was written, was too new. Chile is mentioned in the text only when compared to the other three countries. Munck offers a general bibliography as well as one arranged by country. None of the works in his bibliography is covered in this essay.

Gabriel Gaspar Tapia wrote *Transición en América Latina: los casos de Chile y El Salvador* in 1991. Since the author is a Chilean political scientist who, exiled, teaches at the Universidad Nacional Autónoma de México, I expected some interesting insight. I was disappointed. There are 40 pages for each country and an inadequate 8 pages comparing the two. Gaspar Tapia does not shed any new light on the subject and there is no mention of human rights abuses.

IX. Chile's Transition to Democracy

The human rights violations that occurred under the Pinochet regime is a main theme in the minds of many Chileans during the transition. People wondered what would happen under the new government to those responsible for the abuses of the old. The armed forces were concerned that they would be tried for their actions. Much of the literature about the transition period reflects these concerns.

Most of the books I consulted are anti-Pinochet in bias. The only book I found that was written by a Pinochetista is *Transición a la chilena* by Luciano Vásquez Muruaga (1989). The author is a journalist whom Pinochet named Director of Social Communications in 1979. He also served Pinochet's Chile as an official diplomat of the press in Sweden (1973–1976) and Paraguay (1984–1988). The prologue of Vásquez Muruaga's book recounts Chilean history starting in 1973, proudly toeing the party line. He then presents interviews with Pinochet and eight other men who were campaigning for president (three months before the election).

Luis Ignacio López, a Spanish journalist who had lived in Chile until exiled in November 1973, is definitely not in the same camp as Luciano Vásquez Muruaga. López's *La derrota de las armas* (1989) celebrates that Chile is now preparing itself for free elections. As a returning exile, López addresses the concerns of those living in exile who are now finally able to return to Chile. His descriptions are very emotional.

Journalist Ascanio Cavallo published *Los hombres de la transición* in 1992. Each chapter is dedicated to one of eleven different protagonists in the transition. The well-written, sometimes irreverent, narrative is fun to read. Cavallo attempts to describe pivotal events in the lives of these men from their perspectives. The culmination of the book is Aylwin's inauguration; all the tales describe how these eleven men ended up at Aylwin's inauguration. While an "essential bibliography" is provided, the author does not state if he had personal interviews or inside sources. Perhaps he just projected his feelings and fictionalized events like Pinochet's ascent in the helicopter as he travelled to Valparaiso to hand over the command to Aylwin. Unfortunately, Cavallo does not tell us how he managed to write this book.

Another book focusing on the leaders during the transition is *La otra cara de la Moneda (los cuatro años de Aylwin)* by Emilio Rojo Orrego. This author, also a journalist from Chile, was exiled from 1975 to 1980 and lived in Italy and the former German Democratic Republic. In this book he presents four strange years of Chile, ones in which everyone is overly cautious. He describes the unnatural feeling: "¿Se habrán visto alguna vez en Chile sindicatos tan moderados, gremios tan ponderados, una prensa tan prudente, unos jóvenes tan calmados?" (5).[12] Rojo Orrego presents a chronicle of daily activities in a most unusual administration. He does not mention human rights, which is odd since Aylwin's government created the Commission on Truth and Reconciliation. Evidently, Rojo Orrego was also being moderate, tactful, prudent, and calm.

Since Chile was an economic laboratory under Pinochet, some writers consider the transition in terms of the economy. David E. Hojman discusses the economic policies and successes under Pinochet and contemplates how they can continue in a democracy in his *Chile: The Political Economy of Development and Democracy in the 1990s* (1993). He analyzes whether a democratic government can take the "good" from Pinochet without the "bad," that is, whether the government can continue the economic policies without continuing the repressive measures and human rights abuses. He also wonders aloud if the military will be able and willing to let the democratic government control economic and social policy. His analysis is mostly based on the first year of Aylwin's government and examines the economic policies and conditions. His work is supported by an extensive bibliography and detailed index.

James Petras and Fernando Ignacio Leiva do not perceive that Pinochet saved Chile's economy, nor do they want his economic policies to continue in the democracy. In *Democracy and Poverty in Chile: The Limits to Electoral Politics* (1994), Petras and Leiva focus on the population sectors that are not prospering due to the "economic miracle"; they assert that the "miracle" left 45 percent of Chileans living in poverty. Petras and Leiva also argue that both Pinochet's policies *and* Aylwin's government have only served to widen the gap between the rich and the poor. They blame Pinochet's regime for exasperating the differences between the haves and the have-nots, and they are concerned that Aylwin's policies are doing nothing to improve the situation.

In 1993, Alan Angell and Benny Pollack published an anthology based on papers from "Conference on Democratic Transition and Consolidation in Chile" at the University of Liverpool. *The Legacy of Dictatorship: Political, Economic and Social Change in Pinochet's Chile* focuses on socioeconomic policies developed under Pinochet and the ways they affect the transition. The thirteen brief chapters are, unfortunately, not introduced or tied together in the editors' introduction. Aside from economic policies, many authors express frustration with the pace of the transition. Walter Little's chapter, "Britain, Chile and Human Rights, 1973–1990" (149–163), analyzes the "sensitive" Anglo-Chilean relations complicated by the issue of human rights and the camaraderie of having Argentina as a common enemy. This chapter is especially poignant today. Little points out that the United Kingdom recognized Chile's regime eleven days after the coup (two days before the United States did) (150). At that time, the conservative Tories were running the United Kingdom, and while the liberal Labour Party was anti-Pinochet, it was outnumbered. While Little had no idea at that time that in the near future Pinochet would be detained in London, his chapter provides an interesting background to the United Kingdom–General Pinochet relationship.

Since Chile's transition has been a negotiated process, it has been extremely slow and methodical. Luis Vega in *Estado militar y transición democrática en Chile* (1991) asserts that Chile is still a military state but with two governments, the "elected" one of Aylwin and the "permanent" one comprised of national security, the armed forces, and General Pinochet. While the author has an irritating tendency to use excessive abbreviations (though there is a key), he provides a detailed (sometimes cluttered) analysis of the power structure of the Chilean military and the ways this structure is shaping the transition.

Senator Andrés Zaldívar Larraín was president of the Democracia Cristiana and exiled for three years. He is a strong opponent of Pinochet. In *La transición inconclusa* (1995), he is frustrated that the transition has been so slow, even though he acknowledges that his version of events is subjective since he has been an agent of the transition. His goal in this text is to shake up the population and to make them realize that more work must be accomplished before Chile can really be a democracy. Interestingly, the introduction is by former President Patricio Aylwin. In this forum he expresses more opinions than he was permitted to do during his four years as the country's leader.

Most of the text is actually about the dictatorship. Zaldívar Larraín highlights policies and activities from the military regime that need addressing today in order for Chile to recuperate. He is especially angry about the 1980 plebiscite, since there was no electoral policy and no voter registration. He focuses on this because the 1980 plebiscite, which he argues was not legitimate, is what spelled out the rules that complicate the current transition.

Rafael Otano is also frustrated with the transition. Otano is a Spaniard who moved to Chile in 1969 to study journalism and later went back to Spain (in self-exile?) from 1977 to 1989. In *Crónica de la transición* (1995), he describes the methodical nature of the transition that was allegedly designed to be "painless" and that he finds rather painfully slow as he takes us from the beginning of the transition through Aylwin to Frei. He also presents differing opinions on when the transition started. Some claim it started in 1980 with the Constitution. Others point to the birth of the Alianza Democrática in 1983. There are those who assert that it began with the Acuerdo Nacional in 1985, or the Plebiscite in 1988, or that it will not truly begin until Pinochet steps down in 1998. Otano argues, however, that the transition was set into place in June of 1984 when several prominent leaders (socialists, radicals, Christian Democrats, and members of the military cabinet) met in Tupahue to discuss modifying the 1980 Constitution and calling an open election to end the dictatorship. He interviews eighty-six people involved in the transition, some anonymous and "off-the-record" confessions as he considers different aspects and actors of the events, focusing on the influence of Pinochet through the transition and the subsequent difficulties of Aylwin.

The above texts concentrate on certain aspects of the transition. An excellent collection that attempts to consider many angles and events is *The Struggle for Democracy in Chile,* edited by Paul W. Drake and Iván Jaksi'c (1995). The twelve contributors to this anthology include very familiar names in the fields of Chilean history and politics. The chapters are "Introduction: Transformation and Transition in Chile" (the editors); "The Military in Power: The Consolidation of One-Man Rule" (Arturo Valenzuela); "The Crisis of Legitimacy of Military Rule in the 1980s" (Augusto Varas); "The Political Economy of Chile's Regime Transition: From Radical to 'Pragmatic' Neo-Liberal Politics" (Eduardo Silva); "Entrepreneurs under the Military Regime" (Guillermo Campero); "The Evolving Roles of Women under Military Rule" (María Elena Valenzuela); "Unions and Workers in Chile during the 1980s" (Alan Angell); "The Political Opposition and the Party System under the

Military Regime" (Manuel Antonio Garreton); "External Factors and the Authoritarian Regime" (Carlos Portales); "The Economic Challenges of Democratic Development" (Felipe Larraín B.); and "The Transition to Civilian Government in Chile, 1990–1994" (Brian Loveman).

For the purposes of this bibliography, I will focus on Loveman's contribution to the Drake and Jaksi'c anthology. Loveman addresses civil-military relations, indigenous rights, and the bizarre role of Patricio Aylwin as both the elected leader of the people and the one to have to placate Pinochet. Loveman also addresses the concerns about human rights violations. He describes the founding and work of the Commission on Truth and Reconciliation and explains why Aylwin had to use terms like "justice within the possible" when talking about punishing those responsible for the abuses.

Loveman also explains why people are frustrated today, why Spain fears that Pinochet will never be brought to justice in Chile and that Spain will have to do it itself. Loveman describes the betrayal people felt when Frei "realized that by 1994 most Chileans preferred to forget or repress the past, to continue their lives without allowing the 'human rights issue' to unsettle the consolidation of civilian government. He gave it no mention in the traditional May 21 address to Congress" (315). Many people were offended by that oversight and "In contrast, some political leaders and prominent intellectuals argued that unless the fate of the 'disappeared' was revealed and the guilty named, the political and psychological legacy of the human rights issue would fester for years in the Chilean body politic, preventing real social healing and democratization" (315). This chapter also explains how the military insisted that if they be tried, it be in military courts (where nothing would happen to them). Through the inclusion of this chapter by Brian Loveman, Drake and Jaksi'c have perhaps the most complete description of the transition.

With the transition came new freedoms, one of which was the freedom to talk openly about Pinochet and the events in Chile. Many books gather experts in the field to discuss the multifaceted changes occurring in Chile. The Fundación de Ayuda Social de las Iglesias Cristianas in 1998 published *La transición en Chile: a 25 años del golpe de estado*. In this text the editors interview six prominent Chilean lawyers, asking them to answer the following questions:

1. ¿Qué significado histórico le otorga Ud. al 11 de septiembre de 1973, a 25 años de su conmemoración?

2. ¿Qué balance hace Ud. de las violaciones de derechos humanos ocurridos en Chile durante la dictadura militar?

3. ¿Qué opina Ud. sobre el proceso de transición a la democracia en nuestro país en estos últimos 8 años?

4. ¿Cuál es su opinión sobre el tratamiento que le han dado los gobiernos de los Presidentes Aylwin y Frei al tema de derechos humanos y la impunidad?

5. ¿Cuales son los problemas de derechos humanos que todavía se mantiene pendientes y, como visualiza Ud. la posibilidad de resolución de éstos en la actualidad? (3)

The answers are presented after each question so the reader can easily compare the lawyers' responses. However, there is no dialog with the participants.

El accidente Pinochet offers a dialog as Armando Uribe Arce and Miguel Vicuña Navarro discuss Pinochet as "a phenomenon," a Jungian archetype ("¿de qué? . . . no sabría decirlo," p. 69). Uribe Arce and Vicuña Navarro argue that all sides need Pinochet, even the transition needs him in order to have closure. While I disagree with their assertion that the arrest of Pinochet *created* a polarization of Chileans (looking at the results of Allende's election, the 1988 plebiscite, and the 1999 presidential election, one can see that Chile has been divided for many years and that, sadly, this division continues), the conversation is interesting and intelligent. Their use of spirituality in their observations is intriguing: "la carne del señor Pinochet se ha hecho carne del espíritu nacional chileno, aceptada o denegada" (142). There is no index or any navigational key to this text; the two voices are printed (one in italics) as a transcription of the dialog but without stating which is which.

X. Justice and Reconciliation

Other texts focus entirely on the human rights issue in the transition. While these are not as complete as the Drake and Jaksi'c anthology, they do not pretend to be—they concentrate solely on human rights. Perhaps the *Report on the Commission on Truth and Reconciliation* could also be placed in this category, but I have chosen to include books written after the authors had a year or two to watch Aylwin and reflect on the Chilean situation.

The New York–based organization Americas Watch published their report of Chile's first year of transition in *Human Rights and the "Politics of Agreement": Chile during President Aylwin's First Year* (1991). The principal author is Cynthia Brown, the Americas Watch representative in Santiago. The report, based on information from January 1990 through April 1991, also covers extreme-leftist terrorism such as the April 1, 1991, assassination of Unión Democrática Independiente (UDI) Senator Jaime Guzmán (who helped draft the 1980 Constitution under the military government). This document reports on past abuses and chronicles efforts for justice—noting obstacles to justice such as military jurisdiction and the 1978 Amnesty Law. She credits most of the obstacles to the close relations between the military and judicial systems in Chile. She focuses on how little Aylwin was able to accomplish, and she wryly sums up the armed forces' responses to human rights investigations:

"Most fundamentally, the Army, still loyal to Pinochet, refuses to be criticized for what it considers the patriotic labor of shooting, torturing, clandestinely burying, kidnapping and otherwise tormenting or eliminating certain citizens" (49).

The Comisión Chilena de Derechos Humanos published a "balance sheet" of the human rights situation at the end of the Aylwin presidency. *Las deudas de la transición: balance de derechos humanos* (1994) reviews the duties of the Comisión, its activities, and its conclusion that the country is on the path to reconciliation, but that a great deal of work still needs to be done concerning justice. They report the disturbing month-by-month statistics of torture, arrests, disappearances, and executions from March 1990 to December 1993 (during the transition government). In their essay questioning the amnesty laws ("Derecho de Justicia") and in their discussion of the investigations into crimes by the DINA, one finds a good background for understanding how Chile's hands are tied and why they believe Pinochet will never stand trial at home.

Elin Skaar's master's thesis for the University of Bergen has been published as *Human Rights Violations and the Paradox of Democratic Transition: A Study of Chile and Argentina* (1994). Skaar draws eerie comparisons of Chile and Argentina with disturbing headings such as "Why Argentina was worse." The author compares the "transition by collapse" of Argentina with the "negotiated transition" of Chile and the ways these differing modes of transition create different types of democracy. Many statistics are included regarding the human rights abuses of each country. The author also bemoans the fact that most discussion of transition focuses on the elites and their roles and decisions. Skaar argues that civil society plays an important role and that human rights violations (and how to account for them) are a key concern of the civil society in transition.

Alexandra Barahona de Brito also compared two cases in Latin America for her dissertation, later published as *Human Rights and Democratization in Latin America: Uruguay and Chile* (1997). Her aim is "to shed light on the political conditions which permitted, or inhibited, the realization of policies of truth-telling and justice under these successor regimes" (1). De Brito does not have much faith in "truth-telling" reports because she believes that they are always incomplete and that, unless they are fully forthcoming, justice cannot be all-encompassing. She looks carefully at the truth and justice policies under Aylwin and why they failed to produce satisfactory results.

In *Tarde pero llega: Pinochet ante la justicia española* (1998), Paz Rojas B., Víctor Espinoza C., Julia Urquieta O., and Hernán Soto H. provide background information on the judicial process in Spain. They discuss the extradition process from its beginnings in Spain in 1996. Citing Madrid and Santiago daily newspapers, they track the process in Spain and the reaction in Chile. Published without mention of Pinochet's detention (perhaps it went to press before October of 1998), this book provides useful information about how the Spanish courts gathered information about Pinochet and how they decided to press charges. It also shows how Chile refused to recognize officially what Spain was planning on doing. For many of us, the news of Pinochet's detention in London was a surprise—it came out of the blue. This text demonstrates that it did not come out of the blue, but was a carefully researched attempt to execute justice.

Conclusion

This bibliography is also being composed in the wake of a new transition in Chile. Lagos was inaugurated as president a few short months ago. Spain did not succeed in extraditing Pinochet. However, the former leader of Chile and his actions were put on trial in England and in the court of public opinion. Precedent has now been set for punishing other dictators. And, in Chile, President Ricardo Lagos supports the 13-9 decision of a panel of judges to strip Pinochet of the immunity he enjoyed as a senator-for-life. Appeals from the defense attorneys will probably cause the trials to keep getting postponed until Pinochet's failing health overtakes the aging general.

But, in a way, Pinochet has already stood trial. While he was under house arrest in London and there were sixteen months of hearings challenging the extradition rulings, he was on trial. British courts heard the atrocities allegedly committed during his government. The abuses and actions were entered into public record. Despite the "economic miracle" of Chile, his name has been tainted. And, although it is doubtful that the trials in Chile will come to fruition, this has now set a precedent for other world leaders.

APPENDIX

A Timeline[13]

1970	Socialist Salvador Allende Gossens wins the presidential election with 36 percent of the vote.
March 1973	Congressional elections—44 percent for Unidad Popular (Allende's party); 54 percent for the opposition.
Sept. 11, 1973	Coup d'etat; Allende killed; Pinochet now in command.
Sept. 29, 1974	Former Chilean commander-in-chief of the armed forces and Defense Minister under Allende, General Carlos Prats, and his wife, Sofía, are killed by a car bomb in Buenos Aires (where they were living in exile). DINA (Dirección Nacional de Inteligencia) is suspected.
Sept. 21, 1976	Orlando Letelier and Ronnie Moffit killed in Washington, D.C., by a car bomb. DINA is implicated.
1977	DINA dissolved by Pinochet due to "abuses" and replaced by the CNI (Centro Nacional de Información).
1978	Plebiscite: "yes" or "no" defending Pinochet's authority. While the legitimacy of the plebiscite is questioned internationally, Pinochet uses the victory of the "yes" to justify his presidency. Amnesty Law passed granting amnesty to anyone who had committed a criminal act between Sept 11, 1973, and March 10, 1978.
1980	Plebiscite to ratify Constitution (which among other things said that Pinochet would rule for eight more years at which time there would be another plebiscite). 1980 Constitution also stated that any president to serve a full six-year term would become a "Senator-for-life" after leaving the presidential office.
Oct. 5, 1988	A legitimate plebiscite. Forty-three percent voted "yes" (to keep Pinochet); 55 percent voted "no" (to hold open elections).
Dec. 14, 1989	Open elections. Pinochet did not run, but his party put forth a candidate, Hernán Bücchi. Most opposition parties worked together in a coalition and put forth one candidate, Patricio Aylwin, who won with 55 percent.
March 1990	Aylwin inaugurated; Pinochet steps down as "President," but maintains control of the armed forces.
April 1990	Aylwin's government creates the Commission on Truth and Reconciliation to investigate deaths and disappearances under the dictatorship. They have one year to produce their report.
Dec. 19, 1990	Pinochet, enraged by the work of the Commission, orders the army to arm themselves and await further orders. This "threat" against the democratic government let Aylwin know his limits and set the tone for how the "human rights issue" would be addressed (or not addressed) for as long as Pinochet controls the armed forces.
March 1994	Eduardo Frei Ruíz-Tagle inaugurated as Chile's new President.
March 1998	Pinochet steps down as head of the armed forces.

Oct. 15, 1998	Spain asked Scotland Yard to detain General Augusto Pinochet Ugarte.
Oct. 18, 1998	Pinochet arrested in London while seeking medical detention. Spain wants to extradite him and force him to stand trial against charges of crimes against humanity and genocide.
Oct. 9, 1999	Magistrate ruled that Pinochet could be extradited to stand trial on thirty-five counts of torture and conspiracy to torture.
Nov. 1999	Chilean foreign minister Juan Gabriel Valdés cites Pinochet's minor strokes, heart condition, diabetes, and depression as humanitarian reasons why the general should not be extradited.
Dec. 12, 1999	Chilean presidential election. Neither candidate has clear majority (rightist Joaquín Lavín 47.52 percent, center-left Ricardo Lagos 47.96 percent). A runoff will be necessary.
Jan. 5, 2000	A team of doctors perform a series of tests on Pinochet to determine if he is fit to stand trial.
Jan. 11, 2000	Jack Straw announces that as a result of the medical advice of the team of doctors, Pinochet is declared unfit to stand trial and therefore will not be extradited to Spain.
Jan. 16, 2000	Chilean runoff election. Lavín 48.7 percent, Lagos 51.3 percent.
Jan.–Feb. 2000	Human rights organizations demand to see medical records but are denied. Argentina opens investigation of 1974 death of General Carlos and Sofía Prats.
Feb. 15, 2000	U.K. high court ruled that Straw must give Pinochet's medical reports to any country seeking his extradition. Report is said to state that Pinochet suffers brain damage.
March 2, 2000	Pinochet leaves Britain to return to Chile.
April 27, 2000	Trial begins in Chile to determine whether Pinochet can remain immune for crimes that he might have been responsible for under his reign.
May 24, 2000	Panel of twenty-two judges in Chile decide whether Pinochet can be stripped of his immunity. Official decision to be released after all the judges have signed a written version of the verdict (1–2 weeks).
May 25, 2000	Newspapers (including Guardian Unlimited Online) report that although the official verdict has not yet been released, Pinochet was stripped of his immunity. Some state the judges voted 13-9; others state 12-10.

BIBLIOGRAPHY

Agosín, Marjorie, ed. *Surviving Beyond Fear: Women, Children and Human Rights in Latin America*. Fredonia, N.Y.: White Pine, 1993.

Ahumada, Eugenio, et al. *Chile: la memoria prohibida: las violaciones a los derechos humanos 1973–1983*. Santiago: Pehuén, 1989.

Almeyda, Clodomiro, et. al. *Chile: más allá de la memoria*. Mexico, D.F.: UNAM, 1986.

Angell, Alan, and Benny Pollack, eds. *The Legacy of Dictatorship: Political, Economic and Social Change in Pinochet's Chile*. Liverpool: Institute of Latin American Studies, 1993.

Cassidy, Sheila. *Audacity to Believe*. London: Collins, 1977.

Castillo Velasco, Jaime. *¿Hubo en Chile violaciones a los derechos humanos? Comentario a las memorias del General Pinochet*. Santiago: Editora Nacional de Derechos Humanos, 1995.

Cavallo, Ascanio. *Los hombres de la transición*. Santiago: Editorial Andrés Bello, 1992.

———, Manuel Salazar Salvo, and Oscar Sepúlveda Pacheco. *Chile, 1973–1988: la historia oculta del régimen militar*. 3d ed. Santiago: Editorial Antártica, 1989.

Chuchryk, Patricia M. "Subversive Mothers: The Women's Opposition to the Military Regime in Chile." In Agosín, *Surviving Beyond Fear,* pp. 86–97.

Constable, Pamela, and Arturo Valenzuela. *A Nation of Enemies: Chile under Pinochet*. New York: W.W. Norton and Co., 1993.

Corlazzoli, Pablo. *Los regímenes militares en América Latina: estructuración e ideología: los casos de Brasil, Chile y Uruguay*. Montevideo: Ediciones del Nuevo Mundo, 1987.

Correa, Raquel, and Elizabeth Subercaseaux. *Ego sum Pinochet*. Santiago: Editorial Zig Zag, 1989.

Cueto Román, Patricio. *Atrapado en su red*. Santiago: Sociedad Productora Periodística, 1992.

De Brito, Alexandra Barahona. *Human Rights and Democratization in Latin America: Uruguay and Chile*. Oxford: Oxford University Press, 1997.

Del Solar, Edmundo. *Orlando Letelier: Biographical Notes and Comments*. New York: Vantage, 1978.

Derechos humanos y plebiscito. Santiago: Centro de información y orientación, Comisión chilena de derechos humanos, 1988.

Las deudas de la transición: balance de derechos humanos. Santiago: Editora Nacional de Derechos Humanos, 1994.

Dinges, John, and Saul Landau. *Assassination on Embassy Row*. New York: Pantheon Books, 1980.

Drake, Paul W., and Iván Jaksi'c, eds. *The Struggle for Democracy in Chile*. Rev. ed. Lincoln: University of Nebraska Press, 1995.

Ensalaco, Mark. *Chile under Pinochet: Recovering the Truth*. Philadelphia: University of Pennsylvania Press, 2000.

Fuerzas armadas, estado y sociedad: el papel de las fuerzas armadas en la futura democracia chilena. Santiago: Ediciones Pedagógicas Chilenas, 1989.

García Villegas, René. *Soy testigo: dictadura, tortura, injusticia.* Santiago: Editorial Amerinda, 1990.

Gaspar Tapia, Gabriel. *Transición en América Latina: los casos de Chile y El Salvador.* Mexico, D.F.: Universidad Autónoma Metropolitana, 1991.

Gómez Araneda, León. *Tras la huella de los desaparecidos.* Santiago: Ediciones Caleuche, 1990.

Gurriarán, José Antonio. *Chile: el ocaso del general.* Madrid: El País/Aguilar, 1989.

Handbook of Latin American Studies (HLAS). http://lcweb2.loc.gov/hlas/.

Heinz, Wolfgang S., and Hugo Frühling. *Determinants of Gross Human Rights Violations by State and State-Sponsored Actors in Brazil, Uruguay, Chile, and Argentina 1960–1990.* The Hague: Martinus Nijhoff Publishers, 1999.

Hojman, David E. *Chile: The Political Economy of Development and Democracy in the 1990s.* Pittsburgh, Pa.: University of Pittsburgh Press, 1993.

Human Rights: A Topical Bibliography. Boulder, Colo.: Westview, 1983.

Human Rights and the "Politics of Agreement": Chile during President Aylwin's First Year. New York: Americas Watch, 1991.

Human Rights, Bureaucracy and Public Policy: A Selected Bibliography—1976. Tucson: University of Arizona Press, 1976.

Little, Walter. "Britain, Chile and Human Rights, 1973–1990." In Angell and Pollack, *Legacy of Dictatorship,* pp. 149–163.

López, Luis Ignacio. *La derrota de las armas.* Argentina: Editorial Zeta, 1989.

Loveman, Brian. *Chile: The Legacy of Hispanic Capitalism.* 2d ed. New York: Oxford University Press, 1988.

―――. "The Transition to Civilian Government in Chile, 1990–1994." In Drake and Jaksi'c, *Struggle for Democracy in Chile,* pp. 305–337.

Lowden, Pamela. *Moral Opposition to Authoritarian Rule in Chile, 1973–90.* New York: St. Martin's Press, 1996.

Martínez, Javier, and Alvaro Díaz. *Chile: The Great Transformation.* Washington, D.C.: Brookings Institution, 1996.

Monckeberg, María Olivia, María Eugenia Camus, and Pamela Jiles. *Crimen bajo estado de sitio.* Santiago: Emisión, [1986].

Munck, Ronaldo. *Latin America: The Transition to Democracy.* London: Zed Books, 1989.

O'Brien, Phil, and Jackie Roddick. *Chile: The Pinochet Decade: The Rise and Fall of the Chicago Boys.* London: Latin American Bureau, 1983.

O'Connor, Barry, comp. and ed. *International Human Rights: A Bibliography 1970–1975.* Rev. ed. Notre Dame: Center for Civil and Human Rights, University of Notre Dame Law School, 1980.

Oppenheim, Lois Hecht. *Politics in Chile: Democracy, Authoritarianism, and the Search for Development.* Boulder, Colo.: Westview, 1993.

Otano, Rafael. *Crónica de la transición*. Santiago: Planeta, 1995.

Oyarzún, María Eugenia. *Augusto Pinochet: diálogos con su historia: conversaciones inéditas*. Santiago: Editorial Sudamericana, 1999.

Padilla Ballesteros, Elías. *La memoria y el olvido: detenidos desaparecidos en Chile*. Santiago: Ediciones Orígenes, 1995.

Petras, James, and Fernando Ignacio Leiva. *Democracy and Poverty in Chile: The Limits to Electoral Politics*. Boulder, Colo.: Westview, 1994.

Pinochet Ugarte, Augusto. *Camino recorrido: memorias de un soldado*. [Santiago]: Tallers Gráficos del Instituto Geográfico Militar de Chile, 1990–1994.

Remmer, Karen L. *Military Rule in Latin America*. Boston: Unwin Hyman, 1989.

Report of the Chilean National Commission on Truth and Reconciliation. Translated by Phillip E. Berryman. Notre Dame: University of Notre Dame Press, 1993.

Rodríguez Castañeda, Rafael. *El asasinato de Orlando Letelier*. Mexico, D.F.: Comunicación e Información, 1979.

Rojas, María Eugenia. *La represión política en Chile: los hechos*. Madrid: IEPALA Editorial, 1988.

Rojas B., Paz., et al. *Tarde pero llega: Pinochet ante la justicia española*. Santiago: LOM Ediciones, 1998.

Rojo, Grinor, and John J. Hassett, eds. *Chile: Dictatorship and the Struggle for Democracy*. Gaithersburg, Md.: Ediciones Hispamérica, 1988.

Rojo Orrego, Emilio. *La otra cara de la Moneda (los cuatro años de Aylwin)*. Santiago: Chile América, [1994?].

Rosenberg, Tina. *Children of Cain: Violence and the Violent in Latin America*. New York: Penguin Books, 1991.

Schirmer, Jennifer G. "Chile: The Loss of Childhood." In Agosín, *Surviving Beyond Fear,* pp. 162–167.

Skaar, Elin. *Human Rights Violations and the Paradox of Democratic Transition: A Study of Chile and Argentina*. Bergen, Norway: Chr. Michelsen Institute, 1994.

Sowing Fear: The Uses of Torture and Psychological Abuse in Chile: A Report by Physicians for Human Rights. Somerville, Va.: Physicians for Human Rights, 1988.

Spooner, Mary Helen. *Soldiers in a Narrow Land: The Pinochet Regime in Chile*. Berkeley: University of California Press, 1994.

Teitelboim, Volodia V. *En el país prohibido*. Santiago: Ediciones LAR, 1988.

Terrazas Guzmán, Mario. *¿Quién se acuerda de Sheila Cassidy? (Crónica de un conflicto religioso-político-diplomático)*. Santiago: Ediciones Emete, 1992.

Timerman, Jacobo. *Chile: el galope muerto*. Buenos Aires: Sudamericana/Planeta, 1988.

La transición en Chile: a 25 años del golpe de estado. Santiago: Ediciones FASIC, 1998.

Uribe Arce, Armando, and Miguel Vicuña Navarro. *El accidente Pinochet*. Santiago: Editorial Sudamericana Chilena, 1999.

Valdés, Juan Gabriel. *Pinochet's Economists: The Chicago School in Chile.* Cambridge: Cambridge University Press, 1995.

Varas, Augusto. *Los militares en el poder: régimen y gobierno militar en Chile 1973–1986.* [Santiago]: Pehuén, 1987.

Vásquez Muruaga, Luciano. *Transición a la chilena.* Santiago: Editorial Barcelona, [1989].

Vega, Luis. *Estado militar y transición democrática en Chile.* Madrid: El Dorado, 1991.

Verdugo, Patricia. *Interferencia secreta.* Santiago: Editorial Sudamericana Chilena, 1998.

Verdugo A., Patricia. *Rodrigo y Carmen Gloria, quemados vivos.* Santiago: Editorial Aconcagua, 1986.

Verstappen, Berth, comp. and ed. *Human Rights Reports: An Annotated Bibliography of Fact Finding Missions.* London: Hans Zell Publishers, 1987.

Vicaría de la Solidaridad. *Estudio bibliográfico sobre derechos humanos.* Santiago: Vicaría de la Solidaridad, 1978.

Villegas, Sergio. *El estadio: once de septiembre en el país del Edén.* Santiago: Editora Periodística Emisión, 1990.

Walters, Gregory J. *Human Rights in Theory and Practice: A Selected and Annotated Bibliography.* Metuchen, N.J.: Scarecrow, 1995.

Zaldívar Larraín, Andrés. *La transición inconclusa.* Santiago: Editorial los Andes, 1995.

NOTES

1. The information in this introductory paragraph is taken from a remarkable website by The Guardian at http://www.guardianunlimited.co.uk/Pinochet_on_trial. This site is updated daily and has the most up-to-date information on the Pinochet arrest and subsequent decisions. It also includes articles about the U.S. fears of what could be revealed at a trial as well as editorials by Ariel Dorfman, a Chilean novelist and playwright (now teaching at Duke University), and Sheila Cassidy, a former political prisoner in Chile.

2. According to the 1980 Constitution, all presidents who complete one full term (six years) become "Senators for life" when they step down from office.

3. Rightist candidate Joaquín Lavín (a "Chicago Boy" economist, journalist, and member of the Opus Dei) received 47.52 percent of the vote (the best showing for a rightist candidate since 1932), narrowly losing to the center-left Ricardo Lagos (47.96 percent) in the election of December 12, 1999. Since neither candidate won a majority of the votes, a runoff was on January 16, 2000. The runoff was held in the wake of the announcement that Pinochet would return home from his house arrest in London. Paul W. Drake and Peter Winn wondered if this would affect the election. They wrote: "Polls showed that most Chileans did not consider Pinochet a major issue in the election and while most wanted him returned to Chile because of sovereignty concerns, they also wanted him to stand trial at home because of human rights violations" (8). Each candidate received more votes than in the first round, but this time Lagos was declared victor since his 51.3 percent was more than the required 50 percent (Lavín received 48.7 percent). Information about the 1999/2000 election comes from Paul W. Drake and Peter Winn, "The Presidential Election of 1999/2000 and Chile's Transition to Democracy," *LASA Forum* 31, no. 1 (spring 2000): 5–9.

210   ANNE C. BARNHART-PARK

4. Please see the appendix for a brief timeline of events leading up to the coup d'etat, through the dictatorship and into the transition.

5. An alphabetical listing of all works included in this bibliography can be found at the end of the essay.

6. At the XXII International Congress of the Latin American Studies Association (Hyatt Regency, Miami, Florida, March 16–18, 2000), Brian Loveman shared his next project which is a historical analysis of past Chilean regimes and the history of impunity and amnesty in Chile. This work, previewed in a paper entitled "Political Reconciliation and Chilean 'Exceptionalism': From Lircay (1830) to Chacarillas (1977)," promises to offer a historical context to this transition to democracy.

7. Here is the translation of these two quotes:

[Teitelboim] was the one who wrote the most fantastic fabrications about the place of the relegated. He was an expert in brain-washing the naive Chileans, exposing his demagogic ideology with the appearance of a good ole and affable man, seeming more like a village priest than a Communist. This Soviet agent disguised with impressive ease his betrayal of Chile, and in each opportunity he would find favorable circumstances, he would make the Chileans believe the sweetness of Communism, which he extolled with a soporific "Song of the Siren." [Quoted in Augusto Pinochet U., El dia decisivo: 11 de septiembre de 1973 (Santiago: Editorial Andres Bello, 1980), pp. 49–51.]

The hypocrite and strange character, that Tartuffe, true craftsman of the lie and calumny, who wrote the most fantastic fabrications, expert in brain-washing the naive Chileans demagogue with the appearance of a good ole and affable man, seeming more like a village priest than a Communist, that Soviet agent, who entoned a soporific "Song of the Siren," proposed to enter Chile (7). [translation by the bibliographer with the assistance of James Barnhart-Park]

8. This is a play on the Gabriel Garcia Marquez novel, El general no tiene quien le escriba (Nobody Writes to the General), about Simon Bolivar.

9. "I am not a dictator and my government has not trampled on Human Rights; completely the contrary!"

10. Cardinal Raúl Silva Henríquez died in Santiago on April 9, 1999.

11. Victor Jara was a Chilean folk singer who was politically active under the Allende government and brutally massacred under Pinochet. Lore has it that his hands were broken by the secret police and he was forced to keep playing the guitar and singing his songs until the very end.

12. "Has one ever seen before in Chile unions so moderate, guilds so tactful, a press so prudent, youth so calm?" (my translation).

13. The information in this timeline was gathered from Drake and Jaksi'c, Constable and Valenzuela, Loveman (1988) and Loveman (1995). Information about the extradition case comes from http://www.guardianunlimited.co.uk/Pinochet_on_trial/.

17. We Wirarün (The New Cry): Mapuche Renunciations of State-Imposed Silence

James Barnhart-Park

The Mapuche of Chile have resisted state-imposed silence since the time of independence, but their contemporary struggles stem most directly from certain official policies enacted under the seventeen-year military dictatorship which further fractured the indigenous organizations in attempts to dismantle communal lands and assimilate them into the general population. Their renunciations have expressed themselves through a rebirth of cultural activity during and immediately after the dictatorship. A major gain in this political discourse has been that achieved by a few Mapuche poets, whose works have been recognized throughout Chile and abroad, and who are actively involved in the renunciation of the state-imposed silence. In this paper I will present the obstacles faced by this group of authors, and how they overcame them in order to be heard and acknowledged as voices of the indigenous cultural resistance.

Initial lexical study of the language of the Mapuche, Mapuzugun, by Father Luis de Valdivia in 1606 *(Arte y gramática de la lengua que corre en todo el reyno de Chile, con un vocabulario y confesionario)* makes it one of the earliest indigenous languages to have been transcribed in South America. Following studies by Andrés Febres *(Diccionario Araucano-español* [1764]) and Bernardo Havestadt *(Chilidungu, sive tractatus linguae chilensis* [1777]) showed a continued interest in its complexities and rich expressions. Later transcriptions and studies by Rodolfo Lenz *(Estudios araucanos,* 1895–1897), and by Félix José de Augusta and Sigifredo de Fraunhäusl *(Lecturas araucanas,* 1910) brought Mapuzugun to the foreground of ethnographic and linguistic scholarly research. This brief bibliography, coupled with today's research by both Western and indigenous scholars, documents this cultural and linguistic continuity in Chile and Argentina for over four centuries.

Historically, the Mapuche had maintained territorial autonomy. They had held off the Inca since before the arrival of the Europeans, and after this invasion, the Mapuche forged an independence from the Spanish crown by signing a treaty that recognized them as an independent nation in 1641 (Quillin), and later a border agreement in 1726 (Negrete). Each was disregarded after Chile established its independence, though the Mapuche flag was used to represent the fledgling nation after the initial uprising in 1812—later to be withdrawn after Spain reclaimed the territory and after Chile established final independence. But it was not until 1881 that the Chilean military occupied the region known as the *Araucanía,* and quickly expanded southward, defeating the Mapuche in the questionably named *Guerra de la Pacificación.* Ironically, in the years immediately before the occupation of the Araucanía, Chile's nationalistic discourse used the image of the conquest-period Mapuche warrior, *Caupolicán,* to rally troops in the nation's northern expansion efforts of the *Guerra del Pacífico.* Chile's territorial consolidation affected many indigenous populations, among them the Quechua and Aymara of the northern provinces, and the Mapuche of the south-central valleys, coasts, and highlands.

With this territorial consolidation, the Mapuche were forced into reservation-like settlements called, fittingly, *reducciones.* The reduction of arable lands, for the most fertile were distributed or sold to Chilean and European colonizers as incentives, forced many Mapuche into the cities—a trend that has characterized most of Chile's twentieth-century migration patterns. This migration, while accelerating the assimilation process, also made the Mapuche more evident throughout the somewhat homogenous population. However, they continued to be deprived of representation—they were only folkloric vestiges from the famed epic poem by Alonso de Ercilla y Zúñiga, *La araucana* (1569, 1578, 1589); they were also remembered in the poem written in Chile by the Nicaraguan Rubén Darío called "Caupolicán" (from the 1891 edition of *Azul*). Their presence was felt primarily in Chile's literature, but even then, it was a historical presence—nothing of their current situation or present struggles.

As previously noted, indigenous figures were a source of nationalistic pride, however, the people represented were shunned and dismissed among the government and the social elites. One need not look any further than Chile's Nobel laureates for anecdotes to this effect. Gabriela Mistral and Pablo Neruda both felt the racial undertones of their times. A well-known incident occurred when Neruda was consul in Mexico, where he attempted to begin a journal entitled "Araucanía." The response he received from his superiors was "[c]ámbiele el título o suspéndala. No somos un país de indios." More recently, in a Chilean newspaper article in March of 1997, the journalist and writer Bernardo Subercaseaux wrote: "nuestro país carece de un espesor cultural que reafirme su identidad, apoye su desarrollo y nos distinga como nación," denying any Mapuche influence in the nation's formation—I was told in my Santiago high school that there were no more indigenous peoples in Chile.

Today, the Mapuche comprise nearly 1.5 million of Chile's 13.5 million population. They are located primarily in the ninth and tenth regions, but more than half of their total population resides in the cities, with over 36 percent in Santiago alone. The majority return regularly to their communities for annual rituals or festivals, but they are consistently denied even their cultural autonomy. Urban migration of the late-nineteenth century, and political activism in the early-twentieth occasioned several political organizations to develop in defense of indigenous rights. The most effective of these were the Sociedad Caupolicán (formed in 1910), the Federación Araucana (formed in 1916), and the Unión Araucana (formed in 1926). Others that came along were the Frente Unico Araucano (1939), the Corporación Araucana (1946), and the Asociación Nacional de Indígenas de Chile (1953)—the same year the Primer Congreso Nacional Mapuche took place in Temuco, capital of the ninth region and political center of the Mapuche people. In addition to arguing for the recuperation of lands taken before independence, and up through the present, these organizations vied for equal opportunities in the workplace and the schools.

It is in the latter half of the twentieth century that one begins to see the results of the indigenous organizations' activism. A strong movement toward autonomous representation, both artistic and political, took a more aggressive stance during the 1960s and the first years of the 1970s. However, this resurgence was dispersed and/or annihilated with the brutal repression that followed the 1973 coup. Mapuche student groups had formed before the Allende government took office, and were recognized as a voice within the academic communities. Though as Neruda's experience reveals, publishing was reserved for the economic and social elite in Santiago. This centralized structure greatly reduces the chances of publishing by many authors of the southern and northern regions—an issue being dealt with by educators and authors even today.

Mapuche authors were not published extensively even before the Pinochet regime, except in studies by anthropologists or sociologists who explored the oral nature of Mapuzugun. Magazines and newspapers, where writers sometimes received their initial exposure, were some of the first to be shut down under the dictatorship. A plethora of small, independent, regional newspapers were obliterated by the regime's censorship campaigns. Only recently, a few smaller, independent newspapers are beginning to show signs of economic viability and social functionality. But somehow, Mapuche authors managed to present their materials to the public.

In 1966, a schoolteacher published a small group of poems that are generally considered a starting point by Mapuche and Western critics alike (in terms of indigenous poetry in written form). His name is Sebastián Queulpul, and his work opened the doors for the bilingual poetry that struggled to have itself heard under the repressive censorship of the military. It was not for eleven years that another poet published his work—Elicura Chihauilaf. He was a student of obstetric medicine at the Universidad de Concepción, whose studies were abruptly halted due to the political persecution of his father as a labor leader and the need for his support at home in Quechurewe. In 1977 he published *El invierno y su imagen,* which was dispersed in a series of mostly obscure journals: *Al mirarte* (Talcahuano), *Latrodectus* (Temuco), *Araucaria de Chile* (Spain), *Lar* (Concepción), *Lapislázuli* (La Serena), and *La Castaña* (Santiago), among others. The following years are sometimes viewed as the most repressive of the regime. For the Mapuche, they certainly were. An assault on their rights and lands was part of the economic policies of the neoliberal state, for in 1978, Decreto Ley 2568 was pronounced and reads, in part: "las reducciones mapuches existentes serán divididas y dejarán de llamarse tierras indígenas e indígenas sus habitantes." This blatant attack on the indigenous peoples of Chile was the regime's way of further assimilating this resistant and economically unproductive facet of the population. It also freed lands for the development of private industry and multinational investments. Also enacted, in 1980, was a decree prohibiting the use of Mapuzugun in all public schools (Decreto Ley 4002)—following Spain's model under Franco, and further limiting their autonomy.

But censorship inevitably leads to more varied forms of expression. Through painting and music, artists protested the dictatorship in ever so subtle ways. Eventually, even print regained its viability—although somewhat surreptitiously. The years that intervened are not well documented. It can be assumed that small backroom presses managed to disseminate materials, but this material is difficult to obtain. Chihuailaf published another collection in 1988, *En el país de la memoria,* in a small run of seventy-five copies in Temuco. And boldly, the following year—the same year the Chilean electorate voted in open, democratic elections—a nineteen-year-old poet by the name of Leonel Lienlaf published the first fully bilingual edition (Mapuzugun/Spanish) through a major press: Editorial Universitaria. This text, *Nepey ñi güñün piuke (Se ha despertado el ave de mi corazón),* broke the silence and shook the grounds on which Chile's literary elite rested. A beautiful text, with the Mapuzugun poem faced by the Spanish version, cemented a place for Mapuche literature in Chile's poetic landscape and broke with the European literary conventions.

The Western legacy of Chile's literature was faced with the indigenous elements and its political activism. The transitional candidate, Patricio Aylwin, openly courted the Mapuche vote—eventually bringing the majority into the *Concertación.* Once Aylwin was in office, the new government attempted to rectify some of the injustices of the dictatorship. Besides the official, legalistic means through the new Ley Indígena (no. 19,253) and the establishment of the CONADI (Corporación Nacional para el Desarrollo Indígena)—a state-structured advisory board of elected and appointed indigenous officials—there has been a nationwide organizational effort to mobilize Mapuche communities in opposition to the construction of hydroelectric plants in the upper Bío-Bío river basin, the coastal highway, and other similar development projects. The poorly funded CONADI, and its political appointees causing internal dissent, has made very slow progress in purchasing the lands back from those who stole them either before or during the dictatorship. The Ley Indígena blatantly does not recognize the Mapuche as a nation, but as an ethnic group—limiting their political representation and subverting their claims to territorial autonomy. Their lands are still the focus of environmental issues and political maneuverings by multinational corporations, as well as by state-development projects, wanting to relocate hundreds of families in the name of "progress." These issues are common themes in the works of the Mapuche poets who have had some recognition.

Few others have obtained the recognition awarded Lienlaf—as poetry is not widely read anyway, even in this country of poet laureates. In 1994, Lorenzo Aillapán was awarded the Premio Casa de las Américas in indigenous literature, for his *Hombre pájaro (Uñumche)*. In 1995, the Editorial Universitaria published Chihuailaf's fourth collection, *De sueños azules y contrasueños*. However, others still struggle with the problems of a centralized publishing world, and the limitations of a neoliberal economy. Additionally, there are three alphabets that Mapuzugun authors use. The oldest is named the Alfabeto Unificado and was developed by the Catholic Church for evangelization. A more recent one is the Grafemario Raguileo, developed by a Mapuche linguist who has worked closely with many of the poets mentioned here. A third, and as of yet not widely used, is the AZUMCHEFI, developed by a team of Mapuche and Western scholars at the Universidad Católica in Temuco. This creates problems in editing and transcribing, as many of these poets are self-taught and use a blend of the two primary alphabets. Rayen Kvyeh published her collection of poetry in 1997 entitled *Wvne coyvn ñi kvyeh—Luna de los primeros brotes*. She published this by her own means—since the presses she contacted refused to publish her work if it did not use the Unificado alphabet.

But a new generation of poets is encountering a growing interest in the culture and literature of the Mapuche. Younger Mapuche poets who are getting published in either small artistic or literary journals are almost too numerous to include here, but some are Jacquelin Caniguán, Jaime Luis Huenún, Bernardo Colipán, and Sonia Caicheo (Huenún and Colipán have just recently published collections of their work in Chile). Clearly, the battles for cultural survival continue even beyond the reaches of the Pinochet dictatorship. A more subtle, economic assimilation (of lands and people) is under way, and most of these authors are well aware of what lies ahead. The groundwork for further assimilation was laid via governmental decrees and brutal repression. The Mapuche culture and modes of expression have survived for over four centuries. Other indigenous populations have suffered extinction, but the Mapuche have become a cultural and political force in their own lands. This status has brought upon them much attention, even in the elite literary circles of Chile.

One can point to only a few occasions where the imposed language has been translated into the native, but in Chile, in 1996, the Editorial Pehuén commissioned Elicura Chihuailaf to translate some of Neruda's work, which resulted in the publication of *Todos los Cantos—Ti Kom Vl,* certainly a groundbreaking endeavor worthy of recognition. Lienlaf has helped develop documentaries on environmental and cultural preservation, which helps to preserve the oral nature of his poetry. Aillapán has performed in several short films and one major motion picture based on the novel by Pineda y Bascuñan, *El cautiverio* feliz. Others have chosen various forms of discourse to further the cultural and political goals of the Mapuche of south-central Chile.

Amidst political turmoil, environmental legislations, and multinational progress, the poetry of these authors reveals itself as one of many tactics in their continuing struggle against state-imposed silence—a struggle that has continued for over four centuries and is very much alive today.

BIBLIOGRAPHY

Aillapán Cayuleo, Lorenzo. *Hombre pájaro.* Bogotá: Casa de las Américas, 1994.

de Augusta, Félix José. *Diccionario Mapuche-Español.* Santiago: Ediciones Seneca, 1989.

de Augusta, Félix José, and Sigifredo de Fraunhäusl. *Lecturas araucanas.* Padre las Casas, Chile: Imprenta San Francisco, 1910.

————. *Testimonio de un cacique mapuche.* 1930. Reprint, Santiago: Pehuen, 1983.

Avila Biosca, Ramón, and José Inostroza Ulloa. "Poesía Mapuche." *Stylo* 8, no. 12 (1972): 193–221.

Bengoa, José. *La comunidad perdida.* Santiago: Ediciones Sur, 1996.

————. *Conquista y Barbarie, ensayo crítico acerca de la conquista de Chile.* Santiago: Ediciones Sur, 1992.

————. *Historia del Pueblo Mapuche (Siglo XIX y XX).* Santiago: Ediciones Sur, 1985.

————. "Población, familia y migración mapuche. Los impactos de la modernización en la sociedad mapuche 1982–1995." *Pentukun,* no. 6 (Dec. 1996): 9–28.

Brotherston, Gordon. *Book of the Fourth World: Reading the Native Americas Through their Literature.* Cambridge: Cambridge University Press, 1992.

Calbucura, Jorge. "Ñuke Mapu." http://linux.soc.uu.se/mapuche. Accessed October 12, 1997.

Campos Menchaca, Mariano José. *Nahuelbuta.* Buenos Aires and Santiago: Editorial Francisco de Aguirre, 1972.

Carrasco, Iván. "Dos Epeu de Trabajo y Matrimonio." In *Actas: Jornadas de Lengua y Literatura Mapuche. 29–31 de agosto, 1984.* Metrenco-Temuco, Chile: Küme Dungu, 1984. Pp. 77–88.

————. "Literatura Mapuche." *América Indígena,* no. 48 (1988): 659–730.

————. "Metalenguas de la poesía etnocultural de Chile, I." *Estudios Filológicos* 28 (1993): 67–73.

————."Sistema mítico y relato oral mapuche." *Estudios Filológicos* 20 (1985): 83–95.

Carrasco M., Hugo. "Notas sobre el ámbito temático del relato mítico mapuche." In *Actas: Jornadas de Lengua y Literatura Mapuche. 29–31 de agosto, 1984.* Metrenco-Temuco, Chile: Küme Dungu, 1984. Pp. 115–127.

————. "En torno a los relatos de machi, I." *Estudios Filológicos* 26 (1991): 99–108.

————. "En torno a los relatos de machi, II." *Estudios Filológicos* 28 (1993): 5–18.

Catrileo, María. *Diccionario lingüístico-etnográfico de la lengua mapuche. Mapudungun-Español-English.* 2d ed. Santiago: Editorial Andrés Bello, 1996.

Chihuailaf, Elicura. *De sueños azules y contrasueños.* Santiago: Editorial Universitaria, 1995.

————. *En el país de la memoria (Maputukulpakey).* Temuco, Chile: Quechurewe, 1988.

————. *El invierno y su imagen.* Concepción, Chile: Ediciones LAR, 1977.

————. *El invierno y su imagen y otros poemas azules.* Santiago: Ediciones Literatura Alternativa, 1991.

————. "Mongeley mapu ñi püllü chew ñi llewmuyiñ." *Simpson Siete,* no. 2 (1992): 119–135.

————. "Poesía Mapuche Actual." *Revista Liwen* 1, no. 2 (1990): 36–40.

————, dir. *Kallfvpvllv Espíritu Azul 1: Revista de Arte Mapuche.* Temuko, Chile: Centro de Estudios y Documentación Mapuche LIWEN, 1993.

————, trans. *Todos los Cantos—Ti Kom Vl/Pablo Neruda.* Santiago: Pehuén, 1996.

Citarella, Luca, Ana María Conejeros, Bernarda Espinossa, Ivonne Jelves, Ana María Oyarce, and Aldo Vidal. *Medicinas y culturas en La Araucanía.* Santiago: Editorial Sudamericana, 1995.

Colipán F., Bernardo, and Jorge Velásquez R., eds. *Zonas de Emergencia: Poesía y Crítica.* Valdivia, Chile: Paginadura Ediciones, 1994.

Contreras Hauser, Verónica, and Mabel García Barrera. "La poesía de Bernardo Colipán en 'la búsqueda de los pasos perdidos.'" Temuco, Chile: UFRO, n.d.

Darwin, Charles. *The Voyage of the Beagle.* Garden City, N.Y.: Doubleday & Company, 1962.

Dillehay, T. D. *Monte Verde: A Late Pleistocene Settlement in Chile: Paleoenvironment and Site Context.* Vol. 1. Washington, D.C.: Smithsonian Institution, 1989.

————. *Monte Verde: A Late Pleistocene Settlement in Chile: The Archaeological Context.* Vol. 2. Washington, D.C.: Smithsonian Institution, 1997.

Echaíz, Rene León. *El Toqui Lautaro.* Santiago: Editorial Neupert, 1971.

Editors. "Poesía Mapuche." *Simpson Siete,* no. 2 (1992): 136–154.

Ercilla y Zúñiga, Alonso de. *La araucana.* Mexico: UNAM, 1962.

Erize, Esteban. *Mapuche.* 6 vols. Buenos Aires: Editorial Yepun, 1987–1990.

Faron, Louis C. *Hawks of the Sun: Mapuche Morality and Its Ritual Attributes.* Pittsburgh, Pa.: University of Pittsburgh Press, 1964.

―――. *Los mapuche: su estructura social.* Mexico, D.F.: Instituto Indigenista Interamericano, 1969.

―――. *The Mapuche Indians of Chile.* New York: Holt, Rinehart and Winston, 1968.

―――. *Mapuche Social Structure: Institutional Reintegration in a Patrilineal Society of Central Chile.* Urbana: University of Illinois Press, 1961.

Foerster G., Rolf. *Jesuitas y Mapuches (1593–1767).* Santiago: Editorial Universitaria, 1996.

Foerster G., Rolf, and Sonia Montecinos. *Organizaciones, Líderes y Contiendas Mapuches (1900–1970).* Santiago: Centro Estudios de la Mujer, 1988.

Fuente Duarte, Darío de la. *Diccionario. Raíces Indoamericanas.* Temuco, Chile: Ediciones Universidad de la Frontera, 1996.

Geeregat, Orietta, and Pamela Gutiérrez. "Se ha despertado el ave de mi corazón Texto-Kultrung." In *Actas de Lengua y Literatura Mapuche 5.* Metrenco-Temuco, Chile: Küme Dungu, 1992.

Golluscio de Garaño, Lucía. "Algunos Aspectos de la Teoría Literaria Mapuche." In *Actas: Jornadas de Lengua y Literatura Mapuche. 29–31 de agosto, 1984.* Metrenco-Temuco, Chile: Küme Dungu, 1984. Pp. 103–114.

González Cangas, Yanko. "Nuevas prácticas etnográficas: el surgimiento de la antropología poética." *Alpha* 11 (1995).

Grebe-Vicuña, María Ester. *The Chilean Verso: A Study in Musical Archaism.* Los Angeles: University of California, Los Angeles Press, 1967.

―――. "Cosmovisión mapuche." *Cuadernos de la realidad nacional,* no. 14 (Oct. 1972): 46–73.

―――. "El discurso chamánico Mapuche: consideraciones antropológicas preliminares." In *Actas de lengua y literatura Mapuche 8–10 octubre de 1986. Departamento de Lenguas y Literatura.* Metrenco: Quechurewe, 1986.

―――. "Etnoestética: un replanteamiento antropológico del arte." *Aisthesis,* no. 15 (1983): 19–27.

Grupo de Educación y Desarrollo Indígena. *Nepegñe, Peñi, Nepegñe. Despierta, Hermano, Despierta. Poesía Mapuche.* Santiago: Ñuke Mapu Ediciones, 1997.

Guerrero, Pedro P. "Elicura Chihuailaf: 'Nuestro monumento es la palabra.'" In *El Mercurio, Revista de Libro* (Santiago), no. 416, April 26, 1997. Pp. 4–5.

―――. "La Poesía Mapuche." In *El Mercurio, Revista de Libros* (Santiago), no. 254, March 13, 1997. Pp. 3–5.

Guevara, Tomás. *Historia de la civilización de Araucanía.* Vols. 1, 2. [Santiago], 1898.

Harmelink M., Bryan L. *Manual de Aprendizaje del Idioma Mapuche: aspectos morfológicos y sintácticos.* Temuco, Chile: Ediciones Universidad de la Frontera, 1996.

―――. *Vocabulario y Frases Útiles en Mapudungun.* 3d ed. Temuco: Imprenta Küme Dungu, 1996.

Huenchunao Meza, Oscar E. "La Ley Indígena, Ilusiones y Realidades." *Mapu Ñuke Kimce Wejiñ: Casa de Arte—Ciencia—Pensamiento Mapuche* (octubre–diciembre 1998): 16–19.

Instituto Geográfico Militar. *Atlas Geográfico de Chile para la Educación.* 4th ed. Santiago: Instituto Geográfico Militar, 1994.

Kössler-Ilg, Bertha. *Cuentan los araucanos.* Santiago: Ediciones Mundo, 1996.

———. *Indianermärchen aus den Kordilleren.* Düsseldorf, Germany: Eugen Diederich, 1956.

Kuramochi O., Yosuke. "Los Donantes en *El viejo Latrapai.*" In *Actas: Jornadas de Lengua y Literatura Mapuche. 29–31 de agosto, 1984.* Metrenco-Temuco, Chile: Küme Dungu, 1984. Pp. 89–102.

———. *Me contó la gente de la tierra.* Santiago: Ediciones Universidad Católica de Chile, 1992.

Kvyeh, Rayen. "Modernización versus patrimonio cultural." *Mapu Ñuke Kimce Wejiñ: Casa de Arte—Ciencia—Pensamiento Mapuche* (octubre–diciembre 1998): 13–15.

———. *Mond der ersten Knospen Wvne coyvn ñi kvyeh/Rayen Kvyeh und Carmen Luna.* Stuttgart, Germany: Schmetterling-Verl., 1991.

———. *Wvne coyvn ñi kvyeh. Luna de los primeros brotes.* Temuko, Chile: Ediciones MAPU ÑUKE-Kimce Wejiñ Casa de Arte-Ciencia-Pensamiento Mapuce, 1996.

"LANIC." Latin American Network Information Center of the Institute of Latin American Studies at the University of Texas at Austin. http://www.lanic.utexas.edu/. Accessed May 5, 1996.

Latcham, Ricardo. *La organización social y las creencias religiosas de los antiguos araucanos.* Santiago: Imprenta Cervantes, 1924.

Lenz, Rodolfo. *Estudios araucanos.* Santiago: Imprenta Cervantes, 1895–1897.

Lienlaf, Leonel. "Home page." http://www2.gratisweb.com/lienlaf/. Accessed August 16, 1999.

———. *Se ha despertado el ave de mi corazón.* Santiago: Editorial Universitaria, 1989.

Lipschutz, Alejandro. *La comunidad indígena de América y en Chile.* Santiago: Editorial Universitaria, 1956.

Loncón, Jorge, ed. *"Desde los Lagos" antología de poesía joven, Ivonne Valenzuela, Yanko González, Bernardo Colipán, Harry Vollmer, Marcelo Paredes, Jorge Velásquez.* Santiago: Polígono, 1993.

Manquilef, Manuel. *Comentarios del pueblo araucano (la faz social).* Santiago: Imprenta Cervantes, 1911.

Mansilla, Lucio V. *Una excursión a los indios rangueles.* Madrid: Edicioines de Cultura Hispánica Agencia Española de Cooperación Internacional, 1993.

Mansilla, Sergio. "Poesía Chilena del Sur de Chile (1975–1990). Clemente Riedemann y la Textualización de la Temporalidad Histórica." *Revista Chilena de Literatura* 48 (1996).

Meltzer, David J., Donald K. Grayson, Gerardo Ardila, Alez W. Barker, Dena F. Dincauze, C. Vance Haynes, Francisco Mena, Lautaro Nuñez, and Dennis J. Stanford. "On the Pleistocene Antiquity of Monte Verde, Southern Chile." *American Antiquity* 62, no. 4 (Oct. 1997): 659–661.

Mistral, Gabriela, and Palma Guillén de Nicolau, eds. *Desolación—Ternura—Tala—Lagar.* 5th ed. Mexico City: Editorial Porrúa, 1992.

———. *Poema de Chile.* Edited by Jaime Quezada. Santiago: Editorial Universitaria, 1996.

Moesbach, Ernesto Wilhelm de. *Voz de Arauco.* 4th ed. Temuco, Chile: Editorial Millantu, 1991.

———, ed. *Lonco Pascual Coña ñi tuculpazugun: Testimonio de un cacique mapuche.* Reprint, Santiago: Pehuén Editores, 1984.

Montesino, Sonia. "Literatura mapuche: oralidad y escritura." *Simpson Siete,* no. 2 (1992): 155–166.

Morales T., Leonidas. *Conversaciones con Nicanos Parra.* Santiago: Editorial Universitaria, 1992.

Munizaga, Carlos. *Vida de un estudiante araucano.* Santiago: Universidad de Chile, 1960.

Neruda, Pablo. *Canto general.* Madrid: Ediciones Cátedra, 1990.

———. *Confieso que he vivido.* Buenos Aires: Planeta, 1992.

———. *Cuadernos de Temuco (1919–1920).* Edited by Victor Farías. Buenos Aires: Seix Barral, 1996.

Núñez de Pineda y Bascuñán, Francisco. *Suma y epílogo de lo mas esencial que contiene el libro intitulado Cautiverio Feliz, y guerras dilatadas del reino de Chile.* Edited by José Anadón and Robert A. McNeil. Santiago: Ediciones Universidad Católica de Chile, 1984.

Orellana Rodríguez, Mario. *La Crónica de Gerónimo de Bibar y la Conquista de Chile.* Santiago: Editorial Universitaria, 1988.

Ortega, Emiliano. *Llanto de Maderas. Antología poética de los árboles y los bosques de Chile.* Santiago: MMB Ediciones Integrales, 1994.

Painemal Huenchual, Martin. *Vida de un dirigente mapuche/Martin Painemal Huenchual.* Compiled by Rolf Foerster. [Santiago]: Grupo de Investigaciones Agrarias, Academia de Humanismo Cristiano, [1983 or 1984].

Pewma, Revista de Poesía Joven del Sur. Vol. 1, no. 1 (1994).

Pino Saavedra, Yolando. *Cuentos Mapuches de Chile.* Santiago: Ediciones de la Universidad de Chile, 1987.

Pinto Rodríguez, Jorge, ed. *Araucanía y Pampas. Un mundo fronterizo en América del Sur.* Temuco: Ediciones Universidad de la Frontera, 1996.

Quezada, Jaime, ed. *Gabriela Mistral: Escritos Políticos.* Santiago: Fondo de Cultura Económica Chile, 1994.

Reyes, Bernardo. *Neruda, Retrato de Familia 1904–1920.* Santiago: Dolmen Ediciones, 1997.

Riedemann, Clemente. *Karra Maw'n y otros poemas.* Valdivia, Chile: El Kultrún, 1995.

Rosales, P. Diego de. *Historia General de el Reino de Chile, Flandes Indiano*. Santiago: Editorial Universitaria, 1969.

Sá, Lucia Regina de. "Reading the Rain Forest: Indigenous Texts and their Impact on Brazilian and Spanish-American Literature." Ph.D. diss., Indiana University, 1997.

Salas, Adalberto. "Dieciocho *Kuneo* ("adivinanzas") mapuches." In *Anales de la Universidad de Chile: Estudios en Honor de Rodolfo Oroz*. Edited by Alamiro de Ávila Martel, Luis Merino Montero, and Eduardo Schalscha Becker. Santiago: Ediciones de la Universidad de Chile, 1985. Pp. 459–475.

———. "Dos cuentos mitológicos Mapuches: El *Sumpall y el Trülke Wekufü*. Una perspectiva etnográfica." *Acta Literaria*, no. 8 (1983): 5–36.

———. "Hablar en mapuche es vivir en mapuche: especifidad de la relación lengua/cultura." *Revista de Lingüística Teórica y Aplicada* 25 (1987): 27–35.

———. *Textos orales en Mapuche*. Concepción, Chile: Editorial de la Universidad de Concepción, 1984.

Teillier, Jorge. *Para Ángeles y Gorriones*. Santiago: Editorial Universitaria, 1995.

Teitelboim, Volodia. *Gabriela Mistral: Pública y secreta*. Santiago: Editorial Sudamericana, 1996.

———. *Neruda*. 2d ed. Santiago: Editorial Sudamericana, 1996.

Thayer Ojeda, Tomas. *Las antiguas ciudades de Chile*. Santiago: Imprenta Cervantes, 1911.

Titiev, Mischa. "Araucanian Culture in Transition." In *Occasional Contributions from the Museum of Anthropology of the University of Michigan*, no. 15. Ann Arbor: University of Michigan Press, 1951.

Valdivia, P. Luis de. *Nueve Sermones en Lengua de Chile*. Edited by José Toribio Medina. Santiago: Elzeveriana, 1897 [1624].

Valdivieso, Jaime. *Chile: Un Mito y su Ruptura*. Santiago: Ediciones LAR, 1987.

Valle, Juvencio. *Pajarería Chilena*. Santiago: Dirección de Bibliotecas, Archivos y Museos, 1995.

Vicuña, Cecilia, ed. *Ül: Four Mapuche Poets, An Anthology*. Translated by John Bierhorst. Pittsburgh, Pa.: Latin American Literary Review Press, 1998.

Vivar, Gerónimo de. *Crónica y relación copiosa y verdadera de los reinos de Chile*. Santiago: Editorial Universitaria, 1987.

Vivar, Jerónimo de, and Angel Barral Gómez. *Crónica de los reinos de Chile*. Madrid: Historia 16, 1988.

Zeran, Faride. "En las orillas de un sueño." *La Epoca* (Santiago), April 13, 1997. Pp. 16–17.

———. "La fuerza de la palabra: Elicura Chihuailaf." In *Al pie de la letra: Entrevistas de fin de siglo*. Santiago: Editorial Grijalbo, 1995.

Zurita, Raúl. *Canto a su amor desaparecido*. Santiago: Editorial Universitaria, 1987.

———. *Literatura, Lenguaje y Sociedad (1973–1983)*. Santiago: CENECA, 1983.

18. Elections in Colombia:
A Brief History and Guide to Research

Karen Lindvall-Larson

This paper is part of a larger research project entitled *Latin American Election Statistics: A Guide to Sources*. This publication, which when complete will also include an extensive chronology of elections in nineteen Latin American and Caribbean nations, can be located on the Internet at the address http://dodgson.ucsd.edu/las/index.html. The project grew out of the need for faculty members and students at University of California at San Diego (UCSD) to locate election statistics, and the difficulties encountered along the way. In response to campus interests, UCSD has committed to collecting comprehensively materials on Mexican and Central American elections for the AAU/ARL Latin Americanist Research Resources Project. The University of Notre Dame is complementing this focus with a commitment to do the same for South America. Book dealers throughout Latin America have assisted by locating materials on elections that have facilitated research and made the publication of such a reference work possible. I would especially like to thank Noe Herrera of Libros de Colombia and Fred Morgner and Sandra Pike Raichel of Literatura de Vientos Tropicales and Mexico Norte for their tireless efforts.

In this presentation and in my guide, I include historical information that provides a context for the elections. In the guide I quote from scholars writing about the period in question and include references to statistical sources for elections at the municipal, state, and national levels from independence to the present. In this paper I provide a brief history of elections in Colombia and conclude with a description of sources available for electoral research.

History

Patriots from the Virreinato de la Nueva Granada declared their independence from Spain in 1810, but their final victory over the Spanish troops did not take place until 1819. The political union of present-day Colombia, Venezuela, Ecuador, and Panama was called Gran Colombia, but it was dissolved in 1830. Colombia emerged as a republic, and the colonial era tensions between liberals and conservatives led to the violent political encounters that characterized nineteenth-century Colombian history. By the mid-nineteenth century, voting requirements varied from state to state and each state held its

222

presidential election at a different time. Popular elections were held to select electors, who then voted for the presidential candidates. Many presidential elections were decided in Congress because no candidate won a majority in the secondary elections. Civil wars between the two political factions were frequent and violent, with rural landlords leading their workers to vote or fight for their preferred parties.

The liberal party governed from the 1850s through the 1870s and a conservative government did not return to power until 1880, when the liberal party presidential candidate, Rafael Nuñez, turned to the conservatives after his election. The liberals did not regain the presidency until 1930. The Constitution of 1886 granted the president enormous power, as he was now given the authority to name all state governors, who in turn name all local mayors. This constitution was not replaced until 1991.

The civil wars that pit liberals against conservatives between 1839 and 1902 culminated in the War of the Thousand Days (1899–1902), the result of an ongoing political struggle between Colombian ruling-class factions that was exacerbated by a deepening crisis in the world coffee market. Over 100,000 died, and the country was left bankrupt and the government unable to prevent Panama's secession in 1903.

In 1906 the adoption of proportional representation enabled liberal party candidates to win seats in the various elected bodies. In 1914 national elections were held in which the president was elected by popular vote rather than by electors. In the 1922 presidential election, massive fraud, strong Catholic Church support for the conservative party candidate, and widespread violence again resulted in the election of a conservative party president, but the long powerless liberals did well in urban areas.

Events in 1929 set the tone for what was to come. That summer the Colombian army brutally suppressed a peasant strike in the banana zone. Jorge Gaitán, a liberal congressman, emerged as a champion of the masses and a vocal critic of the conservative government. In 1930, Enrique Olaya Herrera defeated a divided conservative party to become the first liberal president since 1886. The privileges that had belonged to conservative party members throughout the country were now denied. Because of the president's authority to determine governors, the change in the presidential party affected everyone. Violence in the countryside increased, and charges of election fraud and corruption were widespread.

In 1944, Gaitán announced his intention to run for president. The liberal party refused to nominate him as their candidate and the party split, leading to a conservative victory in the 1946 presidential election for the first time in sixteen years. Liberal mobs called for a civil war, but Gaitán called for order and promised to seek election in 1950. Liberals controlled Congress and the conservative president, Ospina, was forced to govern from a minority position.

Appointments of conservative governors and mayors to replace liberals in these positions resulted in violent political conflict, particularly in rural areas. As the chaos increased, moderate liberals left the government and on April 9, 1948, Gaitán was assassinated. Bogotá erupted in the violent riots that came to be known as the *Bogotazo*. The violence in the countryside evolved into a civil war between liberals and conservatives, a war that lasted into the 1960s, claimed over 200,000 lives, and was known as *la Violencia*. General Gustavo Rojas Pinilla overthrew the government in 1953 in an attempt to restore order. In 1954 a constituent assembly unanimously approved an amendment giving women the right to vote and to be elected. Election statistics published since 1957, the year in which women first voted, showed the numbers of women who had voted in each election.

In 1956, leaders of the liberal and conservative parties, disenchanted with the government of Rojas Pinilla, met in Europe to discuss the formation of a coalition government. In December 1957, results of a plebiscite overwhelmingly approved the agreement under which liberals and conservatives would share power. It was known as the Frente Nacional, or National Front. During the National Front period (1958–1974), the two parties agreed to share equally all ministerial, legislative, and bureaucratic positions, and to alternate control of the presidency. While the National Front ended interparty violence, it increased voter apathy and factionalization within the two parties and discouraged the development of alternative parties.

In 1962 the first modern guerrilla organization in Colombia emerged. Officially established in 1964 as the Ejército de Liberación Nacional (ELN), it began with a group of Colombian scholarship students who arrived in Cuba at the time of the Cuban missile crisis. In 1966 the Fuerzas Armadas Revolucionarias de Colombia (FARC) was founded and officially designated a branch of the Colombian Communist Party. In 1968 the Ejército Popular de Liberación (EPL) was formed as the armed branch of the Marxist-Leninist pro-Chinese wing of the same party.

In the presidential elections of April 19, 1970, Gustavo Rojas Pinilla (who had overthrown the government in 1953) received 39 percent of the vote while his opponent Misael Pastrana Borrero (also running on the conservative ticket) received 40.6 percent, a difference of 65,000 votes. There were immediate charges of fraud by supporters of Rojas Pinilla. This was the last election to be held under the provisions of the National Front. In subsequent elections the provisions for parity in elective legislative bodies no longer applied and parties other than the liberal and conservative parties were no longer excluded. In 1972 the Movimiento 19 de Abril (M-19) emerged and took its name from the date on which the leadership believed Rojas Pinilla was fraudulently defeated by Pastrana.

The 1974 presidential election was the first held after the end of the National Front and coincidentally all the major candidates were sons or daughters of former presidents. Liberal Alfonso López Michelsen won the election with 56 percent of the vote, and he was followed in the presidency in 1978 by Liberal Julio César Turbay Ayala, who won 49.5 percent of the vote in an election in which only 39 percent of the electorate voted. During these years the Colombian drug industry emerged as a powerful player on the national scene. In 1982, Conservative Belisario Betancur won the presidency, due largely to voter dissatisfaction with eight years of liberal rule and a split within the liberal party.

In May 1985 the Unión Patriótica (UP) was founded by the FARC as a legal political party. In November 1985, the M-19 seized the Palacio de Justicia and the army responded with massive force, leaving one hundred people dead, including eleven of the twenty-four Supreme Court justices, and the palace destroyed by fire. Increasing social unrest led factions of the liberal and conservative parties to seek ways to modernize Colombia, with reforms including direct election of mayors and the introduction of local referendums. On May 25, 1986, Liberal Virgilio Barco won the presidential election by a margin of 1.6 million votes, the largest in Colombian electoral history.

During the next few years, death squads and paramilitary groups emerged. Mayoral elections were held in 1988 for the first time in over one hundred years in an effort to encourage greater local autonomy. The attorney general was assassinated by drug traffickers, and massacres by paramilitary groups increased. The UP claimed that some five hundred of its leaders have been assassinated since its founding. In 1989, death squads assassinated the UP leader, the governor of Antioquia department, the chief of police of Medellín, and the head of the New Liberalism Movement of the liberal party; and drug traffickers bombed a commercial flight from Bogotá to Cali. The 1990 election saw the assassination by drug-related groups of three of the presidential candidates, including those of the UP, the liberal party, and the M-19. Liberal César Gaviria won the election with 48.1 percent of the vote against a divided conservative party with two candidates. Antonio Navarro Wolf, M-19's candidate, won 12.6 percent of the vote to come in third.

Congressional elections in March 1990 included an extra ballot, the *séptima papeleta,* asking voters to indicate whether they want a constituent assembly to reform the Constitution of 1886. The positive response led to the election of a constituent assembly in December 1990. Four women were elected from a total of seventy seats, with two additional members chosen by indigenous groups and two by demobilized guerrilla groups. Two left-wing candidates, those of the M-19 and the UP, received over 29 percent of the vote.

The constitution promulgated in July 1991 was the first new constitution for Colombia since 1886. It sought to lessen the control of regional party bosses by having senators elected by proportional representation on a nationwide basis, while continuing to have representatives to the lower house of Congress elected in departmental elections. Two Senate seats were reserved for representatives of the indigenous communities, and later changes ensured that the Afro-Colombian communities received two seats in the Chamber of Representatives. The constitution also called for a second round of presidential elections if one candidate did not win an absolute majority in the first round.

The 1994 elections for Congress and for president reflected the failure of the constitutional changes of 1991 to break the continued dominance of the liberal and conservative parties. Although thirty-six parties presented candidates in the congressional elections, liberals won large majorities in both houses of Congress. In the first round of the presidential election, the candidates of the liberal and conservative parties together polled over 90 percent of the vote, although there were sixteen additional candidates. Liberal Ernesto Samper won the runoff election over Conservative Andres Pastrana by less than 2 percent.

Charges of drug cartel financing Samper's election campaign led to efforts to impeach him, and it was not until June 1996 that the Chamber of Representatives voted that there was no evidence that the president knew of the financing of his campaign by the Cali drug cartel. Guerrilla and paramilitary violence escalated, and in the local elections of 1997, thirty-five local council candidates were murdered, two hundred were kidnapped, and thirteen hundred would-be candidates were forced to retire from the campaign. The Consejo Nacional Electoral declared several weeks before the election that voting would be impossible in over 200 of the country's 1,071 municipalities.

The 1998 presidential election was won by Andres Pastrana of the conservative party in the second round, after he lost to the liberal party candidate in the first round. Voter concerns about the liberal and conservative parties' reported corruption and links to drug traffickers opened the field to independent movements like Opción Vida, headed by Noemí Sanín, who won 27 percent of the vote in the first round. There was increasing violence and conflict among all groups: government, military, paramilitaries, drug traffickers, and guerrilla groups.

The new millennium opened with renewed hope for a negotiated peace settlement. Colombia's government negotiators and leftist rebels began the year with a joint tour of democracies in Europe, looking for ways to resolve the country's political and social problems. The many paramilitary groups were seen to be a major obstacle in any peace process, as they also wanted to be involved in any settlement that was reached.

At the same time, documented corruption in Congress reached new heights, and Pastrana called for a referendum for July 2000 to reform or disband Congress. In April, trade unionists, academics, and members of youth, women's, and indigenous movements formed the Frente Social y Política; and the FARC announced a new political party, the Movimiento Bolivariano por la Nueva Colombia. Both groups hoped their efforts would break the historic domination of political power by the liberal and conservative parties.

RESOURCES

Key Works

David Bushnell's many published books and articles are key sources for Colombian political history and his archival research on nineteenth-century elections forms the foundation for nineteenth-century electoral histories and studies. Patricia Pinzón de Lewin has written extensively on twentieth-century elections, and Norma Villarreal focuses on women and politics in Colombia. Dennis Hanratty and Sandra W. Meditz have edited a collection of essays useful for anyone researching Colombian political history. Harvey Kline's books and articles on Colombia should also be consulted. The monumental work edited by Dieter Nohlen, available both in Spanish and German, provides key statistics for national level elections from 1914 through 1991. The larger work on which the present paper is based appears in my research on Colombia in *Latin American Election Statistics: A Guide to Sources,* and directs the scholar to the research and statistical sources related to each Colombian election I could identify from 1810 to 2000.

Subject Headings

The key Library of Congress subject headings for researching elections are "Colombia—elections," "Colombia—politics and government," and "Colombia—political parties." Histories of individual political parties can be found under their names. For information on women's participation, I have found useful general searches under "women—Colombia" and specific searches under "women in politics—Colombia."

Journal Indexes

The bibliographies of books on Colombian elections include valuable references to journal articles. It is also important to review both indexes that are specific to Latin American studies and broader discipline-based indexes. The *Handbook of Latin American Studies* and *HAPI, Hispanic American Periodicals Index* are particularly useful, as are many of the social sciences indexes available in electronic form. The Library of Congress subject headings mentioned above also yield results in these indexes.

Periodical Publications

Among the many useful updates on current events and elections in the Latin American countries are the Economist Intelligence Unit's country profiles and reports; the Latin American Data Base's *NotiSur;* and *Keesing's Record of World Events. Electoral Studies* and the *Boletín electoral latinoamericano* provide useful analyses and in many cases statistics on specific elections. *The Statistical Abstract of Latin America* reproduces a wide variety of electoral statistics published elsewhere and occasionally publishes extremely useful original articles on Latin American elections.

Government Publications

The Registraduría Nacional del Estado Civil is charged by the Consejo Nacional Electoral to run the actual elections and to publish their results. The Departamento Administrativo Nacional de Estadística (DANE) publishes compilations of electoral statistics and includes election statistics in its historical statistical collections.

Internet Sites

Lanic (Latin American Network Information Center) at the University of Texas is the key website for research on Latin American topics. Particularly useful for election research are its "government" section, which includes country-specific and regional resources, and its "Electoral Observatory." The *Political Database of the Americas* at the Georgetown University Center for Latin American Studies provides information on electoral systems, election data, and political parties. Klipsan Press provides election notes, calendars, and results for all Latin American countries.

BIBLIOGRAPHY

Boletín electoral latinoamericano. San José, Costa Rica: CAPEL, IIDH, 1989–.

Bushnell, David. *The Making of Modern Colombia: A Nation in Spite of Itself.* Berkeley: University of California Press, 1993.

Country Profile. Colombia. London: Economist Intelligence Unit, 1986–.

Country Report. Colombia. London: Economist Intelligence Unit, 1986–.

Departamento Administrativo Nacional de Estadística. *Colombia política: estadísticas 1935–1970.* Bogotá: DANE, 1972.

Electoral Studies. Guildford, England: Longman, 1987–.

Estadísticas electorales. Bogotá: Registraduría Nacional del Estado Civil, 1971–.

Handbook of Latin American Studies. Washington, D.C.: Hispanic Division, Library of Congress, 1935–. Available at http://lcweb2.loc.gov/las/.

Hanratty, Dennis M., and Sandra W. Meditz, eds. *Colombia: A Country Study.* Washington, D.C.: Federal Research Division, Library of Congress, 1990.

HAPI, Hispanic American Periodicals Index. Los Angeles: Latin American Studies Center, UCLA, 1975–.

Historia electoral colombiana, 1810–1988. Bogotá: Registraduría Nacional del Estado Civil, Imprenta Nacional de Colombia, 1991.

Keesing's Record of World Events. London: Longman, 1987–.

Kline, Harvey F. *Colombia: Democracy Under Assault.* Boulder, Colo.: Westview, 1995.

Klipsan Press. Available at http://www.klipsan.com/.

Lanic. Austin: University of Texas, Austin. Available at http://lanic.utexas.edu/.

Lindvall-Larson, Karen. *Latin American Election Statistics: A Guide to Sources.* La Jolla, Calif.: Social Sciences and Humanities Library, UCSD, 1998–. Available at http://dodgson.ucsd.edu/las/index.html.

Nohlen, Dieter. *Enciclopedia electoral latinoamericana y del caribe.* San José, Costa Rica: IIDH, 1993.

————. *Handbuch der Wahldaten Lateinamerikas und der Karibik.* Opladen, Germany: Leske and Budrich, 1993.

NotiSur—Latin American Affairs. Albuquerque: Latin American Data Base, Latin American Institute, University of New Mexico, 1991–.

Political Database of the Americas. Washington, D.C.: Georgetown University Center for Latin American Studies. Available at http://www.georgetown.edu/pdba/.

Registraduría Nacional del Estado Civil. *Organización y estadísticas electorales, marzo 15 de 1964.* Bogotá: Reginal Publicaciones, 1965.

Statistical Abstract of Latin America. Los Angeles: Latin American Studies Center, UCLA, 1956–.

Literary Themes

19. "The Feast of the Goat" and Vargas Llosa's Political Fiction

Efraín Kristal

The Feast of the Goat is the most ambitious novel Mario Vargas Llosa has published in almost twenty years. It is a five-hundred-page political novel that explores the corruption of a society under the rule of a dictator. It is an impressively researched novel whose main story lines revolve around the Trujillo regime of the Dominican Republic. The novel explores the humiliating and demoralizing effects of a dictatorship upon an entire society whose basic human and political rights have been undermined by the will of a strongman who exercises power through charisma, intimidation, and corruption. On a secondary level, the novel invites speculation regarding its connections to Vargas Llosa's numerous condemnations, since 1992, of Alberto Fujimori as a dictator who undermined Peru's transition to democracy. It is also clear that the pessimism expressed in the novel about politicians, even those who may be instrumental in assisting a nation in regaining the course towards democracy, coincides with the pessimism Vargas Llosa expressed after his unsuccessful candidacy for the 1990 Peruvian presidential elections.

The Feast of the Goat is not Vargas Llosa's first literary foray into a political situation, but its themes are unprecedented in his narrative fiction. It is Vargas Llosa's first novel about a single individual able to corrupt an entire society, and it may be the only major Latin American novel that condones tyrannicide.

The political content of Vargas Llosa's novels has always been in tune with his political convictions, but his political convictions have changed over the years. To situate *The Feast of the Goat* in the context of Vargas Llosa's political novels, I will first make a few observations with regard to the nature of his political novels in two earlier periods: the 1960s when he was an advocate of the Cuban model for Latin America, and the 1980s when he abandoned his socialist convictions in the name of antiauthoritarian democratic liberalism.

In the 1960s, Vargas Llosa was a committed socialist who believed that violence was a legitimate means to achieve the aims of freedom and justice in Latin America. His novels of the period condemned the evils of capitalism, depicted as an entrenched economic system with corrosive effects on human relations in Peruvian society. In his three first novels, *Time of the Hero, The Green House,* and *Conversation in the Cathedral,* upward mobility is unthinkable without moral degradation because society is too corrupt for reform to be meaningful. The protagonist of *Conversation in the Cathedral*—his first novel about a dictatorship—is Santiago Zavala, a young man who chooses a life of mediocrity in order to shun the lucrative but corrupt activities of his father and the social class to which he belongs.

The novel is set during the Odría dictatorship of the 1950s, and it pays much attention to the regime's repressive apparatus and secret police, but the dictator appears only once, and fleetingly, in the novel. This idea was in keeping with the young Vargas Llosa's socialist convictions that the main goal of a revolution does not entail the elimination of a dictator, but the elimination of the capitalist system in order to establish socialism.

In the 1980s, Vargas Llosa had abandoned his socialist illusions and the messages of his novels reflected this shift. He reconsidered his conviction that violence is a legitimate means to achieve political change. In fact, he began to argue that the violence of political fanatics is a significant impediment to democratic liberalism in Latin America. In this period, his political novels were concerned with the fragility of a society assailed by fanatics, political opportunists, and well-intentioned but misguided idealists who think that violence can make the world a better place. His most important political novel in this period is *The Real Life of Alejandro Mayta,* in which Vargas Llosa explores the negative consequences of revolutionary activity. In the novel the modest and failed insurrection of Alejandro Mayta in 1958 is presented as the starting point of a vortex of violence that has brought Peru to the edge of disintegration. The novel imagines the worst-case scenario for Peru in the light of the Shining Path guerrilla movement: a country in the throes of a devastating civil war plagued with death squads, terrorist activity, and foreign military intervention.

In the novel, a novelist—loosely inspired in Vargas Llosa's own autobiography—encounters the revolutionary Mayta, the man that has inspired the novel he has been writing. In this conversation the novelist tells Mayta that he has willfully invented much about his life that is not true; and that he still feels a need to understand why he had participated in revolutionary activity.

In the early part of the interview, the novelist feels disenchanted because he thinks he knows Mayta's story in more detail than this frail, beaten, abandoned man who was repudiated and betrayed by his old collaborators. Mayta talks about his revolutionary period as if it had been a closed and forgotten chapter of his life. But the novelist discovers, late in the interview, that Mayta's fanaticism has not cooled, that he is still ready and willing to participate in subversive acts, and that he still believes in the ideals that inspired the failed insurrection of 1958. Mayta believes that the only difference between his own revolutionary attempt and Fidel Castro's in Cuba is that one succeeded whereas the other one failed:

> Those things seem impossible when they fail. . . . If they succeed, they seem perfect and well planned to everyone. For example, the Cuban revolution. How many landed with Fidel on the Gramma? A handful. Maybe even fewer than we had that day in Jauja. They were lucky and we weren't.

Twenty-five years after Mayta's failed insurrection in Jauja, Mayta still believes he was right and that he was simply a victim of his circumstances. Mayta's reflection about his revolutionary failure reveals the depth of his fanaticism, as well as Vargas Llosa's cunning in setting the Jauja subversion three years before the historical events that inspired the novel. In the world of the novel, Fidel Castro's triumph cannot provide a justification for Mayta's revolutionary optimism. Thus one can more fully appreciate Mayta's stubborn fanaticism in all its pathetic tenacity.

Mayta failed, but he is not a beaten man because he has not abandoned his political convictions. He is to a tragic figure like Gisors, the Marxist professor in André Malraux's *Man's Fate* who admits "Marxism has ceased to live in me" after the failure of the Shanghai insurrection in which several young Communist militants died, including his own son and some of his dearest disciples.

The story of Mayta is a close relative to Joseph Conrad's *Under Western Eyes:* the narrator of Vargas Llosa's novel, like the language teacher in Conrad's is penetrating in his description of the inner states of those who support and carry out subversive activity, and he ends up equally perplexed about the motivations of those willing to kill for an idea. The perplexity in Mayta, however, is not as in *Under Western Eyes,* in which foreigners gaze at curious individuals (that is to say, a British man gazing at the idiosyncrasies of the Russian revolutionary). It is, rather, the perplexity of one who looks at himself in the mirror. This is why Vargas Llosa does not invent, as Conrad did, a narrator who pretends to give an objective account of a world he does not understand, but one who gives up the objective representation of reality. *Mayta* is not simply a fictionalized account of a revolutionary attempt and its antecedents. It is a fictionalized obsession of a writer who has found in literature, perhaps, a palliative to the same obscure motives that led his protagonist to believe that ideas are worth more than human lives.

Mayta scratches the surface of a dimension of human experience Vargas Llosa has not explored in depth in his novels until *The Feast of the Goat:* the individual who confronts, without illusion or fantasy, the consequences of his own weaknesses and crimes. No one in *Mayta* assumes responsibility for the debacles for which they are liable. At the end of the novel, Alejandro Mayta is as fanatic as he ever was; and the narrator, who used to believe that violence was a legitimate means to accomplish political gains, has channeled his own fanaticism to a work of fiction where no one can attribute moral responsibility to the products of his imagination.

To summarize, Vargas Llosa's novels of the 1980s turned the tables on the themes of his previous political novels. Whereas in the 1960s individuals were abused by the impersonal machinery of capitalism, in the novels of the 1980s society is presented as the victim of the initiative of individuals. In the 1960s, Vargas Llosa was concerned about the corrupting aspects of a political system, but in the 1980s he was more preoccupied with the effects that individuals can have in undermining a society. That being said, in both the 1960s and the 1980s Vargas Llosa was better at identifying the results of corruption and violence than in identifying its sources: in the 1960s an anonymous system called capitalism was responsible for human degradation, and in the 1980s the responsibility for violence are those irrational motivations that goad characters like Mayta into a life of violence.

In *The Feast of the Goat,* Vargas Llosa begins to face the issue of human responsibility in ways that are unprecedented in his fiction. This new development in Vargas Llosa's fiction coincides with a change in his attitude towards politics. After losing the Peruvian elections in 1990, Vargas Llosa has subsumed his critique of the political utopias of the left under a broader critique of governments who do not respect the basic freedoms of their citizens. In the 1990s he continued to condemn the terrorism of revolutionary groups such as the Shining Path, but he began to see them as symptoms rather than causes of social ills. He now attributes the existence of terrorist groups in his country to the authoritarian practices of the Peruvian government and its military institutions, and to the moral and material collapse of the political and civil authorities who have failed to guarantee the human rights of the Peruvian population (especially in the most disenfranchised regions of his nation). It is telling that Vargas Llosa interpreted the 1993 capture of Guzmán—the leader of the Shining Path—as a minor event because he believes that the conditions that accounted for the rise and success of the Shining Path have not been addressed. Furthermore, he believes that Alberto Fujimori's dictatorial tendencies were conducive to political violence and terrorism.

Ever since he lost the elections to Fujimori in 1990, Vargas Llosa has also become more pessimistic about organized politics:

> Real politics, not the kind that one reads and writes and thinks about—the only sort that I had been acquainted with—but the politics that is lived and practiced day by day, has little to do with ideas, values and imagination, with long-range visions, with notions of an ideal society, with generosity, solidarity or idealism. It consists almost exclusively of maneuvers, intrigues, plots, pacts, paranoias, betrayals, a great deal of calculation, no little cynicism and every variety of con game.

The Feast of the Goat reflects Vargas Llosa's political reorientation. In the new novel he returns to the theme of a corrupt society he had treated so extensively in the 1960s, but it is no longer a literary exploration of the machinery of an anonymous repressive political system. Human agency matters in this novel, as it did in the novels of the 1980s, but it is no longer the agency of those fanatics and utopians who undermine social stability: it is the agency, first and foremost, of a individual, the dictator who is directly responsible for the corruption of his nation; and secondly, of the individuals who cannot live with themselves for having participated in a corrupt social regime. Finally, the novel is consistent with Vargas Llosa's skepticism about organized politics and professional politicians because the characters responsible for the Dominican Republic's return to democracy were crafty, amoral individuals of good will who had been willing participants in the dictator's regime.

As in *Conversation in the Cathedral,* in *The Feast of the Goat* the repudiation of a corrupt father by a young person is the vantage point from which Vargas Llosa examines the failures of an entire society. In *Conversation* the failure was that of the capitalistic social order, and in *The Feast of the Goat* the failure is that of a society under the spell of an evil dictator who corrupts the very fiber of the closest human relationships.

The novel's protagonist, Urania Cabral, is Vargas Llosa's best-developed female character in all of his narrative fiction. She is the daughter of a senator who had worked closely with Trujillo and who was a hesitant but willing accomplice in the most traumatic and humiliating experiences of his daughter's life. Senator Cabral was willing to sacrifice his daughter's innocence to regain the favor of the dictator when he had lost grace in the regime. In a novel where the personal and the political are closely intertwined, Urania is the embodiment of the humiliation, shame, and betrayal that the Dominican society suffered at the hands of its dictator and the individuals who served him.

The events of the novel are framed around two chapters that serve as book ends to the novel. In the first chapter, a forty-nine-year-old Urania Cabral returns to the Dominican Republic for a short visit after an absence of thirty-five years. In the last chapter, Urania decides to return to Manhattan where she works as a successful lawyer after an unexpected, cathartic conversation she had with several female relatives, in which she fully reveals the reasons why she had left her country in the first place.

In each of the seven chapters devoted to Urania, Vargas Llosa tells her story by alternating between her visit to the Dominican Republic in the 1990s with the story of her early adolescence. Vargas Llosa invites his readers to wonder why she left the Dominican Republic when she was fourteen years old, and why she feels disgust at the thought of an intimate relationship with any man. It is obvious that the two questions are related and that some traumatic experience had affected her sexuality, but the full dimension of her personal tragedy is not revealed until the last pages of the novel. In the chapters devoted to Urania, Vargas Llosa makes a number of suggestions in increasing order of gravity. At first it appears that Urania might have been affected when she learns that Trujillo expected sexual favors from the wives of his closest associates, and she therefore suspects that the dictator may have been involved with her own mother. Then Vargas Llosa suggests that Urania might have been shocked when a classmate from a wealthy family is forced upon by Trujillo's son and his cronies. Before the final revelation, Vargas Llosa insinuates that she might have been molested by her own father, a theme he had treated in the novel *Who Killed Palomino Molero?* In fact, Urania is psychologically molested by her father because her trust in him was shattered when he was willing to make a sexual present of her virginity to the dictator. In a scene where Vargas Llosa crosses the boundary into pornography, he describes the details of the sexual molestation of the fourteen-year-old girl by an impotent Trujillo.

The second main story line of the novel involves Trujillo in the last months of his life, when he has lost the support of both the United States and the Catholic Church. Trujillo is depicted as a brutal and charismatic narcissist who has no true friends because his only human dealings have been based on fear, intimidation, or patronage. He has no regrets about the crimes he has committed or the lives he has ruined. He thinks of himself as the "savior" of the Dominican Republic because he protected it from any interactions with the blacks from Haiti. His only redeeming feature—when compared to some of his more opportunistic associates and family members—is a relative one: he loves his country. He has not taken any money outside his country, and he wants to die there. There is a sense, however, that his patriotism is an expression of his narcissism because he sees the Dominican Republic as an extension of himself. There is no character in all of Vargas Llosa's narrative fiction who has less scruples than Trujillo.

His primary concern in his dying days are his failing bodily functions. Towards the end of the novel, Trujillo roars with anger at his sexual impotence, and the narrator suggests that he may be literally imploring to the devil himself. Indeed, Trujillo is presented as a diabolical personality who rules from the very top of the political pyramid of power with his conniving and parasitic family (who reap the financial and social benefits of the dictator's reign of terror and corruption), and his two most effective supporters: Abbes, the strongman and head of his secret service, and Balaguer, the president who offers a public front for his power when Trujillo is not the official head of state.

The third main plot of the novel unfolds in a series of chapters in which a number of conspirators plot to murder the dictator. The conspiracy does not come from an organized opposition, and it could not have, because Trujillo's repressive regime has been successful in undermining any opposition with the assistance of his secret police. The conspirators had all been involved in

Trujillo's regime. They come from different walks of life and represent a cross section of Dominican life: army officers, immigrants, pious Catholics, etc. They have little in common save a severe sense of guilt for their participation in a regime that has troubled their conscience. They are all individuals who Trujillo had both rewarded and humiliated to vile submission for they become the tools of the dirty work of his society. After they succeed in murdering the dictator, the dictator's repressive apparatus continues to function without a head, and the majority of the conspirators are captured, brutally tortured, and murdered.

The first three story lines are presented in sequences of three chapters where the stories of Urania, the last months in the life of Trujillo, and the conspiracy to murder the dictator alternate in a recursive pattern. In each of these chapters, Vargas Llosa also moves from the present to the past of his characters: in the Urania chapters Vargas Llosa flashes back to her adolescence as she is narrating her short visit to the Dominican Republic; in the chapters devoted to Trujillo's dying months Vargas Llosa flashes back to Trujillo's political and sexual exploits; and the chapters devoted to the conspiracy alternate with sections about the ways in which each of the conspirators were co-opted and compromised by Trujillo's regime.

With chapter 18 the recursive pattern that had been established earlier comes to an end, and Vargas Llosa ties loose ends and begins the fourth main plot of the novel: the transition to democracy in the Dominican Republic thanks to the crafty Balaguer who bribes Trujillo's family members to leave the country, and manages to outmaneuver Abbes, who is more ruthless, but not as politically savvy as Balaguer.

By the end of the novel, it becomes clear that the conspirators who participated in Trujillo's assassination—even those who anticipate certain death for their role in the conspiracy—have experienced the assassination as a catharsis. More significantly, Urania's confession is a cathartic experience that might begin a healing process of greater significance.

The untold story of the transition into democracy in the Dominican Republic is the silent shame and powerful feelings of betrayal of those victims, like Urania, who represent the most enduring legacy of the dictatorship, decades after Trujillo's regime has been relegated to a minor chapter of Latin American history.

With *The Feast of the Goat*, Vargas Llosa has made a major contribution to the already rich body of literature about Latin American dictators. It is also his most important novel from the perspective of personal responsibility. Even though the ultimate source of the social evils can be traced to the unaccountable Trujillo, several protagonists of the novel try to face up to their own demons: the ones that resulted from their own actions.

20. Arguedas and Dillard: Critical Linkages

Susan H. Shaw

This paper is a quick replay of some of the strategies I used in my thesis[1] to account for striking similarities between two quite different authors, José María Arguedas and Annie Dillard, in the way they regard nature. These strategies may be of interest to Latin Americanist librarians, because there are other people out there doing comparative studies on authors from apparently disparate cultures, and area studies librarians and collections serve as a resource for these researchers. Recent examples include James Nolan in *Poet-Chief: The Native Poetics of Walt Whitman and Pablo Neruda,* John McLaren in *New Pacific Literatures: Culture and Environment in the European Pacific,* and J. Michael Dash in *The Other America: Caribbean Literature in a New World Context.*[2]

In my case, I was originally struck by the similarity in the following passages from Dillard's *Tinker at Pilgrim Creek* and the English translation of Arguedas's *Deep Rivers.*[3] Looking for an explanation for this similarity sent me down many paths, not all of them literary.

> Then one day I was walking along Tinker Creek thinking of nothing at all and I saw the tree with lights in it. I saw the backyard cedar where the mourning doves roost charged and transfigured, each cell buzzing with flame. I stood on the grass with the lights in it, grass that was wholly afire, utterly focused and utterly dreamed. It was less like seeing than like being for the first time seen, knocked breathless by a powerful glance.[4]

> In the dark street, in the silence, the wall appeared to be alive; the lines I had touched between the stones burned on the palms of my hands. . . . The stones of the Inca wall were larger and stronger than I had imagined; they seemed to be bubbling up beneath the whitewashed second story, . . . Then I remembered the Quechua songs which continually repeat one pathetic phrase: yawar mayu, "bloody river"; yawar unu, "bloody water"; yawar wek'e, "bloody tears." . . . The wall was stationary, but all its lines were seething and its surface was as changeable as that of the flooding summer rivers.[5]

Annie Dillard, a United States essayist, novelist, and poet, and José María Arguedas, a Peruvian translator, essayist, novelist, and poet, seem to share what I call permeable boundaries with regard to nature. The subject-object relationship, in other words, is not always one of clear separation. Such permeable boundaries allow the object to act upon the subject, the subject being passive and emptied. For most of us, a lot of the time, the differences between self and other, observer and observed, are easily discerned. But not for Arguedas and Dillard, two authors who come from very different backgrounds and write in different genres. In their respective homelands, Arguedas is considered a neo-indigenist who conveys the Native American cosmovision better than any other non-Indian; Dillard is a nature writer with a mystical turn, a descendant of the transcendentalists. That they are twentieth-century American seems to be the only link between them. Does their commonality have to do with their Americanness, or does the explanation lie elsewhere?

I looked first at Americanness. A focus on the natural world and what it represents has been one of the distinguishing marks of the literature of the New World. Further, this concern with nature and all that it means has been present from the first. Earl Fitz, in expounding a new sort of literary "New Worldism," discusses several themes common to postconquest literatures of the Americas. Six are especially pertinent to the presence of nature in literature: (1) the attempt to recover the preconquest past through rediscovery and revitalization of native literatures; (2) the wonder-filled narrative of discovery and conquest of nature; (3) "miscegenation," not just in the sense of interracial sexual relations, but also in the sense of identity crisis and transculturization; (4) the American brand of modernism, which was one of the pulses driving New Worldism, Indianism, and Indigenism; (5) regionalism; and (6) the conflict between civilization and barbarity.[6]

If Arguedas is considered as a *transculturado* among those who attempt to recover the preconquest past through revitalization of native literatures— Louise Erdrich, N. Scott Momaday, Rosario Castellanos, and Darcy Ribeiro, to name a few—then it is possible to understand why many of his characters have such a special way of perceiving nature. And I do include him here, rather than among earlier *indigenistas*.

The inherent problem of indigenista literature was that it was written by people who did not belong to the world about which they were writing. Not only were the writers not Indian, but as one critic put it, "They used a system of rationalistic thought to try to understand the native culture, which was based on mythical thought or magic."[7] Thus some of the more recent writers, who are not intimately acquainted with native culture, may rely on literary technique rather than personal experience to convey the "mythical thought" of Indian people.

How could a non-Indian begin to write authentically about Indians? This was a question that ate at the heart of Arguedas. He had been nurtured and raised in the Quechua culture, absorbed their language and cosmovision as his "native" one, the one he used to build on later. Arguedas was keenly aware, however, that he was not a member of the Quechua culture. He did not refer to himself as an indigenous writer or as an indigenista. Rather, he considered himself a neo-indigenista and called himself a transculturado, the product of indigenization, which would be the third and final stage of the process Peru must go through in order to really be a nation.[8] His own indigenization he referred to once in an interview:

> I learned their songs, their games. I lived in their world. I believed that the world was as they believed it is. I believed it all, that the river is a god, that the mountains were gods . . . and this indigenous vision of the world I believe in has continued to this day.[9]

Pre-Columbian oral and written literatures were centered in the natural world, as were the lives of the people who produced them. A Navajo chant calls thunder "the voice that beautifies the land"; a Quechua *wanka* personifies a dead tree when asking: "will you never open your eyes again?"[10] The many hundreds of cultures indigenous to the Americas shared and still share a special relationship to nature, a relationship very different from that of Europeans.[11] As best as can be determined, nature for Native Americans was not even a named, separate entity.[12] It did not have tidy hierarchies of relationships all leading up to a one-in-three and ubiquitous but still centralized God. While today one may hear references to a "great spirit" that seem like references to Allah or God or Jehovah, it is not clear that such a monotheistic view existed before contact with Europeans. For indigenous Americans, "godness"—or *wakan,* or *Manitou*—was dispersed throughout creation, and the world around them was peopled with nonhuman beings both organic and inorganic.

Many Latin American literary critics refer to the belief system and way of thinking of the Indians as a "mythological consciousness" or a "magic mentality," using terms (and revealing a way of thinking) currently unfamiliar in Anglo-America. The Quechua belief system seems to be basically the same as those of North American Indians in that it "considers there to be a relation of reciprocity and continuity between man and nature because both are part of a harmonious whole. Nature is a direct reflection of the social relations existing among men."[13] It plays an active role in the lives of people.

People in a highland Indian community, according to anthropologist Catherine Allen,[14] are from earliest childhood made familiar with even the smallest feature of the landscape surrounding the village or town and its fields. They watch for any sort of change or action, believing that an inspirited landscape is watching them, too. The local mountains, hills, and springs constitute a hierarchy of spirits who have specialized jurisdictions and areas of responsibility. The tallest and perhaps slightly distant peak typically incarnates the

Creator of the world who watches over and protects his creatures. The earth itself is *Pachamama*, who tenderly loves and feeds her creatures and makes them fertile, although sometimes her evil alter ego, *Pachatira*, opens up and swallows them.

What inspirits the material world is a particular sort of energy or life source that circulates through everything. Anything that exhibits motion and liveliness, especially flowing water and light, is considered to be a conductor of sorts and is full of this generative force. Rivers circulate it; the sun and stars send it. Rocks are thought to concentrate light, and thus have more of this life force; snow and glaciers, as "concentrated water," also are considered to be higher in content. Some objects are thought to hold even more of this special power: unusual rocks, for instance, or small figures. Bubbly liquids such as beer and soft drinks may have it; musicians and musical instruments also have it.

The people have a respectful approach to nature. For instance, before spring plowing they apologize to Pachamama for the fact that they are about to cut her. They know that, just as the earth feeds them, the earth likes to share what they are eating or drinking, thus the sharing of libations and blood with Pachamama. During annual mock war dances, it is expected that the music and emotions will reach such a pitch that a fight will break out. The blood spilled is regarded as the earth's due.

The Quechua belief system is incorporated into Arguedas's works, which can be appreciated much more by a reader with some idea of those beliefs. For Arguedas, connectedness to nature and to others, not just genealogy, is a sign of Indianness. He shows the Indian aliveness of non-Indians who are open to others and to nature—who have "permeable boundaries"—and the non-Indians' deadness of Indians who have lost heart or soul. Many of Arguedas's characters are Indian and non-Indian highland-dwellers and Quechua speakers who are deeply connected to nature, speaking to it and listening or watching for a response or sign.

In addition to illustrating lives lived in harmony with nature, Arguedas uses nature as a character to comment on what is occurring in the lives of the human characters. Birds appear on the scene to sing or cry; mountains obscure themselves or show off with flower-covered slopes; boulder-strewn rivers roar and murmur; and trees growing by homes droop, starve, or are in their glory, depending on the state of human affairs in their immediate neighborhood.

The origin of Arguedas's mystical attitude toward nature is apparent. But if his permeable boundaries result from his grounding in the Quechua belief system, how can people account for Dillard's similar perception? Dillard is not Native American and does not seem to have any connection with the Native American cosmovision. Critics treat her as a nature writer, or in terms of her gender or spirituality.

Returning to Fitz's categories, one can see that nature writing, a peculiarly Anglo-American phenomenon, must be a descendant of the wonder-filled European discovery narratives by way of natural history. Peter Fritzell attributes the genesis of nature writing partly to a need for control over the unknown and fearsome New World.[15]

Simon Schama talks about the white European male desire to mold nature in the image of man. Mountains have been an especially attractive target in this effort, because they have been the home of the gods and because mountains, more than any other landscape form, show up the small stature of man. "Of all landscapes, then, mountain altitudes were fated to provide a rule against which *men* (for this was a distinctively masculine obsession) would measure the stature of humanity, the march of empires."[16]

Commenting on Mount Rushmore, Schama says, "For Gutzon Borglum, only in the New World empire of America—the most heroic, the most *masculine* since the Greeks'—could such a thing be imagined, let alone executed."[17] Schama contrasts Borglum's attitude with that of the Lakota:

> But to a Lakota shaman, of course, invisibility was the sign of presence, not absence. And for that matter, there was something to be seen: the mountain itself, in which the Great Spirit, *Wakonda,* was indistinguishably embedded with the rock and the scree. To feel its presence and that of all the ancestors buried in such a place required only a kind of respectful annihilation of the human self.[18]

Dillard, though Euro-American, does not seek mastery over the landscape like Borglum. Her approach to nature, "a kind of respectful annihilation of the human self," is more like that of the Lakota shaman. In discussions of nature writers or of the transcendentalists, Dillard is considered to be quite different from the others, more "out on the edge."[19] As it happens, Dillard is the only woman included in such discussions as a self-proclaimed mystic. Thus, to discover the origin of Dillard's way of seeing, I turned to work that might have been done on a connection between gender and perception and to an explanation of mysticism. Along the way, I found more than one link between Arguedas and Dillard.

Perception is now defined as the mind's ordering of sensory data, based on the observer's previous experience and mental and emotional state. Researchers in the 1960s found that perception is affected by ethnicity.[20] Perception is also different today than it was one or two hundred years ago, and it is considered by some to be different in men than in women. The literature on perception is scattered through cultural studies, film and art theory, religion, feminist epistemology, and postcolonial literary criticism. Linda Williams provides a good overview of many of the issues in her introduction to *Viewing Positions: Ways of Seeing Film.*[21]

Jim Cheney's article in *Journal of Feminist Studies in Religion*[22] suggests the difference between the transcendentalists and Dillard at the door of the late-twentieth century and feminism:

> Annie Dillard's postmodernist sensibility is most explicitly stated on 206–8 [of *Pilgrim at Tinker Creek*] where she contrasts the Enlightenment (or Newtonian) epistemology wherein "we gradually roll back the cloud of unknowing" with the Heisenbergian epistemology wherein we "cannot study nature per se, but only [our] own investigation of nature." I take her work as feminist in that it breaks with the dominant masculinist tradition.[23]

Gretchen Legler, Paula Gunn Allen, and Donna Haraway consider the perceptual modes of both females and indigenous peoples to be "outside the norm," the norm being the perceptual mode of the white European male.[24] Paula Gunn Allen asserts that these two ways of perceiving are related when she says:

> Western technological-industrialized minds cannot adequately interpret tribal materials because they are generally trained to perceive their entire world in ways that are alien to tribal understandings. . . . Much of women's culture bears a marked resemblance to tribal culture. The perceptual modes that women, even those of us who are literate, industrialized, and reared within masculinist academic traditions, habitually engage in more closely resemble inclusive-field perception than exclusive foreground-background perceptions.[25]

Whether one credits Paula Gunn Allen's assertion or not, it is worth examining the "dominant masculinist tradition" to which Cheney and Allen refer. They are talking about what is also known as Western thought, including European science, or Euroscience, and epistemology. However, epistemology, the branch of philosophy that studies the nature and possibility of knowledge and how it is acquired, is changing. The approach to determine the validity of knowledge used since the eighteenth century, centered on the concept of a human subject, is in decline.[26] Epistemology has concerned itself until a few decades ago with the question of "objective" reality. Objectivity seems to mean being unbiased, unremarkable, unmarked by strong opinion or discernible point of view.

Feminist critical theory discerns the bias in such objectivity. Donna Haraway and Gretchen Legler talk about situated knowledge, that is, knowledge located in what are termed marked bodies. People who are not white, not middle-class, not heterosexual, and not male have been outside the norm. The points of view of these "others" have not been privileged or considered valid. Those marked as different have been considered closer to nature, or of a lower order, than white middle-class males; and as a matter of fact, they have been much studied and remarked upon in scientific literature. Legler, like Fritzell and others, says that science was a way of establishing control over the world. Legler says it was also used to establish social control.

One area of Euroscience, natural history, is an antecedent of nature writing. Gretchen Legler draws upon Donna Haraway and Peter Fritzell to bring together the threads of Euroscience and situated knowledge as they apply to American nature writers:

> As Peter Fritzell has pointed out, most American nature writers unwittingly write their bodies—their desires, their sexuality, their experience, their race—into the landscape. But instead of paying attention to their being in the natural world, Fritzell writes, the vast majority of American nature writers "have tended to generalize the 'personal' and the 'subjective' in their engagements with nonhuman nature, to render themselves and their environments soundly customary, scientifically and aesthetically clean, and most often morally pure." I want to suggest that this unselfconsciousness of the body of the writer/author/observer is a way of knowing and writing about nature [that] writers inherited from the language and practice of modern science. This way of understanding nature and the place of human bodies in it became codified as the way to write about nature through the work of Henry David Thoreau, the widely acknowledged "father of American nature writing."[27]

The term "consciousness" is important to the discussion of both Dillard and Arguedas. Centuries of schooling in scientific observation resulted in a group of people who took for granted that they were natural and the norm and that their way of confronting the world was rational and normal. That way of confronting the world included bringing to the act of observation as much previously gleaned information as possible about the object being observed. The act of observing is itself a projection or imposition of one's self upon the thing.

Philosopher Caroline Whitbeck explains the importance of developing a feminist metaphysics as a frame of reference for an alternative way of operating in the world; it has at its heart "a conception of the self-other relation that is significantly different from the self-other opposition that underlies much of so-called 'western thought.' . . . Self-other opposition is at the heart of other dualistic oppositions such as . . . culture-nature, spirit-matter, mind-body, human-divine . . . knower-known."[28] Whitbeck says a feminist metaphysics is not gender-based; asserting so would, among other things, continue the dualism of Western thought. "Too often the project of constructing a feminist view is confused with the project of simply affirming the goodness or primacy of the characteristics associated with what masculist dualist thought views as the feminine principle."[29]

Although Dillard's ability to perceive nature in the special way she does may not be due solely to her feminist style of perception, a man steeped in Euroscience would have difficulty letting go of changing. Dillard in *Pilgrim at Tinker Creek* brings in readings from natural history; she examines creek water using a microscope; and she collects pupae. But she is also very conscious of the problem of seeing. Dillard's relationship to nature seems very much like Whitbeck's description of a feminist frame of reference: "in place of an ontology characterized by dualistic oppositions . . . , the self-others relation generates a multifactorial, interactive model of most, if not all, aspects of reality."[30]

Another scholar who contends that a person's relation to nature is made different by adherence to science is historian Lynn White Jr. He argues in one of the foundation essays of ecocriticism that, before the rise of Euroscience in the Middle Ages, a person's relation to nature was much more respectful. The change in attitude toward nature can be traced to the Western, nonmeditative branch of Christianity that spread throughout Europe. Although White fixes the root of the attitude in the Judeo-Christian belief that all creation was made for the benefit of humankind, early Christianity and the Eastern branch of Christianity were more meditative. "Nature was conceived primarily as a symbolic system through which God speaks to men . . . science as we conceive it could hardly flourish in such an ambience."[31]

Latin Christianity developed a natural theology that placed humankind above nature. Nature was to be analyzed, manipulated, and used, not contemplated. One of the few exceptions to this attitude was Saint Francis of Assisi, who believed in a sort of panpsychism in which animals had souls. Another exception would have been those contemplatives or mystics who reached back to the "desert fathers" of the early Church for inspiration. Dillard refers to these desert fathers in *Pilgrim at Tinker Creek*. She also has called herself a Christian mystic.

Panpsychism, the belief that everything animate and inanimate has "psychological" being, is an element in both the early Christian mysticism of Dillard and the tribal shamanism of Arguedas. Here is where the strongest link between these two authors can be found.

Historian of religion Mircea Eliade places shamanism and Christian mysticism along a spectrum of religious experience, whereas others distinguish shamanism from mysticism because of the former's shape-changing aspects.[32] The five ways religious experience, including mysticism, is identified include the awareness of the holy, the sense of being one with the divine, the direct perception of God, the encounter with a reality "wholly other," and the sense of a transforming power as a presence.[33] These qualities or stances are present in works of both Dillard and Arguedas and are the sorts of attitudes or beliefs to which commentators point when they label these authors mystical.

I have drawn a wide circle around Dillard and Arguedas and explored the territory surrounding them, looking for a path that links them. Surely her burning tree and his boiling wall must live somewhere in the same dimension. To continue the mixed metaphor, I have found no direct road between the two territories, but instead an overlapping of both with a third, larger country.

This is the country of the mystical and nonrational, a territory that lies outside Western science. Mystical and nonrational are terms applied to Native American belief systems, to Christian visionaries, and to feminist epistemics, among others. It is inhabited by those who truly see differently, who see more than outward form.

Annie Dillard and José María Arguedas share a nonrational vision that they reached by different routes. Dillard has called herself a mystic, but she may also have a feminist way of seeing. Arguedas said that he retained the Quechua cosmovision in adulthood. Mysticism, feminist epistemology, Native American religion: these are all approaches to reality outside the realm of Euroscience. They could also fall within the very wide circle of ecocriticism.

Dillard says that the whole world is "crackling and buzzing" around us, if we could but see and hear it, and that creation is laden with message from its creator. For Native Americans at the time of the arrival of the Pilgrims, the world was full of nonhuman people, a web of sacred spirit loci. Native Americans today, in spite of centuries of indoctrination in an Enlightenment-based worldview, maintain their connection with the crackling, buzzing world and its messages. And the Euro-Americans' Enlightenment-based worldview, which denied what it could not see or measure, has begun to understand that reality is relative.

As Mircea Eliade explains, the world has been "de-sacralized" for a long time for those of us who are part of modern society. It is thus, perhaps, hard for many to understand that Dillard and Arguedas live in a sacralized one. They are not employing magical realism. They are not writing literature of the fantastic. They are exhorting us to relate to nature in a different way, a way that is shared across the Americas and that traverses boundaries of nationality, language, and ethnic background.

NOTES

1. Susan Helfert Shaw, "The Witness of Landscape: Annie Dillard and José María Arguedas in Accord with Nature" (master's thesis, South Dakota State University, 1997).

2. James Nolan, *Poet-Chief: The Native Poetics of Walt Whitman and Pablo Neruda* (Albuquerque: University of New Mexico Press, 1994); John McLaren, *New Pacific Literatures: Culture and Environment in the European Pacific* (New York: Garland, 1993); J. Michael Dash, *The Other America: Caribbean Literature in a New World Context* (Charlottesville: University Press of Virginia, 1998).

3. Annie Dillard, *Pilgrim at Tinker Creek* (New York: Bantam, 1975); José María Arguedas, *Deep Rivers,* trans. Frances Horning Barraclough (Austin: University of Texas Press, 1978).

4. Dillard, *Pilgrim at Tinker Creek,* p. 35.

5. Arguedas, *Deep Rivers,* pp. 6, 7.

6. Earl E. Fitz, *Rediscovering the New World: Inter-American Literature in a Comparative Context* (Iowa City: University of Iowa Press, 1991).

7. Antonio Cornejo Polar, quoted in Elena Aibar Ray, *Identidad y resistencia cultural en las obras de José María Arguedas* (Lima: Pontificia Universidad Católica del Perú, Fondo Editorial, 1992), p. 87.

8. Reynaldo Jimenez, "Realidad y mitificación: el niño-narrador en *Los ríos profundos,*" *Texto crítico* 5, no. 14 (1979): 104–116.

9. Quoted in Jorge García Antezana, "Estructura del mito en José María Arguedas: el 'zumbayllu' en *Los ríos profundos,*" *Cuadernos americanos* 254, no. 3 (1984): 86, n. 1.

10. George W. Cronyn, ed., *American Indian Poetry: An Anthology of Songs and Chants* (New York: Fawcett Columbine-Ballantine, 1991), p. 69; Abraham Arias-Larreta, ed., *Pre-Columbian Literatures: Aztec—Incan—Maya—Quiché. Book I—History of Indoamerican Literature* (n.p., 1964), p. 72.

11. Dennis Tedlock and Barbara Tedlock, eds., *Teachings from the American Earth: Indian Religion and Philosophy* (New York: Liveright, [1975]), p. xii.

12. Catherine L. Albanese, *Nature Religion in America: From the Algonkian Indians to the New Age* (Chicago: University of Chicago Press, 1990).

13. Aibar Ray, *Identidad y resistencia cultural*, p. 87.

14. Catherine J. Allen, *The Hold Life Has: Coca and Cultural Identity in an Andean Community* (Washington, D.C.: Smithsonian Institution, 1988). The following discussion is drawn largely from this work.

15. Peter A. Fritzell, *Nature Writing and America: Essays upon a Cultural Type* (Ames: Iowa State University Press, 1990).

16. Simon Schama, *Landscape and Memory* (New York: Knopf, 1995), p. 396.

17. Ibid., p. 397.

18. Ibid., p. 398.

19. For example, see Fritzell, *Nature Writing and America;* Stan Goldman, "Sacrifices to the Hidden God: Annie Dillard's *Pilgrim at Tinker Creek* and Leviticus," *Soundings* 74, no. 1/2 (1991): 195–213; Gretchen Tracy Legler, "Toward a Postmodern Pastoral: Contemporary Women Writers' Revisions of the Natural World" (Ph.D. diss., University of Minnesota, 1994); and Scott Slovic, *Seeking Awareness in American Nature Writing: Henry Thoreau, Annie Dillard, Edward Abbey, Wendell Berry, Barry Lopez* (Salt Lake City: University of Utah Press, 1992).

20. Marshall H. Segal, Donald T. Campbell, and Melville J. Herskovits, "Cultural Differences in the Perception of Geometric Illusions," in *Perception: Selected Readings in Science and Phenomenology,* ed. Paul Tibbetts (Chicago: Quadrangle, 1969), pp. 333–339.

21. Linda Williams, introduction to *Viewing Positions: Ways of Seeing Film* (New Brunswick, N.J.: Rutgers University Press, 1995).

22. Jim Cheney, "'The Waters of Separation': Myth and Ritual in Annie Dillard's *Pilgrim at Tinker Creek,*" *Journal of Feminist Studies in Religion* 6, no. 1 (1990): 41–61.

23. Ibid., p. 42, n. 2.

24. Legler, "Toward a Postmodern Pastoral"; Paula Gunn Allen, "Kochinnenako in Academe: Three Approaches to Interpreting a Keres Indian Tale," in *Feminisms: An Anthology of Literary Theory and Criticism,* ed. Robyn R. Warhol and Diane Price Herndl (New Brunswick, N.J.: Rutgers University Press, 1991); Donna Haraway, *Simians, Cyborgs, and Women: Reinventing Nature* (New York: Routledge, 1991).

25. P. Allen, "Kochinnenako in Academe," p. 728.

26. Thomas Mautner, ed., *A Dictionary of Philosophy* (Cambridge, Mass.: Blackwell Publishers, 1996).

27. Legler, "Toward a Postmodern Pastoral," p. 99.

28. Caroline Whitbeck, "A Different Reality: Feminist Ontology," in *Women, Knowledge, and Reality: Explorations in Feminist Philosophy,* ed. Ann Garry and Marilyn Pearsall (Boston: Unwin Hyman, 1989), p. 51.

29. Ibid., p. 55.

30. Ibid., p. 63.

31. Lynn White Jr., "The Historical Roots of Our Ecologic Crisis," in *The Ecocriticism Reader: Landmarks in Literary Ecology,* ed. Cheryll Glotfelty and Harold Fromm (Athens: University of Georgia Press, 1996), p. 11.

32. Mircea Eliade, *Myths, Dreams, and Realities: The Encounter Between Contemporary Faiths and Archaic Realities,* trans. Philip Mairet (New York: Harper, 1967); Sisirkumar Ghose and John Edwin Smith, "Religious Experience," *The New Encyclopedia Britannica. Macropaedia,* 15th ed. (1994).

33. Ghose and Smith, "Religious Experience."

BIBLIOGRAPHY

Aibar Ray, Elena. *Identidad y resistencia cultural en las obras de José María Arguedas.* Lima: Pontificia Universidad Católica del Perú, Fondo Editorial, 1992.

Albanese, Catherine L. *Nature Religion in America: From the Algonkian Indians to the New Age.* Chicago History of American Religion. Chicago: University of Chicago Press, 1990.

Allen, Catherine J. *The Hold Life Has: Coca and Cultural Identity in an Andean Community.* Washington, D.C.: Smithsonian Institution, 1988.

Allen, Paula Gunn. "Kochinnenako in Academe: Three Approaches to Interpreting a Keres Indian Tale." In *Feminisms: An Anthology of Literary Theory and Criticism,* edited by Robyn R. Warhol and Diane Price Herndl. New Brunswick, N.J.: Rutgers University Press, 1991. Originally published in *The Sacred Hoop* (Boston: Beacon Press, 1986).

Arguedas, J. M. *Deep Rivers.* Translated by Frances Horning Barraclough. Texas Pan American Series. Austin: University of Texas Press, 1978. Originally published as *Los ríos profundos* (Buenos Aires: Editorial Losada, 1958).

————. "The Novel and the Problem of Literary Expression in Peru." In *Yawar Fiesta.* Originally published in *Mar del Sur, Revista Peruana de Cultura* (enero/feb. 1950): 66–72.

————. "Puquio: A Culture in Process of Change." In *Yawar Fiesta.* Originally published as "Puquio, una cultura en proceso de cambio," *Estudios sobre la cultura actual del Perú* (Lima: Universidad Nacional Mayor de San Marcos, 1964).

————. *Los ríos profundos.* El Libro del Bolsillo. Madrid: Alianza Editorial, 1981.

————. *Todas las sangres.* Narrativa contemporánéa 9. Lima: Editorial Horizonte, 1987.

————. *Yawar Fiesta.* Translated by Frances Horning Barraclough. Texas Pan American Series. Austin: University of Texas Press, 1985. Originally published as *Yawar fiesta* (Buenos Aires: Editorial Losada, 1941).

Arias-Larreta, Abraham, ed. *Pre-Columbian Literatures: Aztec—Incan—Maya—Quiché. Book I—History of Indoamerican Literature.* N.p., 1964.

Cheney, Jim. "'The Waters of Separation': Myth and Ritual in Annie Dillard's Pilgrim at Tinker Creek." *Journal of Feminist Studies in Religion* 6, no. 1 (1990): 41–61.

Cronyn, George W., ed. *American Indian Poetry: An Anthology of Songs and Chants.* New York: Fawcett Columbine-Ballantine, 1991. Originally published in a somewhat different form as *The Path on the Rainbow: An Anthology of Songs and Chants from the Indians of North America* (Liveright Publishing Corporation, 1934).

Dash, J. Michael. *The Other America: Caribbean Literature in a New World Context.* Charlottesville: University Press of Virginia, 1998.

Dillard, Annie. *Pilgrim at Tinker Creek.* New York: Bantam, 1975.

———. *Teaching a Stone to Talk: Expeditions and Encounters.* New York: Harper Colophon–Harper & Row, 1983.

Eliade, Mircea. *Myths, Dreams, and Realities: The Encounter Between Contemporary Faiths and Archaic Realities.* Translated by Philip Mairet. Harper Torchbook edition. New York: Harper, 1967.

———. *The Sacred and the Profane: The Nature of Religion.* Translated by Willard Trask. New York: Harcourt, 1959.

Fitz, Earl E. *Rediscovering the New World: Inter-American Literature in a Comparative Context.* Iowa City: University of Iowa Press, 1991.

Fritzell, Peter A. *Nature Writing and America: Essays upon a Cultural Type.* Ames: Iowa State University Press, 1990.

García Antezana, Jorge. "Estructura del mito en José María Arguedas: el 'zumbayllu' en *Los ríos profundos*." *Cuadernos Americanos* 254, no. 3 (1984): 86–101.

Ghose, Sisirkumar, and John Edwin Smith. "Religious Experience." *The New Encyclopedia Britannica. Macropaedia.* 15th ed. 1994.

Goldenberg, Naomi R. "Archetypal Theory and the Separation of Mind and Body: Reason Enough to Turn to Freud?" *Journal of Feminist Studies in Religion* 1, no. 1 (1984): 55–72.

Goldman, Stan. "Sacrifices to the Hidden God: Annie Dillard's *Pilgrim at Tinker Creek* and Leviticus." *Soundings* 74, no. 1/2 (1991): 195–213.

Haraway, Donna. *Simians, Cyborgs, and Women: Reinventing Nature.* New York: Routledge, 1991.

———. "Situated Knowledges: The Science Question in Feminism and the Privilege of Partial Perspective." *Feminist Studies* 14, no. 3 (1988): 575–599.

Jimenez, Reynaldo. "Realidad y mitificación: el niño-narrador en *Los ríos profundos*." *Texto crítico* 5, no. 14 (1979): 104–116.

Legler, Gretchen Tracy. "Toward a Postmodern Pastoral: Contemporary Women Writers' Revisions of the Natural World." Ph.D. diss., University of Minnesota, 1994.

Magness, Patricia Kay Phillips. "Contradiction in the Nonfiction of Annie Dillard: Seeing and Seeing Through." Ph.D. diss., Emory University, 1992.

Mautner, Thomas, ed. *A Dictionary of Philosophy*. Cambridge, Mass.: Blackwell Publishers, 1996.

McLaren, John. *New Pacific Literatures: Culture and Environment in the European Pacific*. New York: Garland, 1993.

Nolan, James. *Poet-Chief: The Native Poetics of Walt Whitman and Pablo Neruda*. Albuquerque: University of New Mexico Press, 1994.

Schama, Simon. *Landscape and Memory*. New York: Knopf, 1995.

Segal, Marshall H., Donald T. Campbell, and Melville J. Herskovits. "Cultural Differences in the Perception of Geometric Illusions." In *Perception: Selected Readings in Science and Phenomenology*, edited by Paul Tibbetts. Chicago: Quadrangle, 1969. Pp. 333–339. Originally published in *Science* 139 (1963): 769–771.

Shaw, Susan Helfert. "The Witness of Landscape: Annie Dillard and José María Arguedas in Accord with Nature." Master's thesis, South Dakota State University, 1997.

Slovic, Scott. *Seeking Awareness in American Nature Writing: Henry Thoreau, Annie Dillard, Edward Abbey, Wendell Berry, Barry Lopez*. Salt Lake City: University of Utah Press, 1992.

Tedlock, Dennis, and Barbara Tedlock, eds. *Teachings from the American Earth: Indian Religion and Philosophy*. New York: Liveright, [1975].

Whitbeck, Caroline. "A Different Reality: Feminist Ontology." In *Women, Knowledge, and Reality: Explorations in Feminist Philosophy*, edited by Ann Garry and Marilyn Pearsall. Boston: Unwin Hyman, 1989.

White, Lynn, Jr. "The Historical Roots of Our Ecologic Crisis." In *The Ecocriticism Reader: Landmarks in Literary Ecology*, edited by Cheryll Glotfelty and Harold Fromm. Athens: University of Georgia Press, 1996.

Williams, Linda. Introduction to *Viewing Positions: Ways of Seeing Film*. Edited by Linda Williams. Rutgers Depth of Field Series. New Brunswick, N.J.: Rutgers University Press, 1995.

21. Los archivos de la palabra: la voz de los escritores hispánicos

Ramón Abad

Existe una relación innata entre la literatura y la voz de la palabra escrita y la palabra hablada. Tal vez sea el origen oral de la literatura lo que hace que escuchar una narración o un poema se convierta en una experiencia tan fascinante como la lectura del mismo texto. Y también puede ser la razón por la que, apenas aparecieron los medios de grabación sonora se buscase el modo de registrar la voz de los escritores y los textos por ellos escritos.

En un principio, la grabación de las voces de los escritores tuvieron un propósito fundamentalmente archivístico: crear un archivo sonoro con las voces más prestigiosas del país, como parte del patrimonio nacional. La radio, por su parte, ha sido el principal medio de difusión de la voz hablada, manteniendo su hegemonía hasta el advenimiento de la televisión a partir de los años 50. El cine, la televisión y el vídeo proporcionan imágenes a los textos hablados y crean otro tipo de documentos de los que no nos vamos a ocupar ahora, pero estos inventos, como se puede observar, no han conducido a la desaparición de la grabación del texto leído y de la voz de los escritores. Al poder que todavía conserva la radio, hay que añadir la extraordinaria difusión que las grabaciones sonoras disfrutan gracias a su distribución comercial mediante discos y casetes. El fenómeno de la proliferación de los audiolibros de hoy, si bien responde la demanda específica de un mercado de lectores que utiliza el automóvil como medio habitual de desplazamiento no es ajeno a la fascinación por escuchar un relato bien narrado o un poema en la voz del autor que lo creó.

Fueron las bien surtidas secciones de audiolibros en las librerías de Nueva York las que me movieron a buscar materiales semejantes en lengua española, que completasen la excelente colección de literatura de la biblioteca del Instituto Cervantes en dicha ciudad. La tarea, algunos años después de iniciarse ya ha dado su fruto y es mi propósito ahora tratar de sistematizar la información de que ahora disponemos sobre grabaciones sonoras de tema literario para facilitar a otros bibliotecarios la formación de este tipo de colecciones.

Se trata fundamentalmente de ofrecer un panorama general de los materiales sonoros relacionados con la literatura hispanoamericana y española y de crear un contexto que agrupe y dé cabida a una serie de documentos sonoros de distinto formato (discos de vinilo, cintas magnéticas, discos compactos y grabaciones accesibles a través de Internet) cuyo elemento en común es la voz del autor. Asimismo, se trata de sistematizar dicha información, identificar los proyectos y colecciones más importantes y ofrecer en la medida de lo posible los datos necesarios para su adquisición. Para ello se ha elaborado un cuadro que se presenta como Apéndice al final de este trabajo. En dicho cuadro, ordenado por países, se indican las organizaciones, empresas, proyectos y colecciones que se han ocupado de grabar la voz de los escritores de habla hispana, así como los nombres de los autores incluídos.

Los límites de este trabajo quedan definidos por los siguientes elementos: (1) el *soporte,* es decir, deben ser grabaciones sonoras, en sus diferentes formatos (disco de vinilo, cinta magnetofónica, audiocasete, disco compacto y otros sistemas de almacenamiento digital accesibles a través de Internet); (2) el *contenido,* donde es necesaria la presencia de la voz del escritor; (3) la *disponibilidad,* condición que restringe la oferta a aquellas grabaciones que se han editado comercialmente o que forman parte de proyectos sólidos, desarrollados con ánimo de preservación y accesibles al público interesado.

Fuera de estos márgenes quedan, por tanto, una gran parte de los audiolibros existentes en el mercado, la mayoría de los cuales están leídos por locutores profesionales o famosos actores. Otro campo apasionante dentro de las grabaciones sonoras de tipo literario, pero que no tiene cabida en este trabajo, es el de los textos literarios, fundamentalmente poesía, como letra de canciones a las que se pone música. Desde los famosos "cantautores" que tanto proliferaron en los años 60, a las versiones sinfónicas, como la adaptación musical de Mikis Theodorakis del *Canto General* de Pablo Neruda, pasando por la mismas coplas populares de tradición folklórica. Este tipo de composiciones ha proporcionado en muchas ocasiones a los poetas (sean ellos mismos los intérpretes musicales o no) una popularidad y una difusión imposible de conseguir por medio de las ediciones impresas.

Los archivos de la palabra

Como se ha dicho, ya desde la aparición de los primeros equipos de grabación sonora existió interés en utilizarlos con el propósito de crear archivos de las voces más prestigiosas de la nación. Este interés se verá reforzado con la aparición de la radio en la escena de los medios de comunicación en los años 20 del siglo XX. El papel de las instituciones públicas es esencial en prácticamente todas las iniciativas de este tipo.

En el mundo hispánico, tal vez el primero sea el proyecto que se denominó *Archivo de la Palabra y las Canciones Populares* y que llevó a cabo en España el Centro de Estudios Históricos entre 1931 y 1933. Se trataba de un vasto proyecto de preservación y difusión de la lengua y la cultura españolas, que dió como resultado la recopilación de 1142 grabaciones, en su mayoría de interés lingüístico y folklórico. Veintinueve de estas grabaciones formaban el *Archivo de la Palabra* propiamente dicho, recogidas gracias al trabajo de Tomás Navarro Tomás, en el que se recogen, además de las voces de algunos de los grandes escritores de la época (Valle-Inclán, Unamuno, Pío Baroja, etc.), las de políticos, intelectuales y hombres de ciencia, como Niceto Alcalá Zamora, Fernando de los Ríos o Santiago Ramón y Cajal. Las grabaciones fueron reeditadas comercialmente por la Residencia de Estudiantes en 1990, en disco de vinilo y en 1998 se reeditó en disco compacto.

Con este mismo nombre de "Archivo de la Palabra", se conocen otros proyectos llevados a cabo en América Latina, a través de sus bibliotecas nacionales. Sería el caso de Venezuela, donde la Biblioteca Nacional inició un programa de colaboración con la Universidad Central de Venezuela para este fin, y de Chile, donde se ha llevado a cabo un proyecto similar. Aunque ya he establecido contacto con dichas bibliotecas, todavía no dispongo de información específica sobre dichos proyectos.

En Cuba ha sido la Casa de las Américas la institución que se ha dedicado sistemáticamente a grabar y difundir en casete la voz de los autores de toda América Latina que han colaborado en sus actividades. Una parte de dichas grabaciones se ha publicado en casete en las series tituladas *En vivo en Casa* y *Palabra de esta América*.

En México ha sido la Universidad Nacional Autónoma de México la encargada de difundir en colecciones en casete y disco compacto las grabaciones de sus principales autores, así como de otros famosos escritores latinoamericanos. La UNAM ha difundido comercialmente sus grabaciones a través de sus colecciones *La Voz Viva de América Latina* y *La Voz Viva de México,* ésta última dedicada a escritores y otras personalidades del mundo de la cultura y la intelectualidad mexicanas.

Los proyectos hispanoamericanos no comienzan, por lo general, hasta entrados los años 60, hecho que puede guardar cierta relación con la pujanza de los medios audiovisuales y la aparición en la escena literaria latinoamericana de la generación del "boom".

Perú tuvo en los años 60 un proyecto de archivo de la palabra, que inició de manera privada Juan Mejía Baca. Se titulaba Biblioteca Perú Vivo y llegó a publicar algunos discos. Desgraciadamente, el proyecto no sobrevivió a su creador.

El proyecto más ambicioso y el que más larga duración está teniendo es el que inició la Library of Congress en el año 1942, con el apoyo de la Rockefeller Foundation, denominado *Archive of Hispanic Literature on Tape.* En 1996 el archivo completo—que no sólo contiene autores hispánicos—contenía grabaciones de 620 escritores leyendo selecciones de su obra. No se ciñe exclusivamente al ámbito de la lengua española sino que abarca también la literatura en otras lenguas romances, como el portugués y el catalán, el inglés, el francés, el Caribe y lenguas indígenas de América, como el Nahuatl y el

Zapoteco. En 1974 la Library of Congress publicó *The Archive of Hispanic Literature on Tape: A Descriptive Guide,* catálogo que recoge datos de los 232 autores que componían entonces la colección. Solamente algunas grabaciones se han reproducido para su difusión en discos o casetes. Entre los autores grabados destacan todos los escritores de lengua española ganadores del Premio Nobel desde 1945 (Gabriela Mistral, Juan Ramón Jiménez, Miguel Angel Asturias, Pablo Neruda, Vicente Aleixandre, Gabriel García Márquez, Camilo José Cela y Octavio Paz).

El papel de las radios

El papel de las emisoras de radios en la tarea de difundir y más tarde preservar las voces de los escritores ha sido esencial. Primero por su el papel hegemónico como medio de comunicación que han tenido hasta la aparición de la televisión; luego por su progresiva especialización, que ha favorecido la creación de programas de calidad dirigidos a audiencias específicas, así como su utilización como vehículo educativo.

Las radios han sido y son una cantera inagotable de tesoros en forma de grabaciones únicas. Así lo demuestran los casos como los que se señalan a continuación:

- *Radio Nacional de España (RNE):* Es la radio pública española y cuenta con una larga historia desde sus inicios en 1923. A partir de los años 80 inicia la comercialización de programas a través del Programa de Cooperación Cultural, donde se incluyen algunos excelentes programas de carácter literario, como *Antología Poética Hispanoamericana y Poesía en la Radio,* realizados por el poeta José Hierro (Premio Cervantes), donde se rescatan algunas grabaciones históricas de escritores, sacadas de su excelente archivo sonoro.

- *La Emisora HJCK* de Bogotá es una emisora privada de radio fundada en 1950. Su función difusora de la literatura colombiana e iberoamericana se realiza fundamentalmente a través de la serie discográfica *Colección Literaria H.J.C.K.* y de su colaboración con la Casa de Poesía José Asunción Silva, a la que ha legado una copia de su archivo de voces de poetas, con cerca de 2000 grabaciones, la mayoría autores colombianos, hispanoamericanos y españoles.

- *SODRE* (Servicio Oficial de Difusión, Radiotelevisión y Espectáculos, antes Servicio Oficial de Difusión Radioeléctrica) se creó en 1929 como la radio pública de Uruguay, aunque ahora agrupa otros sectores: televisión, espectáculos, difusión y preservación. Dentro de estas dos últimas funciones hay que incluir la creación del Archivo Nacional de la Imagen y del "Museo de la Palabra", iniciativa similar a archivos de la palabra a los que nos referíamos en el punto anterior, y el lanzamiento de la colección *Los 20 Grandes de la Literatura Uruguaya,* con material de archivo.

Otras Iniciativas: audiolibros, casas discográficas y otras compañías editoras

El propósito principal del audiolibro no es la conservación de la voz original del autor con propósito de archivo sino su difusión comercial utilizando la infraestructura del comercio del libro. No obstante, en el todavía joven mercado del audiolibro en español, es bastante frecuente que las colecciones de audiolibros lanzados por los grandes grupos editores contengan abundantes grabaciones realizadas por los propios autores, mucho más que en el mercado anglosajón. Así, por ejemplo, de los 21 títulos publicados hasta la fecha en España por la editorial Alfaguara en su colección *Alfaguara-Audio,* 13 están leídos por los propios autores. Algo similar ocurre con la colección *Entre Voces,* publicada en México por el Fondo de Cultura Económica o la jovencísima colección de audiolibros publicada en Argentina por Art Net Group.

Dentro del mundo de las editoriales especializadas destacaría, por ejemplo, la editorial española Visor, especializada en poesía, que inició en 1996 la publicación, dentro de su *Colección Visor de Poesía,* de una serie de discos compactos con grabaciones sonoras de importantes figuras de la poesía iberoamericana contemporánea. Asimismo, en Argentina, la Editorial Proa, publica desde 1999 una colección de discos compactos con grabaciones de autores de la literatura hispánica, que se entregan con cada número de la revista.

Hay también un número relativamente abundante de grabaciones editadas por servicios de publicaciones pertenecientes a organismos de la administración, tanto en España como en Hispanoamérica. Generalmente se trata de ediciones producto de iniciativas aisladas, más que parte de una política editorial. Este no sería el caso de los materiales audio que presenta el catálogo del Ministerio de Educación de España, incluídos en colecciones con una clara finalidad educativa.

En los Estados Unidos, concretamente en Nueva York, la actividad coleccionista de la Hispanic Society of America también alcanzó a los materiales audio. De hecho, a finales de los años 60 llevó a cabo la grabación casi íntegra del *Archivo de la Palabra* español descrito al principio de este trabajo. En esta misma época inició la publicación de una serie de grabaciones sonoras en disco, si bien solamente vió la luz el primero, cuyo protagonista era Camilo José Cela y el mismo Theodore S. Beardsley Jr.

La editorial también neoyorquina Spoken Arts publicó una colección de discos relacionados con la lengua y la literatura hispánicas, que incluía grabaciones de autores literarios.

Algunas casas discográficas también han contribuído al mundo literario al incluir en sus colecciones grabaciones con la voz de escritores, fundamentalmente poetas. Algunas de estas casas discográficas ya habían servido de plataforma a "cantautores" o cantantes que ponían música a poemas de escritores conocidos. Es el caso, por ejemplo, de PDI, S.A., en España, con una parte de su catálogo muy enfocado hacia la poesía.

Perspectivas

La literatura en formato audio parece gozar de un buen momento, especialmente, los audiolibros, si bien su mercado en lengua española es todavía muy reducido si se compara con el anglosajón. En cuanto al testimonio oral de los escritores, éste se ha visto completado por la imagen visual, que ha encontrado en la televisión y el vídeo su mejor medio de difusión. La Internet está contribuyendo por su parte a revitalizar los proyectos de archivo sonoro. La facilidad para almacenar y difundir el sonido a través de la red está posibilitando tanto proyectos nuevos como de reconversión de antiguos archivos.

El principal obstáculo, no obstante, para la difusión comercial o la reproducción de este tipo de materiales está en la legislación de derechos de autor. Cuando los autores graban para proyectos institucionales o de archivo no suelen autorizar la reproducción de las grabaciones. Al parecer, la Library of Congress está negociando con los autores que participan en su proyecto la autorización para que pueda accederse al menos a una parte de la grabación a través de Internet.

Mientras tanto, nuevos proyectos aparecen. Así, por ejemplo, en Galicia, España, el Consello da Cultura Galega trabaja desde 1992 en la confección del Archivo Sonoro de Galicia, en una línea muy similar a la que en los años 30 iniciase el Centro de Estudios Históricos, pues trata de abarcar la lengua, la literatura, la música y el folklore de Galicia. Por su parte, la Casa de América en Madrid está desarrollando proyectos para difundir tanto su patrimonio documental, en el que se encuentran abundantes grabaciones sonoras, como sus actividades a través de Internet.

País	Editor/Organización	Colección/Proyecto	Autores	Observaciones
Argentina	Acqua Records	Continente	Pablo Neruda	
Argentina	Art Net Group Paraguay 946 Piso 6-A 1057 Buenos Aires Tel. 4393-2787; Fax: 4328-9590		Ernesto Sábatoa, Pacho O'Donnell	
Argentina	Ediciones Archivo General de la Nación L.N. Alem 246 1003 Buenos Aires Tel. 4331-6642; Fax: 4334-0065		César Tiempo	

País	Editor/Organización	Colección/Proyecto	Autores	Observaciones
Argentina	Ediciones Proa Paraguay 643, 3° A. 1057 Buenos Aires Tel/Fax: 4312-3917; Email: proa@impsat1.com.ar		Jorge Luis Borges, Julio Cortázar, Marco Denevi, Adolfo Bioy Casares, Eduardo Mallea, Pío Baroja, Manuel Peyrou, Alfonso Reyes, Miguel de Unamuno, Manuel Mújica Laínez, Azorín, Héctor A. Murena, Ramón del Valle-Inclán, Jacinto Benavente	CDs que acompañan a la revista "Proa"
Argentina	Editorial Manrique Zago Avenida San Martín 7210 1419 Buenos Aires Tel. 4501-1497; Fax: 4502-7937	Tiempos de Poesía	Marisa Scancarello Augeri	
Argentina	Seix Barral Independencia 1668 1100 Buenos Aires Tel. 4382-4043; Fax: 4383-3793		Ernesto Sábato	CD que acompaña al libro: Sábato/fotografías, selección y textos de E. Longoni. Buenos Aires: Seix Barral, 1994

País	Editor/Organización	Colección/Proyecto	Autores	Observaciones
Chile	Alerce Producciones Fonográficas		Pablo Neruda	
Chile	Editorial Universitaria San Francisco 454 Santiago de Chile		José María Arguedas	
Colombia	Casa de Poesía "José Asunción Silva" Calle 14 Nº 3-41 Bogotá (Colombia) http://www.infomed-co.com/casa-silva/	Fonoteca	Archivo sonoro con cerca de 2000 grabaciones de autores literarios colombianos, latino-americanos y españoles	La Casa Silva de Poesía efectúa grabaciones en colaboración con la emisora HJCK y el patrocinio del Instituto Colombiano de Cultura (Colcultura)
Colombia	Emisora HJCK Carrera 12No. 82-23 A.A. 17161 Bogotá (Colombia) Tel. 571-236-3840; Fax: 571-236-8861; Email: hjck@coll.telecom.com.co; http://www.orquidea.com/hjck/		Albero Lleras, Eduardo Carranza, Jorge Zalamea, Jorge Luis Borges, Raúl Gómez Jattin, Gonzalo Arango, J. Mario Arbeláez, Eduardo Escobar, Jaime Jaramillo, Germán Arciniegas, Arturo Camacho Ramírez, Eduardo Carranza, María Mercedes Carranza, Carlos Castro	

País	Editor/Organización	Colección/Proyecto	Autores	Observaciones
Cuba	Casa de las Américas Tercera y G El Vedado, La Habana 10400 (Cuba) Tel. (537) 323587; Fax: (537) 334554; Email: casa@artsoft.cult.cu	En Vivo en Casa	Julio Cortázar, Eduardo Galeano	
Cuba	Casa de las Américas Tercera y G El Vedado, La Habana 10400 (Cuba) Tel. (537) 323587; Fax: (537) 334554; Email: casa@artsoft.cult.cu	Palabra de esta América	Mario Bendetti, Eliseo Diego, Gabriel García Márquez, Nicolás Guillén, José Lezama Lima, Virgilio Piñera, Angel Gaztelu, Gastón Baquero, Cintio Vitier, Octavio Smith, Fina García Marruz, Dulce María Loynaz, Juan Carlos Onetti	
España	Centro de las Letras Españolas Plaza del Rey 1 28004 Madrid Tel. 34-91-521-3832; http://www.mcu.es		José Hierro	
España	Comunidad de Madrid. Consejería de Educación y Cultura		Pedro Salinas	

País	Editor/Organización	Colección/Proyecto	Autores	Observaciones
España	Consello da Cultura Gallega Pazo de Raxoi, 2° andar. Praza do Obradoiro 17750 Santiago de Compostela Email: asg.ccga@xunta.es; http://www.xunta.es/auto/ccga/paxina_proxecto.html	Arquivo Sonoro de Galicia	Eduardo Blanco Amor, Anxel Fole, Ramón Otero Pedrayo, Ramón Piñeiro, Alvaro Cunqueiro, Ramón Suárez Picallo, Celso Emilio Ferreiro, Rafael Dieste, Manuel Meilán, Ramón Cabanillas	
España	Editorial Alfaguara Torrelaguna, 60 28027 Madrid Tel. 34-91-322-4700; Fax: 34-91-3224771	Alfaguara - Audio	Rafael Alberti, Mario Benedetti, Fernando Fernán Gómez, Carlos Fuentes, Elvira Lindo, Javier Marías, Augusto Monterroso, Manuel Rivas, José Luis Sampedro, Alvaro Mutis	
España	Editorial Alhambra-Longman Núñez de Balboa, 120 28006 Madrid Tel. 34-91-590-3432; Fax: 34-91-590-3448; http://www.awl-elt.com	Fonoteca Literaria	Pedro Salinas, Jorge Guillén, Gerardo Diego, Vicente Aleixandre, Luis Cernuda, Rafael Alberti, Blas de Otero	Antología de la literatura española

País	Editor/Organización	Colección/Proyecto	Autores	Observaciones
España	Galaxia Gutenberg (co-edición con Círculo de Lectores) Princesa 61. 08003 Barcelona Tel. 34-93-458-7600; Fax: 34-93-458-3907; Email: galaxia@galaxiagutenberg.com	Biblioteca Sonora de la Literatura	Camilo José Cela, Octavio Paz	
España	Ministerio de Educación y Ciencia (Hoy Ministerio de Educación y Cultura) Centro de Publicaciones Ciudad Universitaria s/n. 28040 Madrid http://www.mec.es	Archivo de la Palabra	Dámaso Alonso, Carmen Conde, Leopoldo Panero, Gabriel Celaya, Blas de Otero, Francisco García Pavón, Ignacio Aldecoa, Claudio Rodríguez, Rafael Morales, José Hierro, María Zambrano	
España	Ministerio de Educación y Ciencia (Hoy Ministerio de Educación y Cultura) Centro de Publicaciones Ciudad Universitaria s/n. 28040 Madrid http://www.mec.es	Voces Iberoamericanas	Jorge Luis Borges, Camilo José Cela, Luis Rosales, Mario Vargas Llosa	
España	Ministerio de Educación y Ciencia (Hoy Ministerio de Educación y Cultura) Centro de Publicaciones Ciudad Universitaria s/n. 28040 Madrid http://www.mec.es		Juan Ramón Jiménez	Edición conmemorativa en el centenario del nacimiento del poeta

País	Editor/Organización	Colección/Proyecto	Autores	Observaciones
España	PDI, S.A. Passeig de Gràcia, 74 08008 Barcelona		José Agustín Goytisolo, Rafael Alberti	
España	Radio Nacional de España- Programa de Cooperación Cultural Casa de la Radio, Prado del Rey 28223 Madrid Tel. 34-91-346-1406; Fax: 34-91-346-1232; Email: secretario_general.rne@rtve.es	Antología Poética Hispanoamericana	Dámaso Alonso, Vicente Aleixandre, Gerardo Diego, Rafael Alberti, Luis Cernuda, Jorge Guillén, Pedro Salinas, Juan Rejano, Gloria Fuertes, José Hierro, Ramón del Valle-Inclán, Pablo Neruda, Nicolás Guillén, Octavio Paz, Antonio Gala	Programa dirigido por José Hierro
España	Radiotelevisión Española en colaboración con Editorial Planeta	Cien Años de Poesía	Miguel de Unamuno, Juan Ramón Jiménez, León Felipe, Pedro Salinas, Jorge Guillén, Gerardo Diego, Vicente Aleixandre, Dámaso Alonso, Rafael Alberti, Luis Cernuda, Miguel Hernández, Luis Rosales, Gabriel Celaya, Blas de Otero, Carlos Bousoño, Pablo García B.	CD que acompaña al libro "Mil años de poesía española: antología comentada"

País	Editor/Organización	Colección/Proyecto	Autores	Observaciones
España	Residencia de Estudiantes (Consejo Superior de Investigaciones Científicas) Pinar 21. 28006 Madrid Tel. 34-91-261-3200; http://www.residencia.csic.es	Archivo de la Palabra	José Martínez Ruiz "Azorín", Juan Ramón Jiménez, Pío Baroja, Miguel de Unamuno, Joaquín Alvarez Quintero, Serafín Alvarez Quintero, Manuel Cossío, Ramón del Valle-Inclán, Fernando de los Ríos, Ignacio Bolívar, Vicente Medina, Margarita Xirgu, Enrique Borrás, Eduardo Marquina, Mariano Benlliure, Manuel Linares Rivas, Ricardo León, Estrella Sananes, Yojebed Chocrón, Armando Palacio Valdés, José Vera, Lorenzo Rodríguez Castellano, Concha Espina, Jacinto Benavente, José Ortega y Gasset, Miguel Asín y Palacios, Niceto Alcalá-Zamora, Leonardo Torres-Quevedo, Ramón Menéndez Pidal, Santiago Ramón y Cajal	Grabaciones realizadas por el Centro de Estudios Históricos, entre 1931 y 1933
España	Visor Libros, S.L. Isaac Peral, 18. 28015 Madrid Tel. 34-91-549-2655; Fax: 34-91-544-8695; Email: visor-libros@interplanet.es; http://www.libronet.es/editor/visor	Visor de Poesía	Rafael Alberti, Mario Benedetti, Luis Cernuda, León Felipe, Angel González, José Agustín Goytisolo, Juan Ramón Jiménez, Augusto Monterroso, Pablo Neruda, Pedro Salinas, Jaime Gil de Biedma	

País	Editor/Organización	Colección/Proyecto	Autores	Observaciones
México	Fondo de Cultura Económica Carretera Picacho-Ajusco #227 Col. Bosques del Pedregal DF 14200, México Tel. 5-227-4652; Fax: 5-227-4659; Email: gcomercial@fce.com.mx	Entre Voces	Alí Chumacero, Augusto Monterroso, Juan Rulfo, Jaime Sabines	
México	Universidad de Guadalajara-Departamento de Estudios Literarios Publicaciones: Francisco Rojas González 131. Col. Ladrón de Guevara Guadalajara, Jalisco 44600 Tel. 3-615-7589; Fax: 3-615-8192; Email: editorial@udgserv.cencar.udg.mx		Alberto Blanco	
México	Universidad Nacional Autónoma de México (UNAM) Avda. del Imán #5 Col. Ciudad Universitaria DF 04510, México Tel. 5-622-6585; Fax: 5-622-6571; Email: pfedico@servidor.unam.mx	Voz Viva de América Latina	Gabriel García Márquez, Pablo Neruda, Alejandro Rossi	

País	Editor/Organización	Colección/Proyecto	Autores	Observaciones
México	Universidad Nacional Autónoma de México (UNAM) Avda. del Imán #5 Col. Ciudad Universitaria DF 04510, México Tel. 5-622-6585; Fax: 5-622-6571; Email: pfedico@servidor.unam.mx	Voz Viva de México	José Agustín, Carmen Alardín, Griselda Alvarez, Hugo Argüelles, Emmanuel Carballo, Augusto Monterroso, Carlos Monsiváis, Salvador Elizondo, León Felipe, Jaime García Terrés, Jaime Labastida, Enrique Molina, Rubén Bonifaz Nuño, Carlos Fuentes, Salvador Novo, Carlos Pellicer, Juan Rulfo, Jaime Sabines, Tomás Segovia, Jaime Torres Bodet, Luis Villoro, Agustín Yáñez	
México	Universidad Nacional Autónoma de México (UNAM) Avda. del Imán #5 Col. Ciudad Universitaria DF 04510, México Tel. 5-622-6585; Fax: 5-622-6571; Email: pfedico@servidor.unam.mx		Alfonso Reyes, Enrique González Martínez, Ignacio Chávez, Miguel León Portillo, Eduardo Matos Moctezuma, Ramón Xirau	
Perú	Juan Mejía Baca, ed.	Biblioteca Perú Vivo	Sebastián Salazar Bondi, Gustavo Valcárcel	Proyecto no continuado a la muerte del editor

País	Editor/Organización	Colección/Proyecto	Autores	Observaciones
Uruguay	SODRE (Servicio Oficial de Difusión, Radiotelevisión y Espectáculos) Email: info@sodre.gub.uy; http://www.sodre.gub.uy	Los 20 Grandes de la Literatura Uruguaya	Delmira Agustini, Francisco Espínola, Pedro Gigari, Felisberto Hernández, Julio Herrera y Raissig, Sara de Ibáñez, Juana de Ibarbourou, Julles Supervielle, Juan Carlos Onetti, Eliseo Salvador Porta, Horacio Quiroga, Carlos Vaz Ferreira, Eduardo Acevedo, Justino Zavala Muñiz, Juan Zorrilla de San Martín	
USA	Spoken Arts P.O. Box 289 New Rochelle, NY 10802 http://pages.prodigy.com/Spoken-Arts/home.html		Carmen Conde, Pablo Neruda, Manuel Durán, Ricardo Florit	
USA	The Hispanic Society of America 613 West 155 Street New York, NY 10032 Tel. (212) 926-2234	Archive of Record Voice	Camilo José Cela	Charla entre Camilo José Cela y Theodore S. Beardsley Jr.

País	Editor/Organización	Colección/Proyecto	Autores	Observaciones
USA	The Library of Congress http://www.loc.gov/spcoll/018.html	The Archive of Hispanic Literature on Tape	Grabaciones de 620 autores (año 1996) leyendo sus textos en español, portugués, catalán, inglés, francés, quechua, nahuatl y zapoteco, y acompañado de entrevistas y comentarios	Ver el catálogo The Archive of Hispanic Literature on Tape: A Descriptive Guide/comp. by Francisco Aguilera; ed. by Georgette Magassy Dorn. Washington, D.C.: Library of Congress, 1974. Contiene datos referentes a 232 autores
Venezuela	Biblioteca Nacional Zona Industrial de la Trinidad Calle la Soledad con Las Piedrecitas Edificio Rogi, PB Municipio Baruta. Estado Miranda Tel. 941-8622; Email: daudiov@bnv.bib.ve	Archivo de la Palabra		

Cataloging, Bibliographic Control, and Library Services

22. Cataloging Quotas and Flexible Work Schedules at the University of New Mexico

Claire-Lise Bénaud

Introduction

The Flextime Program was implemented at the University of New Mexico General Library Catalog Department in 1998. It replaced accountability for staff from hours spent on the job to productivity as measured by a point system. The previous work culture measured cataloging statistics within a forty-hour week context. The new system measures output in terms of points earned for specific tasks or activities and allows catalogers to set their own schedules. The program, formally called the "Flextime Program and Point System," is based on three premises: productivity is defined in terms of titles cataloged rather than hours on the job; considerable scheduling freedom is allowed; and such flexibility entails production accountability.

External and internal considerations had to be considered in establishing this new model. External issues involved seeking library administrative support, considering impact on other library departments, and ensuring compliance with university and federal regulations. Issues raised within the Catalog Department included catalogers' responsibilities and cataloging productivity, safety, morale, procedures for communication, and flexible schedules. The library personnel and administrative offices and the university's Human Resources Department were consulted extensively and gave the final approval.

Why

Before the point system, individual catalogers reported their monthly statistics by broad categories and worked forty hours per week. Productivity among catalogers varied: some were very productive, others were slower. Before 1998, catalogers were expected to catalog within a range of 75 to 150 non-DLC copy and original records per month. DLC copy catalogers were expected to catalog upward of four hundred titles per month. It was recognized that the amount of original cataloging, the language or script of the piece being cataloged, and the format mattered, but it was unclear how to take into account titles that were difficult to catalog. In addition, the vast majority of catalogers were involved in tasks other than cataloging to different degrees. For example,

some catalogers are selectors, volunteers at public service desks, or participants in committee work. For all these reasons, it was impossible to come up
with a monthly benchmark for all catalogers, since the statistics only measured
the number of titles cataloged. Catalogers were compared to each other in
terms of titles cataloged rather than compared against a clearly established
department goal.

It was clear that staff were interested in more flexible work hours. Before
1998, standard work hours were between 7:00 A.M. and 6:00 P.M., including the
possibility to work a ten-hour day for a compressed four-day week. People
were not allowed to work weekends. If people needed to make exceptions to
this schedule, each request was treated individually. These attempts at flexible
scheduling created lots of red tape (who worked when, make-up time, reporting mechanisms to the supervisor) and there were inconsistencies among
catalogers and supervisors. These attempts were not successful because of
an inadequate reporting and accountability system. To keep track of hours
worked and arrangements for hours not worked and make-up time for some
twenty catalogers was time-consuming, and flexibility was only possible
in special circumstances. Still cataloging managers wanted to provide
more scheduling flexibility. Combined with a need to establish clear productivity benchmarks, this change created a good opportunity at reevaluating
workflow, production quotas, and reporting statistics. The changes occurred in
the fall of 1997.

How

Simply stated, the point system shifted the emphasis completely from
time spent on the job to number of titles cataloged: the forty-hour week
yardstick was replaced with a quota. How catalogers spent their time and its
corollary was a central issue. Since all catalogers spent time involved in
noncataloging activities, these activities had to be identified and had to be
quantified in terms of a point system. Activities were divided into core and
noncore activities, with the recognition that both were essential and took time.

In order to identify which activities belong to which category, the following issues were discussed: which staff meetings were required, how to manage
library-wide meetings, lectures, or receptions; how to factor training time and
formal class work; how to communicate when department members work at
different times; would core hours be necessary; would safety be an issue when
people worked late at night; how to factor sick and annual leave; how to factor noncore tasks, such as ordering supplies and taking care of the photocopy
machine and department printer; how to account for student supervision and
cross-training; how would the point system relate to salary increases; and who
could participate.

These discussions led to the following decisions: all paraprofessionals
could participate; people could work at any time including nights and

weekends, as long as they attended department and section meetings and required training sessions; no core hours would be established; and staff would continue to have a posted schedule indicating when they would likely be at work in order to facilitate communication.

The program could only be adopted for paraprofessional catalogers, who are governed by the university's staff employment manual. Faculty catalogers are governed by a different set of rules and cannot participate. Staff catalogers are divided into two groups, exempt and nonexempt. Exempt staff, who comprise the majority of catalogers, do not fill out time sheets and therefore benefit the most from the program. Nonexempt staff continue to work a forty-hour week, but can now schedule their hours with maximum flexibility.

Based on these premises, work was divided into three categories: cataloging, cataloging support, and generic. Figuring out point values for activities within each category was laborious and complex. It took nearly six months of intense discussions among all members of the Catalog Department. All catalogers were given the opportunity to participate in establishing point values. Because the subject was contentious, most feedback occurred during one-on-one discussions between catalogers and the department head. Group discussions were only used to present and communicate decisions. The vast majority of catalogers had a strong interest in devising a workable system. A few catalogers were not interested because they argued that quantifying cataloging was an anti-intellectual activity. However, even among those who were interested, there were major differences in peoples' sense of how long it took to complete a specific task, and what point value it should receive. Establishing averages was difficult. Catalogers' collective experience as well as benchmark tests were used to establish what would be a realistic point value for a specific task.

What

Cataloging Activities

Point values were based on the average time it takes to catalog a certain type of record. Different point values were assigned for the three major types of records: original, DLC copy, and member copy. Monographs and serials received different point values. Recataloging, retrospective conversion, and contributions to national cooperative programs were also assigned points.

Cataloging Support Activities

Participation in these important activities was quantified in units of time, for conversion into points. The major activity in this category was attendance at staff meetings. Other major activities included NACO revision, special projects, training and cross-training in another department, job-related courses and workshops, and library and university committee work. Selection, student supervision, ordering supplies, and liaison work with OCLC and AMIGOS were also included in this category.

Generic Activities

Points for generic activities are given to all catalogers across the board. There is no need to keep track or report time spent. Generic activities include emailing, reading/writing memos, consulting with co-workers, attending university and library functions, dealing with software and hardware problems, learning to use new network applications, and performing other incidentals. These activities were also quantified in units of time. On average, one and a half hours per day was allotted. This allocation acknowledges that catalogers must invest substantial time to keep current with cataloging rules, rule interpretations, and system updates.

Point System

The point system is calculated based on number of titles cataloged and time spent on activities. It measures cataloging production, cataloging support, and generic activities by converting numbers of titles cataloged and units of time into points. Catalogers are expected to earn an average minimum of 240 points per month.

A month was standardized to twenty working days and the working week was standardized to forty hours, for a total of one hundred and sixty hours per month. As a basic unit, it was decided that 1 point would equal one half hour, meaning that one month would equal 320 points. From this total, 60 points (the equivalent of one and a half hours per day) was subtracted to allow for generic activities. Another 20 points (the equivalent of half an hour a day) was subtracted for breaks, leading to a monthly work activity total of 240 points. Three fourths of the cataloger's time is devoted to cataloging and support activities, and one fourth is devoted to generic activities.

Sick and annual leave receive only 1.5 points per hour, rather than 2. This calculation parallels the 75 percent of time normally devoted to cataloging and support activities while at work. The forty-hour week had to be used as a point of reference to calculate the point system since annual leave, sick leave, and other benefits are calculated by the university in units of time. Even though only a minimum of 240 points is required, it was important to establish the total at 320 points to represent a full-time schedule, thus fulfilling the legal requirement for full-time employment.

Point Values for Cataloging Activities

The following point values reflect the current values, which have been revised since the initial introduction of the project. On average, for AACR2 DLC copy, five titles per hour (0.4 points) was established as a minimum expectation; for other member copy, the minimum was established at one title every thirty-seven minutes (1.2 points). An original title requires an hour and fifteen minutes (2.5 points). Cataloging monographs includes searching, editing, inputting, downloading, authority work, and writing call numbers on items (see table A).

Table A: Point Values for Monographic Cataloging

1 Original title	2.5 points
1 OCLC member copy title/DLC copy title	
(pre-AACR2)/original theses	1.2 points
1 OCLC DLC copy title (AACR2)	0.4 point

In addition, 1 bonus point is assigned for non-book formats and non-Roman titles, taking into account the extra time needed to view, transliterate, and perform physical processing. Extra points are also assigned for upgrading and enhancing bibliographic records and submitting authority records through NACO (see table B).

Table B: Additional Point Values

Non-book title	1.0 point
Non-Roman title	1.0 point
Upgrading a record	0.4 point
Enhancing a record	0.2 point
Creating a NACO personal name record	0.4 point
Creating a NACO corp name/series record	0.8 point

Serials work consists of cataloging new and ceased titles, downloading, item creation, labeling, updating serials check-in, and bibliographic record holding information, as well as solving problems and communicating with branch libraries, the systems office, and acquisitions. On average, for DLC copy, an hour and a half per title (3 points) was established as a minimum expectation; for other member copy and electronic added access, the minimum was established at one title every hour and forty-five minutes (3.5 points). An original title requires two hours (4 points) (see table C).

Table C: Point Values for Serials Cataloging

1 Original title	4.0 points
1 OCLC member copy title	3.5 points
1 OCLC DLC copy title	3.0 points
1 Electronic added access	3.5 points

Point Values for Support Activities

These activities are documented in units of time. They include meetings, workshops, training, selection, and maintaining equipment. For some of these categories, a maximum number of points was established in order to emphasize primary cataloging responsibilities. For example, a selector can only earn up to 30 points a month, the equivalent of fifteen hours, for selection activities.

Conclusion

Initially, there was some anxiety on the part of catalogers whether they could earn a minimum of 240 points. After only two months, most catalogers felt that the 240 point minimum was realistic. For individual catalogers, the greatest benefit was gaining more control over their time. Some people choose to come to work very early, others very late. The stress of getting to work on time is gone. Catalogers no longer take sick or annual leave for medical appointments for themselves, their children, or their parents. And catalogers know exactly what is expected of them. The point system provides an objective measuring tool and allows for more uniformity and fairness in reporting and evaluating production.

For management, the main advantage consists in a 50 percent reduction in sick leave taken, improved morale, and a reduction in red tape. It also afforded the department the opportunity to clarify what constitutes core cataloging activities and activities which are peripheral. An analysis of productivity over six months in 1998 showed a slight productivity increase of 4 percent. This program is now an integral part of the culture of the department. Catalogers feel they have a vested interest in it and do not take lightly the possibility that it could be ended. So far, no other department has adopted this model even though interest has been expressed. An article describing a six-month pilot project testing the effects of the point system was published in a recent issue of *Technical Services Quarterly*.

BIBLIOGRAPHY

Bénaud, Claire-Lise, Sever Bordeianu, and Mary Ellen Hanson. "The Quantification of Cataloging: Documenting Productivity in a Flexible Scheduling Environment." *Technical Services Quarterly* 17, no. 3 (2000): 13–31.

23. Bibliographic Control in Chile: Cooperative Efforts and Standardization

Elizabeth N. Steinhagen

Establishment of the Bibliographic Network, RENIB

Chile has one of the strongest bibliographic traditions among Latin American countries and although most the bibliographies produced in the early times of the Republic were subject listings and various types of catalogs, there had been some effort to bring the total book production under control. Among the more remarkable earlier works up to approximately World War I, there existed the *Anuario de la Prensa Chilena,* published beginning in 1887 by the Biblioteca Nacional, Chile's national library. Its first coverage was 1886 through 1915, published from 1887 to 1927 in thirty-six volumes. It resumed publication in 1963, covering the years 1917 through 1921, and by the mid-seventies, it had caught up with most of the commercial book production. It was an exhaustive record of the nation's bibliographic production, in so far as it reaches the National Library. Although there has been a law of legal deposit on the books since 1834, not every new title had been deposited at the National Library, and noncommercial university publications for instance had not been included. Of course, as any paper tool, it is only an author listing, without subject approach to materials. The seventies brought about official recognition of and support for the nation's bibliographic needs and plans were made to resort to new technology to facilitate the compilation and distribution of the national bibliography. In 1983, Ms. María Teresa Sanz, at the time Coordinator of the National Library, began the project to automate bibliographic processing through the recently donated NOTIS software that had been developed at Northwestern University.

The Red Nacional de Información Bibliográfica (RENIB) was established in August of 1984, by an agreement among the Department of Education; the Directorate of Libraries, Archives, and Museums; and the Committee on Libraries of the Council of University Presidents (Consejo de Rectores). Its main objective was to create a database of the country's bibliographic resources and to improve access to that information. Headquartered in the Biblioteca Nacional, RENIB had been meant, principally, for the production of the national bibliography, but the political realities had added another, much broader dimension to the original plan. After establishing an administrative and organizational structure, its specialized personnel began to examine the standardization of library processes and the creation of union catalogs.

By inviting university libraries to share the responsibility for the creation of a joint union database, the need for standardization was a given, especially as far as bibliographic description and retrieval of information are concerned. Therefore, one of the first activities of RENIB was to create technical committees, with specialists from member institutions, and charged them with developing standards they would agree to follow.

Mission of the Network

The primary mission of RENIB was to integrate libraries into a working group that would oversee and assist with their coordination and interconnection to jointly plan and implement bibliographic control. In addition, this mission included the optimization of access to their collections and to render their services more efficient for the growing information needs of their clientele.

Within RENIB, each library creates its own database, which can be accessed through the network's union catalog mounted on the NOTIS system. Member libraries contribute original catalog records that others can use, which obviously results in savings of time and resources, by avoiding a duplication of effort.

Goals and Objectives

General Goals:

- To increase coverage and to facilitate efficient access to the bibliographic information available in all Chilean libraries.

- To share resources and to develop joint activities in order to face common problems and to provide greater efficiency in the management of libraries, resources, and library processes.

Specific Objectives:

- To develop national bibliographic databases and to create union catalogs of the resources at all member libraries, thereby enabling users to locate and to obtain the required documents.

- To establish standardized bibliographic processes and a controlled vocabulary, based on international standards, in order to facilitate information retrieval and transfer.

- To participate in other national, regional, and international networks.

Standardization

In order to contribute records to RENIB, the joint technical committees define the following standards and require compliance:

- Records must be in USMARC, at a minimal level as defined for monographs, serials, and authorities, including data that is mandatory, required if available, and optional.

- *Anglo American Cataloging Rules,* 2d ed., must be followed, as well as the Library of Congress interpretations, as published and updated in the *Cataloging Service Bulletin.*

- NISO Standard Z39.44 must be used for serial holdings data.

- RENIB's authorities database must be used.

Membership and Cooperation

RENIB's member institutions are committed to add and to maintain information about their collections in the union catalogs. They are also committed to do this following the policies, standards, and formats established by the network and maintain dedicated access to it.

At present there are 15 members, ranging from the National Library, several large public libraries, the Library of Congress (Chile), the National Commission of Scientific and Technological Research (CONICYT), as well as the major academic libraries in the country, which include about 125 departmental libraries, and the Chilean British Cultural Institute.

In addition, there are several associate libraries, which subscribe to access to the databases but do not contribute cataloging. Access to the databases is also possible through the Internet by going to http://www.renib.cl.

Databases

Eight different bibliographic databases are available at this time on the RENIB server. These are separated mainly by area of format of the material they house and contain the bibliographic description as well as holdings information. They are as follows:

- *Union catalog* of member libraries, which contains approximately 700,000 records of monographs, serials, theses, maps, music, audiovisual materials, etc., held in over 120 libraries.

- *Serials union catalog,* which contains about 14,000 records and their detailed holdings in over 120 libraries.

- *Manuscripts catalog,* which contains about 36,000 titles held in the special collections of the National Library.

- *Catalog of the National Archives,* which contains about 31,000 records.

- *Analytics catalog,* which contains approximately 117,000 entries that include bibliographic description of papers in Chilean scientific and cultural serials, in addition to reviews in the national press of Chilean writers.

- *Iberoamerican catalog,* which contains about 32,000 records with information about sixteenth- and seventeenth-century resources at the national libraries of Chile, Argentina, Uruguay, and Paraguay.

- *Catalog of the National Museum of Fine Arts Library,* which contains about 1,500 records of books, serials, exhibit catalogs, and information about Chilean artists.

- *Union catalog of public libraries,* which contains about 43,000 biblio-graphic records of books held in over 200 public libraries.

The above adds up to a total of close to 810,000, of which approximately 81 percent represents monographs, 8 percent manuscripts, about 5 percent serials, and the remaining for music, maps, and AV materials.

Authority Control

Before the establishment of the network, there were no agreements among academic and special libraries in the country relating to the tools, the policies, and the practices used in making their resources known and available to their users. Therefore it was essential for RENIB to work on a consensus among its members on the definition and the development of an authority control practice, which would assure the consistency and integrity of the data contained in the various records and the standardization of access points. This would ensure accurate information retrieval and therefore each bibliographic record entered would be controlled by an authorities structure. Furthermore, this also necessitates a centralized control so the structure would be maintained.

RENIB's authorities database was started in 1986 with about 19,000 subject headings entered from *Lista de Encabezamientos de Materia Bibliográfica (LEMB),* obtained through an agreement with ICFES (Instituto Colombiano para el Fomento de la Educación Superior). These headings were converted to MARC and loaded into NOTIS. To these were added authority records for subjects, names, series, uniform titles, and subdivisions that had formerly been created by the Catholic University and the National Library.

The first authorities database was established in this manner by RENIB with about 28,000 records that were made available online for member libraries. At the same time, discussions started on issues of database maintenance and on general policies and joint practices that all members have agreed to follow, thus contributing to the growth of the database and the quality of its records.

Authorities Database

In development for about fifteen years, the authorities databases today contain well over 400,000 records. Among these, the largest by far is that for personal names, with about 227,000 records, followed by the subject headings list of about 127,000 records. Corporate and geographic names amount to about 28,000 and 20,000, respectively, followed by far fewer conference headings, subdivisions, and references.

These three types of authority headings, that is, authority headings proper, references, and subdivisions, reside in a MARC file and are not linked to the headings in bibliographic records. For this reason, RENIB had to develop a validation software in order to maintain consistency among the various files. Member libraries work online in these files, adding headings, creating cross-references, and, especially, adding the English equivalent from LCSH and a few other thesauri, with an indication of the source. They can update and maintain their own headings, but cannot access the variable fields of records created by others.

The database is used as a source for new headings, and as control for headings already used in bibliographic records, as well as headings that have not yet been used in bibliographic records. At present, the file contains, in addition to the general list for RENIB members, another independent listing of medical subject headings developed by BIREME (Biblioteca Regional de Medicina e Ciências da Saúde in São Paulo), and translated into the MARC format. The coordinating body of all authority file activity is a committee of librarians from member institutions (Authorities Control Unit). This group, composed of catalogers, is the official entity, since 1988, that works out the details of standards and procedures followed for the creation of new headings, as well as for the maintenance of existing ones. Their main responsibilities include resolving conflicts between institutions, validating changes to the file, and requesting global changes in bibliographic records following changes in headings. The libraries nominating members to this body agree to participate actively in the authority work, in order to develop and maintain it. In addition, each library is responsible for the integrity and the consistency of the information it adds to the database. The authorities unit is also empowered to designate subcommittees to work on specific projects. For instance, a group recently composed of lawyers and librarians to work on special subject headings in the legal area and conform them to European legal precepts, based on the Napoleonic law, which is the basis of jurisprudence in Chile. The outcome of this project will be a new thesaurus of legal terminology in Spanish.

Conclusions

It is obvious that neither cooperation nor standardization can exist independently of one another. When libraries and other institutions realize that they can only achieve their missions and go forward by cooperating with one another, real progress is possible. They must of course also agree on a common set of principles to guide their actions, and that is where following certain standards becomes a necessity. International standards for cataloging developed by European and American libraries, such as the *Anglo American Cataloging Rules* (2d ed.), the MARC formats, the use of a controlled vocabulary in the form of authority headings, etc., became, when adopted by Chilean librarians, the norm to follow. This change was not easy, especially when UNESCO began giving away for free the MICROISIS software that had been developed for office automation, and which many United Nations agencies have since used to automate their libraries. Several Chilean libraries, especially smaller special ones, began cataloging on MICROISIS, which was not compatible with MARC, thus making it difficult for larger academic libraries to justify their costs of joining RENIB and continuing to make contributions in time and funding. In addition, given the economic difficulties that the country periodically goes through, political uncertainties at high levels of government, and the availability of free software, it is indeed quite an achievement that RENIB still exists and continues to promote the vision of a joint effort toward a joint goal of making information about the library resources of the country available to all. Indeed, in 1996, publication of the national bibliography was resumed, but this time online, taking advantage of new Internet technologies, and based on the catalog records contributed to RENIB.

BIBLIOGRAPHY

Iglesias Maturana, Maria Texia, and Soledad Fernández-Corugedo. "Chile: El Control y los Servicios Bibliográficos." Paper presented at Seminario Internacional sobre Control Bibliográfico Universal, 1998.

Maturana Salas, Isabel. "Sistema de Autoridades en RENIB." Presented at Reunión Internacional de Usuarios de LEMB, December 1989.

RENIB. Catálogo Colectivo de Publicaciones Seriadas. Assorted documentation.

————. "Manual de Autoridades de Materia en RENIB," 1991.

————. "Pautas para el Procesamiento de Analíticas," February 1992.

————. Various Reports of Authority Control Unit (UCA).

RENIB informa. Nos. 1–11 (January 1988–March 1992).

Saporta Levy, Victoria. "La Automatización en la Biblioteca Nacional." Presented at V. Jornadas Bibliotecarias Nacionales, January 1989.

Steinhagen, Elizabeth N. Interview of María Teresa Sanz, first coordinator of RENIB, and Soledad Fernández-Corugedo, current coordinator, December 1999.

————. "National Bibliography in Chile." Term paper, UW-Madison, School of Library and Information Science, December 1976.

Accreditation in Latin American
Higher Education

24. The Development of Chile's Higher-Education Accreditation System

Ana María Cobos

Introduction

I was in Chile from July 1998 through January 1999 for part of my sabbatical year. During this period I visited several universities[1] and made presentations to Chilean higher-education colleagues about the institutional accreditation model used in North American colleges and universities. I will present some general background for understanding Chilean higher-education reforms followed by some observations about the development of a national accreditation system. I will conclude with an update of the current situation and my own remarks about the role of librarians in this process.

Background

From 1996 to 1998, I became deeply involved in Saddleback College's self-study and accreditation process, which turned out to be a fascinating learning experience. In 1997, I was invited by the Accrediting Commission for Community and Junior Colleges to receive additional training to prepare me for participating in a visiting team to Santa Monica College in March 1998. At the same time, I was aware that Chile's higher-education system was undergoing fundamental structural and financial changes. I did some research; I contacted family, friends, and colleagues in Chile and learned that an accreditation system for higher education was being developed.

These are some characteristics of Chilean higher education through the 1970s: all universities in Chile were either fully or partly funded by the state; a small percentage of students had access to higher education; and the cost of attending the university was nominal, so ability to pay was generally not a factor. While Chilean higher education was recognized and respected in Latin America and Europe and also in the United States, universities in Chile through the 1970s were not required to meet preestablished goals or address sector-defined standards. In other words, there was little or no accountability required of these universities to renew their funding.

In 1981, the higher-education system was totally restructured and the military government decreed the establishment of private higher-education institutions. This 1981 decree is closely related to Chile's neo-liberalist economic policies that have managed, to a great extent, to globalize Chile's economy.[2] In other words, Chile's new economy requires an education system that can produce a well-qualified workforce to make possible effective competition in the global marketplace.

With the advent of private universities, this traditional, elitist, free, no-accountability system was changed forever. The higher-education privatization decree is part of a broader Ministry of Education reform program called MECE or Mejoramiento de la Calidad y la Equidad en la Educación. Primary and secondary education are also being reformed through this policy that seeks to improve instruction and infrastructure, and to introduce accountability measures into the sub-sector. These reforms were recommended in a World Bank Study that was very critical of the overall status of Chile's education system.

Since 1981, private universities, private professional institutes, and private technical training centers have sprouted like mushrooms throughout Chile. When I was there, I was astounded by their advertising presence in newspapers, television, and other media.[3] Indeed, according to the World Bank Project Appraisal Study for a Higher Education Improvement Loan, the new policies have brought about a phenomenal growth and diversification of the higher-education system. Only 8 public or semiprivate universities existed through the 1970s. Remarkably, in 1998, seventeen years after the privatization decree was introduced, the system included 68 universities, 70 professional institutes, and 119 technical training centers. The total number of students served by the system has more than doubled from an enrollment rate of 10.8 percent in 1980 to 27 percent in 1994. Current enrollments exceed 300,000. Most of the expansion has been financed with private sources while the share of higher education in the government's education budget has increased by about 12 percent. This privatized higher-education system, however, no longer provides free access to its public institutions, although a financial aid program has been instituted (World Bank 1998).

While these figures are impressive, has the quality of Chile's higher-education system improved? Are graduates of the system better prepared to meet the requirements of the contemporary Chilean labor market? There are, unfortunately, many reasons for concern.

The most important one is the quality of instruction throughout the system. While the 1981 decree also established a regulatory mechanism for new, private, for-profit universities, too many substandard private universities, professional institutes, or technical training centers were approved. It is true that many of these institutions did not survive the rigors of competition, and yet it is also a well-known fact that many private institutions today are characterized by mediocre or weak curriculum, poor instruction (usually taught by part-time instructors), and inadequate infrastructure (frequently with no library services). Furthermore, intellectual freedom concerns are linked to quality because many of these private institutions are affiliated with political parties, religious groups, or the armed forces.[4] Despite the fact that a handful of the older, more established private institutions (Universidades Diego Portales, Andrés Bello, Gabriela Mistral, and ARCIS) are gaining prestige, the success and employability of their graduates has not been confirmed. All too frequently, graduates who succeed in getting and holding jobs usually are graduates of the traditional, public or semiprivate universities, for example, Universidades de Chile, Católica, and Federico Sta. María.

As previously stated, through the 1980s private higher-education institutions were required to meet certain minimum standards before being allowed to operate. The 1981 decree created a regulatory body but it was not highly successful in ensuring quality. It was not until 1991, with the creation of the Consejo Superior de Educación (http://www.cse.cl), an autonomous body with ties to the Ministry of Education, that the infrastructure was in place to create a more effective system of higher-education accreditation.

This accrediting body has the authority to approve, or not, the institutional plans of new, private institutions, and its membership consists of experts from the "traditional" public universities. While this "peer review" model is similar to the one in North American accrediting bodies, there is one major difference: through 1998, only the institutional plans of new, private higher-education institutions had to be reviewed by experts from the public universities. In other words, public universities were not required to provide evidence that their institutions met the standards demanded of the new, for-profit, private institutions. Clearly, this issue has been controversial. Fortunately, beginning with academic year 1999, all medical and veterinary sciences and engineering programs, whether public or private must be accredited to qualify for public student financial aid programs. This review is "voluntary," although access to government funding is a strong motivation for participating in the process. More programs will be added to this initial list in the coming years. Eventually, all higher-education institutions will have to be evaluated by the accrediting body of the Consejo Superior de Educación to be eligible for public funding. In effect, an oversight environment is now in place, which expects that higher-education institutions will be concerned with public accountability and will strive to meet sector-defined standards.

I arrived in Chile shortly before this "specialized accreditation" was being launched. I was pleased to see that there was public discussion of the issues as evidenced by the numerous articles about accreditation and educational reform in general in the national press as well as conferences on the topic.[5] Discussions with family members and friends (some affiliated with higher education, others not) had a certain level of awareness of the topic. I found, however, that academic staff (faculty and librarians), in general, does not have a clear understanding, and indeed resents and distrusts this "intrusion." Overall, university staff has limited experience with public accountability and the notion of meeting standards. There is widespread distrust, confusion, and fear because implementation of an accreditation system requires nothing less than a radical and fundamental change of the academic culture.

I remind you that the public or so-called traditional universities (Universidad de Chile, Universidad Técnica del Estado, etc.) experienced fundamental structural and financial changes during the Pinochet regime as the military government imposed policies to depoliticize higher education. As a result many faculty lost their jobs, many left the country, many chose to "shut up" to keep their jobs; military officials were appointed to lead universities; and all unions were abolished.

This sense of being under siege, under attack, left many with no choice but to protect their own interests. University salaries generally are inadequate so that many faculty feel compelled to hold one or more other jobs in order to make ends meet.[6] Administrative leadership is elected but these are political elections and the political parties actively support candidates. The result is significant administrative instability because when new leadership is elected, key administrative positions go to political appointments.[7] Then there are the "gremios," the unions that render an already delicate situation even more complex. Cooperation within and between institutions is quite rare.

As a result, I found that this dysfunctional, bureaucratic hierarchy did not possess a sense of common mission. Under these conditions, it is unusual to find staff who is motivated and has a heartfelt sense of commitment to the institutions and to the students. These are among the many legacies of the changes imposed by the military government.

I am presenting a discouraging situation, but I am hopeful. It is truly inspiring to see that good programs and good libraries exist despite these difficult conditions and I believe that the development and implementation of a national accreditation system can and will have positive effects if the system can maintain its independence and autonomy.

Thanks to the magic of email, I have maintained many of my contacts and within the last month I have received updates. These are summaries of the replies:

- The Universidad Católica del Norte is making good progress at the institutional level. Misael Camus, from the Coquimbo campus, reports that a self-study of all undergraduate programs is advancing. A self-study steering committee is active, as are subcommittees for the different undergraduate programs. The self-study of the engineering programs is well underway. They aim to finish all self-studies by 2003. At that point they will be ready to undertake the evaluation of the self-studies by the external team of experts. At the library, colleagues are actively addressing curricular needs and continuing to work towards minimum collection levels, though little progress has been made to bring automation to the library.

- The Universidad de Santiago was among the first to perform a self-study of its engineering programs. Currently, all "facultades" are involved in self-studies, including consultation by foreign experts. These self-studies will have to be validated by external experts from the Consejo Superior de Educación or foreign experts.

- Colleagues at the Sistema de Bibliotecas de la P. Universidad Católica (SIBUC) tell me that they are not aware of any activities at the institutional level (this demonstrates that they expect to be involved, which is an excellent sign). Instead several "unidades académicas" are actively seeking contacts with accrediting organizations, mostly foreign.

- SIBUC colleagues report that since 1998 they have been very active in developing national academic library standards. They expect to revise the 1993 "Estándares para bibliotecas universitarias" authored by the Comisión Asesora de Bibliotecas del Consejo de Rectores. My presentation in November 1998 focused almost exclusively on the ACRL standards and how these relate to accreditation. I am very encouraged that SIBUC staff is actively working in this important area. This revised document should be widely distributed among academic libraries not only in Chile, but also throughout Latin America.[8]

- Dr. Francisco Cala Rodríguez, faculty member from the Universidad Austral, Puerto Montt campus, contacted me recently to ask for my assistance. He has been assigned the responsibility of coordinating the self-study effort at that campus.

As I describe the situation of higher education in Chile, I realize that many of these same issues characterize our own institutions here in North America. Indeed, this was one of my primary motivations: I was trying to learn how universities in Chile are promoting widespread participation in the accreditation process. I was hoping to learn from their experiences.

Concluding Remarks

I have strengthened my initial convictions about the extreme importance of good leadership. I have learned that it is essential for us, librarians, to become knowledgeable about and involved with the accreditation process in our own institutions. In so doing, we gain an in-depth and broad perspective of the institution, and in collaborating with other colleagues, we can become effective advocates for the library and librarians in the institution. Indeed, this is the message I repeated over and over again to my librarian colleagues in Chile. Get involved! We can all be leaders in our own institutions.[9]

I have some reservations about the Chilean process of developing the new accreditation system. Namely, that it is not an independent and completely autonomous one. However, it is clear that Chile is developing its own model, based on its own historical, social, and cultural contexts. I am encouraged and believe the experience has been useful. After all, it took almost one hundred years to develop the model currently used in North America. I believe that Chile has learned from the North American experiences, and I am hopeful that the quality of Chile's higher-education system will improve significantly during the next twenty-five years.

NOTES

1. In northern Chile, I lectured at the Universidad Católica del Norte, Antofagasta, and Coquimbo campuses. In Santiago, I lectured at the Library of the Pontificia Universidad Católica, San Joaquín campus; I participated in two national level conferences sponsored by the Colegio de Bibliotecarios de Chile (http://conicyt.cl:8010). The first was the "Seminario Autoevaluación y Acreditación en las Bibliotecas Universitarias," held at the Universidad de Santiago de Chile; the second was Chile Info '98, the Colegio's annual conference with the Cámara del Libro, whose theme was "Automatización, Estándares y Acreditación, Adquisiciones," held at the Estación Mapocho conference center. On November 25, 1998, 11:00 A.M., I was scheduled to present a lecture at the Facultad de Humanidades y Filosofía, but was postponed at the last minute due to the British Law Lords Pinochet verdict announced at the same time. In the south, I lectured in Concepción at the Universidad del Bío-Bío (organized by the local chapter of the Colegio de Bibliotecarios) and at the Valdivia and Puerto Montt campuses of the Universidad Austral de Chile.

2. Not only are Aetna, Citibank, McDonald's, Pizza Hut, and Blockbuster already in Santiago, Home Depot is opening its doors during the second half of 2000.

3. The *Guía Silber 2000* lists 65 universities of which 49 are private including Stanford University and the University of California's Santiago programs. Articles and advertisements about new universities abound. I collected several education supplements from the Sunday *El Mercurio*.

4. A personal friend who is finishing her studies at the Universidad Andrés Bello tells me that many of the private universities are affiliated with or are influenced by religious groups such as Opus Dei, political parties from the left to the extreme right, the military in general and Pinochet in particular, Freemasons, and newspaper owners. This fact is not widely publicized.

5. I collected many articles from the national press, too many to list in the bibliography. I continue to review *El Mercurio Electrónico* (http://www.elmercurio.cl) and often find articles about accreditation, higher education, or related topics.

6. I recall comments made by librarians, administrative staff, and faculty. These comments indicated how common it is for full-time faculty to be involved in consulting or part-time teaching in order to supplement their insufficient salaries and to supplement their research budgets.

7. Colleagues from Universidad Católica del Norte tell me that their automation efforts have not progressed as quickly as planned due not only to poor funding last year but also "fue año de elecciones y no se hizo mucho . . . las autoridades universitarias cambiaron el año pasado en la U. de Chile y la PUC y aun no se ve nada nuevo."

8. María Luisa Arenas, SIBUC director, recently made a presentation at the XI Seminario Nacional de Bibliotecas Universitarias de América Latina, held in Brazil. What is interesting and encouraging about this activity is that other universities in Chile and Latin America are cooperating in this project.

9. I have some ideas of how to support the work of the Colegio de Bibliotecarios de Chile (http://conicyt.cl:8010). I brought issues of their newsletter and I have membership application forms.

BIBLIOGRAPHY

Acreditación en Chile: la experiencia de un lustro. Santiago: Corporación de Promoción Universitaria (CPU), 1997.

Acreditación universitaria en América Latina: antecedentes y experiencias. Santiago: Centro Interuniversitario de Desarrollo (CINDA), Centro Regional para la Educación Superior en América Latina y el Caribe (CRESALC), 1994. ISBN: 956-7106-15-0, 980-6226-86-0. Currently available from CRESALC. http://www.unesco.org/education/educprog/am/world/uncresal.htm. Accessed June 11, 2000.

Acreditación universitaria en América Latina y el Caribe, informe: seminario técnico internacional, 9, 10, y 11 de diciembre de 1991. Santiago: Programa Políticas y Gestión Universitaria, 1992.

Albornoz, Orlando. *The Latin American University: Facing the 21st Century.* 1994. ERIC, ED 390332.

Arenas, María Luisa, Viena Cobarrubias, Adriana Hermosilla, Francisca Martínes, and Ximena Sánchez, coords. *Estándares para bibliotecas universitarias.* Santiago: Comisión Asesora de Bibliotecas del Consejo de Rectores, octubre 1993.

Ashton, Alvin. *La introducción de un sistema de acreditación en el Caribe de habla inglesa.* Santiago: Corporación de Promoción Universitaria, 1991.

Brovetto, Jorge. "Transformación universitaria y cooperación internacional." *Universidades: Revista de la Unión de Universidades de América Latina* 12 (julio–diciembre 1996): 19–26.

Centro Interuniversitario de Desarrollo. http://www.cinda.cl. Accessed June 11, 2000.

Consejo Superior de Educación. *Autorregulación en la educación superior chilena.* Santiago, 1993.

———. *Criterios de Evaluación de Universidades.* Santiago, 1993.

———. http://www.cse.cl. Accessed June 11, 2000.

———. *Manual para la preparación de informes autoevaluativos.* Santiago, 1993.

———. *Manual para miembros de comisiones de pares evaluadores.* Santiago, 1993.

Cox, Christian. "Higher Education Policies in Chile in the '90s." *Higher Education Policy* 9, no. 1 (March 1996): 29–43. ERIC, EJ 532811.

Esquivel Larrondo, Juan E., coord. *La universidad hoy y mañana: perspectivas latinoamericanas.* México, D.F.: Asociación Nacional de Universidades e Instituciones de Educación Superior, 1995.

Fried, Beatriz, and Mario Abuhadba. "Reforms in Higher Education: The Case of Chile in the 1980s." *Higher Education* 21, no. 2 (March 1991): 137–149.

Iriarte U., Arturo. "Aseguramiento de la calidad en la educación superior por medio de una gestión eficaz y la autoevaluación permanente de la institución." Paper presented at the Tercer Seminario Internacional "El Desafío de la Calidad en la Educación Superior," Santiago, September 23–25, 1998.

Leighton, Federico. *En busca de la excelencia: acreditación de los programas de doctorado.* Santiago: Centro de Estudios Públicos, 1992.

Middle States Accrediting Commission. "El proceso de evaluación y acreditación [*sic*]." http://www.msache.org/poevprs.html. Accessed June 11, 2000.

Miguel López, José Agustín de. *La Asociación Dominicana para el Autoestudio y la Acreditación: una agencia privada de acreditación universitaria.* Santiago: Corporación de Promoción Universitaria, 1991.

Pallán Figueroa, Carlos. "Evaluación, acreditación y calidad de la educación en México: hacia un sistema nacional de evaluación y acreditación." *Universidades: Revista de la Unión de Universidades de América Latina* 12 (julio–diciembre 1996).

Persico, M. Cecilia. "Regulación de la educación superior en Chile." *Estudios Sociales* 83 (Trimestre 1, 1995): 31–49.

Persico, M. Cecilia, and Pablo Persico. *Realidades y mitos de las universidades privadas.* Santiago: Corporación de Promoción Universitaria, 1994.

Project Appraisal Document on a Proposed Loan in the Amount of US $145.45 Million to the Republic of Chile for a Higher Education Improvement Loan. Washington, D.C.: The World Bank, 1998. Report No. 17887 is available from the World Bank at http://www.books@worldbank.org, and an executive summary is available at http://www.worldbank.org/pics/pid/c155481.txt. Accessed June 11, 2000.

Sistema Centroamericano de Evaluación y Acreditación de la Educación Superior, SICEVAES. *Universidades: Revista de la Unión de Universidades de América Latina* 12 (julio–diciembre 1996).

UNESCO World Congress on Higher Education. *Higher Education in the Twenty-First Century: Vision and Action.* http://www.unesco.org/educa-tion/educprog/wche/diaslese.html. Accessed June 11, 2000.

Villegas M., Abelardo, and Magdalena Sosa. "La cooperación internacional en materia de educación en América Latina." *Universidades: Revista de la Unión de Universidades de América Latina* 12 (julio–diciembre 1996).

25. Research on Accreditation in Latin American Higher Education

María Angela Leal

This study is an attempt to assess strengths and weaknesses of U.S. research library collections on the specialized and somewhat technical subject of accreditation in Latin American higher education. The study's raw data, analysis, and conclusions are based on extensive searching and retrieving of bibliographic records in FirstSearch, the user-friendly interface to OCLC, the largest bibliographic database representing the holdings of U.S. research libraries. The primary units of analysis are monographic and serial titles and the number of holdings of these materials. The periodical literature is considered only at the journal or periodical title-level, and not at the article-level. Article databases, such as the ERIC clearinghouse, as well as all other electronic resources, are excluded.

As is the case in other industries or sectors, such as hospitals and laboratories, the literature on accreditation in higher education has a fundamentally practical and empirical focus. In the United States, where accreditation systems are widely established, accreditation is treated as a topic of administrative policy and practice rather than one of educational theory or philosophy. In Latin American higher education, far from being well established, accreditation remains at the developmental stage. While not a subject of international controversy, and while outsiders may not recognize it as being one of Latin America's most pressing educational needs, accreditation is nevertheless a subject of great saliency in Latin America.

Extent of the Literature

To provide a notion of the extent of publications on accreditation unrestricted by geography, publication type, language, or other limits, a search by Library of Congress subject heading term "accreditation universities and colleges" yields 2,260 hits. Adding the term "United States," which may result in excluding materials concerning specific states or regions within the United States, reduces the number of results to just 458 hits.

As an indicator of the extent of publishing on higher education in Latin America, the search under subject heading terms "education, higher latin america" yields 448 hits. Restricting the search to only periodical publications yields 230 hits, of which 183 are in Spanish and 47 in Portuguese.

To retrieve citations on accreditation in Latin America, several searches were tested. The simple search by title word "accreditation," unrestricted by schooling level or school or education type, yielded a total of 54 hits, including a handful of repeated or duplicate titles. By its nature this type of search captures titles from all the Spanish-speaking countries as well as from Latin America as a whole; it is a far more efficient search argument than to search separately the subject heading terms "accreditation Latin America" and "accreditation [each individual country]."

The search by title word "credenciamento," the Portuguese term for accreditation, yielded a total of four unique titles, of which three were published in the 1970s and one in 1986.

For purposes of this study, I generated a representative sample of monograph titles by combining all the results of the following four different kinds of the search arguments: by title word "acreditacion" or title word "credenciamento"; by subject heading terms "universities and colleges accreditation latin america"; by subject heading terms "universities and colleges accreditation [individual country]"; and by subject heading terms "universities and colleges accreditation" limited to "language Spanish" and the same terms limited to "language Portuguese." In analyzing the results, three questions were investigated: (1) How widely held or distributed across owning libraries are the titles? What is the relationship between the breadth of distribution and the subject or genre of the monographs? (2) Which libraries own the most titles? (3) For which countries or regions are the aggregated holdings of libraries the greatest?

The analysis yields several observations and conclusions. The country with the largest number of titles is Puerto Rico, yet these titles are also among the least widely held—being owned by Puerto Rican universities exclusively. The country with the next largest number is Bolivia, with four titles; and these, unlike the Puerto Rican ones, are among the most widely held, averaging five holding libraries each. The most widely held genre or subject categories are the comparative education-type works, which average thirteen holding libraries each, and a work about Mexican medical schools, also with thirteen holding libraries. As for the holding libraries themselves, in descending order, Harvard, UT Austin, U Puerto Rico, the Library of Congress, UC Berkeley, and the New York Public Library top the list in number of titles held, at between seven and nine titles each. Next is Yale University, with six titles; Stanford and Cornell, with four each; and Illinois, UCLA, Massachusetts, Arizona, Duke, Vanderbilt, USC, Florida, NYU, Tulane, Columbia, Wisconsin-Madison and -Milwaukee, UNC-Chapel Hill, Brigham Young University, and the University of Notre Dame, with between one and three each. The overall picture is of a shallow level of collecting on this subject in U.S. research libraries.

Analysis of Periodical Titles and Holdings

The picture of shallowness is repeated when considering periodical titles on higher education in Latin America, the sort of publications where a researcher would look in order to keep current with developments in accreditation as well as other topics. To consider the example of one corporate author, the Quebec-based Inter-American Organization for Higher Education, the University of Texas at Austin is the only U.S. library to own the organization's multilingual bulletin called *Interamerica;* only the University of Arizona owns a copy of the organization's *Anais do IV Seminário Internacional de Administração Universitária;* and only LC, the OAS, and Florida International University own any of the proceedings of the organization's congresses, such as the 1987 congress held in Mérida, Venezuela. In contrast, more than fifty libraries own a copy of the Pan American Union's twenty-page *Latin American Higher Education and Inter-American Cooperation Report and Recommendations,* published in 1961. Could it be that earlier Pan American enthusiasm, from the eve of the Alliance for Progress, has faded to such a degree over the succeeding forty years? My guess is that the holdings of research libraries should not be relied upon for an answer. Rather, I believe it is more likely that there have been significant collecting gaps in this area.

Another example of the state of periodical holdings is the only Latin American title I was able to retrieve that specifically concerns accreditation of universities and colleges. Published since 1995 in Bogotá, Colombia, by the Asociación Colombiana de Universidades, *Cuadernos ASCUN* is held only by Columbia University.

Evidence pointing to further likely gaps in U.S. libraries' collecting emerged from searching under title word "acreditacion." A special 161-page bibliography published in 1998 by the Asociación Nacional de Universidades e Instituciones de Educación Superior in Mexico is held only by the Universidad Autónoma de Ciudad Juárez, and not by any other library in OCLC. Its title is *Evaluación y acreditación en las instituciones de educación superior bibliografía.* Similar gaps likely exist in the related topic of evaluation in higher education. For example, the serial *Avaliação da pós-graduação,* published by Brazil's Coordenação do Aperfeiçoamento de Pessoal de Nível Superior (CAPES), is held only by the University of Texas at Austin. As for periodicals on the general subject of higher education, CAPES's informational bulletin, called *INFOCAPES,* is held only by the University of Kansas, New York Public Library, the University of Texas at Austin, and Stanford University; and the bimonthly *Universidade,* published since 1994 by the Instituto Brasileiro da Qualidade em Serviços, is held only by LC.

Conclusion

Though this study does not pretend to be complete, it nevertheless has uncovered important evidence of spotty and uneven bibliographic coverage of accreditation in Latin American higher education in U.S. research library collections.

Without delving more deeply into the literature available in Latin America, there is no way to tell whether the shallowness of libraries' collecting is at all reflective of the depth and breadth of the literature itself. Yet I think it is fair to say that interest in improving the quality of higher education remains strong in Latin America, as does the interest of U.S. scholars in contributing to this objective. In support of this view I offer the following OCLC citation to a recent U.S. doctoral dissertation: Cristina Rios, "An Assessment Paradigm for Mexican Higher Education Accreditation," Claremont Graduate University, 1999.

Contributors

RAMÓN ABAD, Instituto Cervantes

FERNANDO ACOSTA-RODRÍGUEZ, New York Public Library

MYRA L. APPEL, University of California at Davis

DAVID BLOCK, Cornell University

ANNE C. BARNHART-PARK, Lafayette College

JAMES BARNHART-PARK, Muhlenberg College

CLAIRE-LISE BÉNAUD, University of New Mexico

ANA MARÍA COBOS, Saddleback State College

VIRGINIA GARCÍA, Instituto de Estudios Peruanos

NELLY S. GONZÁLEZ, University of Illinois

MARK GROVER, Brigham Young University

EFRAÍN KRISTAL, University of California at Los Angeles

MARÍA ANGELA LEAL, Catholic University of America

KAREN LINDVALL-LARSON, University of California at San Diego

ENRIQUE MARCHENA CÁRDENAS, Libros Peruanos

MARÍA ROSTWOROWSKI, Instituto de Estudios Peruanos

SARA SÁNCHEZ, University of Miami

SUSAN H. SHAW, San Antonio Public Library

ELIZABETH N. STEINHAGEN, University of New Mexico

PETER A. STERN, University of Massachusetts, Amherst

RAFAEL E. TARRAGÓ, University of Minnesota-Minneapolis

ROBERTO VERGARAY, Iturriaga & Cia.

DARLENE WALLER, University of Connecticut

GEOFF WEST, British Library

Conference Program

Monday, May 29, 2000

9:00–10:00 A.M.   **Inaugural Session**
International IV and V

Opening   *César Rodríguez*
SALALM President
Yale University

Welcome   *Carlos A. Torres*
Director, Latin American Center
UCLA

Janice Koyama
Associate University Librarian-Public Services
UCLA Library

Eudora Loh and *Barbara Valk*
Co-Chairs, Local Arrangements
UCLA

José Toribio Medina Award   *Peter A. Stern*
University of Massachusetts, Amherst

Keynote Speech
María Rostworowski, Instituto de Estudios Peruanos
"Visión general sobre el Incario"

Rapporteur: *Darlene Waller,* University of Connecticut

10:00–11:00 A.M.   Coffee with Book Exhibitors

11:00 A.M.–12:30 P.M.   **Theme Panel I: Research Expeditions: Discovering Historic Andean Collections in the Northeast U.S.**
Moderator: *Denise A. Hibay,* New York Public Library
Rapporteur: *Eileen Oliver,* Kent State University

Peter A. Stern, University of Massachusetts, Amherst
"Recovering the Colonial Past: Researching 'El
Virreinato del Perú' in the Northeast"

Darlene Waller, University of Connecticut
"Masacres, Levantamientos, y Vida Cotidiana: Press
Coverage of 'Campesinado Boliviano' in the Late 19th
Century"

David Block, Cornell University
"Our Man in Peru: The Hiram Bingham Papers at Yale
University"

Fernando Acosta-Rodríguez, New York Public Library
"Preserving Andean Collections: Progress and
Challenges of Microfilm Preservation"

**Workshop I: CRL/LAMP Brazilian Government
Documents Digitization Project: A Final Reckoning**
Moderator: *Scott Van Jacob,* University of Notre Dame
Rapporteur: *Pamela Howard-Reguindin,* Library of
Congress Office, Rio de Janeiro

Presenters:
Scott Van Jacob, University of Notre Dame
James Harper, PFA, Inc.
Chris Harper, PFA, Inc.
Gregory Leazer, UCLA

12:30–2:15 P.M.   Lunch

2:15–3:45 P.M.   **Theme Panel II: Revolución y Contrarevolución en
los Andes: El Sendero Luminoso de Perú y el Caso
Pinochet de Chile**
Subcommittee on Marginalized Peoples and Ideas
Moderator: *Fred G. Morgner,* Vientos
Tropicales/Mexico Norte
Rapporteur: *Molly Molloy,* New Mexico State
University

Peter A. Stern, University of Massachusetts, Amherst
"¿Continuará el Sendero?: The Shining Path after
Guzmán"

Anne C. Barnhart-Park, Lafayette College
"A Still Unreconciled Chile Faces the Millennium:
Selected Resources for Understanding the Pinochet
Crisis"

Marta S. Domínguez Díaz, SEREC, Santiago, Chile
"Chile Con y Después Pinochet: Su Impacto en las
Expresiones Literarias y Culturales"

James Barnhart-Park, Muhlenberg College
"We Wirarün (The New Cry): Mapuche Renunciations
of State-Imposed Silence"

Theme Panel III: Andean Colonial Literature
Moderator: *Mark Grover,* Brigham Young University
Rapporteur: *Micaela Chávez Villa,* El Colegio de
México

Enrique Marchena Cárdenas, Libros Peruanos
"El conocimiento del mundo andino a través de las
crónicas"

Roberto Vergaray, Iturriaga & Cia
"Garcilaso de la Vega, nexo de dos mundos"

Mark Grover, Brigham Young University
"'Nothing in Peru is Permanent': Iturriaga Cia. and the
Peruvian Book"

**Workshop II: Golden Nuggets: Internet Access to
Latin American Resources at the University of
California**
Moderator: *Eudora Loh,* UCLA
Rapporteur: *Mary Jo Zeter,* Michigan State University

Charlotte Brown, UCLA
"Search for 'Ecuador' Produced 300 Hits: An
Introduction to the Online Archive of California"

Walter Brem, University of California, Berkeley
"Mexican Collections in the Online Archive of
California"

David Hirsch, UCLA
"Jewish Communities in Latin America: Some Web
Resources"

3:45–5:15 P.M.

Theme Panel IV: ENLACE Presentations
Moderator: *Adán Griego,* Stanford University
Rapporteur: *Lynn Shirey,* Harvard University

Isabel Miranda Meruvia, UMNSM, Lima
"Acceso a los Servicios de Información a los
Discapacitados del Perú: Su Problemática y la
Necesidad para su Integración y Desarrollo a la
Sociedad"

Socorro Gil Henao, Universidad de Antioquia,
Colombia
"Antioquia, Tierra de Rios"

**Theme Panel V: Andean Resources and
Bibliography, I**
Moderator: *Scott Van Jacob,* University of Notre Dame
Rapporteur: *Olga Espejo,* University of Miami

Virginia García, Instituto de Estudios Peruanos
"La Biblioteca del Instituto de Estudios Peruanos"

Michael Hamerly, Brown University
"Bibliography of Ecuadorian Bibliographies
1885–1999"

Angela Carreño, New York University
"Report from Trip to Peru"

**Workshop III: History of SALALM's Latin
American Information Series**
Moderator: *Laura D. Shedenhelm,* University of
Georgia Libraries
Rapporteur: *Orchid Mazurkiewicz,* Arizona State
University

Laura D. Shedenhelm, University of Georgia Libraries
Latin American Information Series editor

Marianne Siegmund, Brigham Young University
Compiler of LAIS no. 7

Lourdes Vázquez, Rutgers University
Compiler of LAIS no. 6

Tuesday, May 30, 2000

8:00–9:15 A.M.   **Theme Panel VI: Documentaries, Videos, and Audio-Books**
Subcommittee on Audio-Visual Media
Moderator: *Ramón Abad,* Instituto Cervantes
Rapporteur: *Susan H. Shaw,* San Antonio Public Library

Nelly S. González, University of Illinois
"Andean Countries on Video: Bolivia, Ecuador, and Peru"

Angela Carreño, New York University
"Selection and Evaluation of Videos: The SALALM Page Revisited"

Ramón Abad, Instituto Cervantes
"Spanish and Latin American Literature on Sound Recording"

Theme Panel VII: Chile's Accreditation System of Higher Education
Moderator: *Ana María Cobos,* Saddleback State College
Rapporteur: *Gabriela Sonntag,* California State University-San Marcos

María Angela Leal, Oliveira Lima Library, Catholic University of America, Washington, D.C.
"Research on Accreditation in Latin American Higher Education: An Assessment of Collection Strengths of Selected U.S. Libraries"

Ana María Cobos, Saddleback State College
"The Development of Chile's Higher-Education Accreditation System: A Sabbatical Experience and Current Status Report"

Theme Panel VIII: Andean Resources and Bibliography, II
Moderator: *Darlene Waller,* University of Connecticut
Rapporteur: *Peter Bushnell,* University of Florida

Michael Hamerly, Brown University
"Catalog of Peruvian Imprints of the Colonial and
Independence Period"

Geoff West, British Library
"When, Why, and from Whom? The British Library's
Collection of Early Printed Books Containing Andean
Languages"

9:15–9:45 A.M.   Coffee with Book Exhibitors

9:45–11:00 A.M.   **Theme Panel IX: Documenting Peru: One Hundred
Fifty Years of Peruvian Photographic Images**
Moderator: *Guillermo Nañez Falcón,* Tulane University
Rapporteur: *Marian Goslinga,* Florida International
University

Sara Sánchez, University of Miami
"African Legacy in Peru"

Paul Bary and *Guillermo Nañez Falcón,* Tulane
University
"Elites, Stone Monuments, Earthquakes, and a
Contemporary Afro-Peruvian Community: 150 Years of
Peruvian Photographs from the Tulane Collection"

**Workshop IV: Latin American Business and Official
Statistical Sources on the Internet**
Moderator: *Joseph Holub,* University of Pennsylvania
Rapporteur: *Pamela M. Graham,* Columbia University

Daniel Hanne, California State University, Pomona
"Basic Resources for Latin American Business
Research"

Terese Mulkern Terry, Wharton School, University of
Pennsylvania
"Specialized Resources (Free and Fee-Based) for Latin
American Business Research"

Matt Brosius, OECD Washington Center
"The OECD Statistical Database"

12:30–2:00 P.M.   Host Luncheon

2:00–3:30 P.M.   **Theme Panel X: Andean Politics**
Moderator: *Angela Carreño*, New York University
Rapporteur: *John Wright*, Brigham Young University

Linda Rodríguez, UCLA
"Crisis in the Andes: Ecuador 1980–2000"

Karen Lindvall-Larson, University of California, San Diego
"Elections in Colombia: A Brief History and Guide to Research"

2:15–3:45 P.M.   **Theme Panel XI: Andean Literature**
Moderator: *David Block*, Cornell University
Rapporteur: *Bartley Burk*, University of Notre Dame

Efraín Kristal, UCLA
"Mario Vargas Llosa's The Goat's Feast in the Context of his Narrative Oeuvre"

Susan H. Shaw, San Antonio Public Library
"Arguedas and Dillard: Critical Linkages"

Wednesday, May 31, 2000

8:00–9:30 A.M.   **Theme Panel XII: The Enlightenment in the Andes**
Moderator: *Rafael E. Tarragó*, University of Minnesota-Minneapolis
Rapporteur: *Laura D. Shedenhelm*, University of Georgia

Myra L. Appel, University of California, Davis
"'Observaciones sobre la Comida de Lima': Hipólito Unanue's Prescription for an Enlightened Philosophy of Diet"

Rafael E. Tarragó, University of Minnesota-Minneapolis
"Sources about the Vaccination Expedition of Charles IV in the Andes: A Gesture of Enlightened Despotism"

Workshop V: Cataloging and Bibliographic Control Issues
Moderator: *Claire-Lise Bénaud*, University of New Mexico
Rapporteur: *Sarah Leroy*, University of Pittsburgh

Claire-Lise Bénaud, University of New Mexico
"Cataloging Quotas and Flexible Work Schedules: An
Alternative Model at the University of New Mexico"

Elizabeth N. Steinhagen, University of New Mexico
"Bibliographic Control in Chile: Cooperative Efforts
and Standardization"

9:30–10:00 A.M.   Coffee with Book Exhibitors

10:00–11:30 A.M.   **Theme Panel XIII: Asians in the Andean Region:**
Emerging Research and Information Resources
Moderator: *Clara M. Chu,* UCLA Department of
Information Studies
Rapporteur: *Nancy Hallock,* Harvard University

Clara M. Chu, UCLA Department of Information
Studies
"Asians in the Andean Region: Research Resources in a
Digital Age"

Steven Masami Ropp, UCLA Department of
Anthropology
"From Manco Capac to Alberto Fujimori: The
Dynamics of Symbol, History, and Myth in the
Japanese Presence in the Andes"

Jenny Asinc, UCSD Latin American Studies
"Across Two Different Shores: The Life Story of My
Mother"

Workshop VI: Literary Production and Resources:
Argentina
Moderator: *Hortencia Calvo,* Duke University
Rapporteur: *Cecilia Sercan,* Cornell University

Danilo Albero, Fiction Writer, and *Beatriz Colombi,*
Universidad de Buenos Aires
"Literatura e Industria Editorial: El Caso Argentino"

Catharine Wall, University of California, Riverside
"The Jorge Luis Borges Collection at the Harry
Ransom Humanities Research Center at the University
of Texas at Austin"

11:30 A.M.–12:30 P.M.   Town Meeting

12:30–2:00 P.M.   Lunch Break

2:00–3:00 P.M.   Closing General Session

3:00–4:00 P.M.   Executive Board